THE COMBAT MYTH IN THE BOOK OF REVELATION

THE COMBAT MYTH IN THE BOOK OF REVELATION

by

Adela Yarbro Collins

Wipf and Stock Publishers

150 West Broadway • Eugene OR 97401

2001

The Combat Myth in the Book of Revelation

By Collins, Adela Yarbro
Copyright©1976 by Collins, Adela Yarbro
ISBN: 1-57910-716-8

Reprinted by *Wipf and Stock Publishers*
150 West Broadway • Eugene OR 97401

Previously published by Harvard Theological Review, 1976.

Ἰωάννῃ οὐ τῷ θείῳ
ἀλλὰ τῷ Κελτικῷ

TABLE OF CONTENTS

Page

ABBREVIATIONS   xi

PREFACE   xv

INTRODUCTION   1

CHAPTER I.   THE STRUCTURE OF THE BOOK OF REVELATION . . .   5

The Epistolary Framework   5
The Basic Options   8
    The Recapitulation Theory   8
    The Sources Theory 9
    Literary Unity without Recapitulation   9
    The Revival of the Recapitulation Theory   11
Series of Seven as an Organizing Principle   13
    The Overall Plan of the Book   13
    The Technique of Interlocking 16
The Two Scrolls as an Organizing Principle   19
    The Commission of the Seer   20
    The Two Scrolls 21
    The Scroll with the Seven Seals 22
        a. Physical Form   22
        b. Sealed Writings   22
        c. Heavenly Books 24
        d. Relation of Content of Scroll to Visions . .   25
    The Little Scroll 26
        a. The Content of the Little Scroll   26
        b. The Placement of Ch. 10   27
        c. The Unity of Chs. 12-22   28
    Summary 31
Recapitulation in the Book of Revelation   32
    Recapitulation in the Five Series 33
        a. The Seven Seals   33
        b. The Seven Trumpets 34
        c. The First Unnumbered Series   37
        d. The Seven Bowls   38
        e. The Second Unnumbered Series   39
        f. Summary   40
    Recapitulation in the Two Cycles   40
    Why Recapitulation? 43

CHAPTER II.   THE COMBAT MYTH IN REVELATION 12 57

The Pattern of the Combat Myth and Revelation 12 . . .   59
The Dragon's Attack on the Woman   61
    Accadian and Hittite Parallels   61
    Ugaritic Parallels   61
    Egyptian Parallels   62
    Greek Parallels 63
    Revelation 12 65
    Other Recently Proposed Parallels   67
    Conclusion   70

The Woman as Queen of Heaven 71
 The Ephesian Artemis 71
 Atargatis 72
 Isis 73
 Conclusion 75
Mythological Parallels to the Dragon as Chaos Monster 76
 Old Testament Parallels 76
 Ugaritic Parallels 77
 Accadian Parallels 77
 Greek Parallels 78
 Egyptian Parallels 79
 Conclusion 79
The Battle in Heaven 79
 Accadian Myths 80
 Greek Myths 80
 Hittite Myths 80
 Ugaritic Myths 81
 Israelite-Jewish Myths 81
 Conclusion 83
Summary 83

CHAPTER III. JEWISH AND CHRISTIAN USE OF THE COMBAT
MYTH IN REVELATION 12 101

The Literary Unity of Revelation 12 101
 Literary Indications of the Use of Sources 101
 Stylistic Indications of the Use of Sources 103
 Indications of the Use of Sources in the Content
  of Ch. 12 104
 The Relationship of the Two Narratives 107
 The Original Language of the Sources 108
 Redactional Elements in Revelation 12 109
 The Hymn as a Redactional Composition 112
 Conclusion 114
The Function of the Combat Myth in Source I 116
 The Traditional Function of the Dragon 117
 The Associations of the Desert 120
 Revelation 12 as Allegorical Narrative 122
 Implications of the Paradigmatic Narrative 126
 Date and Provenance of Source I 127
The Function of the Combat Myth in Source II 129
The Function of the Combat Myth in the Christian
 Redaction 130
 The Re-use of Source I 130
 The Re-use of Source II 135
 The Hymnic Composition 136
 The New Unity 142

CHAPTER IV. THE ESCHATOLOGICAL ADVERSARY 157

Cosmic Dualism 158
The Role of Satan 161
The Beast from the Sea 161
The Beast from the Abyss 165

The Signification of the Beasts   170
    The Beast as Rome   172
    The Beast as Nero   174
The Nero Legend   176
The Significance of the Nero Legend   183
    Function   184
    The Fusion of Diverse Traditions   186

CHAPTER V.   THE PATTERN OF THE COMBAT MYTH IN THE
BOOK OF REVELATION   207

The Pattern in the First Series of Visions   211
    The Heavenly Scene and the Scroll   211
    The Seven Seals   217
The Pattern in the Second Series of Visions   218
The Pattern in the Third Series of Visions   219
The Pattern in the Fourth Series of Visions   220
    The Seven Bowls   220
    The Babylon Appendix   221
        a. Threat   221
        b. Combat-Victory   221
        c. Victory Shout   222
        d. Sacred Marriage   223
        e. Banquet   224
The Pattern in the Fifth and Last Series of Visions .   224
    Theophany of the Divine Warrior   224
    Banquet   225
    Threat and Combat-Victory   225
    Manifestation of Kingship   226
    Fertility of the Restored Order and Sacred
        Marriage   226
    Temple-Building and Salvation   228
    Sacred Marriage   230
Revelation 12 as Paradigm of the Book of Revelation .   231

APPENDIX   245

BIBLIOGRAPHY   271

ABBREVIATIONS

AB	Anchor Bible
AJA	*American Journal of Archaeology*
ANEP	J. B. Pritchard (ed.), *Ancient Near East in Pictures*
ANESTP	J. B. Pritchard (ed.), *Ancient Near East Supplementary Texts and Pictures*
ANET	J. B. Pritchard (ed.), *Ancient Near Eastern Texts*
APOT	R. H. Charles (ed.), *Apocrypha and Pseudepigrapha of the Old Testament*
Arndt-Gingrich	W. F. Arndt and F. W. Gingrich (eds.), *A Greek-English Lexicon of the New Testament and Other Early Christian Literature*
ATANT	Abhandlungen zur Theologie des Alten und Neuen Testaments
BAR	*Biblical Archaeologist Reader*
BASOR	*Bulletin of the American Schools of Oriental Research*
BEvT	Beiträge zur evangelischen Theologie
Bib	*Biblica*
Blass-Debrunner	F. Blass and A. Debrunner, *A Greek Grammar of the New Testament and Other Early Christian Literature*
BZ	*Biblische Zeitschrift*
BZAW	Beihefte zur Zeitschrift für die alttestamentliche Wissenschaft
CAH	*Cambridge Ancient History*
CBQ	*Catholic Biblical Quarterly*
CIG	*Corpus Inscriptionum Graecarum*, 1828-
CSEL	Corpus scriptorum ecclesiasticorum latinorum
CTA	A. Herdner (ed.), *Corpus des tablettes en cunéiformes alphabétiques*
EBib	Etudes bibliques
Feine-Behm-Kümmel	Werner Georg Kümmel (ed.), *Introduction to the New Testament*, 14th rev. ed.
FRLANT	Forschungen zur Religion und Literatur des Alten und Neuen Testaments
GCS	Griechische christliche Schriftsteller
Greg	*Gregorianum*
HAT	Handbuch zum Alten Testament

Hennecke- Schneemelcher	E. Hennecke and W. Schneemelcher (eds.), *New Testament Apocrypha*
HeyJ	*Heythrop Journal*
HKAT	Handkommentar zum Alten Testament
HNT	Handbuch zum Neuen Testament
HTR	*Harvard Theological Review*
ICC	International Critical Commentary
IDB	G. A. Buttrick (ed.), *Interpreter's Dictionary of the Bible*
IG	*Inscriptiones Graecae*, 1873-
Int	*Interpretation*
JAOS	*Journal of the American Oriental Society*
JBL	*Journal of Biblical Literature*
JHS	*Journal of Hellenic Studies*
JJS	*Journal of Jewish Studies*
JNES	*Journal of Near Eastern Studies*
JSJ	*Journal for the Study of Judaism*
JTS	*Journal of Theological Studies*
KAT	Kommentar zum Alten Testament
LCL	Loeb Classical Library
Meyer	H. A. W. Meyer, Kritisch-exegetischer Kommentar über das Neue Testament
NovT	*Novum Testamentum*
NovTSup	Novum Testamentum, Supplements
NRT	*La nouvelle revue théologique*
NTAbh	Neutestamentliche Abhandlungen
NTD	Das Neue Testament Deutsch
NTS	*New Testament Studies*
OCD	*Oxford Classical Dictionary*
OTS	*Oudtestamentische Studiën*
Pap. Oxy.	*Oxyrhynchus Papyri*
PRU	C. F. A. Schaeffer (ed.), *Palais royal d'Ugarit*
PW	Pauly-Wissowa, *Realencyclopädie der classischen Altertumswissenschaft*
RB	*Revue biblique*
RGG	*Religion in Geschichte und Gegenwart*
RHR	*Revue de l'histoire des religions*
Roscher	W. H. Roscher (ed.), *Ausführliches Lexikon der griechischen und römischen Mythologie*

RQ	*Revue de Qumran*
RSR	*Recherches de science religieuse*
SB	Sources bibliques
SBL	Society of Biblical Literature
SBT	Studies in Biblical Theology
SJT	*Scottish Journal of Theology*
SNGA	*Sylloge Nummorum Graecorum: The Burton Y. Berry Collection* (American Numismatic Society)
SNGB	*Sylloge Nummorum Graecorum* (British Academy)
SNGD	*Sylloge Nummorum Graecorum Deutschland: Sammlung von Aulock*
Strack-Billerbeck	H. Strack and P. Billerbeck (eds.), *Kommentar zum Neuen Testament aus Talmud und Midrasch*
TDNT	G. Kittel and G. Friedrich (eds.), *Theological Dictionary of the New Testament*
ThRu	*Theologische Rundschau*
TLZ	*Theologische Literaturzeitung*
TU	Texte und Untersuchungen
TZ	*Theologische Zeitschrift*
UUA	Uppsala universitets-årsskrift
VTSup	Vetus Testamentum, Supplements
ZAW	*Zeitschrift für die alttestamentliche Wissenschaft*
Zimmern, *Keilinschriften*	H. Zimmern and H. Winckler (eds.), *Die Keilinschriften und das Alte Testament*
ZNW	*Zeitschrift für die neutestamentliche Wissenschaft*

PREFACE

"The Combat Myth in the Book of Revelation" is a dissertation which I defended in September, 1975 before a committee consisting of Dieter Georgi, Frank Moore Cross, Jr., John Strugnell, and George MacRae, S. J. A few references have been added; otherwise the work appears in the form in which it was approved.

John G. Gager's book *Kingdom and Community: The Social World of Early Christianity*, which treats the book of Revelation briefly (pages 49-57), was not accessible to me soon enough to allow for a discussion of his remarks in the dissertation itself. I would like to take this opportunity to note that my work agrees with the line of interpretation he is suggesting. Gager notes a pattern of alternation between symbols of victory/hope and of oppression/despair. Chapters I and V of my work propose that the structure of the book is based on a repeated pattern which moves from visions of persecution/threat to those of salvation/victory. Thus we agree that the key to the book is the repetition of these two major themes. We also agree that this repetition ought to be understood in terms of the function of mythic language. I would not necessarily want to go on to say, as Gager does, that psychotherapy functions in a similar way.

Josephine M. Ford's commentary on the book of Revelation in the Anchor Bible series appeared after my dissertation was completed. Anyone who reads both her book and mine will see that our respective approaches have little in common.

This preface also gives me the welcome opportunity to express my appreciation to my thesis advisor, Dieter Georgi, who stimulated my interest in the book of Revelation and increased my appreciation of the importance of Graeco-Roman religions for understanding the New Testament. The influence of Frank Moore Cross, Jr. on this dissertation is evident. His studies of ancient myths and how they function in the Old Testament have made me aware of the importance of ancient mythic patterns for understanding Revelation. John Strugnell read parts of the

dissertation in draft form and generously shared his great
erudition. I am grateful to him for his many valuable sugges-
tions.

INTRODUCTION

The scroll with the seven seals in Revelation 5 is often used as a symbol of the confusion many readers feel when confronted with the book's profusion of images and apparent lack of structure. The significance and mutual relations of the images used are often obscure. Certain indications are given that the book has a clear structure (the use of the number seven, for example), but the expectations aroused by these signals seem later to be frustrated. Thus Revelation remains a sealed book for many readers.

The problems resulting from the obscurity of Revelation are compounded by certain dogmatic considerations. From Irenaeus and Hippolytus to Hal Lindsey and the "Children of God," the book of Revelation has been interpreted in terms of a literal millenarian eschatology. The popularity of this line of interpretation has made the book offensive to those of a more liberal theological outlook.

Finally, the interpretation of Revelation has been hindered by a variety of dogmatic scholarly positions regarding the background against which the book must be understood. Some insist that it is not necessary to look beyond the Old Testament and Jewish religion for the raw material of Revelation. At the other extreme are those who emphasize the correlations between the book of Revelation and the mythic, astrological and religious-philosophical traditions of the various peoples of the Graeco-Roman world and argue that this Christian apocalypse must be understood primarily from the perspective of Graeco-Roman religion.

The purpose of this study is, first of all, to illuminate the book of Revelation by showing that it has a definite and coherent structure. It is a very carefully planned work with clear indications of its overall plan which have very seldom and never adequately been noticed. Our first chapter will be devoted to a study of this structure.

Much of the difficulty modern readers have with the book of Revelation is due to the fact that its images are unfamiliar.

1

The second way in which this study seeks to elucidate Revelation is to show that its major images and narrative patterns are best understood in the framework of the ancient myths of combat. These myths involve a struggle between two divine beings for universal kingship. One combatant is often a monster representing the forces of chaos. Every major culture of the ancient eastern Mediterranean world had at least one native version of such a combat myth: the battle of Marduk and Tiamat in Babylon; the struggle between Baal and Sea in Canaanite literature; the conflict of Horus and Seth in Egypt; and of Apollo with Python in Greece. The bestial opponent is associated with disorder in society and sterility in nature, while the champion is linked with order and fertility. The conflict between the two thus has universal significance and the order and fertility of the cosmos depend on its outcome. These various versions of the combat myth share many motifs and a basic pattern. When reference is made to the combat myth in this study, these shared motifs and basic pattern are meant.

The basic motifs and pattern of the combat myth play a dominant role in the book of Revelation. Now there was already a long-standing Biblical and Jewish practice of adapting the ancient Near Eastern combat myths to interpret the conflicts in which Yahweh and his people had been engaged. The use of the combat myth in Revelation shows that the book should be understood primarily within this tradition. A number of elements in Revelation show, however, that the Old Testament could not have been the only source of the book's imagery, but that there was still direct contact with Semitic mythology. There are also certain key motifs in Revelation which could not have been derived from Semitic myth alone, but can only be explained as adaptations of Graeco-Roman mythology and political propaganda. But these elements are integrated into an overall pattern which owes most to the Semitic-Biblical tradition.

Revelation 12 has been chosen as the starting point for illustrating the affinities of Revelation with the combat myth because they are most extensive and vivid in that passage. In Chapter II it will be demonstrated that the raw material of Revelation 12 derives from the combat myth. It will then be

shown in Chapter III that this mythic material has been adapted
to interpret a conflict situation and to express confidence
about how that conflict will be resolved. In Chapters IV and V
it will be shown that the conclusions about Revelation 12 apply
to the book as a whole. In the overall context of Revelation,
the combat myth functions to interpret a situation of persecution. The policy advocated by the book is a non-violent course
of action in which martyrdom is idealized. The situation is
depicted as a combat which involves the ultimate defeat of the
adversary. This depiction provides a framework in which the
readers of the book can understand their situation and thus be
strengthened in their resolve to endure.

In the course of this study it will be shown that the
images of Revelation are best understood as poetic expressions
of human experiences and hopes. They are not easy to link with
a specific sequence of historical events of the past or future.
Various visions and different formulations of the same experience or hope are juxtaposed. It would thus seem that the book
is not intended to provide an eschatological timetable. It
should rather be read as a poetic interpretation of human experience in which ancient patterns of conflict are used to illuminate the deeper significance of currently experienced conflict.

CHAPTER I

THE STRUCTURE OF THE BOOK OF REVELATION

The book of Revelation consists primarily of visions and auditions, as even the most casual reader can plainly see. This characteristic would seem to indicate that the book belongs to the general literary category "apocalypse."[1] At the same time, these visions are enclosed in an epistolary framework. In its final form at least, the work was apparently intended to be a circular letter.

The Epistolary Framework

With the exception of the preface (1:1-3), the framework of the book is that of the typical ancient letter. The standard form of the prescript (sender, addressee, greeting) is used in vss. 4-5a.[2] The naming of the sender and addressees contains no elaboration, unlike several of Paul's letters.[3] The greeting (vss. 4b-5a) is elaborated in a way quite similar to the greeting in Galatians (1:3).

Most often in the Pauline and deutero-Pauline letters, the greeting is followed by a thanksgiving or blessing, which reflects early Christian liturgical usage.[4] In the opening of Revelation, a doxology (1:5b-6) follows the greeting. This doxology probably reflects liturgical usage as well.[5] Paul's letter to the Galatians also has a doxology in place of the more usual thanksgiving (1-5).

Two isolated prophetic sayings (Rev 1:7, 8) are appended to the doxology.[6] A similar procedure is followed at the end of the book. Revelation closes in 22:21 with a benediction, which is a typical element in the ending of the conventional ancient letter.[7]

It is not immediately obvious where the last vision ends and these sayings begin. At first glance, the reader is inclined to take at least the first part of 22:6 (And he said to me, "These words are trustworthy and true...") as the statement of the angel who showed the seer the vision of the new Jerusalem (cf. 21:9-10, 15-17, 22:1). But Charles and Lohmeyer

5

understand all of vss. 6 and 7 as words of Christ because (1)
the speaker says, "Behold, I am coming soon" in vs. 7a and (2)
there is no indication in vss. 6-7 of a change of speaker.[8] If
the speaker is Christ, rather than the interpreting angel, it
seems best to take the testimony of reliability of "these
words" in 22:6 as referring to the entire book, rather than to
the preceding vision in particular. Thus the series of sayings
begins with 22:6 and continues through vs. 20. Henceforth this
series of sayings culminating in an epistolary conclusion will
be referred to as the epilogue of the book.[9]

Unlike the typical Pauline letter, the book of Revelation
was intended to be a circular letter, as the address to seven
churches shows (1:4).[10] The messages contain references to the
particular situation of several of the communities addressed,
and the exhortation given applies to that situation. For example, certain false teachers are attacked (2:6, 14, 15, 20-23);
the impending arrest of some believers in Smyrna is mentioned
(2:10), as well as the execution of Antipas in Pergamum (2:13).

Nevertheless, the use of the letter form is superficial.
The vision form is introduced already in 1:9. The seven messages do not follow the conventional letter form. The way in
which the messages are linked to the vision of 1:9-20, and
their highly stylized form (which is very much the same in each
message) shows that they were never independent letters but
were composed for their present context.[11] Furthermore, the
book does not open immediately with the prescript of a letter,
but with a preface or prologue which characterizes the book as
an *apokalypsis* and a *prophēteia* (1:1, 3). Daniel Völter and
other source-critics argued that the preface was added later by
an editor or scribe.[12] The primary argument for this theory is
that it is the only passage in the book which refers to John in
the third person. Bousset rejected this theory as unneces-
sary.[13] The arguments against ascribing the preface to a later
editor are that the language and theology of 1:1-3 are very
much in harmony with the rest of the book. Almost every phrase
occurs elsewhere in the work.[14] The emphasis on the imminence
of the events to be described is in keeping with the general
tone of the book.[15] The preface is most closely linked to the
epilogue (22:6-20), where John, in the first person, testifies

to the reliability of the visions and auditions (22:8) and
where tampering with the text of the book is expressly condemned (22:18-19).[16]

It would seem then that the epistolary framework is of
secondary importance. The question thus arises why it was used
at all. The reason may of course have been purely practical.
The use of the letter form may simply reflect common practice
among Christian communities of the time. There are, however,
two implications of the genre which may have been factors in
its use here.

First, the letter form may have been incorporated in order
to put the work in the proper form for liturgical reading. The
preface refers to the reading of the book in a collective, if
not liturgical, situation (1:3). Among the apparently miscel-
laneous prophetic sayings which make up the epilogue of the
book are several liturgical formulae (22:17-20).[17] Günther
Bornkamm has shown that these are specifically eucharistic formulae, and that their occurrence here at the end of the letter
is paralleled by similar formulae in 1 Cor 16:20-24.[18] Bornkamm and others have argued that the presence of such liturgical formulae at the end of early Christian letters indicates
that they were read at worship services, and that the eucharistic celebration followed the reading.[19]

Second, the letter form may have been adapted in this
apocalyptic work as another means of characterizing its content
as a heavenly revelation. Closely linked to the phenomena (or
conventions) of visions and auditions as means of revelation is
the phenomenon of the reception of revelation in written form.[20]
In Jewish tradition, the tablets given to Moses with the commands inscribed by God and the little scroll given to Ezekiel
to eat come immediately to mind. The command given by Christ
to John--to write what he sees in a book and to send it to the
seven churches--seems to characterize the whole book as heavenly revelation in written form mediated by John. The actual
dictation of the seven messages makes this point even more
clearly (2:1, 8, 12, etc.).

Thus the identification of the book of Revelation as a
letter is helpful in determining the author's intent to some
degree. The letter form is used to make the liturgical reading

of the work possible and to characterize it as heavenly revelation. The observation that the letter form is used does not,
however, provide a key to the plan of the body of the work,
which is a collection of vision accounts (4:1-22:5).

The Basic Options

In current research on the book of Revelation, there is
very little consensus on the overall structure of the work and
how that structure should be interpreted. There are almost as
many outlines of the book as there are interpreters.[21] The
root of the problem is the presence of the numerous parallel
passages and repetitions within the book. Particularly striking are the four series of seven: seven messages, seven seals,
seven trumpets and seven bowls. The parallels between the
trumpets and bowls are especially close and have often been
noted.[22] A number of questions then arise. Do these repetitions indicate the use of sources? Do they refer to the same
events or to a sequence of analogous events? Thus, the problem
of the structure of the book of Revelation cannot be separated
from a variety of interpretive issues.

The interpreter has two fundamental options for explaining
the repetition in Revelation. Either it results (a) from the
compilation of sources, or (b) from the literary design of the
author. Within option (b) are two further alternatives.
First, the literary design of the author may be thought to describe a linear sequence of events. Second, it might be
thought to describe the same events several times in different
ways. This second alternative was called the recapitulation
theory by Bousset.[23]

The Recapitulation Theory

The recapitulation theory was in fact the interpretation
given by the oldest commentator on Revelation whose entire work
is extant, Victorinus of Pettau.[24] According to Victorinus,
both the trumpets and bowls predict the eschatological punishment of unbelievers.[25] This approach was adopted by the Donat-
ist Tyconius and by Augustine and dominated the exegesis of the
book for centuries. The recapitulation theory was used exten-
sively both in the rigorously spiritualizing or allegorical

interpretation of Tyconius and in the chiliastic interpretation of Joachim of Fiore, which encompassed all of world history.[26]

The Sources Theory

The recapitulation theory was eclipsed by the extensive interest in the "literary-critical" approach to Revelation aroused by the appearance of Daniel Völter's analysis of the book in 1882.[27] "Literary-critical" in this context refers primarily to the discernment of written sources contained in a work. An extreme form of this approach is what Bousset called the *Quellentheorie* ("sources theory").[28] This is the theory that the author of Revelation was primarily an editor who simply compiled and superficially edited a number of written sources. Friedrich Spitta's analysis of Revelation is an example of the sources theory. He argued that the seals, trumpets and bowls each reflect a source based on a sevenfold series.[29] By the time Bousset was writing his commentary on Revelation, most critics preferred to explain the difficulties which had previously supported the recapitulation theory with theories about the use of sources.[30]

A recent commentator who takes the source-critical approach is M. E. Boismard.[31] Unlike Spitta, he does not focus on the sevenfold series as the starting point of his source analysis, but he uses repetition as the major criterion for deciding whether or not sources were being used and for distinguishing them.[32]

Literary Unity without Recapitulation

This extreme form of the source-critical approach has been widely criticized because of the unity of style in the book.[33] Thus most exegetes following Bousset have taken the other basic option for explaining the repetitions: they are part of the literary design of the author. The recapitulation theory was not immediately revived however. It was out of favor, apparently because it had most commonly been linked with the theory that the book prophesied the course of history from the time of its composition to the time of the exegete. When the latter

theory was challenged, the recapitulation theory was often rejected as well, although the two are not logically related.[34]
Bousset's history of the interpretation of Revelation shows
clearly that he considered the victory of the eschatological
interpretation over the world-historical interpretation to be
one of the most hard-won and important advances of scientific
scholarship on the book. The association of the recapitulation
theory with the world-historical interpretation as well as the
highly fanciful and arbitrary way the recapitulation was interpreted would seem to explain Bousset's rather negative attitude
toward it.[35] At the same time, he was of the opinion, over
against the source critics, that the interpretation of Revelation cannot totally dispense with the recapitulation theory.[36]

Bousset's balanced point of view on this issue was not
maintained by his successors. The recapitulation theory was
completely rejected by Johannes Weiss and R. H. Charles.[37]

R. H. Charles used source-critical methods in his analysis
of Revelation, but was of the opinion that the structure of the
book was carefully planned by the author.[38] Charles' interpretation is an example of the theory that the literary design of
the author describes a linear sequence of events. He argued
that most of the visions in the book are in strict chronological order. The exceptions are ch. 12, which recounts past
events to prepare for those described in ch. 13, and three
"proleptic" visions which interrupt the orderly unfolding of
events to encourage the readers by reference to the more dis-
tant future (7:9-17; 10:1-11:13; 14).[39] These significant exceptions already raise the question of the adequacy of the se-
quential interpretation. The adequacy of this approach is also
called into question by the fact that Charles was forced to
posit the activity of an editor who rearranged the text which
the author had left.[40] This editor was "a very unintelligent
disciple" of the author and "profoundly ignorant of his mas-
ter's thought."[41] According to Charles, the traditional order
of 20:4-22 "exhibits a hopeless mental confusion and a tissue
of irreconcilable contradictions."[42] But it is not only the
latter passage which Charles thought to be in disorder. He
listed nearly a dozen passages in 1:1-20:3 which he felt had

been put out of order by the editor.[43] When such machinations
are necessary to maintain a theory, the viability of that theory is highly questionable.

The Revival of the Recapitulation Theory

The recapitulation theory was revived and established as
an acceptable scholarly theory by Günther Bornkamm in an article which first appeared in 1937.[44] Bornkamm's attempt to illuminate the structure of the book as a whole is based first of
all on the argument that most of the body of the work, the collection of visions, is meant to be the revelation of the content of the scroll with seven seals.[45] Since the scroll cannot
be read until the seventh seal is broken (8:1), the revelation
of what it contains can only begin with 8:2. One is at first
inclined to say that, since 8:2 begins the series of the seven
trumpets, the content of the scroll is identical to that series
and thus ends with 11:19. Bornkamm rejects this interpretation, since he sees a close parallel structure between 8:2-14:
20 and 15:1-19:21. According to his interpretation, the former
segment describes the same series of events as the latter, but
in a mysterious, fragmentary, and proleptic manner. Because of
the relationship between these two segments, Bornkamm argues
that the content of the scroll with the seven seals covers 8:2-
22:6.[46]

In arguing for the parallel structure of 8:2-14:20 and
15:1-19:21, Bornkamm points first of all to the fact that each
section begins with a cycle of seven: the former with the seven
trumpets, the latter with the seven bowls. He shows, as others
have done, that the two cycles are similar, not only in their
seven part structure, but also in content, and that the bowls
bring about an intensification of the plagues of the trumpets.[47]

Secondly, Bornkamm argues that chs. 17-18 were composed in
conscious contrast to chs. 12-13. The queen of heaven in ch.
12 is contrasted with the harlot of ch. 17. One is the mother
of the heavenly child; the other, the mother of harlots and of
earth's abominations. One flees to the desert where she has a
place prepared by God; the other is also seen in the desert,
but riding on the scarlet beast. The similarities between the

dragon and the first beast of chs. 12-13, on the one hand, and the beast of ch. 17, on the other, are pointed out as support for the argument that chs. 17-18 are parallel to chs. 12-13. Finally, the unlimited power of the two beasts in ch. 13 is contrasted with the fall of Babylon in ch. 18.[48]

Thirdly, Bornkamm points out parallels between 14:1-20 and 19:1-21. 14:1-5 describes in a restrained way the heavenly outcome which is fully depicted in 19:1-8. 14:6-12 has no parallel in ch. 19 because it describes in a fragmentary and mysterious manner events which are about to be related in full in ch. 19. 14:13 and 19:9 each begin with the command to the seer that he write, followed by a beatitude. The former beatitude calls those blessed who die in the Lord because their bliss is foreseen; the latter shows the experience of that bliss.[49]

Fourthly, Bornkamm demonstrates that both 14:14-20 and 19:11-21 describe the judgment of the messiah on the powers of the earth. He notes first of all the general similarities: both depict the appearance of a heavenly being (one like a son of man on a white cloud and a figure on a white horse in the heavens) and both use the image of treading the wine press for the wrath of God. Next he shows that certain fragmentary and mysterious elements in 14:14-20 are illuminated if the passage is interpreted as an allusion to 19:11-21. The remark that the wine press was "outside the city" (14:20) is clarified by the reference to the lake of fire in 19:20. The latter is probably Gehenna, whose entrance was traditionally located in the valley outside Jerusalem. The abrupt references to blood and to a horse's bridle (14:20) are mysterious in their context, but are clarified if the image of vintage in ch. 14 is an allusion to battle, as it is in 19:11-21.[50]

Thus Bornkamm's interpretation is that the visions of the book of Revelation are organized into two large sections (8:2-14:20 and 15:1-19:21) which are parallel in structure and content.[51] The strength of this theory is mainly in the recognition of the close and very likely intended parallels between the seven trumpets and the seven bowls and between 14:14-20 and 19:11-21. The weakness of the theory lies first of all in the fact that it excludes the seven seals, which clearly belong to

the vision section. Secondly, the recapitulation in the book
is far more extensive than Bornkamm's theory shows. This point
will be elaborated below. Finally, there does not seem to be a
clear literary signal that 15:1 marks the beginning of the second half of the visions. There is, however, a literary signal
of a midpoint in the visions sections, but not at 15:1. This
point will also be taken up again below.

Series of Seven as an Organizing Principle

The Overall Plan of the Book

Many exegetes have pointed out that the first key to the
plan of the visions of the book of Revelation is the fact that
they are, to a great extent, organized in series of seven.[52]
This observation was the starting point of Austin Farrer's analysis in his first book on Revelation, *A Rebirth of Images*.[53]
In that work he linked the series of seven with the days of
creation and with the Jewish festal calendar and lectionary.
Farrer's theory that the series of seven in Revelation reflect
the calendar and the lectionary is highly speculative and did
not win general acceptance. In his commentary, he shifted his
emphasis from liturgical parallels to the correspondences between the series of seven in Revelation and the "Danielic half-
week of tribulation." This interpretation is no less arbitrary. In spite of his failure to formulate a satisfactory
interpretation of the structure of Revelation, the analysis of
that structure suggested in *A Rebirth of Images* is still the
most faithful to the indications of literary organization within the book of those which have been so far proposed.[54] According to his schema, the book is divided into six sections,
including chs. 1-3, and each is based on the number seven. The
following represents his view of the major sections of the
book:

seven messages	1-3
seven seals	4-7
seven trumpets	8:1-11:14
seven unnumbered visions	11:15-14:20
seven bowls	15-18
seven unnumbered visions	19-22 [55]

Farrer's method for distinguishing the individual visions
in the two unnumbered series is basically formal. The visions
between the trumpets and bowls are isolated simply by counting
the introductory formulae of the vision accounts. Visions are
usually introduced with *eidon* or *ōphthē*.[56] Using this method,
we arrive at the following sequence:

1.	The woman and the dragon	12:1-17
2.	The beast from the sea	13:1-10
3.	The beast from the earth	13:11-18
4.	The Lamb and the 144,000	14:1-5
5.	The three angels	14:6-13
6.	One like a son of man	14:14-20
7.	The seven angels with seven plagues	15:1 [57]

Farrer notes that in ch. 12 there are actually two occurrences of *ōphthē*, the introductory formula, in vss. 1 and 3.
This does not mean, however, that there are two distinct visions in ch. 12. Rather, the formula is used in this case to
introduce each of the two main figures whose interaction forms
a single vision account.[58] Farrer does not notice, however,
that the introductory formula *eidon* occurs twice at the beginning of ch. 15 (in vss. 1 and 2). The reason for the repetition is that 15:1 is actually the introduction to the series of
the seven bowls, while 15:2-4 is the seventh vision of the unnumbered series. We shall return to this point below.

This first series of unnumbered visions (12:1-15:4) is
quite easily distinguished, since it is bounded by the clearly
numbered series of trumpets and bowls. Beginning with 17:1,
however, the numbering ceases, and thus the distinguishing of
series and individual visions becomes more difficult.

Farrer argues quite plausibly that ch. 17 should be included in the bowls section, since (1) it is introduced by the
appearance of one of the angels of the bowls to the seer immediately following the activity of those angels, and (2) its
content is an elaboration of the effect of the seventh bowl,
the fall of Babylon (cf. 16:19 with 17:1, 5). Rev 17:1 prom-
ises to describe the judgment of the harlot. But this judgment
is only briefly described in 17:16. The more elaborate commentary on her downfall finally comes in ch. 18, which therefore
should also be included in the bowls section. Rev 19:1-10 is

the heavenly celebration of the judgment described in ch. 18
and is thus the climax of the series involving the seven
bowls.[59]

We are then left with 19:11-22:5 as the second unnumbered
series of visions. Farrer's analysis of this last series is
based on the close parallel between 17:1-3 and 21:9-11. In
each case, one of the angels who had the seven bowls comes to
the seer and says, "Come, I will show you...." In both passages, the seer is then carried to his vantage point by the
Spirit. This parallel contrasts two women--the harlot and the
bride, and two cities--Babylon and Jerusalem, in an antithetical parallelism. Just as 17:1-19:10 elaborates the destruction
of Babylon in 16:19, so also 21:9-22:5 is an elaboration of the
announcement in 21:2 of the descent of new Jerusalem adorned as
a bride. Farrer labels these two passages the Babylon appendix
(17:1-19:10) and the Jerusalem appendix (21:9-22:5).[60]

These two passages border on the last series of vision accounts, 19:11-21:8. Distinguishing each individual vision
again by noting the introductory formulae, we arrive at the
following series:

1. The second coming of Christ   19:11-16
2. Call to the "banquet"   19:17-18
3. The final battle   19:19-21
4. The binding of Satan   20:1-3
5. The thousand year reign   20:4-10
6. The last judgment   20:11-15
7. The new creation and new
   Jerusalem   21:1-8 [61]

One would expect the first three elements of this schema,
and possibly the fourth as well, to belong to a single vision
because of the continuity of content. The repeated use of
eidon is an indication, however, that they are to be distinguished as a series of images. The situation is different in
the seventh vision. This vision is of the new heaven and the
new earth (21:1). The *eidon* is repeated in 21:2 (*Kai tēn polin
tēn hagian Ierousalēm kainēn eidon katabainousan...*). The repetition of *eidon* in this case does not seem to be the indication of a new vision for two reasons. First, the introduction
of the new Jerusalem is not a change of subject, but rather an
elaboration of 21:1. The new Jerusalem is the only aspect of

the new creation which is described in detail. Secondly, each of the seven visions opens directly with *kai eidon*.... In contrast, the *eidon* of 21:2 follows the object. This lack of emphasis on the *eidon* in 21:2 is an indication that in this occurrence it is not functioning as an introductory formula.

A number of criticisms of this overall plan of the book as formulated by Farrer must be made. The points at which he divides the book into the six major sections (see the table above) reflect his theory that several of the series begin with what he calls a sabbath-vision, i.e., a heavenly scene involving liturgy. According to Farrer, there are four such sabbath-visions: 8:1-6, which introduces the seven trumpets; 11:15-19, which introduces the first series of unnumbered visions; 15:1-16:1, which sets the scene for the seven bowls; and 19:1-10, which leads into the final series of visions.[62] Farrer confuses the structure of the book by claiming that these visions introduce what follows. This claim overlooks the fact that at least two of these sabbath-visions function as the end and climax of the series which precedes them. The series of the seals, for example, does not end with ch. 7, as Farrer implies on his chart, since the seventh seal is only opened in 8:1. In the same way, the series of the trumpets does not end with 11:14, as Farrer indicates, since the seventh angel blows his trumpet only in 11:15. The confusion is apparent in his discussion of 19:10, which he describes as both the climax of the Babylon appendix and the beginning of the last series of visions.[63]

The Technique of Interlocking

Farrer might have avoided these anomalies if he had recognized one of the key literary devices of the book, i.e., the technique of interlocking.[64] This device is first used in the opening section. The seven messages of that section have a dual literary function. On the one hand, they are the logical continuation of the epistolary introduction (1:4-6). The seven messages fulfill the literary expectation aroused by the prescript. On the other hand, the messages are part of the initial vision and audition introduced by 1:9 and described in

1:10 and following. The seven messages thus continue the letter in terms of content, but belong formally to the visions.
The messages of chs. 2-3 thus allude back to and continue 1:4-
8, while the introduction to the initial vision in 1:10 points
forward to ch. 4. Ch. 4:1 alludes back to 1:10 by repeating
the motifs of the voice sounding like a trumpet and of the
seer's being *en pneumati*. Chs. 1:9-3:22 then is the first example of an interlocking or transitional passage in Revelation.
In this case the use of the technique does not obscure the fact
that 4:1 marks the beginning of the next section. There is no
need to modify Farrer's schema at this point.

The device of interlocking is used again in the transition
from the seven seals to the seven trumpets (8:1-5). The
seventh unsealing has three effects: the silence of about half
an hour (8:1), the appearance of the seven angels with the
seven trumpets (8:2), and the vision of the angel with the
golden censer (8:3-5). The interlocking device is used here in
two ways. First, since one of the effects of the seventh unsealing is the introduction of the seven trumpet angels, the entire series of trumpets is linked to the preceding section as
the result of the opening of the seventh seal. Second, the
vision of the angel with the golden censer is inserted between
the introduction of the trumpet angels in vs. 2 and the description of their activity which begins in vs. 6. This insertion (8:3-5) is a transitional vision because it alludes back
to the fifth seal and forward to the first four trumpets. With
the mention of the altar and the prayers of the saints (8:3),
two key motifs of the vision following the fifth seal (the
souls beneath the altar) are repeated. The vision of the angel
offering incense in 8:3-5 thus repeats the prayer for vengeance
of 6:9-11 in different images and language. The casting of
fire upon the earth in 8:5 foreshadows the catastrophes of the
first four trumpets. Thus 8:3-5 also interlocks the seals and
the trumpets by alluding back to 6:9-11 and forward to 8:6-12.

There are a number of difficulties involved in the interpretation of the literary integration of the trumpets and the
seals. The significance of the silence is a crucial point.[65]
Bousset interpreted the silence as a literary technique to

build suspense for the blowing of the seven trumpets.[66] But
the silence has the effect of breaking the momentum from seals
to trumpets. The symbolic significance of the silence seems to
be some sort of mysterious End.[67] This impression is supported
by the use of the image in 4 Ezra 7:30, where a cosmic silence
represents the return of the world to its original state. The
primary impact of the seventh seal is the sense of an Ending.
There is thus discontinuity between the seals and the trumpets.
This element of discontinuity precludes the idea that a sequen-
tial relationship between the two series is implied, that is,
that they form a continuous chain of events in chronological
order.[68]

The device of interlocking is thus used here in two ways:
(1) the seven trumpets are linked to the seven seals as the result of the opening of the last seal; (2) the vision of 8:3-5
refers back to the fifth seal and forward to the first four
trumpets.

The use of the interlocking technique in this case creates
an overlap between the seals and the trumpets, which Farrer's
scheme does not reflect. The overlap should be expressed by
designating the series of the seven seals 4:1-8:5 and the trumpet series 8:2-11:19.

So far we have seen that the technique of interlocking has
been used to link the seven messages with the vision which follows and to link the seven seals with the series of trumpets.
The trumpet visions are not linked to the series of unnumbered
visions which follows in as clear and firm a manner. But there
is a link between the two sections. This link is made by the
abrupt introduction of the beast from the abyss in 11:7. The
beast plays a major role in the action of ch. 11, but the
reader is not informed about the nature of this beast until
chs. 13 and 17, i.e., in the next series of visions.

The transition from the first series of unnumbered visions
to the series of the seven bowls is also characterized by the
interlocking technique. In Farrer's list of the seven visions
in this series, the seventh is the appearance of the angels
with the seven plagues in 15:1. Actually the introductory
formula *eidon* occurs twice in this passage, in 15:1 and 15:2 as

we noted above. The function of 15:1 is to introduce the
series of the seven bowls, which actually begins in 15:5 with
the third occurrence of *eidon*. Thus 15:2-4 constitutes a separate vision of the faithful in heaven, which has been inserted
into the introduction to the seven bowls (15:1, 5-8). Ch. 15:
2-4 is therefore the seventh vision of the first unnumbered
series and interlocks that series with the seven bowls. The
placement of 15:2-4 is similar to that of 8:3-5. The latter,
as was shown above, is inserted between the appearance of the
trumpet angels (8:2) and the beginning of their activity (8:6).
So also 15:2-4 is inserted between the appearance of the angels
with the plagues (= bowls; 15:1) and the beginning of the narrative involving them (15:5).

The series of the seven bowls is linked to the second
series of unnumbered visions by the parallel introductions to
the Babylon and Jerusalem appendices and by the antithetical
parallelism of their content.

A final modification which should be made in Farrer's plan
is the distinction of the prologue (1:1-8) and epilogue (22:6-
21) from the visions.

The overall plan of the book of Revelation is thus structured to a great extent in sevenfold series of visions. The
divisions of the book indicated by the above discussion are as
follows:

1. Prologue   1:1-8
     preface   1:1-3
     prescript and sayings   1:4-8
2. The seven messages   1:9-3:22
3. The seven seals   4:1-8:5
4. The seven trumpets   8:2-11:19
5. Seven unnumbered visions   12:1-15:4
6. The seven bowls   15:1-16:20
     Babylon appendix   17:1-19:10
7. Seven unnumbered visions   19:11-21:8
     Jerusalem appendix   21:9-22:5
8. Epilogue   22:6-21
     sayings   22:6-20
     benediction   22:21

The Two Scrolls as an Organizing Principle

In the critique of Bornkamm's theory on the structure of
Revelation in the section on basic options above, it was

objected that there is no indication that 15:1 is the midpoint
of the book of Revelation. The purpose of this section is to
show that there are indeed literary indications that the work
is presented in two great halves, namely, 1:9-11:19 and 12:1-
22:5. These indications are (1) the parallel between the commission of the seer in 1:9-3:22 and his recommission in ch.
10; (2) the parallel and contrast between the scroll with the
seven seals in ch. 5 and the open scroll given to the seer in
ch. 10. The way in which these parallels are integrated into
the structure of the work points to 12:1 as the midpoint of the
book.

The Commission of the Seer

In the initial vision of the book (1:9-3:22), the seer is
commissioned twice by Christ who appears to him as the Danielic
son of man with attributes of the ancient of days as well.[69]
In 1:11 he is told to write what he sees in a scroll (*biblion*)
and to send it to the seven churches. In 1:19 the commission
is resumed (*grapson oun*). He is told to write "what he saw and
what is and what is about to take place hereafter." The last
clause of this commission is picked up again in 4:1. The seer
is shown an open door in heaven and he hears the same voice
which he had heard in the first vision, saying, "Come up here,
and I will show you what must take place hereafter." The resumption of the commission of 1:19 in 4:1 shows that the seer
was ordered to communicate not just the seven messages but the
visions which begin in 4:1 as well.

In the vision of the mighty angel in ch. 10, the seer is
commissioned a second time. In vss. 8-9 he is told to take the
little scroll from the mighty angel and to eat it. His com-
pliance is described in vs. 10. The eating of the scroll here
is of course a symbolic action which expresses in a concrete
way the idea that the message communicated by the prophet does
not originate with himself, but has a divine origin. A similar
symbolic action is related in Ezek 2:8-3:3.[70] The commission
to prophesy follows the symbolic action in Ezek 3:4-11. So
also in Rev 10:11, a command to prophesy follows the eating of
the scroll. The image whereby the angel gives the seer a

scroll to eat implies that the angel conveys to the seer the message he is to communicate.

Chs. 1 and 10 thus are parallel because they each describe the appearance of a revealing figure who commissions the seer to communicate what is being revealed to him. They each involve the idea of the reception of revelation in written form. The wording of the commission in 10:11 implies that the first commission has already been fulfilled and that a new one is being issued: "You must *again* prophesy about many peoples and nations and tongues and kings."

The Two Scrolls

There are several indications that ch. 10 was composed as a parallel not only to ch. 1 but to ch. 5 as well. The first indication is the fact that the angel who appears to the seer in ch. 10 is deliberately linked to the angel in ch. 5 who asks, "Who is worthy to open the scroll and to break its seals?" (5:2). The latter is called *aggelon ischyron*; the angel of ch. 10 is introduced as *allon aggelon ischyron* (10:1).[71] The second indication that ch. 10 is meant to be a parallel to ch. 5 is the fact that both visions involve a heavenly writing. In both cases the scroll is at first in the hand of a heavenly being. In 5:1 the scroll is in the hand of the enthroned deity. In 10:2, 8 the scroll is in the hand of the angel. There also seems to be a deliberate contrast made between the *biblion...katesphragismenon* of 5:2 and the *biblion to ēneōgmenon* of 10:8. In ch. 5 the action of the Lamb is described: "And he went and took [the scroll] from the right hand of him who was sitting on the throne. And when he had taken the scroll...." (5:7-8). In ch. 10 the action of the seer is similar: "And I went to the angel....And I took the little scroll from the hand of the angel...and when I had eaten it...." (10:9-10).

The significance of the parallel between chs. 5 and 10 depends of course on the nature of the scroll with the seven seals of ch. 5 and on how much of the work is devoted to the revelation of its content.

The Scroll with the Seven Seals

a. *Physical Form*. Most exegetes agree that the *biblion* of
Revelation 5 should be understood as a scroll rather than a codex.[72] There has been much inconclusive speculation about the
further physical attributes of the scroll.[73] One theory which
has won a number of adherents is that the description of the
scroll fits a form of legal document consisting of two parts
(*Doppelurkunde*). One part would be sealed and thus legally
binding. The contents of the sealed part of the document would
also be written on a second, open portion, which could be easily consulted.[74] The most recent detailed presentation of this
hypothesis was made by Otto Roller, who was followed by Bornkamm.[75] This theory, however, is based on a reading which most
text critics today regard as secondary; i.e., *biblion gegramme-
non esōthen kai exōthen* (5:1). The reading *esōthen kai opis-
then* is to be preferred because it best explains the rise of
the other readings.[76] If the reading *exōthen* is excluded,
there is no hint that the scroll of ch. 5 has an open readable
part. The statement that the scroll was inscribed "inside and
on the back" is best understood as a reference to a scroll
which has writing on both sides, i.e., an *opisthographon* (*biblion*). The writing on the back would still be visible when
such a scroll was rolled up.[77]

The most then that can be said about the physical nature
of the *biblion* of Revelation 5 is that it is a scroll with
writing on both sides, rolled up and sealed with seven seals.

b. *Sealed Writings*. The motif of sealing occurs in two
basic forms: (1) in connection with legal documents, and (2) in
various metaphorical senses. Legal documents that would be
sealed in the ancient world include deeds, wills and certifi-
cates of debt. Jer 32:9-15 is an example of the practice of
sealing in connection with the sale of land. The purchaser is
given two copies of the deed. One is the official copy, which
is sealed, while the other is open for easy reference. In this
case, the purpose of the sealing is to prevent falsification of
the document. The seal makes a document legally valid.[78]

A number of types of legal documents have been proposed as
the significance of the scroll in Revelation 5. Some have

suggested that the sevenfold sealing in ch. 5 derives from the Roman custom of sealing an official will with the seals of seven witnesses.[79] But given the significance of the number seven in the book of Revelation, it is more likely that the seven seals are part of the general reverence and preference for that number.[80] In any case, there is no internal evidence that the scroll of Revelation 5 is meant to be a testament.[81]

Otto Roller, whose thesis about the physical nature of the scroll in ch. 5 was discussed above, also proposed that it should be understood as a certificate of debt or guilt (*Schuldurkunde*).[82] There is, however, insufficient internal evidence to support this thesis.[83]

Isa 8:16-22 is an example of the metaphorical use of the motif of sealing: "Bind up the testimony, seal the teaching among my disciples" (vs. 16). Probably no written document is meant; the "sealing" indicates that the disciples will be the guarantors of the tradition.[84]

In Daniel, the seer is ordered to seal up the book containing the revelations just given to him "until the time of the end" or "because [they] pertain to many days hence" (8:26; 9:24; 12:4, 9). This sort of language is part of the literary fiction of pseudonymity, and explains why a revelation allegedly given in antiquity had not been known hitherto.[85]

Books of judgment are often described as sealed until the day of judgment. Such books are explicitly said to be sealed in 1 Enoch 90:20 (cf. 89:61-64, 68-71). The statement elsewhere, that at the time of judgment, "books were opened," probably thus implies that until then these books were sealed. Such a statement occurs in Dan 7:10, 4 Ezra 6:20, 2 Apoc Bar 24:1 and Rev 20:12.

There is no internal indication that Revelation 4-5 is a judgment scene. There are thus no grounds for saying that the scroll with the seven seals is a book of judgment.

So the fact that the scroll of ch. 5 is sealed, taken in isolation, does not allow us to identify the type of document it is. Since this sealed scroll is also a heavenly book, it must be interpreted in the general context of the ancient idea of heavenly books or tablets.

c. *Heavenly Books.* This concept was current from ancient Sumer to New Testament times in a variety of forms.[86] The major types of heavenly books are (1) the roster of the elect kept in heaven;[87] (2) books of judgment in which deeds are recorded;[88] (3) books of destiny in which future events are inscribed.[89]

The first type, the roster of the elect, occurs in Revelation as the book of life.[90] The scroll of Revelation 5 has been identified with this book of life.[91] This theory has been correctly rejected by most exegetes.[92] Its only support is the fact that the scroll of Revelation 5 is put under the jurisdiction of the Lamb (vss. 5-10), as the book of life is linked specifically to the Lamb in 13:8 and 21:27. In 13:8, as well as in 5:6, 9, 12, it is the *slain* Lamb who has power over the book. But there is no reason why the slain Lamb might not have jurisdiction over several types of heavenly books. The identification of the scroll of ch. 5 with the book of life is untenable in light of the explicit significance given to the book of life in 3:5, 20:15 and 21:27. Christ will confess the names of those who are in the book before God and the angels (3:5). Only those whose names are in the book of life will enter the new Jerusalem (21:27); all others will be thrown into the lake of fire (20:15). These passages make clear that the book of life in Revelation is associated with the quite specific context of the last judgment and eternal salvation or punishment. As was noted above, the heavenly scene of chs. 4-5 is not characterized as a judgment scene. The events which follow the seven unsealings are too varied to fit the rubric of the last judgment. Thus the identification of the scroll in Revelation 5 with the book of life should be rejected.

The only interpretation of the scroll with seven seals which fits the context is that it is a book of destiny, type (3) of those listed above. In other words, it is a heavenly book in which future events are recorded.[93] This concept is widespread in apocalyptic literature.[94] The manner in which the motif is used in Revelation 5 still reflects the roots of this idea in the ancient combat myth, where the possession of the tablets of destiny is associated with kingship. The seven

seals then emphasize the intensity of the secret of the knowledge of future events.[95] That only the Lamb is "worthy" to
open the seals implies (1) the death and resurrection of Christ
is the essential prerequisite for the unfolding of the eschatological events; (2) only Christ can mediate knowledge of the
future.[96]

    d. *Relation of Content of Scroll to Visions*. A great deal
of discussion has focussed on what part of Revelation corresponds to the content of the scroll with the seven seals of Revelation 5. It has been quite logically noted that a scroll
sealed with seven seals in the usual way could not be read until all the seals were broken.[97] However, the breaking of each
seal is followed by an event of an eschatological character.
The events which follow each of the seven trumpets are more intense than those of the seven seals, but certainly not fundamentally different in kind. No reference is made to the actual
reading of the scroll after the opening of the seventh seal.
Thus, it seems that the image of the scroll is not used in such
a way that a strict correlation is set up between the reading
of the scroll and the revelation of the events written therein.
A comparison of the way the image of the heavenly book is used
here with its use in the Apocalypse of Weeks may clarify the
issue. In the latter text Enoch is allowed to read the heavenly books and then communicate their content to others (1 Enoch
93; cf. 81:1-3). In Revelation 5-6, the seer is *shown* the content of the scroll by means of a series of visions. The basic
intent of the image is the same in both cases. But in contrast to 1 Enoch, neither the Lamb nor the seer is said to actually read the scroll in Revelation. Since the scroll is not
read, the point at which the scroll is readable is irrelevant.
Thus there is no reason to suppose that only what follows the
seventh unsealing can be understood as the revelation of the
content of the scroll.

    The question then arises how much of the book of Revela-
tion is associated with the scroll of ch. 5. Ch. 1:9-3:22 and
certainly chs. 4-5 are associated with the scroll in that they
set the scene and prepare for the opening of the scroll and the
revelation of the events associated with it. In 1:19 Christ

commissions John to write, among other things, "what is about
to take place hereafter." This clause is repeated in 4:1 and
thus associated with the visions which follow. This resumption
of the statement does not of course exclude the possibility
that the seven messages also refer to future events. But it
does show that the vision of the scroll and its unsealing is an
important part of the revelation which the seer is commanded to
communicate in 1:11 and 19.[98]

The visions which follow the seven unsealings belong to
the revelation of the content of the scroll of Revelation 5 as
was noted above. The visions associated with the seven trumpets also belong to that revelation, since the seven trumpets
are part of the effect of the seventh unsealing.

The end point of the material associated with the scroll
of ch. 5 seems to be 11:19. This is indicated by the fact that
only the vision sequence of the seven trumpets is integrated
compositionally with the opening of the seals. There is thus a
natural break between 11:19 and 12:1. This break might not be
considered significant except for the fact that ch. 10 presents
a new commission parallel to that of ch. 1 and a new scroll
parallel to that of ch. 5. Before we can conclude that 12:1-
22:5 was composed as a parallel to 1:9-11:19, we must consider
the relation of the little scroll of ch. 10 to the visions
which follow.

The Little Scroll

a. *The Content of the Little Scroll*. As was noted above
in the section on the commission of the seer, he receives a new
commission in 10:11: "You must *again* prophesy about many peoples and nations and tongues and kings." The question naturally arises as to when the seer begins to fulfill this new commission. As noted earlier, the eating of the little scroll
(10:8-10) and the command to prophesy belong together. The
scroll is an image for the transmission of the message which is
to be announced by the prophet. Therefore, it is not legitimate to argue, on the one hand, that the content of the little
scroll is 11:1-13, but that the command to prophesy, on the
other hand, refers to ch. 12 or 17.[99]

In any case, ch. 11 does not seem to be the continuation
of ch. 10. Ch. 11:1-13 cannot be the presentation of the content of the little scroll of 10:8-10, i.e., it cannot be the
message which goes with the symbolic act of eating the scroll,
because 11:1-2 is a *new* symbolic act. The command to measure
the temple in 11:1-2 is the symbolic act which is associated
with the message of 11:3-13.[100] Ch. 11 then should not be used
to illuminate the nature and content of the little scroll of
ch. 10.[101]

Chs. 10 and 11 interrupt the series of the seven trumpets
between the sixth and the seventh. Ch. 10, as we have noted,
seems to have been composed as a parallel to chs. 1 and 5.
There are a number of indications that a written source lies
behind ch. 11.[102] The placement of this source after ch. 10 is
understandable without the assumption that 11:1-13 represents
the content of the little scroll. Ch. 11 was placed within the
trumpet series for a literary purpose, i.e., to interlock the
trumpet series with the visions which follow by the cryptic
reference to the beast from the abyss (11:7). It should also
be noted that the two symbolic acts of eating a scroll and measuring the temple were already combined in the book of Ezekiel,
so their combination here would be natural.

If therefore, the revelation of the content of the little
scroll is not 11:1-13, the most natural assumption is that the
revelation in question begins in 12:1, after the completion of
the trumpet series. This theory is supported by the wording of
the commission in 10:11, whose reference to many kings seems to
allude to chs. 13 and 17.[103] If the revelation of the content
of the little scroll and the fulfillment of the new commission
only begin in 12:1, the question arises as to why ch. 10 was
placed where it is.

b. *The Placement of Ch. 10.* The placement of ch. 10 is
another example of the interlocking device discussed above.
Just as 11:7 with its mention of the beast from the abyss
points ahead to chs. 13 and 17, ch. 10 also announces proleptically that after the seventh trumpet, the seer will "again
prophesy about many peoples and nations and tongues and kings"
(10:11). By resuming and paralleling chs. 1 and 5 and at the

same time pointing ahead to chs. 13 and 17, ch. 10 firmly links the new series of visions with what precedes.

We have already noted that 12:1 begins a new series of seven unnumbered visions. The parallel of ch. 10 with chs. 1 and 5 would seem to indicate that 12:1 also begins a second great cycle of visions. We have seen that 1:9-11:19 is a tightly knit unity. The question naturally arises whether 12:1-22:5 is also a unified whole.

c. *The Unity of Chs. 12-22.* We noted in the section on series of seven as an organizing principle that 12:1-22:5 consists of three series of visions: the first unnumbered series (12:1-15:4), the seven bowls plus the Babylon appendix (15:1-19:10), and the second series of unnumbered visions plus the Jerusalem appendix (19:11-22:5). The first two of these series are interlocked in the same way as the series of seals and trumpets; this was shown in the section above on the interlocking technique. It was also noted that the second and third series are linked by the parallelism of the two appendices.

The three series of the second great cycle of visions are also linked by the continuation of certain narrative elements which have their starting points in ch. 12. There are a number of open-ended elements in the narrative of ch. 12. The messianic office of the child is announced in vs. 5 as his *future* function: *hos mellei poimainein ktl.* In the present, redacted form of the chapter the "child" has actually taken office as messiah: *arti egeneto...kai hē exousia tou Christou autou...* (vs. 10). But the continuation of that verse--*hoti eblēthē ho katēgōr tōn adelphōn hēmōn...*--as well as the general context imply that this office is as yet fully exercised only in heaven. The actual fulfillment of the particular messianic function announced in vs. 5--shepherding the nations with an iron rod--is finally narratively described only in 19:11-21 and 20:4-6 (specifically, 19:15). The relationship between 12:5 (prediction) and 19:11-21, 20:4-6 (fulfillment) thus functions as a kind of literary bracket, framing the material in between and qualifying it as the eschatological period between the heavenly installation and earthly manifestation of the messiah.

The rescue of the woman is also open-ended. She is to be nourished in the desert for a predetermined and limited length of time (vss. 6, 14). The implication of the time limit is that her sojourn in the desert is a prelude to a further event. The fact that the *desert* is the place of sojourn also implies that something more is to come. In post-Maccabean Judaism, especially in eschatologically oriented groups, flight to the desert or sojourn in the desert was typologically understood as a New Exodus which would be followed by a New Conquest.[104] This particular element of narrative open-endedness is not picked up again and rounded off with the explicitness of the element concerning the messianic office of the child. It is not said later in a further narrative section that the woman is brought forth from the desert. But the expectation evoked by this element is later satisfied. The New Exodus of ch. 12 is followed by the New Conquest of 19:11-21. The limited rescue or salvation of ch. 12 is followed by the ultimate rescue or salvation of 21:1-22:5. The function of the open-endedness of the rescue of the woman then is to create a tension of expectation in the reader which is finally resolved in chs. 21-22.

The defeat of the dragon in ch. 12 is also an open-ended feature of the narrative because the defeat is only partial. This partiality is expressed in spatial terms. The dragon = Satan is defeated in heaven (vss. 8-9), but the immediate effect of that defeat is that he exercises a more direct and wrathful control over the earth (vs. 12). Since Satan has lost access to the heavenly court, he no longer has the opportunity to influence directly the ultimate destinies of human beings by accusing them before the divine judge. Henceforth he must work through earthly persons, institutions and events to achieve his aims.

A further explicit signal that the defeat of the dragon is only partial is the statement that his time is short (vs. 12). The reader is signalled to expect a burst of activity on Satan's part to follow. This expectation is partly fulfilled already in vs. 17 when it is said that the dragon went away to make war on the rest of the seed of the woman, i.e., on the followers of Jesus. This activity is continued, or rather described, in the following statement: *kai estathē epi tēn ammon tēs thalassēs. Kai eidon ek tēs thalassēs thērion anabainon....* (12:18-13:1).[105] The dragon raised up a beast which will be his instrument of war against the seed of the woman. This viceroyship of the beast for the dragon is made explicit in 13:2 and 4. The rebellious activity of the dragon is continued in 16:13-14 by the assembling of the kings of the whole world (*tēs oikoumenēs holēs*) for the war of the great day of God the Pantocrator.

These activities constitute a second rebellion of Satan against God (the first being the attack on the woman and her child in ch. 12). This second rebellion is also put down by an angel, this time unnamed, in 20:1-3. The defeat is again a partial one. The partiality is expressed here in temporal terms. The dragon will be bound, confined to the abyss for a limited time, a thousand years. The third rebellion consists in the assembling of Gog and Magog and instigating their attack on the camp of the saints as they enjoy the messianic reign (20:7-9). This final rebellion is also suppressed by heavenly means (fire from heaven--vs. 9). This time the defeat of Satan is definitive. He is thrown into the lake of fire and sulphur, where he will be tormented *eis tous aiōnas tōn aiōnōn* (vs. 10).

There is a further element which unifies the second cycle of visions, the theme of the persecution of the faithful. Unlike the other narrative elements discussed above, it also occurs in the first cycle of visions.[106] But like the others, it is introduced (in the second cycle) by a statement in ch. 12; i.e., that the dragon went away to make war on the rest of the seed of the woman (12:17). This theme is explicitly picked up again in 13:7 where it is said that the beast, Satan's instrument, was allowed to make war on the saints and to conquer them. This statement is elaborated in 13:10 with an allusion to Jer 15:2 and/or 43:11--If anyone is for captivity, to captivity he goes. If anyone is to be killed by the sword, he is to be killed by the sword.[107] The second beast also has the power to slay those who refuse to worship the first beast (13:15). In the next series of visions, the seven bowls plus the

Babylon appendix (15:1-19:10), this theme is enunciated several
times. In 16:4-7, the plague of the third bowl is characterized as punishment for shedding the blood of the martyrs. In
17:6 the harlot is said to be drunk with the blood of the
saints and of the martyrs of Jesus. A similar point is made in
18:24. When the harlot-city is destroyed the blood of prophets
and saints was found in her. The exhortation in 18:20--Rejoice
over her, O heaven, and saints and apostles and prophets because God has given judgment for you against her--is a further
implication that she has persecuted the faithful. This judgment against 'Babylon' in 19:2 is then explicitly linked to the
persecution of the servants of God. This theme also occurs in
the third series in this cycle (the second unnumbered series of
visions plus the Jerusalem appendix--19:11-22:5), i.e., in the
vision of the resurrection of those who had been beheaded on
account of the testimony of Jesus (20:4). It is also resumed
in the attack led by Satan on the saints in 20:7-10. This persecution theme is a further example of an element in the narrative of ch. 12 which initiates narrative action to be unfold-
ed in the following chapters, and which functions in such a way
as to give thematic unity to the second great cycle of vision
accounts (12-22:5).

The prediction of the messianic function of the child in
ch. 12, which is fulfilled in 19:11-21 and 20:4-6, links the
first and third series of visions in this cycle. The revolt of
Satan, described in chs. 12, 13 and 16 and definitively quelled
in 20:10, links all three series, as does the theme of persecution as shown above.

Summary

We have seen that the book of Revelation is organized in
two great cycles of visions, 1:9-11:19 and 12:1-22:5. Each
cycle consists of three series of seven: (1) the seven messages, seals, and trumpets; (2) seven unnumbered visions, the
seven bowls, and a second series of seven unnumbered visions.
The first cycle is introduced by the vision of 1:9-3:22 in
which the seer is commissioned, and it concerns the revelation

of the content of the scroll with seven seals. The second cycle is introduced by the vision of ch. 10 in which the seer is commissioned a second time. The revelation contained in this cycle is symbolized by the little scroll of ch. 10.

Recapitulation in the Book of Revelation

In the discussion of basic options for interpreting the book of Revelation, it was noted that Bornkamm had made a significant contribution by reinstating the recapitulation theory.[108] Two criticisms were made of his application of that theory: (1) we could not accept his structural arguments that the revelation of the content of the seven scrolls begins only with 8:2, and that 15:1 begins the second great cycle of visions; (2) it was indicated that the recapitulation in Revelation is more extensive than Bornkamm realized.

The purpose of this section is to show how the conclusions argued above regarding the structure of Revelation relate to the principle of recapitulation. It was argued that, aside from the prologue and epilogue, the book is divided into six sections, each characterized by seven numbered or unnumbered elements. The recapitulation does not extend into all six of these sections, but begins with the revelation of the content of the scroll with the seven seals, i.e., at 6:1. There are thus five series of visions which manifest recapitulation:

1. The seven seals   6:1-8:5
2. The seven trumpets   8:2-11:19
3. Seven unnumbered visions   12:1-15:4
4. The seven bowls   15:1-16:21
   Babylon appendix   17:1-19:10
5. Seven unnumbered visions   19:11-21:8
   Jerusalem appendix   21:9-22:5

The most regularly recurring motifs in the five series are the following elements: (a) persecution, (b) the punishment of the nations, followed by (c) the triumph of God, the Lamb, and/or the faithful. The second great cycle of visions also recapitulates the first. Bornkamm's theory concerning the relationship of the two great cycles was that the first tells the story in an allusive, fragmentary and veiled way, while the second presents the same basic story in a more straightforward manner,

more clearly and with more detail. We will show that this
theory is even more applicable to the two cycles as we have
delimited them. The first is vague, mysterious and fragmentary
at a number of points. For this reason, its primary symbol is
the sealed scroll. The second cycle clarifies the issues
hinted at in the first. Therefore, it is characterized by the
open scroll.

Recapitulation in the Five Series

As was noted above, there are five series of visions in
Revelation, each of which recapitulates the threefold pattern
described above: (a) persecution, (b) punishment of the nations, and (c) triumph of God, the Lamb, or the faithful. The
five series are the seals, the trumpets, the first unnumbered
series, the bowls, and the second unnumbered series.

a. *The Seven Seals.* The seven seals are divided into two
groups by the association of the first four with four horses.
Aside from the enigmatic first vision (6:2), the events following the first four unsealings comprise traditional eschatological motifs.[109]

The fifth seal, with its vision of the souls of those
slain on account of the word of God and the witness which they
held, is a clear allusion to persecution (6:9). Their oppres-
sors are referred to quite generally as "those who dwell upon
the earth" (vs. 10). The reference to persecution is thus
clear, but no information about the nature of the conflict is
given.

The sixth unsealing is followed by a description of the
great day of wrath of the enthroned one and of the Lamb (6:12-
17). This "day of wrath" is described with the language traditionally associated with the theophany of the divine warrior.[110] The wrath seems to be directed against all humanity:
the kings of the earth, the great, the generals, the rich, the
strong, every slave and every free person (vs. 15).

This passage is followed by two vision accounts (7:1-8 and
9-17) which are not associated with an unsealing, but are inserted between the sixth and the seventh seals. The placement

of these two visions is thus analogous to the placement of ch.
10 and 11:1-13. The analogy would lead us to expect that the
two visions of ch. 7 are so placed for a literary reason. They
do not seem to have an interlocking function, so it would seem
that their placement is intended to single them out for emphasis.

Each of these visions describes the salvation of the
elect. Ch. 7:1-8 relates the sealing of the 144,000 to preserve them from the plagues which are about to come upon the
world (cf. 7:2-3, 9:4). The following vision (7:9-17) describes the salvation and triumph of "those who come out of the
great tribulation" (vs. 14). They stand before the throne of
God and in the presence of the Lamb (vss. 9, 15); they partici-
pate in the heavenly liturgy by serving in the temple (vs. 15)
and by hymning the deity and the Lamb (vss. 10, 12).[111] Since
the faithful are sealed to protect them from the plagues of divine wrath, the "great tribulation" (vs. 14) is probably a reference to persecution. As in 6:9-11, no details are given
about this persecution.

In the series of the seven seals, the elements which are
elaborated and emphasized are: (a) persecution (the fifth seal
and 7:14), (b) the punishment of the nations, which is here
alluded to by the manifestation of the wrath of God against all
humanity (the sixth seal), and (c) the triumph of the faithful,
which takes the form of the description of their salvation
(7:1-8 and 9-17).

b. *The Seven Trumpets.* The vision which interlocks the
series of the seals with the trumpet series (8:3-5) alludes to
persecution by resuming the motifs of the altar in heaven and
the prayers of the saints from the vision of the fifth seal
(6:9-11).[112] The juxtaposition of the symbolic act of casting
fire upon the earth with the offering of the prayers of the
saints implies that the plagues of the seven trumpets which
follow are divine acts of judgment executed as vengeance for
the suffering of the faithful.[113] This motif is explicit in
the third bowl vision, as we will see below.

Like the seals, the seven trumpets are divided into two
groups. The last three trumpets are singled out as three woes

(8:13). The first four trumpets are followed by plagues on various parts of the natural world. These plagues are reminiscent of those wrought by Moses against Egypt.[114] They are briefly described, as are the events following the first four unsealings. The only vision in the series of the seals whose destruction is quantified is the fourth, where Death and Hades are allowed to kill one-fourth of humanity. The eschatological woes which follow the first four trumpets express an intensification over the seals, in that one-third of the elements affected are destroyed. The two sets of four are distinguished insofar as the seals involve humanity, while the trumpets affect the natural world.

The last three trumpets, designated as three woes, are followed by longer and more elaborate visions than those following the first four trumpets. Thus, in both of the series, it is the later visions which are emphasized (the fifth and following in both cases).

The vision which follows the fifth trumpet (9:1-11) is a bizarre transmutation of the eighth plague against the Egyptians, the swarm of locusts (Exod 10:12-20). The Exodus motif is fused with images from Joel, where a natural plague is described with various metaphors, and is associated with eschatological holy warfare (cf. Rev 9:7a and 9b with Joel 2:4-5; Rev 9:8b with Joel 1:6).[115] The apocalyptist mythicizes the image even further by characterizing the locusts as beings from the abyss led by the angel of the abyss (9:2-3, 11).[116] Strangely, these locusts are not to devour the green plants of the earth, but to torture human beings by stinging them (9:4-6, 10). One aspect of the grotesque and highly mythological picture are the clear military allusions: the locusts appear as horses arrayed for battle (vs. 7), their chests are like iron breastplates, i.e., military armour (vs. 9). They have human characteristics: human faces and hair (vss. 7-8) and crowns like gold (vs. 7). The crowns of course bring kings to mind.

The vision which follows the sixth trumpet (9:13-21) is also a mythological collage involving angelic beings (vss. 14-15) and torture of individual human beings (vss. 18-19). The military dimension is also present here. It is less veiled

than in the preceding vision. The four angels bound at the
Euphrates are the leaders of troops of cavalry (vs. 16) whose
riders wear breastplates (vs. 17).[117]

In neither of these visions is an actual battle described.
The vision following the sixth trumpet, however, seems to be a
cryptic allusion to a battle described later in the book. The
vision following the sixth bowl (16:12-16) corresponds to 9:13-
21 as the sixth in a series. It also mentions angelic-demonic
beings (*pneumata tria akatharta*--16:13; *pneumata daimoniōn*--16:
14), who are to assemble the kings of the world for battle.
These kings (at least in part) will approach via the Euphrates,
which will be dried up as a passageway for them. The vision
ends before the battle takes place (16:16). The fact that
these spirits and kings are associated in the vision of the
sixth bowl with the dragon and the two beasts of ch. 13 shows
that this vision is a fragmentary description of the great battle of 19:11-21. Because of the parallels between the visions
of the sixth trumpet and the sixth bowl, it would seem that
9:13-21 (the sixth trumpet) is a cryptic allusion to the final
battle.[118]

The series of trumpet visions ends with an emphatic description of the last things (11:15-19):

1. The manifestation of the kingdom of God and Christ
   in the world (vss. 15, 17)
2. The destruction of the nations and the destroyers
   of the earth (vs. 18)
3. The judgment of the dead (vs. 18)
4. The reward of the faithful (vs. 18)

Like the vision of the salvation of the faithful in 7:9-17,
this account is also set in heaven and contains a heavenly
liturgy (vss. 17-18).

The element of persecution (a) is alluded to in the vision
which interlocks the series of the seals with that of the trumpets (8:3-5). The final conflict involving the punishment of
the nations (b) is alluded to in the sixth trumpet (9:13-21)
and proclaimed in the heavenly scene associated with the seventh trumpet (11:18). The reward of the servants of God and
the triumph of God and Christ (c) is celebrated in that heavenly scene also (11:15, 17, 18).

c. *The First Unnumbered Series.* The first series of unnumbered visions opens with a vision which interprets the persecution faced and expected by the first readers of the book by
placing it within the framework of a cosmic conflict (ch.
12).[119] The two visions of ch. 13 further characterize this
conflict.[120]

The fourth and fifth visions are preliminary announcements
of salvation and judgment. The fourth (14:1-5) depicts the
144,000 redeemed from the earth and with the Lamb. The mention
of the throne, the four living creatures, and the elders implies that the setting is heaven (vs. 3), but the explicit locale given is Mt. Zion (vs. 1). The new song which the redeemed have learned is mentioned but not quoted (vs. 3). The
fifth vision (14:6-13) announces the judgment of Babylon (vs.
8) and of those who worshipped the beast (vss. 9-11).

The sixth vision in this series (14:14-20) alludes to the
final defeat of the earthly powers. It does so in a veiled
way, as Bornkamm has shown.[121] The angel, one like a son of
man, sitting on a white cloud, is not Christ, but would inevi-
tably bring to mind the second coming of Christ as Son of Man
for the earliest Christian readers. The image of the harvest
of grain (vss. 15-16) was used in at least one other early
Christian writing as a metaphor for the gathering in of all
people for the last judgment.[122] The trampling of the grapes
in the winepress was a well-known image for battle (cf. Isa
63:3, Joel 4:13). Both the harvest and vintage images appear
in Joel 4:13 as metaphors for the final battle of the divine
warrior against the nations. The mention of blood and a
horse's bridle in vs. 20 makes the allusion to battle explicit.
The parallels between 14:17-20 and 19:11-16 indicate that the
battle of 14:14-20 is identical with the defeat of the nations
by Christ as heavenly warrior described in ch. 19. The former
account is veiled in that metaphors for battle are used for the
most part, and in that the warriors are angels. But the explicit reference to battle in vs. 20 and the links with ch. 19
show that an allusion to ch. 19:11-21 is intended.[123]

The seventh vision of this series (15:2-4) describes those
who have conquered the beast standing at the edge of the

crystal sea, i.e., in the presence of God (cf. 4:6). Like 7:
9-17 and 11:15-19, the setting is heaven, and the focus is a
hymnic liturgy (15:3-4). This final vision climaxes the series. The characterization of the faithful proclaims their victory over the threat of persecution elaborated in ch. 13 ("the
conquerors of the beast and its image and the number of its
name"--15:2). The song which they sing (15:3-4) celebrates the
revelation of the judgments of God, i.e., those announced in
14:6-13 and allusively described in 14:14-20.

The first unnumbered series of visions thus begins with
three visions which depict persecution (a). It ends with (b)
an allusion to the final defeat of the earthly powers (14:14-
20), followed by (c) a description of the triumphant faithful
in heaven (15:2-4).

d. *The Seven Bowls*. The first four bowls are closely parallel to the first four trumpets. A new element in the bowls
is that an interpretation is given to one of the plagues (the
third--16:4-7). The plague on the rivers and the fountains of
water by which they are turned to blood is interpreted as vengeance for the blood of the martyrs.[124]

The fifth bowl is similar to the fifth trumpet in the motifs of darkness and physical anguish of individuals. The
fifth trumpet, as shown above, makes a veiled reference to armies, kings and battle. The fifth bowl, by its mention of the
throne and kingdom of the beast, alludes to the conflict of
Christ and his followers with the beast, and thus indirectly
to the persecution which that conflict involves.

The vision of the sixth bowl (16:12-16) recapitulates that
of the sixth trumpet as noted above. The former is a clear,
though fragmentary, description of the final battle.

The actual defeat and punishment of the powers of the
earth (the cities of the nations--16:19) is related in the vision of the seventh bowl (16:17-21). This act of judgment involves Rome in particular (= Babylon--16:19) and is elaborated
in chs. 17-18.[125]

In light of the pattern seen in the other series so far,
we expect a description of salvation to follow this depiction
of vengeance. That we find it in 19:1-10 supports the

hypothesis that 17:1-19:10 belongs with the seven bowls series
as an appendix.

In 19:1-10 we find, as in the previous corresponding passages, a heavenly scene and a heavenly liturgy. The liturgy in
this case consists of five acclamations or hymns (vss. 1b-2,
3b, 4b, 5b, 6b-8a). These acclamations, taken as a whole, parallel 11:15-19 in the proclamation of the establishment of the
reign of God (cf. 19:6b with 11:15, 17), of the punishment of
the nations (cf. 19:2, 3b with 11:18) and of the reward of the
faithful (cf. 19:1 and 9 with 11:18).

In the series of the seven bowls, the element of persecution (a) appears in the vision of the third bowl (16:4-7). The
punishment of the nations (b) is alluded to in the sixth bowl
(16:12-16) and described in the seventh bowl (16:17-21). The
triumph of God and the salvation of the faithful are proclaimed
in the heavenly scene which climaxes the appendix to the bowls
(19:1-10).

e. *The Second Unnumbered Series.* Several unique features
of the second series of unnumbered visions become apparent upon
comparison with the previous four. The events which were alluded to in veiled language or only partially told in the earlier sections are here described in a continuous narrative.
Two of the elements traced in the earlier series, (b) the decisive punishment of the nations and (c) the final triumph and
salvation, here comprise nearly the entire section rather than
its later stages alone. Finally, and most strikingly, there is
even a recapitulation within this section itself.

The penultimate battle (19:11-21) results in the slaughter
of the "kings of the earth" and their armies and in the confinement and punishment of the beast and his ally, the pseudo-
prophet. Linked to their downfall is the (temporary) confinement of Satan (20:1-3). This vengeance phase is followed by a
salvation phase, i.e., the first resurrection and the thousand
year reign of Christ (20:4-6). The persecution of the faithful
(a) is mentioned in 20:4 to show that their state of blessed-
ness is both a triumph (a victory over the persecutors in the
battle of which the persecution was part) and a reward.

The first recapitulation of the judgment-salvation sequence within this series then is in 19:11-20:6. The first or judgment phase of the second recapitulation is 20:7-15. It consists of a renewed threat by Satan against the saints and a renewed conflict which ends in the final defeat and confinement of Satan (vss. 7-10) and the last judgment (vss. 11-15). The last judgment is held over *all* the dead, but only the punishment of the wicked is described. This second judgment phase (20:7-15) is then followed by a second salvation phase (21:1-8), which involves a new creation (vss. 1, 5) and the establishment of God's dwelling among his people (21:2-4, 7). The Jerusalem appendix which follows (21:9-22:5) is the elaboration of this second salvation phase.

f. *Summary*. The five series then each depict the eschatological woes and their resolution. The description of the woes vary from series to series, especially in the earlier parts. But a recurring pattern is clearly present in each of the series which consists of (a) persecution of the faithful, (b) divine judgment on their adversaries, followed by (c) their triumph and salvation. This pattern is illustrated on the following chart.

Recapitulation in the Two Cycles

We have seen that each of the five series of visions, beginning with the revelation of the content of the scroll with the seven seals, recapitulates the same pattern of eschatological events. There is also recapitulation in the second great cycle of visions of the content expressed in the first. This recapitulation is such that what is merely alluded to in the first cycle is clarified in the second.

This parallelism is evident when chs. 4-5 are included as the immediate introduction to the series of the seven seals. Each of the introductory passages (chs. 4-5 and ch. 12) consists of a heavenly vision which functions as the backdrop or framework of the visions which follow. Chs. 4-5 focus on the symbolic act of opening a sealed scroll. The scroll is not explicitly identified. The Lamb is not given any clear title,

SEVEN SEALS	SEVEN TRUMPETS	UNNUMBERED (1)	SEVEN BOWLS	UNNUMBERED (2) (A)	(B)
Persecution fifth seal (6:9-11) (cf. 7:14)	[Persecution] interlocking vision (8:3-5)	Persecution first three visions (chs. 12-13)	Persecution third bowl (16:4-7)	Persecution fifth vision (20:4)	[Persecution] sixth vision (20:9)
	[Armies Assembling for Final Battle] sixth trumpet (9:13-21)		Armies Assembling for Final Battle sixth bowl (16:12-16)		
Day of Wrath sixth seal (6:12-17)	Destruction and Judgment seventh trumpet (11:18)	[Judgment and Destruction] sixth vision (14:14-20)	Destruction seventh bowl (16:17-20)	Battle and Destruction first four visions (19:11-20:3)	Battle and Judgment fifth and sixth visions (20:7-15)
Salvation inserted visions (7:1-8 and 9-17) a. heavenly scene (vss. 9-17) b. liturgy (vss. 10-12)	Salvation seventh trumpet (11:18) a. heavenly scene (vss. 15-19) b. liturgy (vss. 15-18)	Triumph and Salvation seventh vision (15:2-4) a. heavenly scene (vss. 2-4) b. liturgy (vss. 3-4)	Triumph and Salvation appendix (19:1-10) a. heavenly scene (vss. 1-10) b. liturgy (vss. 1-8)	Salvation fifth vision (20:4-6)	Salvation seventh vision and appendix (21:1-22:5)

nor is his function clarified beyond his worthiness to open the
scroll. Ch. 12 also relies heavily on symbolic and mythic language. But the hymn of ch. 12 (vss. 10-12) clarifies the function of this language to a greater extent than the acclamations
of ch. 5. We are told that Christ has become sovereign in
heaven and defeated Satan by his death (and exaltation). This
heavenly victory, however, means that the battle will continue
even more intensely on earth in the immediate future. The hymn
of ch. 12 thus not only provides the context for the visions of
the second cycle, but also illuminates the import of the
"worthiness" of the Lamb in ch. 5 and the function of the
scroll. The "worthiness" of the Lamb is an allusion to his
heavenly victory and the unsealing of the scroll corresponds to
the battle with Satan which is still to be waged on earth.

The clear reference to persecution following the fifth
seal (6:9-11) was noted above, as well as the fact that no par-
ticulars regarding the nature of the persecution are given. In
ch. 8:3-5 the motif reappears, but in veiled language. In the
second cycle of visions, the persecution is a major theme; ch.
12 places it in the context of a cosmic dualism. The ultimate
cause of the persecution is the activity of Satan. In chs. 13
and 17 it becomes clear that the proximate adversary is the
Roman empire.

The final battle in which the powers of the earth are to
be judged and destroyed is alluded to in a veiled manner in 6:
12-17 and proclaimed briefly in the heavenly liturgy of 11:15-
19. The allusions become progressively more detailed and more
clear in the second cycle, until the full depiction in the last
series of visions (19:11-20:15).

The salvation of the elect is described very fully in 7:9-
17 from the point of view of the blessed state of the individual or worshipping community and of their fellowship with God
and the Lamb (cf. vss. 15-17). The reference to the reward of
God's servants in 11:18 is again a matter of salvation limited
to the believing community. It is only in the second cycle
that salvation is a cosmic event involving a new creation (21:
1-22:5).

The relationship between the two great cycles of visions
is thus characterized by the fact that each of the major recurring elements is sketched in the first cycle and then described
more fully in the second. It does not thus seem to be accidental that the sealed scroll characterizes the earlier visions,
while an open scroll introduces the later series.

Why Recapitulation?

The phenomenon of recapitulation is not unique to the book
of Revelation. In fact, it seems to be characteristic of a
number of writings with an eschatological interest. The oracles of the third sibyl regularly manifest an eschatological
pattern consisting of (a) idolatry or some other form of rebellion against God which will lead to (b) cosmic disasters, which
will be followed by (c) the arrival of a divinely ordained
king.[126] The major oracles of the fifth sibyl recapitulate a
common structure: (a) oracles against nations, (b) Nero's return as the eschatological adversary, (c) a saviour figure, and
(d) a destruction, usually by fire.[127]

The visions of the book of Daniel repeat the same basic
sequence of events in four parallel accounts: (1) 7:1-18, (2)
7:19-27, (3) 8:1-25, (4) 10:12-12:3. The pattern shared by
these accounts consists of (a) events prior to Antiochus Epiphanes, (b) the career of Antiochus, and (c) the eschatological
outcome.[128]

In 4 Ezra 3:1-9:22 a threefold pattern is used to structure the dialogues between the seer and the revealing angel.
This pattern is comprised of (a) the seer's expression of distress at the destruction of Jerusalem, (b) the seer's complaint
to the Most High, and (c) a vigorous dialogue between the seer
and the interpreting angel. This pattern occurs three times.
Each of the three dialogues ends with a discussion of the signs
of the end.[129]

The dream visions of 4 Ezra are structured on a fourfold
pattern: (1) the dream vision itself, (2) the seer's response,
(3) the angelic interpretation, and (4) a narrative section
which relates the vision to the overall narrative of the
book.[130] This pattern occurs twice in chs. 11:1-13:58. The

repetition in 4 Ezra combined with the fact that the seer's
questions are never given satisfactory, direct responses evokes
the impression that the specific details of the dialogues and
visions are not important in themselves. Rather, it is the impact of the repetition of the pattern which is significant.
Earl Breech has suggested that the repetition serves the purpose of depicting a movement from distress to consolation in the
book as a whole. The consolation derives especially from the
dream-visions which reaffirm the power of the Most High.[131]

The phenomenon of recapitulation, the repetition of the
same basic pattern in a variety of specific formulations, is
not limited to eschatological writings, but seems to be an essential characteristic of mythic language. According to Paul
Ricoeur, myth is condemned by its very nature to division into
multiple cycles. The reason for this is that myth aims at the
intuition of a cosmic whole, its intent is the restoration of
a wholeness which is not *given*, but simply *aimed at*. Thus its
method must be symbolic, and no act of signifying is equal to
its aim.[132] The totality of the various formulations thus
represents the message more fully than any single expression.

According to Claude Lévi-Strauss, myths and other types of
oral literature so often repeat the same sequence because the
function of the repetition is to make the structure of the myth
apparent.[133]

Wayne Meeks has made use of this insight of contemporary
anthropology to explain the repetition of sayings and even
whole discourses in the gospel of John. Meeks refers to Edmund
Leach's formulation of the theory, which uses an analogy from
electronic communications. If a message is to be conveyed in
the presence of distractions, "noise," the communicator must
resort to "redundance." The signal must be repeated, as many
times as possible, in *different* ways. The repeated impact of
varying signals communicates the basic structure which they
have in common.[134]

It would seem then that the pattern isolated in the last
section is the message which underlies the sometimes overwhelming diversity of visions in Revelation. The primary impact of
the book is the movement from persecution to salvation through
combat.

NOTES

CHAPTER I

[1]In fact the modern scholarly term derives from the use of the word *apokalypsis* in Rev 1:1. See Johann M. Schmidt, *Die jüdische Apokalyptik: Die Geschichte ihrer Erforschung von den Anfängen bis zu den Textfunden von Qumran* (Neukirchen-Vluyn: Neukirchener Verlag des Erziehungsvereins, 1969) 87. On modern attempts to define apocalyptic, see Schmidt, *Die jüdische Apokalyptik*, 171-94, 215-44, 277-303; Klaus Koch, *The Rediscovery of Apocalyptic: A Polemical Work on a Neglected Area of Biblical Studies and Its Damaging Effects on Theology and Philosophy* (SBT, second series 2; Naperville, Ill.: Allenson, [1972]) 18-35; D. S. Russell, *The Method and Message of Jewish Apocalyptic: 200 BC-AD 100* (Philadelphia: Westminster, 1964) 104-39. That Revelation belongs to the genre "apocalypse" has been disputed recently by James Kallas, "The Apocalypse--An Apocalyptic Book?" *JBL* 86 (1967) 69-80; Bruce W. Jones, "More about the Apocalypse as Apocalyptic," *JBL* 87 (1968) 325-27.

[2]See Robert W. Funk, *Language, Hermeneutic, and Word of God: The Problem of Language in the New Testament and Contemporary Theology* (New York: Harper and Row, 1966) 257; William G. Doty, *Letters in Primitive Christianity* (Guides to Biblical Scholarship, New Testament Series; Philadelphia: Fortress, 1973) 14.

[3]Cf. Rom 1:1-7a, 1 Cor 1:1-2, 2 Cor 1:1.

[4]See the studies of James M. Robinson cited by Funk, *Language, Hermeneutic, and Word of God*, 256-57.

[5]See Elisabeth Schüssler Fiorenza, *Priester für Gott: Studien zum Herrschafts- und Priestermotiv in der Apokalypse* (NTAbh N. F., 7; Münster: Aschendorff, 1972) 174, 212.

[6]See Ernst Lohmeyer, *Die Offenbarung des Johannes* (HNT 16; Tübingen: Mohr, 1926) 10-11; R. H. Charles, *A Critical and Exegetical Commentary on the Revelation of St. John* (ICC; New York: Scribner's, 1920) 1. 17; on Rev 1:7 see also Norman Perrin, "Mark 14:62: The End Product of a Christian Pesher Tradition?" *A Modern Pilgrimage in New Testament Christology* (Philadelphia: Fortress, 1974) 12, 13, 14, 15, 16, 17, 34-35.

[7]Funk, *Language, Hermeneutic, and Word of God*, 257; Doty, *Letters in Primitive Christianity*, 14.

[8]Lohmeyer, *Offenbarung des Johannes*, 174; Charles, *Revelation of St. John*, 2. 217-18.

[9]A recent study on the structure of the book of Revelation argues that 22:6-20 is the epilogue and conclusion of the entire book (Ugo Vanni, *La struttura letteraria dell'Apocalisse* [Alosiana scritti...8; Rome: Herder, 1971] 107-15); for a

46

different opinion, see Charles H. Giblin, "Structural and Thematic Correlations in the Theology of Revelation 16-22," *Bib* 55 (1974) 487-504.

[10]See Henry Barclay Swete, *The Apocalypse of St. John*, 2nd ed. (London: Macmillan, 1907) xli.

[11]On the dissimilarity of the messages to letters, see ibid.; Lohmeyer, *Offenbarung des Johannes*, 37-38. On the links between the messages and the vision and on the form of the messages, see E. B. Allo, *Saint Jean: L'Apocalypse*, 4th ed. rev. (EBib; Paris: Gabalda, 1933) 29; G. B. Caird, *A Commentary on the Revelation of St. John the Divine* (New York: Harper and Row, 1966) 27.

[12]See the discussion in Wilhelm Bousset, *Die Offenbarung Johannis* (Meyer 16; 5th ed.; Göttingen: Vandenhoeck und Ruprecht, 1896) 212-13.

[13]Ibid.

[14]Cf. 1:9, 19; 2:16; 3:11; 4:1; 22:6, 7, 12, 16, 20.

[15]Cf. 2:16; 3:11; 11:14; 22:6, 7a, 10, 12, 20.

[16]On the parallels between the prologue and the epilogue, see Swete, *Apocalypse of St. John*, xlvi-xlvii.

[17]See Lohmeyer, *Offenbarung des Johannes*, 178-79.

[18]Günther Bornkamm, "On the Understanding of Worship," *Early Christian Experience* (New York: Harper and Row, 1969) 169-79.

[19]Ibid., 169; see also R. Seeberg, "Kuss und Kanon," *Aus Religion und Geschichte: Gesammelte Aufsätze und Vorträge* (Leipzig: Deichert, 1906) 1. 118-20; Hans Lietzmann, *Mass and Lord's Supper: A Study in the History of the Liturgy* (Leiden: Brill, 1955) 186; Karl-Martin Hofmann, *Philema Hagion* (Gütersloh: Der Rufer Evangelischer Verlag, 1938) 23-25.

[20]Franz Boll, *Aus der Offenbarung Johannis: Hellenistische Studien zum Weltbild der Apokalypse* (Stoicheia 1; Leipzig: Teubner, 1914) 7-8; see also L. Röhrich, "Himmelsbrief," *RGG*, 338-39 with bibliography; Geo Widengren, *Muhammad, The Apostle of God, and His Ascension (King and Saviour V)* (UUA 1955:1; Uppsala: Lundequistska, 1955) 115-39.

[21]See the synoptic chart provided by John W. Bowman, "The Revelation to John: Its Dramatic Structure and Message," *Int* 9 (1955) facing 444; see also André Feuillet, *L'Apocalypse: Etat de la question* (Studia Neotestamentica Subsidia 3; Paris: Desclée, 1963) 19-30; Heinrich Kraft, "Zur Offenbarung des Johannes," *ThRu* N.F. 38 (1973) 81-98. Studies devoted entirely or in part to the structure of Revelation include Günther Bornkamm, "Die Komposition der apokalyptischen Visionen in der

Offenbarung Johannis," *ZNW* 36 (1937) 132-49; reprinted in
*Studien zu Antike und Urchristentum: Gesammelte Aufsätze Band
II* (BEvT 28; Munich: Kaiser, 1959) 204-22 (the latter will be
cited hereafter); Stanislas Giet, *L'Apocalypse et l'histoire:
Etude historique sur l'Apocalypse johannique* (Paris: Presses
Universitaires de France, 1957) 146-85; Elisabeth [Schüssler]
Fiorenza, "The Eschatology and Composition of the Apocalypse,"
CBQ 30 (1968) 537-69; Vanni, *La struttura letteraria* (see
above, note 9); F. Rousseau, *L'Apocalypse et le milieu prophé-
tique du Nouveau Testament: Structure et préhistoire du texte*
(Montreal: Bellarmin, 1971). See also Allo, *L'Apocalypse*,
XCVII-CXI.

[22]Bousset, *Offenbarung Johannis*, 463; Bornkamm, "Komposition," 206 (who refers to Boll's analysis).

[23]Bousset, *Offenbarung Johannis*, 57.

[24]Victorinus flourished circa 275-300; his *Commentarius in
Apocalypsin* was edited by Iohannes Haussleiter (*Victorini Episcopi Petavionensis Opera* [CSEL 49; Leipzig: Freytag, 1916]).

[25]Ibid., 84, line 14 - 86, line 7.

[26]See Bousset, *Offenbarung Johannis*, 64-65, 66, 84-85,
108-10.

[27]See the discussion of Völter's various works on Revelation in ibid., 128-30.

[28]Ibid., 149-50.

[29]Ibid., 135-36.

[30]Ibid., 142.

[31]M. E. Boismard, "'L'Apocalypse,' ou 'les apocalypses' de
S. Jean," *RB* 56 (1949) 507-27.

[32]Ibid., 508.

[33]This criticism was already made by Bousset, *Offenbarung
Johannis*, 150; see also Charles, *Revelation of St. John*, 1.
lxxxviii-lxxxix.

[34]See, for example, the criticism of Franciscus Ribeira
(fl. 1578) and Ludovicus ab Alcasar (fl. 1614), the great
Jesuit commentators described by Bousset (*Offenbarung Johannis*,
103-5, 106-7).

[35]Ibid., 57-58, 107-9.

[36]Ibid., 142.

[37]Johannes Weiss, *Die Offenbarung des Johannes: Ein Beitrag zur Literatur- und Religionsgeschichte* (FRLANT 3; Göttingen: Vandenhoeck und Ruprecht, 1904) 150-51; Charles, *Revelation of St. John*, 1. xxiii.

[38]Charles, *Revelation of St. John*, 1. xxii.

[39]Ibid., xxiii.

[40]Ibid., xxii-xxiii, 1-lv.

[41]Ibid., xxii.

[42]Ibid., 1.

[43]Ibid., lix.

[44]Bornkamm, "Komposition" (see note 21 above).

[45]Ibid., 204-5.

[46]Ibid., 205.

[47]Ibid., 205-6; see note 22 above; see also Charles, *Revelation of St. John*, 1. 220.

[48]Bornkamm, "Komposition," 206-7.

[49]Ibid., 207, 210-12.

[50]Ibid., 208, 212-14.

[51]Bornkamm notes other parallel sections which describe basically the same event (notably 9:1-11, 9:13-21 and 20:1-3, 7-10), but he does not relate these passages to his overall view of the book (ibid., 215-16).

[52]Lohmeyer, *Offenbarung des Johannes*, 181-85; Charles, *Revelation of St. John*, 1. xxiii-xxv; Bousset, *Offenbarung Johannis*, 152-53; Eduard Lohse, *Die Offenbarung des Johannes* (NTD 11; 10th ed.; Göttingen: Vandenhoeck und Ruprecht, 1971) 8-9.

[53]Austin Farrer, *A Rebirth of Images: The Making of St. John's Apocalypse* (Westminster: Dacre, 1949) 36-58; he later produced a commentary (*The Revelation of St. John the Divine* [Oxford: Clarendon, 1964]).

[54]For Farrer's comparison of Revelation with the motif of the half-week, see *Revelation of St. John*, 7-13. In this work, Farrer maintained much of his earlier analysis of the structure, but argued that there are only four sections to the book, corresponding to the four numbered series. To maintain this theory, he is forced to argue that 12:1-14:20 and 19:11-21:9 are attached to the trumpets and bowls, respectively. This argument is not compelling for reasons which will be evident in the discussion which follows.

[55]Farrer, *Rebirth of Images*, 45.

[56]"I saw" or "x appeared to y" are typical and very old introductory formulae of vision accounts; cf. Exod 3:2, Amos

9:1, Isa 6:1. See Moses Sister, "Die Typen der prophetischen
Visionen in der Bibel," *Monatsschrift für Geschichte und Wissenschaft des Judentums* 78 (1934) 399-430.

[57]This sequence is based generally on Farrer's conclusions
(*Rebirth of Images*, 47-49).

[58]The fact that no introductory formulae are used at 12:7
and 13 is an indication that vss. 7-9 and 13-17 are meant to
continue the vision of vss. 1-6, rather than to introduce new
visions. In vs. 10, the auditory formula *ēkousa* does not introduce something new, but rather a commentary on the event of
vss. 7-9. Thus Lohmeyer's division of ch. 12 into four visions
is not justified (*Offenbarung des Johannes*, 94-101; see the
chart in Bowman, "Dramatic Structure," facing 444).

[59]Farrer, *Rebirth of Images*, 55-56.

[60]Ibid., 55-57.

[61]Ibid., 57-58.

[62]Ibid., 40-41, 56.

[63]Ibid., 56.

[64]The term "interlocking" used here is adapted from Allo's
term *loi de l'emboîtement*. Allo's use of the term is more
general than that intended here. He refers to the technique of
preliminary allusion to what will be described in further detail later in the work; e.g., the reference to the fall of
Babylon in 14:8, which is then further discussed in 16:19 and
ch. 18 (*L'Apocalypse*, LXXXII-LXXXV).

[65]Farrer interprets the silence as an allusion to the Sab-
bath rest (*Rebirth of Images*, 37-38); Charles argues that the
silence is a cessation of the continual heavenly worship so
that the prayers of the saints can be heard (*Revelation of St.
John*, 1. 222); Lohmeyer's interpretation is similar (*Offenbarung des Johannes*, 70), as is Caird's (*Commentary on Revelation*,
106-7).

[66]Bousset, *Offenbarung Johannis*, 339.

[67]So also Caird, *Commentary on Revelation*, 104.

[68]Contra Bousset, *Offenbarung Johannis*, 339-40.

[69]See Charles, *Revelation of St. John*, 1. 27-28.

[70]See also Jer 15:16.

[71]This parallel is noted by Charles (*Revelation of St.
John*, 1. 258) and by Caird (*Commentary on Revelation*, 125).

[72]Charles, *Revelation of St. John*, 1. 136-37; Lohmeyer,
Offenbarung des Johannes, 50; Caird, *Commentary on Revelation*,
70.

[73]See the summaries in Charles, *Revelation of St. John*, 1.
137; Bousset, *Offenbarung Johannis*, 298. A recent but equally
inconclusive suggestion is that the *biblion* of Revelation 5 is
a *get mekushshar*, i.e., a document folded and tied once for
each witness. A minimum of three witnesses were required for
such a document (see J. Massingberd Ford, "The Divorce Bill of
the Lamb and the Scroll of the Suspected Adulteress. A Note on
Apoc. 5, 1 and 10, 8-11," *JSJ* 2 [1971] 136-37).

[74]This theory was first suggested by A. Deissmann and then
argued in detail by K. Staritz; see the discussions by Bornkamm
("Komposition," 204-5) and Heinrich Kraft (*Die Offenbarung des
Johannes* [HNT 16a; Tübingen: Mohr, 1974] 105).

[75]Otto Roller, "Das Buch mit sieben Siegeln," *ZNW* 36
(1937) 98-113; Bornkamm, "Komposition," 221-22.

[76]See Bruce M. Metzger, *A Textual Commentary on the Greek
New Testament* (London: United Bible Societies, 1971) 737.

[77]Charles, *Revelation of St. John*, 1. 137; Bousset, *Offenbarung Johannis*, 297.

[78]Gottfried Fitzer, "*Sphragis*," *TDNT* 7 (1971) 945; Otto
Procksch, *Jesaia I* (KAT 9, 1; Leipzig: Deichert, 1930) 140.

[79]Gottlob Schrenk, "*Biblos, biblion*," *TDNT* 1 (1964) 618,
note 16; Joachim Marquardt, *Das Privatleben der Römer* (Handbuch
der römischen Alterthümer 7; 2nd ed.; Leipzig: Hirzel, 1886);
E. Huschke, *Das Buch mit sieben Siegeln in der Offenbarung St.
Johannis 5, 1 u. folg.* (Leipzig: Naumann, 1860); W. Sattler,
"Das Buch mit sieben Siegeln. Studien zum literarischen Aufbau
der Offenbarung Johannis. II. Die Bücher der Werke und das Buch
des Lebens," *ZNW* 21 (1922) 51.

[80]So Lohmeyer, *Offenbarung des Johannes*, 50.

[81]This theory is rejected by Charles, *Revelation of St.
John*, 1. 137-38.

[82]Roller, "Das Buch mit sieben Siegeln," 107-8.

[83]See Bornkamm's criticism of this suggestion, "Komposition," 221-22. Ford's suggestion (that the scroll with the
seven seals is a bill of divorce by which the Lamb puts aside
his unfaithful betrothed [Jerusalem], so that he might marry
the new Jerusalem) has even less relation to the immediate context ("The Divorce Bill of the Lamb," 137-38).

[84]Procksch, *Jesaia I*, 140. See also Isa 29:11-12.

[85]Another theory is that this motif of sealing in Daniel
was part of a growing reverence for and keeping of esoteric
books (Russell, *The Method and Message of Jewish Apocalyptic*,
107-18).

[86]See Charles, *Revelation of St. John*, 1. 138-39; F.
Nötscher, "Himmlische Bücher und Schicksalsglaube in Qumran,"
RQ 1 (1959) 405-11; see also Chapter V, *The Heavenly Scene and
the Scroll*.

[87]Cf. Exod 32:32-33; Isa 4:3; Mal 3:16; Ps 69:29; Dan
12:1; Jubilees 19:9, 30:20, 22; 1 Enoch 47:3; Luke 10:20; Phil
4:3; Heb 12:23. At first this roster symbolized just member-
ship in the people of God; later, it came to represent those
destined for eternal life (e.g., Dan 12:1).

[88]Books of judgment were discussed above as one example of
the metaphorical use of the motif of "sealing." See also Isa
65:6; Ascension of Isaiah 9:22; 1 Enoch 81:4, 98:7-8, 104:7.

[89]For example, Dan 10:21; 1 Enoch 81:1-3, 93:1-3, 103:1-3,
106:19-107:1, 108:7. See also Charles, *Revelation of St. John*,
1. 138.

[90]As *biblos tēs zōēs* in 3:5, 20:15; as *biblion tēs zōēs* in
13:8, 17:8, 20:12, 21:27.

[91]This interpretation was combined by Sattler in the article cited above (note 79) with the theory that the scroll is a
testament ("Das Buch mit sieben Siegeln," 43-50). Nötscher
also identifies the scroll of Revelation 5 with the book of
life ("Himmlische Bücher," 406).

[92]Mathias Rissi, *Was ist und was geschehen soll danach:
Die Zeit- und Geschichtsauffassung der Offenbarung des Johannes*
(ATANT 46; Zürich: Zwingli, 1965) 46, note 158; Caird, *Commen-
tary on Revelation*, 70-71.

[93]So Bousset, *Offenbarung Johannis*, 297; Charles, *Revelation of St. John*, 1. 138; Caird, *Commentary on Revelation*, 72-
73; Kraft, *Offenbarung des Johannes*, 103.

[94]See note 89 above.

[95]On the relation of Revelation 5 to the combat myth, see
Chapter V, *The Heavenly Scene and the Scroll*. That the content
of the scroll with the seven seals is considered to be secret
knowledge about future events is shown by the oath of the angel
in 10:6-7, that in the days of the seventh trumpet, the *mystērion tou theou* would be completed. This interpretation presupposes that the events associated with the seals and trumpets
reveal the content of the scroll of ch. 5. On the background
and use of *mystērion*, see Raymond E. Brown, *The Semitic Background of the Term "Mystery" in the New Testament* (Facet Books,
Biblical Series 21; Philadelphia: Fortress, 1968); Günther
Bornkamm, "*Mystērion, myeō*," *TDNT* 4 (1967) 802-28.

[96]On the motif of "worthiness," see W. C. van Unnik,
"'Worthy is the Lamb.' The Background of Apoc 5," *Mélanges
bibliques en hommage au R. P. Béda Rigaux* (eds. A. Descamps
and A. de Halleux; Gembloux: Duculot, 1970) 445-61.

[97] Bousset summarizes this opinion, held by Hofmann, and rejects it (*Offenbarung Johannis*, 297-98); the theory was revived by Bornkamm, "Komposition," 205.

[98] On the interpretation of "what you saw, and what is, and what is about to take place hereafter" (1:19), see Heinrich Schlier, "Vom Antichrist: Zum 13. Kapitel der Offenbarung Johannis," *Theologische Aufsätze: Karl Barth zum 50. Geburtstag* (ed. E. Wolf; Munich: Kaiser, 1936) 110-23; reprinted in *Die Zeit der Kirche: Exegetische Aufsätze und Vorträge*; 2nd ed. (Freiburg im Breisgau: Herder, 1958) 16-17 (the latter will be cited hereafter); see also Caird, *Commentary on Revelation*, 26.

[99] This approach was taken by Charles (*Revelation of St. John*, 1. 269, 292) and Lohmeyer (*Offenbarung des Johannes*, 84).

[100] See Rudolf Bultmann's review of Lohmeyer (*Offenbarung des Johannes*): *TLZ* 52 (1927) 507.

[101] Contra Charles, *Revelation of St. John*, 1. 260; and Schlier, "Antichrist," 18, who was followed by Bornkamm, "Komposition," 216-18.

[102] See Chapter IV, *The Beast from the Abyss*.

[103] So Bousset, *Offenbarung Johannis*, 368; Charles, *Revelation of St. John*, 1. 269.

[104] See Chapter III, *The Associations of the Desert*.

[105] Some manuscripts read *kai estathē*, while others read *kai estathēn*. Decisions on the variants have influenced the verse numbering and chapter division. See Metzger, *Textual Commentary*, 748. There are three reasons for preferring the reading *estathē*. Firstly, it has the better attestation from the point of view of the reliability of the witnesses involved. Secondly, it is easier to explain a change from *estathē* to *estathēn* than vice versa. *Estathēn* could have arisen as an accommodation to the following *eidon* (so Metzger). Further, the *estathē* might have been suppressed in favor of *estathēn* in a conceptual assimilation of the passage to Dan 10:4. Thirdly, the reading *estathē* gives the impression that the dragon has called forth the beast from the sea, an idea which is supported by 13:2 and 4.

[106] Cf. Rev 2:10, 13; 6:9-11.

[107] There are a number of variant readings for this verse. The major difficulty is determining whether the assimilation of the Jeremiah allusion to Matt 26:52 is original. See Metzger, *Textual Commentary*, 749-50, and the discussion in Charles, *Revelation of St. John*, 1. 355-57. If the assimilation to the Matthew passage is original, the passage is an explicit rejection of the militant revolutionary position over against Rome. If such an explicit rejection is not original, the use of the Jeremiah passage in this context at least implies that the elect are to take a passive role in a context of persecution.

[108]Allo recognized a limited degree of recapitulation in the book, and explained it as a conscious literary device which he called the *loi des ondulations*. He referred to the device by which a schematic vision is related first, followed later by a more extended account which gives the message more precision and clarity (*L'Apocalypse*, LXXXV-LXXXVI).

[109]A variety of interpretations have been proposed for the first horseman; see the summaries by Bousset (*Offenbarung Johannis*, 309-10) and Charles (*Revelation of St. John*, 1. 163-64). The two most widely proposed interpretations are (1) the first horseman is a veiled reference to the second coming of Christ and thus parallel to 19:11-16 (so Bornkamm, "Komposition," 219), and (2) he represents the eschatological invasion of the west by the Parthians (so Bousset, *Offenbarung Johannis*, 310). Charles and Lohmeyer accept (2) as a secondary significance of the vision, but hold that its primary meaning is the eschatological spread of war in general (Charles, *Revelation of St. John*, 1. 163; Lohmeyer, *Offenbarung des Johannes*, 57). Rissi argues that the first horseman is an image for the Antichrist (*Zeit- und Geschichtsauffassung*, 77). On the traditional nature of the eschatological motifs in the visions of the other three horsemen, see Bousset, *Offenbarung Johannis*, 308; Charles, *Revelation of St. John*, 1. 161; Rissi, *Zeit- und Geschichtsauffassung*, 77; Giet, *L'Apocalypse et l'histoire*, 150-51, 188.

[110]See Chapter V, *The Seven Seals*.

[111]On the hymnic material in Revelation, see Gerhard Delling, "Zum gottesdienstlichen Stil der Johannes-Apokalypse," *NovT* 3 (1959) 107-37; Reinhard Deichgräber, *Gotteshymnus und Christushymnus in der frühen Christenheit: Untersuchungen zur Form, Sprache und Stil der frühchristlichen Hymnen* (Studien zur Umwelt des Neuen Testaments 5; Göttingen: Vandenhoeck und Ruprecht, 1967) 25-40; J. J. O'Rourke, "The Hymns of the Apocalypse," *CBQ* 30 (1968) 399-409; Klaus-Peter Jörns, *Das hymnische Evangelium: Untersuchungen zu Aufbau, Funktion, und Herkunft der hymnischen Stücke in der Johannesoffenbarung* (Studien zum Neuen Testament 5; Gütersloh: Mohn, 1971).

[112]Ch. 8:3 refers explicitly to an altar in heaven ("before the throne"). The altar in 6:9-11 is doubtless also the heavenly altar (see Charles, *Revelation of St. John*, 1. 172).

[113]The motif of an angel's casting celestial fire on the earth as an image of judgment occurs in Ezek 10:2. There it is the temple which is marked for destruction. On the juxtaposition of the prayers and the image of judgment, see Charles, *Revelation of St. John*, 1. 232.

[114]See Charles, *Revelation of St. John*, 1. 233-37; Lohmeyer, *Offenbarung des Johannes*, 72.

[115]The motif of eschatological holy warfare is clear, for example, in Joel 2:1-17; cf. Patrick D. Miller, *The Divine Warrior in Early Israel* (Harvard Semitic Monographs 5; Cambridge: Harvard University Press, 1973) 139.

[116]On the mythological character of the descriptions, see Hermann Gunkel, *Zum religionsgeschichtlichen Verständnis des Neuen Testaments* (FRLANT 1, 1; Göttingen: Vandenhoeck und Ruprecht, 1903) 51-53; Boll, *Aus der Offenbarung*, 68-77; Bousset, *Offenbarung Johannis*, 350-53.

[117]Bousset notes that the description of hordes from the East calls the Parthians to mind and that the mythological material is applied to that political-military threat (*Offenbarung Johannis*, 358). Giet interprets the sixth trumpet as a reference to the expedition of the governor of Syria, Cestius Gallus, into Judaea in 66 C.E. (*L'Apocalypse et l'histoire*, 34-36; cf. Emil Schürer, *The History of the Jewish People in the Age of Jesus Christ (175 B.C.-A.D. 135)* [eds. G. Vermes and F. Millar; Edinburgh: Clark, 1973] 487-88).

[118]Bornkamm interprets the fifth trumpet (9:1-11), the sixth trumpet (9:13-21), and the fourth and part of the fifth visions of the last series (20:1-3, 7-10) as variant descriptions of the same battle ("Komposition," 215-16).

[119]See Chapter III, *The Re-use of Source I* and *The New Unity*.

[120]See Chapter IV, *The Significance of the Nero Legend*.

[121]Bornkamm, "Komposition," 210-14.

[122]Matt 3:12; 13:24-30, 36-43.

[123]G. B. Caird (*Commentary on Revelation*, 189-95), followed by A. Feuillet ("La moisson et la vendange de l'Apocalypse (14, 14-20). La signification chrétienne de la révélation johannique," *NRT* 94 [1972] 225-50), has argued that the harvest refers to the ingathering of the elect by the Son of Man and his angels and that the vintage represents the deaths of the martyrs. Of the passages which Caird cites to support his interpretation of the harvest, only one (Matt 13:24-43) combines the image of the harvest with the coming of the Son of Man. In this passage the harvest is the gathering of *all* people for judgment. The other texts have only one of the two motifs and are thus not real parallels to Rev 14:15-16 (Matt 9:37-38, Mark 4:29, Luke 10:2, John 4:35-38, Mark 13:27, Matt 24:31, 1 Thes 4:15-17). Caird's interpretation of the vintage is weak; firstly, because both the Old Testament sources of the winepress imagery (Isa 63:1-6 and Joel 3:13) and the parallel in Rev 19:11-16 use the image for vengeance on the adversaries of the Lord. Secondly, if it were the martyrs' blood in the winepress of God, the same group of angels who gathered the elect would also be responsible for the deaths of the martyrs. Elsewhere in the book, their deaths are ascribed to Satan (cf. 2:10, 12:17). Thus, Caird's interpretation is not compatible with the book's dualistic framework (see Chapter IV, *Cosmic Dualism*).

[124]The term "martyr" is used here to refer to a person who has died rather than speak or act contrary to his or her

religious convictions. It is not implied that *martys* is already a technical term in Revelation. On this terminological issue, see A. A. Trites, "Martys and Martyrdom in the Apocalypse: A Semantic Study," *NovT* 15 (1973) 72-80; N. Brox, *Zeuge und Märtyrer* (Munich: Kösel Verlag, 1961).

[125]See Chapter IV, *The Signification of the Beasts*.

[126]John J. Collins, *The Sibylline Oracles of Egyptian Judaism* (SBL Dissertation Series 13; Missoula, Mont.: Scholars Press, 1974) 37.

[127]Ibid., 74.

[128]John J. Collins, "The Son of Man and the Saints of the Most High in the Book of Daniel," *JBL* 93 (1974) 54-55.

[129]Earl Breech, "These Fragments I Have Shored against My Ruins: The Form and Function of 4 Ezra," *JBL* 92 (1973) 270.

[130]Ibid., 272-73.

[131]Ibid., 269, 273.

[132]Paul Ricoeur, *The Symbolism of Evil* (Boston: Beacon, 1969) 167-68.

[133]Claude Lévi-Strauss, "The Structural Study of Myth," *Structural Anthropology* (New York: Basic Books, 1963) 229.

[134]Wayne Meeks, "The Man from Heaven in Johannine Sectarianism," *JBL* 91 (1972) 48.

CHAPTER II

THE COMBAT MYTH IN REVELATION 12

Although the book of Revelation is presented as a heavenly
letter, its imagery did not simply fall out of the sky. Few
interpreters today hold the opinion that the entire book was
dictated word for word to the seer or that he simply wrote down
mechanically what he heard and saw. Even if the book is based
on actual ecstatic experience, it is clear that the seer made
use of traditional images and forms to communicate that experience.[1] The traditional character of the imagery also places a
limitation on our understanding of the nature of the seer's
creative genius.

Most of his images are not metaphors created by an individual poetic mind in isolation, but are traditional images
with a long history and a rich variety of connotations and
associations. In order to understand these images, one must be
aware of their traditional character and become familiar with
the connotations they carry with them.

The underlying pattern of Revelation and much of its
imagery have strong affinities with a mythic pattern of combat
which was widespread in the ancient Near East and the classical
world. The pattern depicts a struggle between two divine beings and their allies for universal kingship. One of the com-
batants is usually a monster, very often a dragon. This monster represents chaos and sterility, while his opponent is associated with order and fertility. Thus, their conflict is a
cosmic battle whose outcome will constitute or abolish order in
society and fertility in nature.

In the first century C.E., this basic pattern was current
in a variety of forms; nearly every major ethnic tradition had
one or more versions of its own. The pattern can be found in
Jewish, Syro-Phoenician, Egyptian and Graeco-Roman tradition.
Joseph Fontenrose, in his study of Delphic mythological traditions, has argued that these various combat myths are historically related, i.e., that they derive from a common prototype.[2]
He argues that the Apollo-Python and the Zeus-Typhon myths are

closely related variants of an earlier combat myth which came
to Greece from Syria and Cilicia and which may have been of
Semitic or Sumerian origin.[3] According to Fontenrose, the
Egyptian Horus-Osiris-Seth cycle is a national variant of the
same prototype.[4] Other variants of the same basic combat myth
include the conflict between the storm god and (the) *illuyankas*
(i.e., the "dragon" or "serpent") in Hittite tradition;[5] the
struggle of Baal with Yamm in the Canaanite-Ugaritic literature;[6] the battles of a hero-god with the dragon Labbu and the
bird Zu[7] and of Marduk with Tiamat[8] in Accadian literature.

The question of the historical interrelationships of these
myths is not directly relevant to our study. The point of interest here is that there were a number of combat myths in cir-
culation in the first century C.E. and that they had a common
pattern, as will be shown below. It is this pattern that is
meant when reference is made to "the combat myth" in this
study. The use of the term does not imply any particular theory of historical origin and interrelationship of the individual versions of the myth.

In this study of the imagery of Revelation, it will be
shown that the various motifs could not have derived from a
single tradition. Much of the imagery can be understood
against a Semitic background. The term "Semitic" is used here
to refer to the OT, non-canonical Jewish literature, and Mesopotamian, Ugaritic, and Syro-Phoenician mythology. But a number of motifs, including some quite central ones like the dragon's pursuit of the woman in ch. 12 and the wounded head of
the beast in ch. 13, cannot be adequately understood against
this background. It would seem that the author of Revelation
was consciously attempting to be international by incorporating
and fusing traditional elements from a variety of cultures.

The passage in Revelation which best illustrates these
characteristics--the traditional nature of the images, the affinities with the combat myth, and the fusion of diverse tradi-
tions--is ch. 12. Revelation 12 reflects the combat myth in a
more extensive and vivid manner than any other passage of the
book. The dragon's attack on the woman reflects the phase of
the combat myth in which the rebel (the dragon) has power and

is trying to prevent the one destined to be king (the child of the woman) from eventually wresting that power from him. The battle between Michael and the dragon in heaven strongly reflects the form of the combat myth in which the rebel god (the dragon) and his allies ("his angels") attempt to seize kingship of the gods, but are defeated and expelled from heaven. That ch. 12 most clearly reflects the combat myth was recognized, in effect, already at the end of the last century by Hermann Gunkel in his famous work, *Schöpfung und Chaos in Urzeit und Endzeit.*[9] It was this insight into the nature of Revelation 12 which led him to focus his study of the mythic background of Revelation on that passage.

The study of the imagery of ch. 12 which follows begins with the demonstration that the events related in the narrative of that passage reflect the pattern of the combat myth. Next the confrontation between the woman and the dragon is investigated to see what particular form of the combat myth it most closely resembles. The motifs which constitute the description of the woman as Queen of Heaven in 12:1 and the dragon as chaos monster in 12:3-4 are then examined. Finally, the associations of the battle between Michael and the dragon are explored.

The Pattern of the Combat Myth and Revelation 12

Fontenrose demonstrates the similarity among the various combat myths by showing that many of the same themes occur in each of them.[10] These basic themes, arranged in their usual sequence, form the following pattern:

A. *The Dragon Pair* - the opponent is often a pair of dragons or beasts: (1) husband and wife and/or (2a) brother and sister or (2b) mother and son.
B. *Chaos and Disorder* - forces which the opponent represents.
C. *The Attack* - the opponent wishes (1a) to keep the chief god (or younger gods) from coming to power, and/or (1b) to overthrow him after he has attained power.
D. *The Champion*
E. *The Champion's Death*
F. *The Dragon's Reign* - while the god is dead and confined to the underworld, the dragon rules destructively: (1) he plunders and satisfies his various lusts; in particular (2) he attacks the god's wife or mother.

    G. *Recovery of the Champion* - (1) the god's wife,
       sister and/or mother strives to recover him (a)
       by magic, or (b) by seducing the dragon, or (c)
       by going herself to fight the dragon; or (2) his
       son helped him (a) by recovering the god's lost
       potency, or (b) by taking the champion role upon
       himself.
    H. *Battle Renewed and Victory*
    I. *Restoration and Confirmation of Order*[11]

In Revelation 12 the opponent (A) is a single dragon (vs.
3); the motif of a multiplicity of bestial adversaries does occur in ch. 13. The fact that the dragon of ch. 12 is associated with chaos and disorder (B) is shown by his threat to the
order of the cosmos expressed by his sweeping stars from heaven
to earth (vs. 4a). The attack of the dragon (C) consists in
his attempt to devour the child (vs. 4). It is implied that
the dragon's aim was to prevent the fulfillment of the child's
destiny: "to rule all the nations with a rod of iron," i.e.,
to prevent the young hero from coming to power.

The champion (D) is introduced with the mention of his
birth in vs. 5. The allusion to Ps 2:9 indicates that he is a
messianic figure.[12] The champion's death is not described in
ch. 12. On the contrary, the narrative depicts his rescue from
the dragon (vs. 5). But the removal of the child to the throne
of God would of course bring the death and exaltation of Jesus
to mind for Christian readers.

The theme of the recovery of the champion (G) follows immediately on the champion's "removal" (E) in Revelation 12.
Ch. 12 is distinctive in that the champion's role in fighting
the dragon is not taken by the hero, his female ally (wife,
sister, mother or daughter), nor by his son, but by an angelic
ally, Michael (vs. 7). The battle renewed and victory (H) are
described in vss. 7-9--the battle in heaven and the casting of
the dragon out of heaven. The restoration and confirmation of
order (I) are announced and celebrated in the hymn and associated with "the kingdom of our God and the authority of his
Christ" (vs. 10).

Order is restored, however, only in heaven, as the woe on
the earth of vs. 12 indicates. In vss. 13-18, we have the dragon's reign (F) expressed by his attack on the hero's mother
(F2).

The pattern of the combat myth is thus present in Revelation 12 in the following form:

A. The Dragon (vs. 3)
B. Chaos and Disorder (vs. 4a)
C. The Attack (vs. 4b)
D. The Champion (vs. 5a)
E. The Champion's "Death" (vs. 5b)
G. Recovery of the Champion (vs. 7a)
H. Battle Renewed and Victory (vss. 7b-9)
I. Restoration and Confirmation of Order (vss. 10-12a)
F. The Dragon's Reign (vss. 12b-17)

We have seen that the overall pattern of Revelation 12 corresponds to the basic pattern of the combat myth. The question then arises as to what form or forms of the combat myth Revelation 12 resembles most closely. We shall approach this question first of all by investigating the parallels to the description of the dragon's attack on the hero's mother.

The Dragon's Attack on the Woman

There are two basic ways in which a goddess associated with the champion may function in the combat myth. She may appear in the dragon's reign (F) as the hero's wife or mother under attack by the dragon (F2); or she may function as the ally of the champion, either by fighting alongside him in battle (H), or by bringing about his recovery and/or fighting the dragon in his stead (G1).[13]

Accadian and Hittite Parallels

In the Accadian Myth of Zu, the hero is encouraged and apparently given concrete aid by his mother, the goddess Mah or Mammi.[14] The goddess Inaras makes possible the storm god's conquest of the dragon in the Hittite Myth of Illuyankas.[15] Inaras was apparently considered to be the daughter of the storm god.[16] In both of these traditions the goddesses play a role in the recovery of the champion (G1) or in the victory (H), but not in the dragon's reign (F).

Ugaritic Parallels

There is little evidence that the theme of the dragon's attack on the champion's consort was current in Canaanite mythology. Such an attack can be an expression of the dragon's lechery. The only evidence for such a motif in Canaanite myths are traditions about Typhon's lustful pursuit of Aphrodite, an event located near the Euphrates or Ascalon. The association of the tradition with the East may be an indication that the myth originally concerned Yamm and Anat.[17]

In the Ugaritic texts which deal with the battles of Baal with Yamm and Mot, Anat is the champion's goddess-ally. She is both sister and wife to him.[18] She assists him first of all in the battle with Yamm and his allies (H).[19] When Baal is defeated and killed by Mot, Anat performs elaborate acts of mourning for him.[20] She then battles Mot herself to avenge Baal.[21] The texts imply that the effect of Anat's victory over Mot was to bring Baal back to life, i.e., that Anat enables Baal to return from the underworld where he had been imprisoned.[22]

The theme of the dragon's attack on the consort of the champion as an expression of the "dragon's reign" (F) does not occur in the currently available Ugaritic texts. Anat's role, therefore, does not belong to the dragon's reign, but to the themes of the recovery of the champion (G1c) and of the battle and victory (H).

Egyptian Parallels

A number of the themes which occur in the Ugaritic myths occur also in the Egyptian. Like Anat, Isis is sister and wife to the champion, Osiris.[23] She also performs elaborate acts of mourning upon the death of her consort.[24] Isis restores Osiris to life; not to his former state as universal king, but she makes possible his resumption of life in a new state as king of the underworld.[25]

Like Anat in the Ugaritic myths, Isis appears as the goddess-ally of the champion, assisting him in combat. In this case it is not the recovered Osiris who does battle; his son Horus takes on the role of champion (G2b). In the earliest Egyptian literature, the Pyramid texts, there is no tradition about Isis aiding Horus in his battle with Seth.[26] This theme, however, becomes quite prominent in the middle kingdom, and is referred to in the Coffin Texts and other literary remains of the middle and new kingdoms.[27] Diodorus Siculus, writing about 60 B.C.E., but probably dependent on earlier written materials,[28] accords an active role to Isis in the combat: *tēn de Isin...metelthein ton phonon, synagōnizomenou tou paidos autēs Hōrou, anelousan de ton Typhōna....*[29]

Egyptian tradition also contains the theme of the attack of Seth-Typhon on Isis as an expression of the "dragon's reign."[30] This attack is sometimes motivated by lechery. Seth's sexual advances to Horus and Anat are well-known.[31] There are also traditions which tell of Seth's lust for Isis and his amorous pursuit of her.[32]

Most commonly in Egyptian tradition, however, Seth-Typhon's pursuit of Isis is motivated by a desire to prevent the birth or the coming of age of Horus, the hero's son, because the latter would aid or avenge his father when strong enough. According to a tradition of the middle kingdom, Isis sought Ra's protection for the child in her womb against Seth.[33] The later traditions tell of Seth's imprisoning Isis, his search for the infant Horus, and his attempt to murder the latter.[34] Thus, in these versions of the myth, the attack of the "dragon" on the hero's wife is not only an aspect of the "dragon's reign" (F), but is also a renewed "attack" (C), in that it is motivated by the same desire for kingship which led to the original attack on Osiris.

In the mythological material preserved by Herodotus and on the Metternich stele (c. 378 B.C.E.), Isis' role in the struggle against Seth-Typhon is to bear and protect Horus until he is old and strong enough to fight Seth.[35] Plutarch's discussion of the role of Isis in the mythic cycle is closest to that of Herodotus and the Metternich stele. He indicates a general hostility between Isis and Seth, but limits her active role to the bearing and nurturing of Horus.[36]

Greek Parallels

The aid afforded to Zeus and Apollo by female allies is a minor theme in the Greek versions of the combat myth. According to Nicander, quoted by Antoninus Liberalis (28.2), and

Valerius Flaccus (*Argonautica* 4.237-38) Athena aided Zeus
against Typhon. Artemis was sometimes mentioned or depicted
as Apollo's ally in the battle with Python.[37]

The theme of the dragon's attack on the wife of the champion during the "dragon's reign" is reflected in Nonnos' version of the Zeus-Typhon myth. Typhon's lechery was a threat
to nymphs and goddesses alike.[38] His wish to wed Hera seems to
be founded on a lusty desire to humiliate Zeus.[39]

In most versions of the Apollo-Python-Leto myth, features
(E), the "champion's death," and (F), the "dragon's reign," do
not occur, although there is some evidence that they were part
of the myth at an earlier stage.[40] In any case, in most extant
versions, the pursuit of the hero's mother belongs to the stage
of the original attack of the dragon. One would expect the motivation of this attack to be the prevention of Apollo's coming
to power.

Some traditions tell of Apollo's conflict with Python
simply as a struggle for control of the oracle at Delphi.[41]
Others link the battle with his birth and describe the slaying
as an act of vengeance for the dragon's attack on Leto, either
while she was pregnant with her twin offspring, Apollo and Artemis,[42] or after the birth.[43] W. F. Otto's opinion, that the
versions which link the dragon fight with Delphi are secondary,
is supported by the fact that many localities besides Delphi
claimed Apollo's dragon fight as a local legend.[44]

When an explicit motivation for Python's attack is given
in the traditions which link the dragon fight with the birth or
infancy of Apollo, it takes one of two forms. Python is sometimes said to have been one of Hera's emissaries charged with
the prevention of Leto's giving birth to the child or children
of Zeus.[45] The implication is that Hera acted out of jealousy,
probably both of the favors of Zeus and of the potential accom-
plishments of Leto's offspring. The other explanation, sometimes only implied by juxtaposing a reference to Apollo's taking over the oracle with his slaying Python, is that Python's
attack was intended to prevent Apollo from doing just that.[46]

If Otto is correct that the linking of the dragon fight
with the Delphic oracle is a secondary development, those

traditions which speak of an alliance between Python and Hera
are primary. Her role then in the Python-Apollo myth is analogous to that of the goddess Ge in the Zeus-Typhon myth. After
the defeats of her elder children, the Titans and the Giants,
Ge brought forth Typhon and incited him to attack and overthrow
Zeus and the other gods.[47] Hera is also said to be the mother
of Typhon.[48] Thus, at an earlier stage in the development of
the Apollo-Python-Leto myth, the purpose of the attack may have
been to prevent Apollo's accession to the rule over the gods,
i.e., to universal kingship.

Revelation 12

Turning our attention once again to Revelation 12, it is
evident that the role of the woman is not that of the goddess
ally, which belongs to the theme of the recovery of the champion (G) or to the theme of battle and victory (H). She is
rather the threatened mother of the hero, a role which belongs
to the theme of attack (C) or of the reign of the dragon (F).
Thus, her nearest analogues are not Anat of the Baal cycle,
nor Isis in her role as avenger of Osiris and ally of Horus in
the contest with Seth,[49] but rather the Isis of the Metternich
stele and related traditions, and Leto.[50] The woman in Revelation 12, like the latter two goddesses, is depicted as the
mother of a heroic figure under attack by a dragon because of
the threat posed by the child.

The thematic similarities among Revelation 12, the Python-
Leto-Apollo and the Seth-Isis-Horus myths can be best elucidated by listing and comparing the basic themes of each. We will
use Hyginus *Fabulae* 140 as our starting point for the Leto tradition, since it is the most complete witness to that myth in
narrative form.[51] There is, unfortunately, no comparably systematic narrative of this aspect of the Isis cycle. The *Hymn
of Amen-Mose* and the Metternich stele will be relied upon here
as the most complete witnesses to the overall sequence of
events. Comments made by Herodotus, Plutarch and Aristides indicate that the mythic pattern so reconstructed was known outside of Egypt from the fifth century B.C.E. down at least to
about 140 C.E.

    I. The Python-Leto-Apollo myth

       1. Motivation of Python's attack (possession of the oracle; *Fab*. 140.1; cf. 2,3)
       2. Leto pregnant by Zeus (140.2)
       3. Python pursues Leto with intent to kill her (140.2)
       4. By order of Zeus, the north wind rescues Leto (140.3)
          Poseidon aids Leto (140.3,4; cf. Lucian, *Dial. Mar.* 10)
       5. Birth of Apollo and Artemis (140.4)
       6. Apollo defeats Python (140.5)
       8. Apollo established Pythian games (140.5)

   II. The Seth-Isis-Horus myth

       1. Motivation of attack by Seth-Typhon on Osiris (kingship)
       2. Isis pregnant by Osiris
       5. Birth of Horus
       3. Seth-Typhon persecuted Isis and child in order to kill child
       4. Isis aided by Ra and Thoth
       6. Horus defeats Seth-Typhon
       7. Kingship of Horus[52]

  III. Revelation 12

       2. A woman about to give birth (vs. 2)
       3. A dragon intends to devour the child (vs. 4)
       5. Birth of the child (vs. 5)
       7. Kingship of the child (vs. 5)
       4. Woman is aided by God (vs. 6)
                      by the great eagle (vs. 14)
                      by the earth (vs. 16)
       6. Michael defeats the dragon (vss. 7-9)

The motivation of the dragon (1) is not explicit in Revelation 12, but the description of the child's destiny in vs. 5 ("who is to rule all the nations with a rod of iron....") implies that universal kingship is at stake.

While the order varies, we see that a number of the same themes occur in all three narratives: the attack by the dragon on the mother of the hero with the intent to kill the child (3); the birth of the hero (5); the mother of the hero is given divine aid (4).

The narrative of Revelation 12 thus has a clear affinity with the themes of one form of the combat myth. This particular form of the myth depicts a time when the dragon is in power. During this time he attacks the mother of the hero in an attempt to destroy her son, his prospective rival.

If we ask which example of this form of the combat myth most closely resembles Revelation 12, the answer is clearly the Leto myth. The similarity between Revelation 12 and Hyginus' version of the Leto myth is striking. Both depict the attack of a serpentine monster on a woman big with child. The flight of the woman in Revelation 12:14 with the two wings of the eagle is analogous to Leto's flight from Python with the help of the north wind. The aid of the personified earth in vs. 16 is analogous to that afforded Leto by Poseidon, god of the sea. The ultimate source of the woman's aid in Revelation 12 is God himself, as the reference to "a place prepared for her by God" shows (vs. 6). This motif is analogous to Zeus' role in the Leto myth: she is rescued *Jouis iussu* (140.3).

The similarities between the two narratives are too great to be accidental. They clearly indicate dependence. Since the Leto myth is the older of the two, we must conclude that Revelation 12, at least in part, is an adaptation of the myth of the birth of Apollo.

Other Recently Proposed Parallels

The discovery and gradual publication in recent decades of the sectarian Jewish documents from Qumran and the Gnostic writings from Nag Hammadi have provided a wealth of new material for the study of the environment and history of the early Christian movement. Two compositions, one from each of these new sources, have been pointed out recently as parallels to Revelation 12.

The first of these is a hymn from Qumran (1QH 3:3-18):

(3) ...for me you have illuminated my face...
(4) ...for you in eternal glory with all ...
(5) ...your mouth and you delivered me from...and from...
(6) ...now [my] being...they reckoned me and they made [my] being like a ship in the depths [of the sea]
(7) and like a fortified city in the face of...I was in distress like a woman giving birth, bearing for the first time, when [her pangs]
(8) and grievous pain have come with her birth throes to cause writhing in the womb of the pregnant one, when children have come to the throes (waves) of death.
(9) And the one pregnant with a man-child suffers distress in her pains because in the throes (waves) of death she will be delivered of a male-child and in pains of Sheol he will burst forth

(10) from the womb of the pregnant one, a wonderful coun-
selor with his might, and a man-child will be saved
from the throes (waves) in the one pregnant with him. All
(10/11) throes and violent pains have come quickly at
their (masc.) births, and trembling came upon those pregnant with them (masc.), and all pangs will come upon
(12) the womb of the pregnant one at his birth. And she
who is pregnant with a viper is given over to violent
pain and the throes (waves) of the pit are for all the
works of trembling and wall foundations
(12/13) will crumble like a ship on the surface of the
waters and clouds will disperse with a tumultuous sound,
and those who dwell on dry ground
(14) will be terrified by the noise of the waters like
those who travel on the waters and all their wise men
will be like seamen in the depths (of the sea),
(15) for all their wisdom will be swallowed up in the
roaring of the seas, when the depths seethe over above
the springs of water, (and) the waves and the breakers
of the waters with their roaring sound
(15/16) will be forced up on high. And while they are
raging, [Sheol...] will open (pl.)...the arrows of the
pit are not
(17) with their step. They will make their sound heard
as far as the abyss. And the gates [of Sheol] will open
[for all] the works of the viper.
(18) And the gates of the pit will shut behind the one
pregnant with wickedness and the eternal bolts behind
all the spirits of the viper.[53]

The text is fragmentary and ambiguous. There is very
little consensus on the interpretation of the hymn.[54] The
point of comparison with Revelation 12 is the description of a
woman pregnant with a male-child (9-10). This description (a
woman in labor for the first time) is an image which is one of
three metaphors used by the hymnist to describe his present
distress (6-7). In the description of the birth of the child,
there is an allusion to Isa 9:5 (10). Some commentators have
concluded on the basis of this allusion that the child is identified with the messiah.[55] Over against this image of a woman
pregnant with a man-child is set that of a woman pregnant with
a viper (12).

The similarity between this text and Revelation 12 consists only in the fact that they share two very commonplace
images: a woman giving birth and a serpentine figure in the
general role of adversary. The distinctive characteristic of
Revelation 12 is the way in which these two motifs are related
narratively by the dragon's attack on the woman. This

narrative theme is totally lacking in the Qumran hymn. The
Isis and Leto myths discussed above, however, share not only
the two motifs which the Qumran hymn has in common with Revelation 12, but this narrative theme as well. The hymn, therefore, cannot be reckoned as a true parallel to ch. 12.[56]

The second text which has been pointed out recently as a
parallel to Revelation 12 is the Apocalypse of Adam 78:6-26:

> And the second kingdom says about him that he came
> from a great prophet. And a bird came, took the
> child who was born, brought him onto a high mountain.
> And he was nourished by the birds of heaven. An
> angel came forth there. He said to him: "Arise! God
> has given glory to you." And thus he came upon the
> water.
> The third kingdom says of him that he came from a
> virgin womb. He was cast out of his city, he and
> his mother; he was brought to a desert place. He
> was nourished there. He came. He received glory
> and power. And thus he came upon the water.[57]

These passages are two of thirteen brief stories which depict
the coming of a savior figure, the illuminator (*Phōstēr*). The
Apocalypse of Adam contains no explicitly Christian material,
so the first commentators concluded that it represents a pre-
Christian, Jewish Gnosticism with signs of Iranian influence.[58]
There is no clear indication of date.

The parallel between the passages cited above and Revelation 12 has been seen in the common sequence of pregnancy,
birth, removal and nourishing. The last element, however, is
not actually parallel, since in Revelation 12 the mother is
nourished, while in the Apocalypse of Adam it is always the
child who is nourished. The parallel thus lies in the sequence
of pregnancy, birth, and removal. In both cases the child is
removed temporarily. In Revelation 12 it is implied that the
child will one day "rule all nations with a rod of iron" (vs.
5). In the Apocalypse of Adam the child will return by "coming
upon the water," which presumably marks the beginning of the
Illuminator's saving mission.

There does seem to be shared tradition here. The removal
of the child in both cases should probably be understood in the
context of the Jewish tradition of "translation," whereby a
figure is taken up to heaven in order that he might return to

fulfill an eschatological function. Examples of this concept
are the traditions about the return of Elijah and about the
ascension and second coming of Christ.[59] A parallel to the
Apocalypse of Adam and Revelation passages, where the savior
is translated immediately after birth, is the rabbinic legend
about Menachem (*Berakhoth* 2:4).[60] According to this legend,
Menachem, the messiah, was born on the day the temple was destroyed, but shortly thereafter he was carried off by a storm
wind. The implication is that he will return at the proper
time; an Israelite had comforted the child's mother earlier in
the story: "...if, because of his advent, the temple is destroyed, it will also be rebuilt by him...."

Revelation 12 and the Apocalypse of Adam 78:6-26 draw upon
a common tradition for the motif of the removal of the child-
savior. This is, however, a quite limited point of contact and
is not sufficient to consider the Gnostic text a true parallel
to Revelation 12. The distinctive narrative theme of ch. 12,
the dragon's attack on the mother of the savior-hero, is totally lacking in the Apocalypse of Adam passage.

Conclusion

We have seen that Revelation 12 shares certain motifs with
1QH 3:3-18 and with the Apocalypse of Adam 78:6-26. Neither of
these passages, however, shares the most striking characteristic of Revelation 12, i.e., the attack of the dragon on the
woman in an attempt to destroy the child and his pursuit of the
mother of the child. The myths of the births of Horus and
Apollo, on the other hand, do not simply share isolated motifs
with Revelation 12 but have the same basic narrative pattern in
common.

The closest parallel to ch. 12, as pointed out above, is
the Leto-Apollo myth. The numerous thematic similarities between the two narratives makes the conclusion of dependence
highly probable. It would seem, therefore, that the author of
Revelation 12 was familiar with the Leto-Apollo myth and
adapted it for a new purpose.

There is a considerable body of literary and monumental
evidence which shows that the Leto-Python-Apollo myth was

well-known in western Asia Minor during the first centuries
B.C.E. and C.E. A representative collection of this data is
offered in the appendix at the end of this book to show that
this myth would have been known to an apocalyptist living in
that area in the relevant period. In Chapter III, the function
of the Leto-Python-Apollo myth in Revelation 12 will be discussed.

The Woman as Queen of Heaven

A second striking feature of Revelation 12 is the fact
that the woman is described as a Queen of Heaven. In spite of
all the partial parallels from Old Testament figures of speech
which can and have been collected,[61] it is difficult to escape
the conclusion that the image portrayed in 12:1 is that of a
high-goddess, a cosmic queen conceived in astral categories:[62]
the moon is a mere footstool for her; the circle of heaven, the
zodiac, her crown;[63] and the mighty sun, her garment. Such language is the ultimate in exaltation. Only a few goddesses of
the Hellenistic and early Roman periods were awarded such
honors, for example, the Ephesian Artemis, the Syrian goddess
Atargatis, and Isis.

The Ephesian Artemis

From the fourth century B.C.E. onwards, the Ephesian Artemis was associated with the goddess Selene.[64] She appears with
the crescent moon and stars on coins of Ephesus;[65] a crescent
moon is part of the ornamentation of the upper torso of one of
her cult images.[66] In reliefs found in the Celsus library of
Ephesus, Artemis is depicted as Selene, sometimes with Apollo
Helios.[67] She apparently was never directly associated with
the sun in her own right. The scholiast on Aristophanes' *Pax*
(line 410), writing in the first century B.C.E., remarks that
at Ephesus, Artemis is a moon-goddess with the half-moon and
stars as her "symbols."[68]

The subordination of the entire zodiac as a divine attribute was relatively rare in the Graeco-Roman world. In the
official iconography of the Roman imperial period, the zodiac
was most frequently associated with some form of the male

high-god: Zeus, Zeus-Juppiter, Helios, or Sarapis-Zeus.[69] In
the exceptional cases in which the zodiac is associated with a
lone goddess, she is usually a minor figure; e.g., Nike, Provi-
dentia, Aeternitas.[70] A notable, though late, exception is the
description of Juno in a fifth century C.E. treatise by Marti-
anus Capella (1.75), where she is a heavenly goddess wearing a
crown whose twelve stones are explicitly associated with the
zodiac.[71]

The zodiac was a standard part of the iconography of the
Ephesian Artemis. All twelve signs of the zodiac never appear,
probably for aesthetic reasons in view of the limited space.
The signs which are pictured appear frequently on the cult
images of the great goddess, either just below or above the
large garland which she regularly wears.[72]

Atargatis

The second goddess mentioned above, Atargatis, was one of
the major goddesses of northern Syria in the Hellenistic period. Her name is a combination of 'Atar and 'Ata, i.e., Astarte and Anat.[73] She was known as Aphrodite Ourania to the
Greeks.[74] A Roman republican coin, dating from 68/66 B.C.E.
and issued by Q. Pomponius Musa, depicts a female figure, probably Aphrodite Ourania, and a globe with the band of the zodiac.[75]

Atargatis was known to the Romans as the Dea Syria (cf.
the treatise *Peri tēs Syriēs theou* by Lucian of Samosta).[76]
Her major cult place was the temple at Hierapolis-Bambyke,
about which Lucian wrote, but she was also worshipped in Damascus, Ascalon, Dura Europos, Heliopolis-Baalbek, Palmyra, and
Delos.[77]

Lucian remarks that "Hera" (Atargatis) resembles the Greek
moon-goddess, Selene (32).[78] He goes on to say that *epi tē
kephalē aktinas te phoreei*. This would imply that she was associated, if not identified, with the sun.

Atargatis was apparently identified with *Allāt*, the high
goddess of the Nabataeans, and influenced the latter's iconography.[79] In his book on Nabataean architecture and iconography, Nelson Glueck argues that the representations of the

high-goddess (*Allāt*-Atargatis) from the temple of Khirbet Tannur are equivalent to those of a *Tychē*-like goddess also found there.[80] It is known that most Semitic goddesses were first understood as the protectresses of a people or city along with their consorts.[81] In keeping with such an origin, Atargatis was regularly depicted in the East as a *thea poliouchos*, i.e., wearing a mural crown.[82] But occasionally *Tychē* and the high-goddess (Atargatis or Astarte) were worshipped side-by-side in the same locale, each with her own cult.[83] It is unclear whether the two were distinct at Khirbet Tannur during Glueck's period III, to which the relevant sculpture fragments date (100-125 C.E.). In any case, given the nature of Atargatis elsewhere as a *thea poliouchos*, it is likely that even if *Tychē* had a separate cult at Khirbet Tannur in the relevant period, her function and iconography derived from those of Atargatis.

This Atargatis (*Tychē*) then is depicted on a high relief from Khirbet Tannur with a crescent moon over her right shoulder and holding a two-pronged wand with a crescent moon at the end of one prong. This bust with its two accompanying symbols is enclosed in a circular relif depicting the signs of the zodiac, all of which are distinguishable.[84]

The Dura relief of Hadad and his consort Atargatis portrays her wearing a radiate mural crown (as Lucian describes the goddess of Bambyke) and holding the same type of wand described above, topped by a crescent moon.[85]

Isis

The third great goddess mentioned above is Isis. In his *Metamorphoses* 11.2, Apuleius (writing about 170 C.E.) has Lucius pray to the moon-goddess at the time of her rising for deliverance from his plight.[86] He first addresses her as *regina caeli* and then with various names in an attempt to find the most pleasing one. In 3-6, the goddess appears to Lucius in a dream and reveals to him her *verum nomen: regina Isis* (5). The description of the goddess in 3-4 is in keeping with her epithet *regina caeli*: her figure, rising from the sea, is called *pellucidum simulacrum*; she has a *plana rotunditas in modum lunae* on the midpoint of her forehead; her *palla* resembles the night sky: it is shining black and covered with stars, in the midst of which appeared the moon in mid-month.

Plutarch, writing about a half-century earlier (c. 120 C.E.), reports traditions which identified Isis with the moon (*On Isis and Osiris* 43, 44, 52).[87] Since there is little evidence for a lunar Isis in Egypt,[88] and a great deal in Graeco-Roman literature and iconography,[89] it is clear that her association with the moon was a Graeco-Roman development under the influence of the identification of Osiris-Sarapis with Helios.[90]

There is little concrete evidence that the zodiac itself was an attribute of Isis in her iconography. She appears with Zeus-Sarapis and the zodiac on a coin of Antoninus Pius issued in Alexandria in 144/5 C.E. But in light of the conception of Isis as mistress of fate,[91] it is likely that the zodiac was considered to be under her power. For example, in lines 13 and 14 of the Isis aretalogy from Cyme (first or second century C.E.) she proclaims:

13. *Egō astrōn hodous edeixa.*
14. *Egō hēliou kai selēnē[s] pore(i)an synetaxamēn.*[92]

These two great deeds give support to the claims made in lines 55 and 56:

55. *Egō to himarmenon nikō.*
56. *Emou to heimarmenon akouei.*

In *Met.* 11.15 the point is made clearly that the goddess Fortuna has no power against the will of Isis, who is called *Fortuna, sed videns, quae suae lucis splendore ceteros etiam deos illuminat.* In 25 Lucius hails the goddess and her right hand *qua fatorum etiam inextricabiliter contorta retractas licia, et Fortunae tempestates mitigas, et stellarum noxious meatus cohibes.* The last statement especially indicates that Isis was considered to have more power over human destiny than the planets and the zodiac.

As Jan Bergman has pointed out, Isis was regularly associated with the sun in the late kingdom in Egypt. This association is clearly evidenced by the epithets given her in temple inscriptions: "female sun," "second sun," "companion of the sun," "mistress of heaven," "mistress of the stars," "mistress of the entire radius of the sun," "mistress of the four regions of heaven."[93]

In the Cyme aretalogy mentioned above (line 45), Isis claims that she accompanies the sun in his journey through the sky: *Egō paredreuō tē(i) tou hēliou poreia(i)*. Thus the association of Isis with the sun extended beyond Egypt in the Roman period, even though Plutarch sees the association as a very indirect one (through Osiris and Horus).[94]

Conclusion

All three of the goddesses discussed above were explicitly associated with the moon. The Ephesian Artemis was associated indirectly with the sun through her cult-partner and brother Apollo. Isis and Atargatis were associated with the sun both indirectly through their consorts and in their own rights. Atargatis as *Tychē* and the Ephesian Artemis were associated explicitly with the zodiac. There is little direct evidence for such an association for Isis, but in light of her titles "queen of heaven," and "mistress of fate," we can conjecture that the association was made.

Thus, any one of the three high goddesses might have served as the model for the description of the woman of 12:1. The astral attributes with which she is endowed seem to belong to the typical depiction of a high goddess.

This typical image was undoubtedly familiar to anyone living in western Asia Minor in the first centuries B.C.E. and C.E. The cult of the Ephesian Artemis dominated Ephesus and was well-known outside the city. The worship of Isis was well-established and widespread in Asia Minor. The aretalogy which associates Isis with the sun, moon and stars was found in a city on the west coast of Asia Minor (Cyme). It is somewhat more likely that Revelation 12:1 was influenced by the iconography of Isis than of the other two goddesses mentioned. Atargatis was not as well-known in western Asia Minor. Artemis was not associated with the sun in her own right.

In Revelation 12 then we seem to have a fusing of Leto and Isis traditions. Such a combination is not surprising since analogous birth stories were associated with the two goddesses. The narrative of ch. 12 reflects the pattern of these myths, particularly the pattern of the Leto myth. The description of the woman reflects the typical image of Isis.

Mythological Parallels to the Dragon as Chaos Monster

Old Testament Parallels

The use of the term *drakōn* for the monster in Revelation 12 shows that he is related to the OT serpentine sea-monster referred to in Isa 27:1 and elsewhere, namely, *livyāthān*, rendered by *drakōn* in the LXX. Leviathan and related beasts (Rahab – Job 9:13, 26:12, Isa 51:9, Ps 89:10 and Tannin – Ps 74:13) in the OT clearly reflect the opponent of Baal, Yamm (Sea) and the sea-monster Lotan of Canaanite mythology, as a number of studies have pointed out.[95] Particularly striking is the verbal similarity of the description of Leviathan in Isa 27:1 to that of the sea-dragon slain by Anat. The Hebrew is *nāḥāš ʿaqalātôn*; the Ugaritic is *ʿqltn*. The Hebrew *livyāthān* is clearly derived from the Ugaritic *ltn*, the name given to the same serpent in another passage.[96]

In Revelation 12 the dragon is associated with both fire (he is fire-colored or red--vs. 3) and water (vs. 15). The same combination is found in Job 41 with regard to Leviathan. The color of his body is not mentioned, but in vss. 10-13 his eyes are said to give forth light, and his nostrils and mouth to expel fire.[97] In vss. 23-24 his movements are said to stir up the primordial subterranean waters (the *tᵉhôm*).

The remark that the dragon sweeps down one-third of the stars of the heaven and casts them on the earth is not an integral part of the narrative of Revelation 12 as it stands. It functions as part of the description of the dragon, and it is assumed that the readers will understand the reference. This motif is closely related to the self-magnification of the little horn in Dan 8:10-11, which is said to have caused some of the stars to fall to the earth, and to have challenged the prince of the host. Now, as Hermann Gunkel has argued persuasively, the visually concrete idea of the dragon sweeping

down stars with his tail in Revelation 12 could not have been
directly derived from Dan 8:10.[98] Rather, the two passages
seem to derive independently from a myth which tells of a battle in heaven and which involves stars. There is a possible
parallel to this motif in an Accadian myth and a clear parallel
in a late version of the Zeus-Typhon myth, as will be shown below.

Ugaritic Parallels

The description of the dragon in Rev 12:3 as seven-headed
is paralleled by the description of Lotan in the Ugaritic texts
as Shilyat (šlyṭ) of the seven heads.[99] The tradition that
Leviathan had several heads is reflected in Ps 74:14, though
their number is not mentioned.

The fiery element is also associated with Yamm and Lotan
(cf. Rev 12:3). The messengers of Yamm are said to flash forth
fire from their eyes, thus terrifying the assembled gods.[100]
Anat boasts that, after destroying the sea-dragon, she slew two
female goddesses, apparently his allies, called Fire and
Flame.[101]

Accadian Parallels

The Babylonian tradition includes the motif of a serpentine monster with seven heads.[102] Heinrich Zimmern has noted
references to the mušruššu tâmtim, which he would translate
either the "furious" or the "red-shining dragon."[103] He explains this term, as well as the reference to the serpent with
the seven heads cited above, as variant descriptions of Tiamat.

The Accadian text mentioned above which may reflect the
motif of the attack on the stars is the fragmentary Myth of
Labbu, a dragon associated with Tiamat. This myth is similar
to another Accadian document, the Myth of Zu. Both tell of a
conflict between the gods and a chaos monster over kingship.[104]
The Labbu text is interesting for Revelation 12 becuase in line
13 the dragon is said to lift its tail. Unfortunately, the
second half of the line is lost, so what the dragon does with
its tail is unclear. But at least it is an important part of

his terrifying appearance, since in the next two lines the gods of heaven are said to prostrate themselves.

Greek Parallels

The myth about Zeus' battle with Typhon also involves an attack on the stars, at least in the later stages of its development. In the accounts of Hesiod and Apollodorus, the battle is over kingship of the gods (Hesiod *Theog*. 836-38; Apollodorus 1.2.1, 6.3).[105]

The battle between Zeus and Typhon is told much more elaborately by Nonnos, a mythographer from Panopolis in Egypt of the fifth century C.E.[106] He treats this myth in the first two books of his forty-eight volume work, the *Dionysiaca*.[107] According to R. Keydell, his source for the section dealing with this battle was the *Hērōikai theogamiai* of Peisander of Laranda, who wrote about 200 C.E.[108]

The most striking characteristic of Nonnos' account is that, like Dan 8:10-11, one of the major acts of rebellion is an attack on the stars. Typhon stretched his hands to the upper air and seized the various constellations, dragging them from their places and even knocking them out of the sky. He dragged the two fishes (the zodiacal sign Pisces) out of the sky and threw them into the sea (*Dion*. 1.163-64, 180-81).

According to Nonnos' version of the story, Typhon's rebellion had two related aims. One was to gain the throne and sceptre of Zeus, i.e., rule over heaven (*Dion*. 2.361-62). The other is like that implied by the Zeus-Typhon story in Hesiod and the Accadian Zu myth: Typhon's rebellion was an attempt to return the world to chaos. He threatened to create confusion by mixing earth and sky, water and fire, sea with Olympus (*Dion*. 2.271-72, 296-315, 337-41).

The fact that Typhon is associated with Mount Cassius (which is Baal's Mount Zaphon[109]) in Apollodorus 1.6.3 may be an indication that the Typhon myth was Canaanite in origin. The association may, however, be due to later syncretism. At least it shows that the combat myths of Syro-Phoenicia and of Greece were associated by the first or second century C.E.

Egyptian Parallels

The adversary of Isis and Horus, Seth, was identified with Typhon in the Graeco-Roman period.[110] Plutarch regarded Seth-Typhon as symbolic of destructiveness (On Isis and Osiris 43). He interprets the name Seth as "oppressive and compulsive" (41).

When Seth was identified with Typhon, he would of course have been considered as a dragon.[111] He was frequently described in animal form in Egyptian tradition.[112] At times Seth was identified with the Apophis snake.[113]

Seth-Typhon was also equated with the sea according to Plutarch. The Egyptian priests are said to hold the sea in abomination and to call salt "the spit of Typhon" (On Isis and Osiris 32).

The color red was consistently associated with Seth-Typhon beginning at least in the late Egyptian period.[114] In his battle with Horus, according to texts of the Ptolemaic period, Seth took the form of a red hippopotamus or of a red steer.[115] According to Plutarch, the Egyptians believed that Seth-Typhon was red in color (pyrros; On Isis and Osiris 22, 30-31).

Conclusion

The attributes of the dragon described in Rev 12:3-4 are attested in a variety of traditions. The motif of the seven heads seems to be Semitic in origin.[116] The association with water (Rev 12:15 and the connotations of the term drakōn) and the red or fiery color are found in Egyptian tradition as well as in Semitic. The attack on the stars is attested both in Greek and Semitic tradition.[117] The description of the dragon in Revelation 12 would thus have been intelligible in a Semitic, Graeco-Egyptian or Graeco-Roman context.

The Battle in Heaven

In the section on the dragon's attack on the woman, it was noted that the defeat of the dragon by Michael in Rev 12:7-9 corresponds to the defeat of Python by Apollo and of Seth-Typhon by Horus. The description of the battle in vss. 7-9 has further connotations which relate it to other forms of the

combat myth as well. These connotations are associated with
(1) the motif of the heavenly armies: Michael and his angels
battling Satan and his angels;[118] and (2) the motif of the expulsion of the vanquished combatant from heaven by the victor:
the casting of Satan down to earth.[119]

Accadian Myths

The combat between two gods is often depicted as the central encounter of a struggle between two groups or generations
of deities. In the Accadian *Enuma elish*, Tiamat and her newly
chosen consort Kingu join in battle against the gods of heav-
en.[120] After Marduk, as the representative of the gods of
heaven, defeats the couple and their allies, he consigns Kingu
to Uggae, the god of death; i.e., he assigns him to the underworld.[121]

Greek Myths

In Greek tradition, Ge functions like Tiamat in that she
is the mother of the gods and yet produces monsters to overthrow the ruling gods of heaven.[122] The battles of Zeus and
his allies with the Titans (Hesiod *Theog.* 617-735) and with the
Giants (Apollodorus 1.6.1-2) are analogous to the battle of
Marduk with Tiamat, Kingu and their allies.[123] When Zeus defeated the Titans, he consigned them to Tartarus (*Theog.* 717-
35). After their defeat, certain of the giants were confined
under islands (Apollodorus 1.6.2).

The battle of Zeus with Typhon was perhaps understood as
the central encounter of the gigantomachy.[124] According to
Hesiod, Zeus cast Typhon into Tartarus after conquering him.[125]

Hittite Myths

The Greek mythic pattern according to which Kronos over-
threw Uranos and became ruler of the gods, and was later over-
thrown in turn by his son Zeus probably derives from a Hurrian-
Hittite myth about the sequence of the kings of heaven. This
Hittite myth seems to be dependent on Babylonian myth.[126]
Alalu is the first king of heaven mentioned in the Hittite

version. He was served by Anu, the first of the gods, who
eventually challenged him in battle; Alalu was defeated and
suffered the fate of the vanquished god: he fled before Anu and
went down to the Dark Earth.[127] Anu is in turn overthrown by
Kumarbi, who is apparently superseded by other gods, although
the fragmentary nature of the text prevents clarity on this
point.

Ugaritic Myths

When Baal was defeated by Mot, he was confined in the underworld.[128] The period during which Baal was so confined constituted the "dragon's reign" of Mot.[129]

There seems to have been a Canaanite myth about the attempt of an astral deity to succeed Baal as king. Such a myth
can be reconstructed from a fragmentary Ugaritic text in con-
junction with Isa 14:12-20.[130] This deity is called *'Athtar* in
the Baal poems and is identified with the morning star in
Canaanite religion.[131] According to the Ugaritic text, Athtar
attempted to take over Baal's rule, at the suggestion of his
mother, Athirat/Asherah.[132] This attempt occurred while Baal
was a prisoner of Mot in the underworld.[133] Athtar ascended
Mount Zaphon and Baal's throne, but proved inadequate. He thus
left Baal's abode, and went down to reign on earth instead.

Israelite-Jewish Myths

The names applied to the taunted addressee in Isa 14:12
show that this passage (14:12-20) reflects the myth of Athtar:
he is called *hêlēl* and *ben-šaḥar*, i.e., Morning Star and Son of
Dawn, the two being equivalent. The myth is used in Isaiah 14
as a taunt of the king of Babylon in which his fall from power
is compared to that of Athtar.[134]

In the version of the myth reflected in Isaiah 14, the
rebellion motif is clear:

> You said in your heart,
>   'I will ascend to heaven;
> above the stars of God
>   I will set my throne on high;
> I will sit on the mount of assembly
>   in the far north;

> I will ascend above the heights of
>   the clouds,
> I will make myself like the Most
>   High.' (Isa 14:13-14)

The failure of the rebellion is equally clear in the explicit
references to the consignment of the rebel to Sheol in vss. 9-
11 and 15.

The myth reflected in Isa 14:12-20 was applied to Satan,
probably by the first century C.E. This application is no
doubt responsible for his epithets *Phōsphoros* and Lucifer,
i.e., Morning Star.[135] The result of this application is the
myth about the rebellion of Satan against God.

In the course of a revelatory speech in 2 Enoch, in which
God recounts for Enoch the events of creation, the casting of
"Satanail" and the order of angels under him out of heaven is
described (29:4-5). The brief account is clearly dependent on
the same myth as is Isa 14:13-14: the rebellious desire of the
angel was to place his throne above the clouds and to be equal
in power to God. The action taken by God is analogous to that
of Marduk and Zeus against their enemies: he threw Satan down
from the height, and the latter thenceforth flew continuously
in the air over the "bottomless."[136]

According to the Life of Adam and Eve 12-17 God required
the angels to worship Adam as the image of God. The devil and
the angels under him refused. This act of disobedience is conceived in terms of the rebellion described in Isaiah 14: when
Michael warns the devil that God will be angry if he persists
in his disobedience, he replies, "If he is angry, I will set my
seat above the stars of heaven and will be like the Highest."
As punishment, God banished the devil and his angels from heav-
en, and they were hurled down to earth.[137]

We see then that at least one strand of Jewish apocalyptic
tradition conceived of the primordial fall of Satan and a whole
class of angels in terms of the struggle of two rival divini-
ties for power. The battle is sometimes fought by God himself,
as in 2 Enoch,[138] and sometimes by an angel or angels acting on
his behalf, as is implied by the Life of Adam and Eve 16. This
primordial battle did not by any means result in the total defeat of Satan, but like Athtar, Seth-Typhon and Mot, he

continued to exercise power, though in a limited way. This
continued activity of Satan is illustrated in the Life of Adam
and Eve by Satan's leading them into sin (9-11, 16); so also
2 Enoch 31.

Conclusion

The battle in heaven of Rev 12:7-9 is related to the combat of Marduk against Tiamat, of Zeus with the Titans, Zeus
with the Giants (including his conflict with the Giant Typhon),
of Anu with Alalu, and of Baal with Mot. In many of these
myths, the combat is between two heavenly "armies" or generations of deities. The myth of the rebellion of Athtar is related to these in that the vanquished combatant in each case is
expelled or flees from heaven to the earth or to the underworld.

The closest parallel to Rev 12:7-9 is the myth of Satan's
rebellion against God, which results in Satan's expulsion from
heaven. This myth, as shown above, derives from the Canaanite
myth of Athtar who attempted to usurp Baal's throne.

Summary

We have seen that the narrative of Revelation 12 reflects
the basic pattern of the combat myth. All the typical themes
appear:

A. The Dragon (vs. 3)
B. Chaos and Disorder (vs. 4a)
C. The Attack (vs. 4b)
D. The Champion (vs. 5a)
E. The Champion's "Death" (vs. 5b)
G. Recovery of the Champion (vs. 7a)
H. Battle Renewed and Victory (vss. 7b-9)
I. Restoration and Confirmation of Order (vss. 10-12a)
F. The Dragon's Reign (vss. 12b-17)

The particular form of the combat myth which most closely re-
sembles Revelation 12 is that exemplified by the myths of Seth-
Typhon's attack on Isis and Horus and of Python's pursuit of
Leto. The striking similarities between Revelation 12 and the
Python-Leto myth led to the conclusion that Revelation 12 is
an adaptation of that myth.

The depiction of the woman in 12:1 was compared with the
typical descriptions of three high goddesses: Atargatis, the
Ephesian Artemis, and Isis. Of these, the cult and iconography
of the latter two were well-known in Asia Minor in the first
centuries B.C.E. and C.E. The typical depiction of Isis is the
better parallel to Rev 12:1. We concluded, therefore, that
Revelation 12 reflects the pattern of the Leto myth, but in
such a way that the goddess has been assimilated to the high-
goddess Isis.

It was then noted that the description of the dragon in
Rev 12:3-4 contains motifs attested in various cultural traditions. The seven-headed character of the monster is a particularly Semitic motif. The red or fiery color is a motif current
in both Semitic and Egyptian myths. The dragon's attack on the
stars is found both in Semitic and in Greek myths.

The battle in heaven, often a struggle for kingship of the
gods, is a motif current in Accadian, Greek, Hittite, Ugaritic
and Jewish myths. Two elements which Rev 12:7-9 (Michael's
defeat of the dragon) shares with most of these myths are the
combat between two groups of heavenly beings (heavenly "armies") and the expulsion of the vanquished combatant from heav-
en. The closest parallel to Rev 12:7-9 is the Jewish myth
about the rebellion of Satan, which derives from Canaanite
myth.

The results of this investigation raise two further questions. Both are related to the defeat of the dragon by
Michael. The first question relates to the pattern which Revelation 12 shares with the Leto myth. We noted that Michael's
victory over the dragon corresponds to Apollo's victory over
Python. There is an obvious difference between the two stories, however. In the Leto myth (as in the Isis myth) it is the
offspring of the woman under attack who eventually defeats the
dragon. In Revelation 12 it is not the son of the woman, but
an angel who takes this role. Why does this shift in function
occur?

The second question relates to the extensive associations
of the battle described in Rev 12:7-9. Does this battle really
cohere with the narrative about the woman and the dragon?

These two questions raise the issue of the unity of Revelation 12. This question of literary unity will be addressed in Chapter III.

NOTES

CHAPTER II

[1]On the question of ecstatic experience versus literary activity, see Johannes Lindblom, "Die Gesichte der Johannes-apokalypse," *Gesichte und Offenbarungen: Vorstellungen von göttlichen Weisungen und übernatürlichen Erscheinungen im ältesten Christentum* (Skrifter utgivna av Kungl. Humanistiska Vetenskapssamfundet i Lund 65; Lund: Gleerup, 1968) 206-39.

[2]Joseph Fontenrose, *Python: A Study of Delphic Myth and Its Origins* (Berkeley and Los Angeles: University of California Press, 1959) 2-3, 145, 176, 262.

[3]Ibid., 145.

[4]Ibid., 177-93. See also J. Gwyn Griffiths, *The Conflict of Horus and Seth, from Egyptian and Classical Sources* (Liverpool: Liverpool University Press, 1960); H. Te Velde, *Seth, God of Confusion: A Study of His Role in Egyptian Mythology and Religion* (Probleme der Ägyptologie 6; Leiden: Brill, 1967) 27-80.

[5]See *ANET*, 125-26; see also Hans Güterbock, "Hittite Mythology," in *Mythologies of the Ancient World* (ed. Samuel N. Kramer; Garden City, N.Y.: Doubleday, 1961) 148, 150-51.

[6]*CTA*, 2, 3; *ANET*, 130-31, 135-38. See also Cyrus H. Gordon, *Ugaritic Literature* (Rome: Pontificium Institutum Biblicum, 1949) 9-56; idem, "Canaanite Mythology," in Kramer, *Mythologies*, 183-218; G. R. Driver, *Canaanite Myths and Legends* (Old Testament Studies 3; Edinburgh: Clark, 1956); John Gray, *The Legacy of Canaan: The Ras Shamra Texts and Their Relevance to the Old Testament* (VTSup 5; Leiden: Brill, 1957) 18-72; Arvid S. Kapelrud, *Baal in the Ras Shamra Texts* (Copenhagen: Gad, 1952) 98-109; Fontenrose, *Python*, 129-38.

[7]It is not clear which god or gods defeat Labbu and Zu, since the texts are fragmentary. On the Myth of Labbu, see Alexander Heidel, *The Babylonian Genesis: The Story of Creation* (2nd ed.; Chicago: University of Chicago Press, 1951) 141-43. On the Myth of Zu, see ibid., 144-47; *ANET*, 111-13.

[8]*Enuma elish* I-V; *ANET*, 60-68; *ANESTP*, 501-3. See also Samuel N. Kramer, "Mythology of Sumer and Akkad," in *Mythologies*, 120-37; Heidel, *Babylonian Genesis*; Thorkild Jacobsen, "Mesopotamia," in *The Intellectual Adventure of Ancient Man* (by H[enri] Frankfort et al.; Chicago: University of Chicago Press, 1946) 125-219; Fontenrose, *Python*, 148-51. Jacobsen has argued that the battle of Marduk and Tiamat derives from a west Semitic myth ("The Battle between Marduk and Tiamat," *JAOS* 88 [1968] 104-8).

[9]Hermann Gunkel, *Schöpfung und Chaos in Urzeit und End-zeit: Eine religionsgeschichtliche Untersuchung über Gen 1 und Ap Joh 12* (Göttingen: Vandenhoeck und Ruprecht, 1895).

[10]By "theme," Fontenrose means "a recurrent feature or episode of traditional stories" (*Python*, 6). See his outline of the themes of the combat myth and his discussion of their transformations (ibid., 6-11). On the themes which the Egyptian combat myth has in common with the Greek, see ibid., 177-93.

[11]Ibid., 262-64.

[12]Cf. the allusion to Ps 2:9 in Pss Sol 17:26(24), where the passage is applied to the Davidic messiah.

[13]Fontenrose, *Python*, 11 (7D), 263 (F2, G1).

[14]*ANET*, 111-12.

[15]*ANET*, 125-26.

[16]Güterbock, "Hittite Mythology," in Kramer, *Mythologies*, 148 and note 10.

[17]Diognetos Erythraeus cited by Hyginus *Astron*. 2.30; Ovid *Fasti* 2.461-64; Manilius 4.580-81, 801; see also Franz Cumont, "Dea Syria," PW 4. 2241; Fontenrose, *Python*, 84, 143 note 46, 190.

[18]Kapelrud, *Baal*, 66.

[19]*CTA*, 3.3; *ANET*, 136-37; see also W. F. Albright, "Anath and the Dragon," *BASOR* 84 (1941) 14-17.

[20]*CTA*, 6; *ANET*, 139.

[21]*CTA*, 6; *ANET*, 139-40.

[22]See Gordon, "Canaanite Mythology," 212-13.

[23]*Hymn of Amen-Mose* 14-15; English translation in E. A. Wallis Budge, *From Fetish to God in Ancient Egypt* (Oxford: Oxford University Press, H. Milford, 1934) 422-23; German translation in Günther Roeder, *Urkunden zur Religion des alten Ägypten* (Religiöse Stimmen der Völker; Jena: Diederichs, 1915) 24. See also Plutarch *On Isis and Osiris* 12.

[24]*Hymn of Amen-Mose* 14-15; Plutarch *On Isis and Osiris* 14.

[25]The immortality of Osiris was made possible by the gathering up of the scattered parts of his body by Isis; see E. A. Wallis Budge, *The Gods of the Egyptians; or, Studies in Egyptian Mythology* (Chicago: Open Court, 1904; reprinted in New York: Dover Publications, 1969), 2. 139-40, 204.

[26]Maria Münster, *Untersuchungen zur Göttin Isis: Vom Alten Reich bis zum Ende des Neuen Reiches* (Münchner Ägyptologische Studien 11; Berlin: B. Hessling, 1968) 13.

[27]Ibid., 13-17.

[28]Griffiths, *Conflict*, 99.

[29]Diodorus Siculus 1.21.3; see also 1.88.4, 6; 1.27.1.

[30]The opponent in the various forms of the combat myth is not invariably a dragon, i.e., a serpentine monster, but is usually non-human, i.e., bestial in appearance. Seth was identified with many animals; one of these was a serpent and it seems that Seth as opponent was assimilated to Apep (Apophis), the serpentine enemy of Ra. See Fontenrose, *Python*, 185-88. On Seth-Typhon's "dragon's reign," see Plutarch *On Isis and Osiris* 27.

[31]On Seth's sexual advances to Horus, see J. Gwyn Griffiths, *Conflict*, 41-46; Te Velde, *Seth*, 33-52. On Seth's sexual relations with Anat, see Griffiths, *Conflict*, 42 note 5; Te Velde, *Seth*, 37. According to Plutarch (*On Isis and Osiris* 31), Seth-Typhon is characterized by lust. In *The Contendings of Horus and Seth* (or *The Contest of Horus and Seth for the Rule*), the goddess Neith suggests that Seth be compensated for the rejection of his claim to kingship by the doubling of his property and the gift of Anat and Astarte (3.4-5; *ANET*, 15).

[32]*The Contendings of Horus and Seth* 6.5-7. Seth is said to be wildly in love with Isis when she appears as a beauteous maid; Seth pursues Isis with obviously amorous intent according to the Papyrus Jumilhac 3.1-3 (cited by Te Velde, *Seth*, 41).

[33]In a spell used a number of times in coffins of the twelfth dynasty (2000-1800 B.C.E.), Isis rejoices over her pregnancy; she predicts that the child, Horus, will slaughter Seth, the enemy of his father, and take over the latter's rule. She states that Seth would destroy the child while still "an egg" if he could, but proclaims that Ra has guaranteed the child's safety. Cf. spell 148 in Adriaan de Buck, *The Egyptian Coffin Texts* (The University of Chicago Oriental Institute Publications 49; Chicago: University of Chicago Press, 1938) 2.209c; a partial translation is given by Griffiths in *Conflict*, 52-53; a more complete one by Münster, *Untersuchungen*, 6-8.

[34]The *Hymn of Amen-Mose* (c. 1400) implies that Seth was hostile to the child Horus: "she (Isis) made an heir, she suckled the child in lonliness, the place where he was being unknown (to any) and she brought him forward when his arm was mighty into the abode of Gebb" (16); translation by Budge, *Fetish to God*, 423; cf. Roeder, *Urkunden*, 24. See also Herodotus 2.156: Isis gave Apollo (Horus) to Leto when Typhon (Seth) came seeking everywhere for the son of Osiris. On the identification of Leto with the Egyptian goddess Wedfoyet, see

Griffiths, *Conflict*, 93-95. Seth's attempts to kill Horus are reflected in the Metternich stele, dating from 378-360 B.C.E.; see the partial translation by Te Velde, *Seth*, 38. The same tradition is implicit in the *Apology* of Aristides 12 (c. 140 C.E.); see J. Rendel Harris, *The Apology of Aristides on behalf of the Christians* (Texts and Studies 1,1; Cambridge: University Press, 1891) 45.

[35]C. E. Sander-Hansen, *Die Texte der Metternichstele* (Analecta Ägyptiaca 7; Copenhagen: Munksgaard, 1956); the text was first published by Vladimir S. Golenishchev with a partial translation in *Die Metternichstele in der Originalgrösse* (Leipzig: Engelmann, 1877); a transcription of the text was published by E. A. Wallis Budge with an English translation in *Egyptian Literature*, vol. 1: *Legends of the Gods: The Egyptian Texts* (London: K. Paul, Trench, Trübner, 1912), 142-44. The translation cited here is that of Budge in *Fetish to God*, 491-503; see also Roeder, *Urkunden*, 82-97.

[36]Plutarch *On Isis and Osiris* 2, 27, 40.

[37]Clearchos of Soli 46.2.318m; *Anth. Pal.* 3.6: Seneca *Medea* 700; Pausanias 2.7.7. According to Pausanias (3.18.15), Artemis also aided Apollo in the punishment of Tityos, whose attack on Leto is related to that by Python; see Fontenrose, *Python*, 22-24.

[38]Nonnos *Dionysiaca* 2.113-62, 208-36.

[39]*Dionysiaca* 2.314-33, 581-86.

[40]Fontenrose, *Python*, 85-89.

[41]*Homeric Hymn* 3.182-387; Simonides frag. 26A (Bergk), *VH* 3.1; for further references, see Fontenrose, *Python*, 15 notes 5 and 6.

[42]*Schol. Dan. Aen.* 3.73; Lactantius Placidus *Theb.* 5.533 and *Ach.* 206; Lucan 5.79-81; Lucian *Dial. Mar.* 10; Hyginus *Fab.* 140; for further references, see Fontenrose, *Python*, 18 note 9.

[43]Euripides *IT* 1239-51; Clearchos of Soli 46.2.318m; for further references, see Fontenrose, *Python*, 18 note 8.

[44]Walter F. Otto, "Mythen von Leto, dem Drachen und der Geburt," in *Das Wort der Antike* (Stuttgart: Klett, 1962) 107-8. See also the studies by Theodor Schreiber, *Apollon Pythoktonos: Ein Beitrag zur griechischen Religions- und Kunstgeschichte* (Leipzig: Engelmann, 1879) and Otto Gruppe, *Die griechischen Culte und Mythen in ihren Beziehungen zu den orientalischen Religionen*, vol. 1: *Einleitung* (Leipzig: Teubner, 1887) 532-40; see also Albrecht Dieterich, *Abraxas: Studien zur Religionsgeschichte des spätern Altertums* (Leipzig: Teubner, 1891) 111-26.

[45]*Anecd. Bach.* 351.14-21; *Schol. Dan. Aen.* 3.73; Lactantius Placidus *Theb.* 5.533 and *Ach.* 206; Macrobius 1.17.50-52.

[46]Hyginus explains Python's attack by saying that he had received an oracle that the offspring of Leto would slay him (*Fab.* 140); cf. Euripides *IT* 1239-51; Lucan 5.79-81.

[47]Apollodorus 1.6.3; see also H. J. Rose, *A Handbook of Greek Mythology including Its Extension to Rome*, 2nd ed. (London: Methuen, 1933) 56, 73 note 73.

[48]*Homeric Hymn* 3.305-55.

[49]See above notes 27 and 29.

[50]Albrecht Dieterich was the first to propose that Revelation 12 was modeled on the Python-Leto-Apollo myth (*Abraxas*, 116-22); in a recent study of social and religious life on Patmos in the Hellenistic and early Roman periods, H. D. Saffrey, O.P., has called attention once again to Dieterich's thesis which he accepts ("Relire l'Apocalypse à Patmos," *RB* 82 [1975] 416-17).

Gruppe (*Culte und Mythen*, 1. 534) has argued that there was a Syro-Phoenician myth similar to the Leto-Python-Apollo myth. His evidence for such a myth is contained in the mythological material preserved by Eusebius (*Praep. evang.* 1.9-10; see Karl Mras, ed., *Die Praeparatio evangelica* [*Eusebius Werke* 8; GCS 43, 1-2; Berlin: Akademie, 1954-56]). Eusebius is citing Philo Byblius who gives Sanchuniathon as his source. The motifs referred to by Gruppe are: (1) the defeat of Uranos followed by the capture of his concubine, who gives birth to his son Demarus after she has been given by the victor to Dagon in marriage (*Praep. evang.* 1.10.18-19); (2) a battle between Uranos, assisted by Demarus, and Pontus; Demarus is defeated (apparently temporarily) by Pontus (1.10.28). Pontus (Sea) may be related to the chaos monster. The texts to which Gruppe refers, however, do not constitute a pattern at all similar to the Leto myth. The concubine of Uranos gives birth to Demarus before Pontus is born (cf. 1.10.18-19 with 10.26). The birth is not said to have been threatened at all, certainly not by a monster or god associated with chaos.

[51]H. J. Rose, ed., *Hygini Fabulae*, 2nd ed. (Lugduni Batavorum: A. W. Sythoff, 1963) 102-3.

[52]Element (1) is implied in the *Hymn of Amen-Mose* 14-15 (see Budge, *Fetish to God*, 422; Roeder, *Urkunden*, 24) and in the Metternich stele 52 (Budge, *Fetish to God*, 491, 498; Roeder, *Urkunden*, 88). The story is told in detail by Plutarch (*On Isis and Osiris* 13); cf. also Diodorus Siculus 1.21 and Aristides 12 (Harris, *Apology of Aristides*, 45). On element (2) see the *Hymn of Amen-Mose* 16; Plutarch *On Isis and Osiris* 18-19; cf. the Metternich stele 168-69. On element (5) see the *Hymn of Amen-Mose* 16; Metternich stele 169-71; Plutarch *On Isis and Osiris* 65. On element (3) see Metternich stele, 48-54; 89-100, 169-201; cf. Herodotus 2.156. On element (4) see Metternich stele 48-50, 206-47; see also spell 148 of the Coffin Texts (see above note 33), especially 217c-219b (Münster,

92

Untersuchungen, 7). On element (6) see *Hymn of Amen-Mose* 22;
spell 148.213ab, 222d; Plutarch *On Isis and Osiris* 19; Aristides 12; cf. Diodorus Siculus 1.21.3, 88.6. On element (7)
see *Hymn of Amen-Mose* 17-25; Metternich stele 48-50; spell 148.
212cd, 214a-d, 221a-d, 222d; Herodotus 2.144; Diodorus Siculus
1.25.7; Manetho quoted by Eusebius *Chron.* 1.

[53]Translation by the writer. See the studies by J. Baumgarten and M. Mansoor, "Studies in the New *Hodayot* (Thanksgiving Hymns) - II," *JBL* 74 (1955) 188-95; Otto Betz, "Die Geburt
der Gemeinde durch den Lehrer," *NTS* 3 (1956/57) 314-26; idem,
"Das Volk seiner Kraft: Zur Auslegung der Qumrân-hodajah III,
1-18," *NTS* 5 (1958) 67-75; F. M. Braun, "La Femme vêtue de
soleil (Apoc. XII): Etat du problème," *Revue Thomiste* 55 (1955)
639-69; W. H. Brownlee, "Messianic Motifs of Qumran and the
NT," *NTS* 3 (1956/57) 12-30, 195-210; J. V. Chamberlain, "Another Qumran Thanksgiving Psalm," and "Further Elucidation of a
Messianic Thanksgiving Psalm from Qumran," *JNES* 14 (1955) 32-
41, 181-82; Matthias Delcor, "Un Psaume messianique de Qumran,"
in *Mélanges bibliques rédigés en l'honneur de André Robert*
(Travaux de l'Institut Catholique de Paris 4; Paris: Bloud et
Gay, 1957) 334-40; A. Dupont-Sommer, "La Mère du Messie et la
mère de l'aspic dans un hymne de Qoumrân," *RHR* 147 (1955) 174-
88; André Feuillet, "Le Messie et sa mère d'après le chapitre
XII de l'Apocalypse," *RB* 66 (1959) 55-86; idem, *L'Apocalypse:
Etat de la question* (Studia Neotestamentica Subsidia 3; Paris:
Desclée de Brouwer, 1963) 92-94; Altfrid Th. Kassing, *Die
Kirche und Maria: Ihr Verhältnis im 12. Kapitel der Apokalypse*
(Düsseldorf: Patmos Verlag, 1958) 138-46; Sigmund Mowinckel,
"Some Remarks on Hodayot 39:5-20," *JBL* 75 (1956) 265-76; L. H.
Silberman, "Language and Structure in the Hodayot (1QH 3)," *JBL*
75 (1956) 96-106; A. S. van der Woude, *Die messianischen Vor-
stellungen der Gemeinde von Qumrân* (Studia Semitica Neerlandica
3; Assen: Van Gorcum, 1957); Hildegard Gollinger, *Das "Grosse
Zeichen" von Apokalypse 12* (Stuttgarter Biblische Monographien
11; Würzburg: Echter Verlag, 1971) 138-46.

[54]See the discussion of the various interpretations by
Gollinger, *Grosse Zeichen*, 140.

[55]F. M. Braun, "La Femme," 643-44; Kassing, *Kirche und
Maria*, 78, 141; Dupont-Sommer, "La Mère," 184; Chamberlain,
"Thanksgiving Psalm," 182; Brownlee, "Messianic Motifs," 26-28;
Delcor, "Psaume messianique," 337, 339.

[56]Herbert Braun rejects the identification of the child in
1QH 3:10 with the messiah. He argues that, if the child is not
the messiah, 1QH 3:1-18 and Revelation 12 share only the use of
the image of a woman in labor for the messianic woes. There is
thus, according to Braun, no reason to suggest 1QH 3:3-18 as a
source for Revelation 12 (*Qumran und das Neue Testament* [Tü-
bingen: Mohr, 1966] 1.317). Eduard Lohse sees no relation between the two passages other than the common use of OT language
(*Die Offenbarung des Johannes* [NTD 11; 3rd ed.; Göttingen: Vandenhoeck und Ruprecht, 1971] 70).

[57]The parallel was pointed out by James M. Robinson, "On the *Gattung* of Mark (and John)," in *Jesus and Man's Hope* (Pittsburgh Theological Seminary Festival on the Gospels; Pittsburgh: Pittsburgh Theological Seminary, Perspective, 1970) 119-23. The translation quoted here is that of George MacRae cited by Robinson (119). The text was edited by Alexander Böhlig and Pahor Labib, *Koptisch-gnostische Apokalypsen aus Codex V von Nag Hammadi*... (*Wissenschaftliche Zeitschrift der Martin-Luther-Universität Halle-Wittenberg*, Sonderband; Halle: Martin-Luther-Universität Halle-Wittenberg, 1963) 96-117.

[58]Böhlig-Labib, *Apokalypsen aus Codex V*, 95; George W. MacRae, "The Coptic Gnostic Apocalypse of Adam," *HeyJ* 6 (1965) 27-35 (supporting the theory that the Apocalypse of Adam is pre-Christian, but urging caution on the question of Iranian influence); see also Kurt Rudolf, review of Böhlig-Labib, *TLZ* 90 (1965) 359-62. The theory of the pre-Christian nature of the work was disputed by Antonio Orbe, review of Böhlig-Labib, *Greg* 46 (1965) 169-72; and Jean Daniélou, *RSR* 54 (1966) 291-93. See also MacRae, "The Apocalypse of Adam Reconsidered," in *The Society of Biblical Literature...Book of Seminar Papers*... (ed. Lane C. McGaughy; Missoula, Mont.: SBL, 1972) 2. 573-79; here MacRae suggests that "non-Christian" rather than "pre-Christian" be used of the Apocalypse of Adam.

[59]The removal of Enoch and Elijah to heaven so that they might not see death, but be in the presence of God was a special favor bestowed on them; Paul expected faithful Christians to share this fate at the eschaton; cf. 1 Thes 4:17 with Gen 5:24; see also Sir 44:16; Heb 11:5; 2 Kgs 2:11; 1 Mac 2:58; 1 Enoch 89:52, 93:8. See Ulrich B. Müller's discussion of the eventual connection between removal to heaven and eschatological function in *Messias und Menschensohn in jüdischen Apokalypsen und in der Offenbarung Johannes* (Studien zum Neuen Testament 6; Gütersloh: Mohn, 1972) 184-87; cf. Mal 3:23-24; Sir 48:9-10; 4 Ezra 6:26; 2 Apoc Bar 13:3, 76:2; Jub 4:17-25; 1 Enoch 90:31. The pagan Tribonian said of emperor Justinian: *hoti ouk apothaneitai, alla meta sarkos eis ouranous harpagēsetai*; see Walter Bauer, *A Greek-English Lexicon of the New Testament*, 4th ed. rev. (trans. and adapted by W. F. Arndt and F. W. Gingrich; Chicago: University of Chicago Press, 1957) 108. On removal to heaven and heavenly journies in antiquity and on the ascension of Jesus, see Gerhard Lohfink, *Die Himmelfahrt Jesu: Untersuchungen zu den Himmelfahrts- und Erhöhungstexten bei Lukas* (Munich: Kösel Verlag, 1971). In apocalyptic vision accounts the seer was sometimes transported to heaven; see 2 Cor 12:2, 4; cf. Rev 17:3 with 4:1-2; 1 Enoch 14:8-9; 71:1, 5; 3 Apoc Bar 2:1-2; T Levi 2:6-7. The Apocalypse of Adam, though he did not cite it, supports Müller's thesis that translation to heaven was often understood as preparation for an eschatological function. In six of the fourteen accounts of the birth or coming to be of the *Phōstēr*, he is said to have been nourished and to have received glory and power in various special localities. In three accounts, the newly-born *Phōstēr* is removed from the place of his birth to heaven; 77:28-78:5, 79:19-27, 80:9-20.

[60]This text was pointed out as a parallel to Revelation 12:5 (with a reference to Schürer) by Eberhard Vischer, *Die Offenbarung Johannis: Eine jüdische Apokalypse in christlicher Bearbeitung* (TU 2, 3; Leipzig: Hinrichs, 1886) 27; see the translation by Moses Schwab, *The Talmud of Jerusalem*, vol. 1: *Berakhoth* (London, 1886; reprinted, New York: Hermon, 1969) 44-45; an English translation is also given by James Drummond, *The Jewish Messiah*... (London: Longmans, Green and Co., 1887) 279-80.

[61]For the personification of Israel as a woman, see Hosea 1-3; Ezekiel 16, 23; Isaiah 54, 60, 62, 66; Mic 4:9-10; see the discussion by Gollinger, *Grosse Zeichen*, 48-49. For the sun and moon as attributes, see T Naph 5:3-4; Ps 103 (104):2. For the use of the number 12, see Gen 35:22-26, 37:9; Rev 21:12. For the image of a woman in travail, see Ps 48:6 (7); Isa 13:8, 21:3, 37:3; Jer 49:22, 50:43; cf. also 1 Enoch 62:4. In some cases the motif of personified Israel is combined with that of travail, so that Jerusalem or Israel is addressed as a woman and her punishment predicted, which will be like the pangs of childbirth; see Jer 4:31, 6:24, 13:21, 22:23, 30:6; Mic 4:9-11.

[62]Franz Boll, *Aus der Offenbarung Johannis: Hellenistische Studien zum Weltbild der Apokalypse* (Stoicheia 1; Leipzig: Teubner, 1914) 98-117; E. Dupuis, *L'Origine de tous les cultes* (Paris, 1794) 3, 49.

[63]On the equivalence of star and constellation, see Boll, *Aus der Offenbarung Johannis*, 99 note 1.

[64]Charles Picard, *Ephèse et Claros: Recherches sur les sanctuaires et les cultes de l'Ionie du Nord* (Bibliothèque des écoles françaises d'Athènes et de Rome...123; Paris: Boccard, 1922) 368.

[65]Ibid.; Théodore Edme Mionnet, *Description de médailles antiques, grecques et romaines* (Paris: Impr. de Testu, 1806-13) 3.215, 361, 400. Artemis appeared between the sun and moon on coins from Pergamum and Stratonikeia, and simply with the crescent moon on coins from a number of towns; see K. Wernicke, "Artemis," in PW 2. 1438. She was depicted with a half moon and star on a coin from Tabai (Caria) dating from the second or first century B.C.E. (*Sylloge Nummorum Graecorum Deutschland: Sammlung von Aulock*, vol. 7: *Karien* [Berlin: Mann, 1962] plate 86, no. 2703).

[66]Hermann Thiersch, *Artemis Ephesia: Eine archäologische Untersuchung*, part 1: *Katalog der erhaltenen Denkmäler* (Abhandlungen der Gesellschaft der Wissenschaften zu Göttingen, phil-hist Kl. 3, 12; Berlin: Weidmann, 1935) plate VII.

[67]Picard, *Ephèse*, 368.

[68]Willem J. W. Koster, ed., *Scholia in Aristophanem* (Groningen: Wolters, 1960-62).

[69]Hans Gundel, "Zodiakos: Der Tierkreis in der Antike," PW 10A. 617, no. 17; 666, no. 178; 667, no. 183; 668, nos. 185-87; 669, nos. 188, 192, 193; 675-78.

[70]Ibid., 617, nos. 14-15.

[71]Cited by Boll, *Aus der Offenbarung Johannis*, 40, 99; see Percival R. Cole, *Later Roman Education in Ausonius, Capella and the Theodosian Code* (New York: Teachers College, Columbia University, 1909; reprinted, New York: AMS, 1972).

[72]Franz Miltner, *Ephesos: Stadt der Artemis und des Johannes* (Vienna: F. Deuticke, 1958) 41, fig. 31; 100-4, figs. 87-89; Robert Fleischer, *Artemis von Ephesos und verwandte Kultstatuen aus Anatolien und Syrien* (Etudes préliminaires aux religions orientales dans l'empire romain 35; Leiden: Brill, 1973) 70-72, plates 18-19, 28, 34.

[73]Wolfgang Röllig, "Atargatis," in *Götter und Mythen im Vorderen Orient, Wörterbuch der Mythologie*, vol. 1,1; (ed. Hans Wilhelm Haussig; Stuttgart: Klett, 1965) 245.

[74]Aphrodite Ourania and Venus Caelestis were the Greek and Roman equivalents of the Phoenician Astarte, the Arabian Allat, and the Syrian Atargatis; see *OCD*, 67; E. Oberhummer, "Urania," PW 9A[1]. 935-41.

[75]Gundel, "Zodiakos," 617 no. 13; published by Herbert A. Grueber, *Coins of the Roman Republic in the British Museum* (London: Printed by order of the Trustees, 1910) 2638.

[76]See the translation by Herbert Strong and John Garstang, *The Syrian Goddess: A Translation of Lucian's 'De Dea Syria' with a Life of Lucian* (London: Constable, 1913); see now also Harold W. Attridge and Robert A. Oden, eds., *De Dea Syria* (SBL Texts and Translations; Missoula, Mont.: Scholars Press, 1976); Robert A. Oden, "Studies in Lucian's *De Syria Dea*," (Ph.D. dissertation, Harvard University, 1975; soon to appear in the Harvard Semitic Monograph series).

[77]Röllig, "Atargatis," 245; Franz Cumont, "Dea Syria," PW 4. 2237-39.

[78]Strong, *Syrian Goddess*, 41 note 2.

[79]Marie Höfner, "Allat (Lāt, 'Ilat)," in Haussig, *Wörterbuch*, 423.

[80]Nelson Glueck, *Deities and Dolphins* (New York: Farrar, Straus and Giroux, 1965) 284-85; 108, plate 46.

[81]Cumont, "Dea Syria," 2239.

[82]Ibid., 2237, 2239; Lucian *Peri tēs Syriēs theou* 32.

[83]Ed. Meyer, "Astarte (*Astartē*)," in Roscher, 1. 651.

[84]Glueck, *Deities and Dolphins*, 107-10, plates 46-48.

[85]For references to reproductions, see ibid., 597 note 655.

[86]See J. Gwyn Griffiths, *Apuleius of Madauros: The Isis Book (Metamorphoses, Book XI)* (Etudes préliminaires aux religions orientales dans l'empire romain 39; Leiden: Brill, 1976).

[87]See the edition with an introduction, translation and commentary by J. Gwyn Griffiths, *Plutarch's "De Iside et Osiride*," (n.p.: University of Wales Press, 1970).

[88]Hans Bonnet, *Reallexikon der ägyptischen Religionsgeschichte* (Berlin: de Gruyter, 1952) 328, 472; W. Drexler, "Isis: ausserägyptische Kulte," in Roscher, 2. 437-39.

[89]Griffiths, *Plutarch*, 497, 501 note 4.

[90]Bonnet, *Reallexikon*, 328, 472; Griffiths, *Plutarch*, 501.

[91]Dieter Müller, *Ägypten und die griechischen Isis-Aretalogien* (Abhandlungen der sächsischen Akademie der Wissenschaften zu Leipzig, phil-hist Kl. 53, 1; Berlin: Akademie, 1961) 86-87, 91.

[92]The text and a discussion of the literary relationships of the sources are given by Jan Bergman, *Ich bin Isis: Studien zum memphitischen Hintergrund der griechischen Isisaretalogien* (Acta Universitatis Upsaliensis, Historia Religionum 3; Uppsala: Universitetet, 1968) 13-18, 301-3; see also Werner Peek, *Der Isishymnus von Andros und verwandte Texte* (Berlin: Weidmann, 1930); R. Harder, *Karpokrates von Chalkis und die memphitische Isispropaganda* (Abhandlungen der preussischen Akademie der Wissenschaften zu Berlin, phil-hist Kl. 14; Berlin: de Gruyter, 1943); A.-J. Festugière, "A propos des arétalogies d'Isis," *HTR* 42 (1949) 209-34; Müller, *Isis-Aretalogien*.

[93]Bergman, *Ich bin Isis*, 162.

[94]Plutarch *On Isis and Osiris* 51-52; cf. Diog. Laert. 10.

[95]Gunkel recognized the mythological character of Leviathan et al. before the discovery of the Ugaritic texts (*Schöpfung und Chaos*, 29-114); on their relation to Canaanite mythology, see Marvin Pope, *Job* (AB 15; Garden City, N.Y.: Doubleday, 1965) 30, 40-41, 70, 166, 276-79; Gray, *Legacy of Canaan*, 19, 27 note 1, 209; see also Otto Kaiser, *Die mythische Bedeutung des Meeres in Ägypten, Ugarit und Israel* (BZAW 78; Töpelmann, 1959; 2nd ed., 1962); see the review by J. Greenfield, *JBL* 80 (1961) 91-92; see also Howard Wallace, "Leviathan and the Beast in Revelation," *BAR* (Garden City, N.Y.: Doubleday, 1961) 290-98; Mary K. Wakeman, *God's Battle with the Monster: A Study in Biblical Imagery* (Leiden: Brill, 1973).

[96]Cf. Isa 27:1 with *CTA*, 3. 3. 37-38; *ANET*, 136-37; see
W. F. Albright's translation of the text in "Anath and the
Dragon," 15-17; see also Frank M. Cross, Jr., *Canaanite Myth
and Hebrew Epic: Essays in the History of the Religion of Israel* (Cambridge: Harvard University Press, 1973) 119. On Lotan
see *CTA*, 5. 1. 1-5; *ANET*, 138; see W. F. Albright, "Are the
Ephod and the Teraphim Mentioned in Ugaritic Literature?" *BASOR*
83 (1941) 39-42; Cross, *Canaanite Myth and Hebrew Epic*, 119.

[97]This motif is also found in the Greek myth of Typhon;
see Hesiod *Theog.* 827-28; Apollodorus 1.6.3.

[98]Gunkel, *Schöpfung und Chaos*, 243.

[99]*CTA*, 5. 1. 1-5; *ANET*, 138.

[100]*CTA*, 2. 1. 30-33; *ANET*, 130.

[101]*CTA*, 3. 3. 42-43; *ANET*, 137; see the translation of
Albright, "Anath and the Dragon," 17.

[102]*ANEP*, 220 no. 691; Archibald H. Sayce, *Babylonian Literature* (London: S. Bagster and Sons, [1877]) 34; Eberhard
Schrader, *Die Keilinschriften und das Alte Testament*, 3rd ed.
(ed. Heinrich Zimmern and H. Winckler; Berlin: Reuther und
Reichard, 1903) 504, 512. The tradition persists in the Odes
of Solomon 22:5; Pistis Sophia 66; Kiddushin 29b.

[103]Zimmern, *Keilinschriften*, 503.

[104]See note 7 above; the text is given by Zimmern, *Keilinschriften*, 498-99; in addition to Heidel's translation, see
Robert W. Rogers, *Cuneiform Parallels to the Old Testament* (New
York: Eaton and Mains, 1912) 61-63; a German translation is
given in Gunkel, *Schöpfung und Chaos*, 417-19. On the myths of
Labbu and Zu, see Fontenrose, *Python*, 147-48. It is unclear
whether the beast was called "lion" (*labbu*), "dog" (*kalbu*), or
"rahab(?)" (*ribbu*); see Zimmern, *Keilinschriften*, 498-99.

[105]Ge bore Typhon in revenge for Zeus' defeat of the Titans
and Giants, her previous offspring. The struggle between Zeus
and the Titans was also for kingship (Hesiod *Theog.* 881-85).
H. J. Rose (*Greek Mythology*, 58) argues that the Typhon myth
is of Semitic origin and that it came to the Greeks via Anatol-
ia, as the consistent association of Typhon with Cilicia shows;
cf. Fontenrose, *Python*, 70-76.

[106]*OCD*, 610; Rudolf Keydell, "Nonnos (15)," *PW* 17. 904-20;
Paul Collart, *Nonnos de Panopolis: Etudes sur la composition et
le texte des Dionysiaques* (Le Caire: Impr. de l'Institut français d'archéologie orientale, 1930).

[107]Nonnus Panopolitanus, *Dionysiaca* (ed. Rudolfus Keydell;
Berlin: Weidmann, 1959); Reinhold Koehler, *Über die Dionysiaka
des Nonnos von Panopolis* (Halle: Pfeffer, 1853); Viktor Stegemann, *Astrologie und Universalgeschichte: Studien und*

Interpretationen zu den Dionysiaka des Nonnos von Panopolis
(Stoicheia 9; Leipzig: Teubner, 1930) 107-22.

[108]Rudolf Keydell, "Eine Nonnos-Analyse," *L'Antiquité classique* 1 (1932) 173-202; idem, "Peisandros (12)," PW 37.
145-46; see also idem, "Zur Komposition der Bücher 13-40 der Dionysiaca des Nonnos," *Hermes* 62 (1927) 393-434; L. R. Lind, "Un-Hellenic Elements in the Subject Matter of the Dionysiaca of Nonnos," *Classical Weekly* 29 (1935) 17-20; idem, "Un-Hellenic Elements in the Dionysiaca," *L'Antiquité classique* 7 (1938) 57-65.

[109]Richard J. Clifford, *The Cosmic Mountain in Canaan and the Old Testament* (Harvard Semitic Monographs 4; Cambridge: Harvard University Press, 1972) 32, 58, 60; A. Goetze, "The City Khalbi and the Khapiru People," *BASOR* 79 (1940) 32-33; W. F. Albright, "Baal-Zephon," in *Festschrift Alfred Bertholet* (ed. Walter Baumgartner et al.; Tübingen: Mohr, 1950) 2 and note 4.

[110]Plutarch *On Isis and Osiris* 41; Griffiths, *Plutarch*, 259.

[111]Fontenrose, *Python*, 70.

[112]Rudolf Anthes, "Mythology in Ancient Egypt," in Kramer, *Mythologies*, 38.

[113]Ibid., 76.

[114]G. Roeder, "Set," Roscher, 4. 776.

[115]Ibid., 777; see also Kees, "Seth," PW 2, 4. 1907-8.

[116]Contrast the Greek tradition (Hesiod *Theog.* 820-22), according to which Typhon has one hundred heads of a snake.

[117]Since the specification that one-third of the stars were knocked down is not paralleled in any of the related traditions, it is probable that the quantity derives from the apocalyptist's general numerological scheme; cf. Rev 8:7, 9-12; 9:15, 18. See Allo, *L'Apocalypse*, 179.

[118]Cf. Fontenrose's theme 7 G (*Python*, 11).

[119]Cf. Fontenrose's theme 10 A (ibid.).

[120]*Enuma elish* I; *ANET*, 61-63.

[121]*Enuma elish* IV:119-20; *ANET*, 67.

[122]Cf. *Enuma elish* I:1-20 with Hesiod *Theog.* 116-56; *Enuma elish* I:125-45 with *Theog.* 183-87, 207-10, 624-28, 820-22; Apollodorus 1.6.1, 3.

[123]On Zeus' battle with the Giants, see Rose, *Greek Mythology*, 57-58.

[124]Nonnos refers to Typhon as *gigas* (*Dion.* 1.176, 220 etc.).

[125]Hesiod *Theog.* 868. According to Apollodorus (1.6.3) Zeus cast Mount Aetna in Sicily upon Typhon to confine him after his defeat; this is a fate similar to the one he ascribes to two of the giants (1.6.2). See the comments of Rose, *Greek Mythology*, 56-57, 60.

[126]Hesiod *Theog.* 164-82, 492-506; see Güterbock, "Hittite Mythology," 155-75; Albrecht Goetze, "Hittite Myths, Epics, and Legends," *ANET* 120-28; Güterbock, "The Hittite Version of the Hurrian Kumarbi Myths: Oriental Forerunners of Hesiod," *AJA* 52 (1948) 123-34, especially 124-25; idem, *Kumarbi* (Istanbuler Schriften 16; Zürich: Europa Verlag, 1946) 110-15; Albin Lesky, *Hethitische Texte und griechischer Mythos* (Anzeiger der Öster- reichischen Akademie der Wissenschaften 9 [1950] 137-59); Hein- rich Otten, *Mythen vom Gotte Kumarbi* (Deutsche Akademie der Wissenschaften zu Berlin, Institut für Orientforschung 3; Ber- lin: Akademie, 1950).

[127]*Kingship in Heaven* 1.15; *ANET*, 120.

[128]*CTA*, 5. 2. 1-5; *ANET*, 138; see also *CTA*, 5. 6. 20-33; *ANET*, 139. On the former text, see Cross, *Canaanite Myth and Hebrew Epic*, 116-17.

[129]*CTA*, 6. 2. 20-25; *ANET*, 140.

[130]*CTA*, 6. 1. 52-65; *ANET*, 140.

[131]The form ʾAštar is also used; see Marvin H. Pope, "ʾAttar," in Haussig, *Wörterbuch*, 249-50.

[132]See Marvin H. Pope, "Atirat," in Haussig, *Wörterbuch*, 246-49.

[133]Athtar's abortive attempt to succeed Baal is followed by Anat's dealings with Mot aimed at rescuing Baal: *CTA*, 6. 2. 4-35; *ANET*, 140.

[134]Otto Procksch, *Jesaia 1* (KAT 9; Leipzig: Deichert, 1930) 193-200; Cross, *Canaanite Myth and Hebrew Epic*, 180 note 148.

[135]The application is made or used by the author of 2 Enoch. According to Charles, this document dates before 70 C.E. (*APOT*, 2.429). For the epithets *Phōsphoros* and Lucifer, see Sib Or 5:516, 527; cf. Luke 10:18.

[136]There was a tradition in the intertestamental period, attested in 1 Enoch, that in pre-Noachic times the Watchers were confined by God or his angels under the earth, in an abyss, pit or valley; see 1 Enoch 10:4-6, 11-12; 88:1-3; Jub 5:5-7.

[137]Charles, *APOT*, 2. 137. According to the Apocalypse of Moses 27-29 (Charles, *APOT*, 2. 148), angels drove Adam and Eve out of paradise; the deity may have delegated the casting down of Satan to angels as well in this tradition. In the Life of Adam and Eve 28:3-4 (Charles, *APOT*, 2. 140), it is said that Michael cast Adam out of heaven.

[138]This form of the myth is also attested in the Book of Adam and Eve 1.6; see Charles, *APOT*, 2. 447.

CHAPTER III

JEWISH AND CHRISTIAN USE OF THE COMBAT MYTH

IN REVELATION 12

The preceding study of the relationship of Revelation 12
to the combat myth has raised some questions about whether the
passage is a unified composition. It will be shown in this
chapter that Revelation 12 is not a unitary composition, but
that it is a Christian adaptation of two Jewish sources. The
first was a narrative describing the conflict between a woman
with child and a dragon; the second, a depiction of a battle in
heaven. The Christian redactor combined these two narratives
and adapted them for his own purposes by making certain changes
and additions, notably the hymnic passage of vss. 10-12.

The conclusion that the woman-dragon story is an adaptation of the Leto-Python-Apollo myth raises the questions how
this mythic pattern was adapted by the author of the first
Jewish source, and what significance it had for himself and his
community. After a treatment of these issues, discussion will
focus on the second source, the narrative of the battle in
heaven, and how this form of the combat myth must have functioned in its Jewish context, prior to its incorporation into
Revelation 12. Finally, this chapter will examine the questions how the Christian redactor has modified his sources and
how the new unity, the redacted ch. 12, should be understood.

The Literary Unity of Revelation 12

Literary Indications of the Use of Sources

A number of characteristics of Revelation 12 suggest that
it is not the unitary composition of a single author at a particular point in time. First of all, the narrative does not
seem to be a unified one. In vss. 1-6 a story about a dragon's
attack on a woman and her child is presented. This story
reaches a resolution with the rescue of the child (i.e., his
removal to heaven in vs. 5) and with the flight of the woman to
a place of refuge in the desert (vs. 6). Then suddenly in vs.

101

7 is a new beginning of another story: "And a war arose in
heaven...." This battle is not linked to the confrontation between the dragon and the woman and her child in any way except
by juxtaposition. This loose connection between vss. 6 and 7
suggests that the account of the battle in heaven (vss. 7-9)
was originally distinct from the story of the woman and the
dragon.

Secondly, there are literary indications that vss. 10-12
are not of a piece with the rest of the chapter. First, they
are set off from what precedes by a new introductory formula:
"and I heard a great voice in heaven saying...." As opposed to
the rest of the chapter, these three verses are not narrative,
but as the introductory formula shows are proclamatory or ac-
clamatory speech.

The hypothesis that vss. 7-9 constitute an originally independent story is supported by the way in which the account
of the conflict between the dragon and the woman is resumed
after the hymnic passage (vss. 10-12). The substance of vs. 6
(with which the woman-dragon story had concluded) is repeated
in vs. 14 with considerable verbal similarity:

> *kai hē gynē ephygen eis tēn erēmon, hopou echei ekei*
> *topon hētoimasmenon apo tou theou, hina ekei trephōsin*
> *autēn hēmeras chilias diakosias hexēkonta* (vs. 6).

> *kai edothēsan tē gynaiki hai dyo pteryges tou aetou*
> *tou megalou, hina petētai eis tēn erēmon eis ton*
> *topon autēs, hopou trephetai ekei kairon kai kairous*
> *kai hēmisy kairou apo prosōpou tou opheōs* (vs. 14).

Such repetition is a common redactional device for returning to
the major source after making an insertion.[1] Vs. 13 also seems
to have a primarily transitional purpose, namely, to reintro-
duce the two major characters and to re-establish the situation
of confrontation between them.[2] If vs. 13 were not redactional, but were the continuation of a single, unitary story, we
would expect the account of a new confrontation to follow it.
But that is not the case. Instead, vss. 14-16 describe the
same event as vs. 6, merely giving more detail.

Finally, the narrative of ch. 12 as it now stands is unclear at certain points. The dragon confronts the woman *in*
heaven according to vs. 4. The monster is cast down to earth

(vs. 9) and proceeds to pursue the woman (vs. 13). But we are
not told how or why the woman comes to be on earth.

The abruptness of the transition from vs. 6 to 7, the
formal distinctiveness of the hymnic passage (vss. 10-12), the
repetition in vss. 6 and 14, and the unclarity about the
woman's movement from heaven to earth might be taken as signs
of the use of sources. They might, on the other hand, be understood as peculiarities of the compositional technique of the
author of Revelation. The repetition in vss. 6 and 14, for
example, could be explained as a characteristic of the author's
style.

Since these literary indications are not decisive in themselves, we must look to other criteria for determining whether
sources have been used in the composition of ch. 12, namely,
style (diction, word order, syntax) and content.

Stylistic Indications of the Use of Sources

R. H. Charles argued that the style of ch. 12 deviates in
four places from the ordinary usage elsewhere in Revelation.
In fact two of these so-called deviations in style occur in
other passages of the book. The two remaining cases, however,
do contrast notably with alternative constructions which are
used consistently outside ch. 12. The first alleged stylistic
deviation pointed out by Charles is the description of the
woman in vs. 1, which includes the phrase *epi tēs kephalēs
autēs stephanos*. Charles argued that the use here of the genitive of *kephalē* with *epi* is contrary to the style of the final
author.[3] Ch. 14:14 is a likely counter-example, although the
textual witnesses are divided.[4] In any case, it is doubtful
whether we can expect the author of Revelation to have been
absolutely consistent in using the accusative of *kephalē* with
epi, since he sometimes uses the genitive of *thronos* with *epi*
(5:1, 7:15) and sometimes the accusative (4:2, 4).

The second stylistic deviation noted by Charles is the
pleonastic construction *hopou...ekei* in vss. 6 and 14. This
formulation is distinctive. *Hopou* occurs six times elsewhere
in the book and without *ekei* in each case.[5]

Charles' third stylistic argument is unconvincing. He argued that the construction *oude topos heurethē autōn* (vs. 8) is an indication of the use of a source, because the genitive of the possessive pronoun is separated from its noun. The author of Revelation, according to Charles, never makes such a separation. However, we find similar constructions in 18:14 and 22:12. Charles explains these by referring the former to a source and the latter to the editor who put the finishing touches on the work.[6] Such a line of argumentation is dubious. Charles' hypothesis of a final editor is particularly suspect.

The fourth of Charles' stylistic arguments refers to the use of *tou* with the infinitive in vs. 7. The use of a source in possibly indicated here because vs. 7 is the only well-attested occurrence of this construction in Revelation.[7]

We have noted four points at which the style of ch. 12 differs from the typical usage elsewhere in the work. We have judged that two of these cases (*kephalēs* with *epi* in vs. 1; *autōn* separated from its noun in vs. 8) are not significant. In the other two cases we have constructions which occur only in ch. 12 (*hopou...ekei* in vss. 6 and 14; *tou* with the infinitive in vs. 7). These stylistic data are far from overwhelming. But the occurrence of these two constructions, both of which go against the author's usual practice, does add some force to the argument that the repetition and abruptness noted above should be taken as signs of the use of sources. The compositional and stylistic arguments are suggestive, but not yet decisive. We look then finally to see whether the content of ch. 12 might furnish a decisive answer to the question of sources.

Indications of the Use of Sources in the Content of Ch. 12

Revelation can be and obviously has for many centuries been read from a Christian point of view. But the probabilities are clearly against the theory that the chapter as a whole was originally composed by a Christian.[3] The allusion to Ps 2:9 in vs. 5 (*hos mellei poimainein panta ta ethnē en rabdō sidēra*) is a clear indication that the child is a messianic figure.[9]

The question then may be expressed in the following terms: Does
the description of the messiah and his role in these verses
conform well enough with the early Christian kerygma to make it
probable that the passage was formulated by a Christian? Or,
are the anomalies great enough to make it more likely that the
passage was formulated in a Jewish context, and only later read
from a Christian point of view?

The anomalies are serious enough to indicate that the passage was not originally formulated by a Christian. The story
is concerned with the *birth*, not with the *death* of the messiah.
The child is translated to God to rescue him from a threat at
the time of his *birth*. Since the translation takes place immediately following that birth, it could not have been intended
originally as a reference to the ascension of Christ (which is
the usual--ancient and modern--Christian understanding of the
passage).[10] The absence of any reference to the life or deeds
of the messiah, especially the lack of any notice of a redemp-
tive death, and the complete projection of the messianic office
of the child into the future, make it quite unlikely that the
narrative concerning the woman, the dragon and the child was
originally composed to suit a Christian context.[11]

This conclusion is supported by the fact that the attempt
to give a Christian interpretation to the woman, the mother of
the child, is problematic. In the ancient church, controversy
arose over the question whether she is to be understood as an
individual (the Marian view: the woman is the mother of Jesus)
or as a collective (the ecclesiological view: the woman is the
Church).[12]

The strength of the Marian view is that it is the most natural interpretation of vss. 1-5 in a Christian context. For
Christians familiar with the infancy narratives of Matthew and
Luke, the statement "and she brought forth a son, a male
(child), who will rule all the nations with a rod of iron (vs.
5)," would naturally bring to mind the birth of Jesus from
Mary. But this theory stumbles on vss. 13-17, which describe
the dragon's pursuit of the woman after the removal of the
child. This pursuit is most probably to be read as a symbolic
reference to persecution. But what historical or hortatory
significance would the persecution of Mary have?

The ecclesiological interpretation fits vss. 6 and 14-17 quite well. The woman would then be a symbolic representation of the Church undergoing persecution instigated by Satan, and guaranteed safety by God. But this interpretation is very problematic for vss. 1-5. In its present Christian context, the birth described in vs. 5 is most naturally understood as that of Christ, since the allusion to Ps 2:9 applied here to the child is applied to Christ at his second coming in 19:15. In what sense then can it be said that the Church gives birth to Christ? Unless the interpreter resorts to an artificial allegorization of the child, the interpretation of the woman as the Church is untenable.

The most common approach to the interpretation of the woman is the attempt to formulate the ecclesiological view in such a way as to overcome the anomaly of the Church as the mother of Christ. It is most often suggested that the woman in vss. 1-5 represents the people of God of the old covenant from whom Christ came according to the flesh. In vss. 6 and 14-16, however, she is the people of God of the new covenant undergoing persecution.[13] This theory is both old and ingenious, but is clearly an artificial attempt to smooth over the difficulties inherent in the attempt to give a consistent Christian interpretation to the chapter. Besides its artificiality, this interpretation in effect fragments the image of the woman into two. The shift in her signification which this theory requires is not justified by the text; in vs. 13 it is explicitly said that the dragon pursued the woman who had borne the child. Thus an interpretation which could suggest a consistent referent of the woman would be preferable.

The major difficulty in the interpretation of the woman from a Christian point of view is how to reconcile her role as mother of the messiah with her apparent symbolic significance as the Christian community or Church undergoing persecution. The tension between these roles exists only when the passage is read in a Christian context. This tension would seem to indicate that the image of the woman expressed in the narrative of 12:1-6 and 13-17 is not a Christian creation, but an adaptation which only partially fits its new context. From a

Jewish point of view, however, the woman has a coherent symbolic
significance. She represents the persecuted people of God from
whom comes the messiah.

The symbolic significance of the woman and the characterization of the child as messiah are both better understood as
Jewish formulations, secondarily adapted for a Christian context. It would seem then that at least the portion of Revelation 12 concerned with the woman, the child and the dragon,
i.e., vss. 1-6, 13-17, is derived from a Jewish source.

It must then be asked whether vss. 7-9 were most probably
formulated by a Christian or a Jew. The passage features
Michael the archangel as victor in the battle of heaven. It
is he who defeats the dragon and not Christ. If a Christian
were freely formulating a depiction of an end-time heavenly
battle, we would expect to find Christ in the role of the champion. Thus it is more likely that the Christian apocalyptist
was drawing upon a Jewish source here, than that he was composing freely.

The Relationship of the Two Narratives

The next question to be raised concerns the relation of
the passage depicting the battle in heaven (vss. 7-9) to the
rest of the chapter. It was noted in Chapter II that Michael's
defeat of the dragon is compatible with the narrative about the
woman and the dragon, because the mythic pattern of the dragon's attack on the woman normally includes the defeat of the
monster. It is usually the child of the woman, however, who
slays the dragon. The observation of this deviation from the
usual pattern led us to raise the question of the literary
unity of ch. 12. The abrupt transition from vs. 6 to 7 and the
purely external relationship between the attack of the dragon
on the woman and the battle in heaven indicate that the two
narratives (vss. 1-6, 13-17 on the one hand, and vss. 7-9 on
the other) were originally independent. The question of their
relationship then must focus on when the two stories were combined. The alternatives are: (1) vss. 7-9 constituted a second
source which the Christian redactor combined with the first
(vss. 1-6, 13-17); (2) the two originally independent

narratives were already combined in a single source which the
redactor had at his disposal.

As noted above, the narrative regarding the woman and the
dragon was apparently formulated to express Jewish messianic
expectations. If this story were combined in a Jewish context
with the narrative about the battle in heaven, the effect would
be a depiction of the eschatological defeat of Satan. The expectation of the definitive defeat of Satan in the last times
was a common theme in Jewish eschatology during the Hellenistic
and Roman periods. This ultimate defeat of Satan was often described with battle language.[14] But the final, complete victory over Satan is not described in Jewish texts as the casting
of Satan out of heaven to earth. Where this motif does occur
it is in a primordial context.[15] In 1 Enoch we find the idea
of a preliminary defeat and punishment of Satan combined with
thàt of an eschatological, definitive defeat. The latter is
described as binding and as casting into an abyss of fire.[16]

Charles argued that all the necessary elements for the
idea of an eschatological expulsion of Satan from heaven were
already present in Judaism.[17] Since the idea is not actually
attested in Jewish writings, the probabilities favor the theory
that the transformation of the casting down of Satan from a
primordial to an eschatological conception was accomplished by
the Christian redactor of Revelation 12. The transformation
was accomplished by combining two Jewish sources--one regarding
the messiah, the other depicting the fall of Satan--in such a
way that the eschatological character of the former transformed
the originally primordial character of the latter.

The Christian redactor of Revelation 12, therefore, probably made use of two Jewish sources. The conclusion that
sources were used does not necessarily imply confidence in our
ability to determine whether those sources were written or oral
and what the original language of these sources was, nor to
reconstruct those sources in detail.

The Original Language of the Sources

Charles argued that most of ch. 12 is a translation from
a Semitic language.[18] Two of the constructions Charles lists

as Semitisms conform with regular Greek usage. The expression *en gastri echousa* for pregnancy occurs in Herodotus (3.32) as well as in the Pauline corpus (1 Thes 5:3).[19] The phrase *hōs potamon* is standard Greek. A number of Charles' alleged Semitisms reflect the usage of the LXX. The construction *apo prosōpou tou opheōs* (vs. 14) need not be explained as a translation of *mpny hnḥš* meaning "because of the serpent."[20] The more usual meaning "away from (the presence of) the serpent" fits the context. This construction occurs in 2 Thes 1:9 and reflects the LXX of Isa 2:10, 19, 21. The phrase *huion arsen* is good Greek and reflects the LXX of Isa 66:7.[21] Even the pleonastic construction *hopou...ekei* is not unheard of in classical and later Greek.[22]

The major flaw in Charles' argument is that he does not distinguish between translation Greek and Greek which was composed in conscious imitation of the LXX in order to create a hieratic, "Scriptural" effect.[23] Since there are no unequivocal translation errors in ch. 12, a case cannot be made for earlier, Semitic versions of the sources used in the chapter.

Redactional Elements in Revelation 12

There are some clear indications of redactional activity in Revelation 12. Given the associations of the battle in heaven (vss. 7-9) with the primordial event of Satan's fall, we would expect the opponent of Michael in vs. 7 to be called Satan, Azazel or some other appropriate epithet for an angelic figure. The designation of the opponent as the *drakōn* is probably due to the redactor's assimilation of the second source (vss. 7-9) to the first. But the redactor clearly wanted his readers to identify the dragon with Satan as the aside within vs. 9 shows: "the ancient serpent,[24] who is called 'devil' and 'satan,' the deceiver of the whole world was cast down."[25] There are two indications that this clause is redactional. First is the repetition of *eblēthē*, an indication of a redactional seam.[26] Second is the fact that three of the epithets mentioned in vs. 9 reappear in 20:2, again applied to the dragon. The effect of this aside is to associate the motifs of the deceiver and the judicial adversary with the dragon.

　　　As noted earlier, vs. 14 repeats the substance of vs. 6.
Such repetition is frequently a sign of redactional activity.
Since vs. 6 is a proleptic conclusion to the story, which is
then told in more detail in vss. 14-16, it is likely that vs.
6 is redactional; i.e., that the redactor has summarized the
ending of the story in vs. 6 as a transition to the battle in
heaven. Vs. 13 must then be redactional, at least in part, in
order to make the transition back to the story about the woman
and the dragon.

　　　Regardless of the decision on the textual variant in vs.
18 (*estathē* or *estathēn*), the verse clearly sets the scene for
ch. 13. Its mention of the sea prepares for the beast which
rises from the sea in 13:1. If we accept the better attested
reading *estathē*,[27] vs. 18 then also has the function of linking
the dragon of ch. 12 with the beast of ch. 13. In that case it
is clearly a redactional addition to the source which tells of
the woman and the dragon.

　　　The assignment of vs. 17 or parts of it to source or redaction has been much debated.[28] It is clear that at least the
phrase *tōn tērountōn tas entolas tou theou kai echontōn tēn
martyrian Iēsou* was added to the source by the redactor.[29] But
vs. 17a is more problematic. The crucial point is the interpretation of *tōn loipōn tou spermatos autēs*. It was argued
above that the narrative about the woman and the dragon was
formulated in a Jewish context before it was incorporated into
this Christian apocalypse. The emphasis on persecution, especially in vss. 14-16, combined with the motif of the nourishing in the desert, imply that the woman is an image or a symbolic representation of the people. The reference to "the rest
of her seed" disrupts the symbolic function of the woman implied in the rest of the chapter, where she seems to be identified with the people. It introduces a different way of con-
ceiving the symbolic significance of the woman.[30] The tension
between vs. 17a and the apparent symbolic function of the narrative indicates that vs. 17a, as well as 17b, is an addition
of the redactor. The only other passage in ch. 12 which identifies a character in the story is vs. 9b, which is redactional, as we have seen. The meaning of vs. 17 in the Christian
redaction will be discussed below.

A certain unclarity in ch. 12 was noted above about how
and why the woman came to be on earth. The problem seems to
have resulted from the combination of the two sources. The
present lack of clarity in the text can be explained by the
assumption that the woman-dragon story was originally set on
earth. Such a location is required in fact by the statement
that the child *ērpasthē...pros ton theon kai pros ton thronon
autou* (vs. 5). Such language regularly means translation from
earth to heaven.[31] When the dragon-woman story was combined
with the battle story, i.e., the account of the casting of
Satan out of heaven, it was necessary to set part of the woman-
dragon story in heaven (vss. 1-5) and part on earth (vss. 14-
16). The modification, not a perfectly consistent one, resulted in the unclarity about the location of the desert which
served as the woman's refuge, and in the lack of an explanation
as to how the woman came to be on earth.

It would seem then that we should assign all the elements
in vss. 1-6 which imply a distinction between heaven and earth
to the redactor. The opening clause of the vision (*kai sēmeion
mega ōphthē en tō ouranō*) and the corresponding clause in vs. 3
which place the two main characters of the first narrative in
heaven are redactional additions. Support for this conclusion
is given by the fact that the vision of the seven bowls begins
in a very similar way (*kai eidon allo sēmeion en tō ouranō mega
kai thaumaston...*15:1). If we remove the other elements in
vss. 1-6 which refer to heaven, we are left with a coherent
narrative which leads smoothly into vs. 14 (see the chart below). Thus the depiction of the woman as Queen of Heaven (vs.
1) is most likely a contribution of the redactor. The motif
of the dragon's sweeping down stars (vs. 4) is not part of the
narrative about his attack on the woman, but belongs to the
description of the monster. It would seem then that the dragon's attack on the stars (vs. 4a) is also a redactional addition.

The question naturally arises whether the redactor has
added any other elements to the description of the dragon. The
dragon's seven heads and ten horns are paralleled by those of
the beast in 13:1 and 17:3. Both elements are traditional.

The seven heads belong to the typical Semitic depiction of the chaos monster. The ten horns derive from Dan 7:7.[32] There-fore, the occurrence of these motifs elsewhere in Revelation is not an argument against assigning them to the source. The phrase *epi tas kephalas autou hepta diadēmata*, however, is not a traditional motif, but is paralleled in 13:1 (ten diadems) and 19:12 (many diadems). It is somewhat more probable then that the motif of the diadems is redactional than that it was part of the source.

The Hymn as a Redactional Composition

It was noted above that the hymnic composition (vss. 10-12) is distinguished from the rest of the chapter by literary form; it is proclamation while the rest of ch. 12 is narrative. Vss. 10-12 is audition, the rest of the chapter is vision. This literary suggestion of independence is reinforced by the difference in content between the song and the narratives. In the narrative of the battle in heaven (vss. 7-9) the victory over Satan is ascribed to Michael. In the song, the victory is ascribed to Christ and to his followers: "and they have con-quered him by the blood of the Lamb and by the word of their testimony, for they loved not their lives even unto death" (vs. 11).

The adversary is not referred to as the dragon in the hymn. Rather the names given him in vss. 10-12 pick up and elaborate the identifications made in the redactional addition to vs. 9. In vs. 9 he is called the ancient serpent (Gen 3:1), the devil, satan and the deceiver of the world. In the hymn he is called the *katēgōr* of our brethren (vs. 10) and devil (vs. 12). Like "satan," *katēgōr* is a judicial term.[33] His deeds, however, are described with verbs influenced by the combat lan-guage of the battle in heaven (*eblēthē* - vs. 10; *katebē* - vs. 12).[34] The use in the hymn of epithets related to the inter-pretative comment of vs. 9 indicates that the hymn is also re-dactional. The use of verbs related to the narrative estab-lishes continuity between the story and the song.

It would seem then that the hymn (vss. 10-12) is a compo-sition of the redactor. This hypothesis is supported by the

fact that such hymnic passages are characteristic of the book
as a whole, and seem rather to have been composed for their
present context than to have been borrowed from liturgy.[35]
Further support lies in the fact that the opening lines of the
song ("Now the salvation and the power and the kingdom of our
God and the authority of his Christ have come..." vs. 10) are
typical of the language used in other hymnic passages in Revelation.[36] Several motifs of vs. 11 are typical of the particular theological perspective of the author of Revelation: "conquering," the blood of the Lamb, *martyria*, and faithfulness
unto death.[37] The reference to *hoi en autois [ouranois]*
skēnountes in vs. 12 occurs also in 13:6 (*tous en tō ouranō*
skēnountas). The term *thymos* occurs ten times in Revelation.[38]
In at least two cases (15:1 and 16:1) the use of the term is to
be attributed to the redactor, since these two passages introduce and explain the significance of the seven bowls.

Charles argued that most of vs. 10 and all of vs. 12 were
not composed by the redactor, but rather belonged to one of the
sources used by him. Thus Charles took vss. 7-10 and 12 as a
unity, a Jewish source, originally in a Semitic language, but
found by the redactor in Greek. The redactional modifications
were, according to Charles, "not improbably" the addition of
ho ophis ho archaios...eblēthē to vs. 9,[39] the substitution of
tōn adelphōn hēmōn for something like *tōn dikaiōn* in vs. 10,[40]
and the composition and addition of vs. 11.[41]

Charles' main argument against ascribing vs. 12 to the redactor is the use of the plural *ouranoi* here which is unique in
the work.[42] It is striking that a similar expression occurs in
18:20 with *ourane*. Neither passage is a Scriptural quotation,
though they both may well be allusions to one or more Scriptural passages (the LXX of Isa 44:23, 49:13, for example, both of
which have *ouranoi*). In such a situation, it would not be surprising if the wording of the passage alluded to influenced the
diction of the author of Revelation on one occasion, while he
preferred his usual style on another. In any case, the variation is not sufficient reason to ascribe the verse to the
source, given the considerations discussed above.

A further argument against ascribing vss. 10-12 to the
source containing the battle in heaven can be made on the basis
of content. It was pointed out above that the story of Satan's
expulsion from heaven is in Jewish tradition a primordial
event. Vss. 10 and 12 both refer to that expulsion, however,
as an eschatological event. Vs. 10 connects it with the establishment of the *exousia tou christou autou* (antecedent of *autou*
being *theou*). In a Jewish source, we would not expect the
exousia of the messiah to be active as yet. Compare, for example, the Jewish source containing the woman-dragon story, where
the messianic office of the child is not yet exercised. The
oligon kairon of vs. 12 also makes clear that an eschatological, not primordial event is meant.

Furthermore, the transition from vs. 11 to vs. 12 is not
as abrupt as has often been argued.[43] The *dia touto* does not
necessarily refer directly back to the *egeneto* and *eblēthē* of
vs. 10. Therefore, there is no reason to see vs. 11 as a redactional intrusion into a source where vs. 12 had followed
immediately upon vs. 10.

Conclusion

Thus the hypothesis which best explains the literary
anomalies and substantive tensions within Revelation 12 is the
theory that the Christian redactor of the chapter, who was most
likely the author of the book as a whole, made use of two Jewish sources. These were (1) the story about the woman and the
dragon (roughly vss. 1-5, 14-16; hereafter referred to as
source I); and (2) the story of the battle in heaven (roughly
vss. 7-9; hereafter source II). The redactor combined these
two narratives by composing a hymnic commentary on the battle
in heaven and appending it to that narrative, and then insert-
ing source II with its hymnic appendix into source I.

Having determined as far as possible the additions made
by the Christian redactor, these additions can now be distinguished from the material derived from the sources. The isolation of such material is not equivalent to a reconstruction of
these sources, since certainty about how they began and ended
is not attainable.

Source I

Source Material	*Redactional Additions*
[kai idou] gynē	kai sēmeion mega ōphthē en tō ouranō
	peribeblēmenē ton hēlion, kai hē selēnē hypokatō tōn podōn autēs, kai epi tēs kephalēs autēs stephanos asterōn dōdeka
en gastri echousa, kai krazei ōdinousa kai basanizomenē tekein.	kai ōphthē allo sēmeion en tō ouranō
kai idou drakōn pyrros megas echōn kephalas hepta kai kerata deka	kai epi tas kephalas autou hepta diadēmata kai hē oura autou syrei to triton tōn asterōn tou ouranou, kai ebalen autous eis tēn gēn.
kai ho drakōn hestēken enōpion tēs gynaikos tēs mellousēs tekein, hina hotan tekē to teknon autēs kataphagē. kai eteken huion, arsen, hos mellei poimainein panta ta ethnē en rabdō sidēra. kai hērpasthē to teknon autēs pros ton theon kai pros ton thronon autou.	
	kai hē gynē ephygen eis tēn erēmon, hopou echei ekei topon hētoimasmenon apo tou theou, hina ekei trephōsin autēn hēmeras chilias diakosias hexē-konta. [source II and hymn]
	kai hote eiden ho drakōn hoti eblēthē eis tēn gēn, ediōxen tēn gynaika hētis eteken ton arsena.
kai edothēsan tē gynaiki hai dyo pteryges tou aetou tou megalou, hina petētai eis tēn erēmon eis ton topon autēs, hopou trephetai ekei kairon kai kairous kai	

hēmisy kairou apo prosōpou
tou opheōs. kai ebalen ho
ophis ek tou stomatos autou
opisō tēs gynaikos hydōr hōs
potamon, hina autēn potamo-
phorēton poiēsē. kai eboēthē-
sen hē gē tē gynaiki, kai
ēnoixen hē gē to stoma autēs
kai katepien ton potamon hon
ebalen ho drakōn ek tou stomatos autou.

kai ōrgisthē ho drakōn epi tē
gynaiki, kai apēlthen
poiēsai polemon meta tōn
loipōn tou spermatos
autēs, tōn tērountōn tas
entolas tou theou kai
echontōn tēn martyrian
Iēsou. kai estathē epi
tēn ammon tēs thalassēs.

Source II

Source Material   *Redactional Additions*

kai egeneto polemos en tō
ouranō ho Michaēl kai hoi
aggeloi autou tou polemēsai
meta tou [satana]   drakontos

kai ho [satanas] epolemēsen
kai hoi aggeloi autou, kai
ouk ischysen, oude topos
heurethē autōn eti en tō
ouranō

kai eblēthē ho [satanas] eis   drakōn ho megas, ho ophis ho
tēn gēn, kai hoi aggeloi   archaios, ho kaloumenos
autou met' autou   diabolos kai ho satanas,
eblēthēsan.   ho planōn tēn oikoumenēn
                                     holēn, eblēthē

[hymn= vss. 10-12]

The Function of the Combat Myth in Source I

The affinities of Revelation 12 with the pattern of the
combat myth show that the images of ch. 12 are not the result
of the creativity of two individual poetic geniuses. They are
rather ancient symbols, already available to the authors em-
bodied in traditions which were widely familiar in the cosmo-
politan culture of the eastern Mediterranean in the Graeco-Roman

period. These symbols are not isolated images, but belong to
an ancient and venerable story, the combat myth.

The Traditional Function of the Dragon

In its archaic form, exemplified by the Ugaritic myths involving Baal, Yamm and Mot, the combat myth functioned to interpret the tensions between fertility and sterility, order and
chaos. The victory of Baal was thus understood to be cosmogonic in an indirect and repeatable sense.[44] In the *Enuma elish*,
this cosmogonic aspect is explicit in the depiction of the victor's creation of the cosmos from the body of the vanquished
Tiamat. This cosmogony also seems to have been understood as a
repeatable event as the cultic use of the *Enuma elish* implies.
The victory of order over chaos, fertility over sterility was
not something which happened once and for all *in illo tempore*,
but must be won repeatedly with the ebb and flow of the seasons
and of dynasties.

The combat myth also has a cosmogonic character when it
appears in the Hebrew Bible. In a number of passages the myth
functions primarily to express the present awesome power of the
deity by recalling his mighty cosmogonic deeds. This emphasis
is characteristic of the dialogues of Job (e.g. 26:5-14).[45]
The present, timeless and repeatable aspect of the combat myth
is emphasized in a number of psalms of the royal cult. The
combat myth in these psalms functions in such a way as to link
the temple and the Davidic kingdom with their heavenly arche-
types. In the cult Yahweh was celebrated as king and creator,
as legitimator, model and patron of the monarchy.[46] The language of the combat myth was also drawn upon by the poets and
prophets of the OT to interpret events. The most striking example is perhaps Isa 51:9-11, where the crossing of the Reed
Sea is interpreted in terms of Yahweh's cosmogonic battle with
Yamm.[47] The mythic pattern of combat also lent itself to the
expression of the universal and transcendent significance of
Israel's wars of conquest, the wars of the period of the
judges, and later her conflicts with her internationally power-
ful neighbors.[48] In this framework, political independence and
stability is what is constituted by the creative act, the

cosmogonic battle. The interference of a foreign power is expressed as the threat of chaos. This particular way of interpreting political events in a mythic framework is characteristic of the prophetic literature.

The author of the hymn of Habakkuk 3 apparently made use of an ode praising Yahweh as the divine warrior doing battle with cosmic powers, particularly *nhr* and *ym* (vss. 8-15). Vss. 12-14 show that a military defeat of an enemy of Israel is expressed in terms of the cosmogonic battle.[49] In Nahum 1:4 the fall of Nineveh is celebrated as the victory of Yahweh over Yamm. The absolute character of the threat posed by Israel's enemies was expressed by the identification of Egypt with Rahab.[50] We also find the rulers of hostile foreign powers identified with Yahweh's serpentine adversary, Tannin (LXX - *drakōn*).[51]

Although the terminology is different, the basic pattern in the treatment of Antiochus Epiphanes in Daniel 7 and 8 is of the same type. His association with a beast from the sea expresses in a mythical way that his dealings with the Jews were experienced as the threat of chaos against divinely established order. The motif of the hostile ruler's rebellious pride, which is part of the pattern in the prophetic passages mentioned above,[52] also occurs in the description of Antiochus Epiphanes in Daniel.[53]

The capitulation of Jerusalem to the Romans in 63 B.C.E. is reflected in the second Psalm of Solomon. Roman power was manifested in the person of Pompey, and it is he (like Nebuchadnezzar and Antiochus Epiphanes before him) who is cast in the role of the adversary of the divine warrior. The psalmist prayed that God would change *hyperēphanian tou drakontos en atimia*.[54] The motif of rebellious pride is also clearly present.[55]

The attitude toward the Romans in the Psalms of Solomon is relatively mild. In Pss Sol 2:3-19 the fall of Jerusalem to Pompey is said to have been a deserved punishment on the sons and daughters of Jerusalem.[56] In strong contrast to this restrained reaction to the Romans is the point of view expressed in the fifth book of the Sibylline Oracles, which is one of bitter opposition.[57] This collection of oracles was written between the destruction of the temple in 70 C.E. and about 135 C.E.[58] Although this work originated in Egyptian Jewish circles, it seems to be representative of the anti-Roman sentiment of a significant segment of the Jewish population of the empire in that period.[59] Two factors made the milder attitude of the Psalms of Solomon difficult for at least the more nationalistic Jews to maintain: the destruction of the temple and the Roman claims to divinity.

In the fifth sibyl the hostility to Rome takes shape in a mythicization of Nero and his career. This involves the adoption and inversion of the popular legend of Nero's return as Savior-King into an eschatological myth in which Nero functions as the adversary of God.[60] The traditional motif most emphasized in Nero's portrayal is that of rebellious pride, the claim to be god.[61] The description of Nero as *deinos ophis* may reflect his association with the beast of watery chaos.[62]

This brief survey of the function of the dragon motif is intended to show that, in the first century C.E., a Jew reading about a *drakōn pyrros megas* would place that image in a political context. The dragon would carry associations with a long line of national enemies, foreign powers often personified in a particular ruler whose deeds were perceived as especially infamous or threatening.

The association of the dragon with Satan in Revelation 12 belongs only to source II and to the redactional stage. The apparent allusion to the story of Genesis 3 also belongs to the redactional stage. Without these associations, there is no reason intrinsic to the story of source I to associate the dragon with Satan. Rather, as was shown above in tracing the history of the motif, the cosmogonic conflict was regularly drawn upon to interpret political conflict in the prophetic tradition. Thus, the most natural way to read source I, especially since its pattern is one of conflict and confrontation, is as a figurative expression of a situation of political and religious conflict.

The Associations of the Desert

A number of details in the woman-dragon story evoke Exodus traditions. One is the motif of the nourishing of the woman. Among the mighty deeds of the Lord during the desert sojourn was the miraculous feeding of the people with manna, water from the rock, and quails.[63] A second element is the method of rescue of the woman in vs. 14: she is given the two wings of the great eagle in order that she might fly into the desert. It was noted in Chapter II that this motif is analogous to Leto's rescue from the attack of Python by being carried out of his reach by the north wind. This allusion to non-Jewish myth, however, does not exclude the possibility that the choice of eagle's wings as the method of rescue was intended to evoke the traditional metaphor for the Exodus event: "You have seen what I did to the Egyptians, and how I bore you on eagles' wings and brought you to myself" (Exod 19:4).[64]

A further element which recalls the Exodus is the place of refuge taken by the woman, the desert. As noted above the dragon as chaos beast is a motif which often functioned to interpret political-religious conflict. In the Hellenistic and early Roman periods, desert traditions, especially when combined with the idea of a New Exodus, often had political implications.

As Martin Hengel has pointed out, the motif of a retreat into the desert was very widespread in post-Maccabean Judaism, both as concept and deed.[65] Its significance varied somewhat. Hengel suggested four possible motivations for such a retreat, of which two are particularly relevant here:

1. Flight from the political-religious oppression of the ruling power;
2. A sort of typological thinking according to which "Endzeit gleicht Urzeit"; thus, the eschatological retreat to the desert was seen as "the New Exodus."

The first motivation was already a traditional motif by the first century C.E. The flight of the woman to the desert in source I would recall for its earliest readers the flight of Mattathias and his sons into the hills from the power of Antiochus and the withdrawal of the pious ones to the desert to escape Pompey.[66]

The Exodus typology was an important part of the self-
understanding of the Qumran community.[67] It is especially
clear in the War Scroll that the dwelling of the community in
the desert was understood as a prelude to a great final battle
which would purge foreign elements and Jewish apostates from
the land.[68] Their sojourn in the desert was modeled on the
wandering in the desert under Moses, and the final battle was
conceived of as a Holy War constituting the New Conquest.

This Exodus typology was not confined to the Qumran community. In about 44 C.E. a certain Theudas, claiming to be a
prophet, led a large number of people down to the Jordan, and
promised to cleave the waters for them. This projected deed
was intended at least to legitimate himself as a prophet, and
perhaps as Moses redivivus.[69] The promised sign makes clear
that Theudas expected the Lord to act decisively through himself in a way analogous to the Exodus event. Our sources do
not provide explicit information about whether he predicted a
New Conquest, which would have led to the defeat of the Romans.
The action taken by the Roman procurator, however, shows that
he viewed the movement as a threat to the authority of Rome.[70]

About a decade later, during the procuratorship of Felix,
an Egyptian (presumably a Jew) behaved in a way reminiscent of
Joshua. He assembled his followers in the desert, led them to
the Mount of Olives, promising that at his command, the walls
of Jerusalem would collapse.[71] The political significance of
the Exodus-Conquest typology is very clear. After the collapse
of the walls, the Egyptian promised to take power into his own
hands, and to install his allies as a bodyguard.

It would seem then that the description of the rescue of
the woman and her refuge in the desert are intended to evoke
the expectation of a new, eschatological Exodus and desert sojourn, which would be followed by the appearance of a savior
figure who would free the Jewish people from the power of Rome.
This savior would of course be the messiah whose birth and
translation were depicted in vs. 5. The implication of his
translation is that he would remain in the presence of God until the time when he would be sent on his eschatological mission.[72]

The use of the time designation *kairon kai kairous kai hēmisy kairou* borrowed from Daniel is compatible with the interpretation given above.[73] That time limit in Daniel designates the amount of time left to Antiochus, the little horn, to exercise his power. At the end of this period, the great time of trouble would occur which would entail the defeat of Antiochus and the exaltation of the people of the saints of the Most High.[74] In the same way, the phrase as used in source I indicates the amount of time which would pass until the avenging of the woman and the defeat of the dragon, i.e., the appearance of the child in his messianic role and the end of Roman power.

There is a rabbinical text, citing traditions ascribed to rabbis of the fourth century, which links the New Exodus with the eschatological time period of Daniel. It reads:

> As the first redeemer (Moses), so the last redeemer (Messiah). As the first redeemer first revealed himself to them and then hid himself, so will the last redeemer....And how long will he hide himself from them?...45 days. And from the time that the Tamid offering was removed and the abomination of desolation set up, it will be 1290 days. Blessed is he who waits and reaches the 1335 days (Dan 12:11).... And where does he (Messiah) lead them? Some say: in the desert of Judah....[75]

Here we have an independent tradition which combines an Exodus typology (Moses and the desert sojourn) with the motif of the temporarily hidden messiah. The length of time during which the messiah is hidden is linked with the calculations of the length of the time of woe found in Daniel. It is thus a rather striking parallel in content to our source I.

An objection which might be raised to the interpretation of source I given above is that there is no explicit indication in the text that it refers to political conflict with Rome. This potential objection raises the question of the nature of symbolic narrative and the legitimacy and scope of allegorical interpretation.

Revelation 12 as Allegorical Narrative

Revelation 12 is a figurative narrative whose relation to historical events, whether past or future, has been variously

interpreted. The narrative has been read as a continuous historical allegory, in which each episode in the story corresponds to a particular historical event. According to H. B.
Swete, the woman represents the Church of the Old Testament in
the first part of the chapter and the Christian Society beginning with vs. 13.[76] The removal of the child (vs. 5) represents the ascension of Jesus, corresponding to Acts 1:2 and
1 Tim 3:16. The flight of the woman to the desert (vs. 6) corresponds to the escape of the Jerusalem Church to Pella.[77] The
reference to Satan as *katēgōr* (vs. 10) recalls the *delatores*
who attacked the Christians of Asia Minor under Domitian.[78] In
vs. 13 the verb *ediōxen* clearly has the secondary hostile sense
and thus is a reference to the beginning of the era of the Roman persecution of Christians begun by Nero in 64 C.E.[79] The
dragon's attack with the flood of water (vs. 15) represents the
persecutions of Nero and Domitian and foreshadows those of
Decius and Diocletian.[80]

This type of continuous allegorical interpretation was
also proposed by J. Wellhausen.[81] The dragon is meant to recall the Roman Empire. The three and a half years (vs. 14)
correspond to the length of the Jewish war with Rome. The
child is the messiah expected by the Jews. The woman who flees
to the desert represents the Pharisaic group among whom Revelation 12 originated. This group left Jerusalem during the Jewish War because, unlike the Zealots, they placed their confidence in divine intervention rather than armed revolution. The
rest of the seed of the woman (vs. 17) are those who remained
in Jerusalem, who would be destroyed by the Romans. The battle
in heaven (vss. 7-9) is but the shadow which the earthly events
cast before them, i.e., the poetic expression of the belief in
predestination derived from Daniel, whereby earthly events were
determined by their heavenly counterparts. The defeat of Satan
in heaven is thus the foreshadowing of the defeat of the
earthly world-power.

This type of allegorical interpretation has been recently
revived by S. Giet, who argued that the purpose of Revelation
12 as it now stands is to recall the messianic past in order to
place the Jewish war with Rome of 66-70 C.E. at the heart of

Christian history.[82] The woman is the people of Israel with
whom the Christians, as the true Israel, could identify. The
child is the messiah, for the Christian readers, Jesus. The
one thousand two hundred and sixty days (vs. 6) correspond to
the length of the Jewish war. Giet interprets the water with
which the dragon attacks the woman (vs. 15) by analogy with
17:15, where the "waters" are interpreted as "peoples." The
flood of water thus symbolizes either the "nations" who flocked
to Jerusalem, the troops who besieged the holy city, or those
which traversed Peraea. The swallowing up of the water by the
earth represents the destruction of the nations who came to
Jerusalem or the preservation of the true Israel from the
troops.

This sort of continuous allegorical interpretation has not
found wide acceptance because the narrative of Revelation 12
does not contain any clear signal or explicit reference to indicate that the story is meant to correspond to any specific
historical events. It does not encourage the reader with clear
hints, as does the Animal Apocalypse, for example, to look for
a continuous series of historical events to which the story
corresponds.

E. Lohmeyer's interpretation of Revelation 12 takes a very
different approach to the question of the relation of the passage to historical events. According to Lohmeyer, the vision
does not relate to past events at all; it does not refer to the
historical birth of Jesus. Rather, the entire vision depicts
the birth of the divine logos from lady wisdom and is purely
eschatological.[83] Lohmeyer does not simply mean by "eschatological" a future historical event. He can speak of the birth
of this child both as "eschatological" and as "timeless."[84]
The reason for this is Lohmeyer's view, which he believes is
also the view of Revelation, that religiously significant
events are all timeless insofar as they reflect a "timeless
order," i.e., a transcendent reality.[85] Thus events of the
past, present and future which are of religious significance to
Christians have a similar structure; they are typologically
related to each other. This view does not dissolve Christian
faith into a timeless mysticism, however. Something new is

presumed by eschatological expectation. According to Lohmeyer,
Revelation 12 depicts the future manifestation of the messiah
to the world. This event can be described as the birth of the
messiah because it is typologically related to the birth and
ministry of Jesus.

The interpretation proposed by Lohmeyer clearly does not
take Revelation 12 as a continuous historical allegory. There
are of course other types of allegorical narrative. We might
call a narrative allegorical whose tangible images and narrative patterns point beyond themselves to intangible realities.
As Edwin Honig has put it:

> We find the allegorical quality in a twice-told tale
> written in rhetorical, or figurative language and
> expressing a vital belief....The twice told aspect
> of the tale indicates that some venerated or proverb-
> ial antecedent (old) story has become a pattern for
> another (the new) story....The relating of the new
> and the old in the reflective nature of both language
> and theme typifies allegorical narration. The tale,
> the rhetoric, and the belief work together in what
> might be called a metaphor of purpose.[86]

In source I the old story is the combat myth in the form of the
threatened birth of god Apollo. The birth of this god and his
defeat of the dragon was associated with the dawning of a new
era. His kingship meant peace and fertility as Virgil's fourth
ecologue shows:

> Now the last age by Cumae's Sibyl sung
> Has come and gone, and the majestic roll
> Of circling centuries begins anew:
> Justice returns, returns old Saturn's reign
> With a new breed of men sent down from heaven.
> Only do thou, at the boy's birth in whom
> The iron shall cease, the golden age arise,
> Befriend him, chaste Lucina; 'tis thine own
> Apollo reigns....[87]

But how are we to understand the new story? In Lohmeyer's interpretation, it is really only the birth of the child which
has any real significance. The function of Revelation 12 as a
whole in his view is to express the eschatological hope for the
cosmic manifestation of the messiah. This is certainly an important aspect of the function of our source I. But this interpretation does not do justice to the story's emphasis on the
role of the woman nor to much of the narrative detail.

The interpretation proposed here is that source I is not a
continuous historical allegory, but that it is a figurative expression of an historical conflict and its projected resolution. Because of the story's lack of specificity in historical
detail and its masterful use of a venerable older story, it is
flexible in application. That the narrative did originally
refer to an historical situation is implied by its use of
images which were traditionally and contemporaneously associated with political conflict. The image of the dragon in and
of itself would naturally call the contemporary ruling power
to mind, as was shown above. A number of motifs in the story
(refuge in the desert, nourishing, rescue on eagle's wings)
evoke the contemporary expectation of a New Exodus and a New
Conquest, which were often associated with withdrawal from the
ruling power and hope for its overthrow.

The narrative of the woman and the dragon might be characterized as a paradigmatic story. By this term is meant a
story which is allegorical only in a general sense. The story
is not intended to be applied to one or even several specific
historical events exclusively. It is not thus an explicit nor
a continuous historical allegory. But the story is also not
the expression of universal truths. It contains motifs which
are historically rooted and which relate to a discernible time
and place. The purpose of such a story is to interpret the
situation of its intended readers by placing it in a broader
context. The characters and events in the story have an implicit relation to the historical situation of the readers. The
particular situation is not represented in detail, it is rather
typified. It is this typical character of the story which the
term paradigmatic is meant to express.

The confrontation between the woman and the dragon typi-
fies the conflict of the Jewish people with Rome in the first
centuries B.C.E. and C.E. The depiction of the rescue of the
woman and the birth of the messiah would, in such a context,
awaken the hope of deliverance from subjugation to the Romans.

Implications of the Paradigmatic Narrative

What does the apparently paradigmatic nature of the narrative of source I tell us about the political stance of the

Jewish author and his community? Combat language is meaningful for the author and presumably for his audience. An actual battle is not described at least in the part of source I which has been incorporated into Revelation 12. Such a battle however is implied. The translation of the child and the time limit announced for the desert sojourn imply the expectation of a future turning point. Since the images and pattern of the narrative derive from the combat myth, that turning point would most likely have been conceived of as a battle.

The example which the story sets for the readers is not a violent one, however. The woman, with whom they would identify, has a passive role. She is rescued and she sojourns in the desert until the final turning point, presumably a battle in which the messiah would defeat the dragon. There is no indication that the author advocates that his readers adopt a Zealot position by taking up arms against the Romans. The stance advocated is similar to that of the Essene community at Qumran: sojourn in the desert awaiting the divine intervention.

The function of the narrative at the Jewish stage seems to have been to console and to exhort endurance in a time of conflict. It does this in two ways. First, it reveals that the messiah has already been born and is being preserved in heaven until the appropriate time. Second, the description of the woman's rescue evokes the hope of the community's rescue in a New Exodus and sojourn in the desert. The hope is given this form by the use of the motifs of the eagle's wings and of the nourishment in the desert. Finally, the veiled time reference of vs. 14 is an indication that the sojourn in the desert would be of a divinely determined length of time, presumably to be followed by some form of a New Conquest which would mean the defeat of Rome.

Date and Provenance of Source I

The identity of the adversary depicted in the narrative of the woman and the dragon would of course depend on the date of composition of source I. There is no clear internal indication of date. We can only be certain that it was composed before the final redaction of the book of Revelation, which most

likely occurred in the latter part of Domitian's reign (90-
95).[88] Our working hypothesis has been that source I originated in the same general context, i.e., the domination of the
East by Rome.

There is no clear reference to the destruction of the temple in 70 C.E. in source I. Given the allusive style of the
narrative, however, which avoids explicit allegory, we may not
draw the conclusion that it was written prior to that event.

The dependence of our source on a Graeco-Roman myth is of
some help in discerning its provenance. While it certainly
would have been possible for a Jewish visionary to come in contact with and adapt such a myth in Judaea or its culturally
rather diversified environs, it is much more likely that such
a process took place in the diaspora. In a context of the latter type, the synagogue would have been in more direct competition, if not in dialogue with other institutions which called
for adherence or full allegiance.

Since there is a strong tradition, as well as good internal evidence,[89] for associating the book of Revelation with
western Asia Minor, that region presents itself as a likely
location for the origin of source I. The Appendix below provides evidence that this area was an ideal setting for the kind
of religious syncretism which would have encouraged such an
adaptation of myth, and that the Leto-Python-Apollo myth was
widespread and culturally significant enough to have been known
to Jewish communities in the region.

To suggest that a Jew adapted a Graeco-Roman myth to express the current situation of conflict and his messianic expectation is not to propose a process without precedent. Jesus
ben Sirach made use of language apparently borrowed from an
aretalogy of Isis in composing a hymn to wisdom (Sir 24:3-6).[90]
An Egyptian Jew, writing about the middle of the second century
B.C.E., expressed his messianic hopes in language derived from
Egyptian mythology: "And then from the sun God shall send a
king..." (Sib Or 3:652).[91] It is likely that another Jewish
oracle in the third sibyl (3:350-80) contains language influenced by the Isis-aretalogies. These images borrowed from the
mythology of Isis are used in this oracle to articulate

eschatological expectations.[92] Two other second century Jews, Pseudo-Eupolemos and Artapanus, apparently made a conscious attempt to fuse Hebrew traditions with Greek, Babylonian and Egyptian mythology.[93]

Even where mythic language is borrowed from non-Jewish sources and used positively, the result is not a levelling sort of syncretism. The borrowing tends rather to reinforce the authority of the mother-faith. Rather than an acknowledgment of Isis, the application of *aretai* of the goddess to wisdom has the effect of claiming for Sophia the universal significance attributed to Isis. In Chapter IV it will be argued that the application of the Apollo myth to the messiah has a similar effect; i.e., it attributes the cosmic peace and fertility of the reign of Apollo to the rule of the messiah.

The Function of the Combat Myth in Source II

The form of the combat myth most similar to source II (the battle in heaven--vs. 7-9 exclusive of redaction) is the Jewish myth of the rebellion of Satan. This Jewish myth is closely related to the Canaanite myth of the fallen stellar god Athtar.

In the Jewish intertestamental works where the motif of Satan's fall from heaven occurs, it is conceived of as a primordial event. In the Life of Adam and Eve, the fall of Satan is placed chronologically between the creation of Adam and Eve and their fall. Satan and his angels are cast out of heaven because of their refusal to worship Adam. The seduction of Eve was Satan's revenge.[94] Michael functions as Satan's adversary in this story, though it is not explicitly said that Michael hurls Satan out of heaven.

In 2 Enoch, the fall of Satan is not associated with the story of Adam and Eve, but is said to have occurred on the second day of creation. The Lord created ten orders of angels and commanded them to stand in their orders. The cause of Satan's expulsion was his refusal to obey this command.[95]

In its original Jewish context, the primordial myth of the fall of Satan functioned as an aetiological or speculative myth, which attempted to explain the origin of evil. Functionally speaking, it belongs to the same category as the myth

of original sin and the myth about the fallen angels, the
Watchers.[96]

The existential significance of these myths is ethical
rather than political. The effect of Satan's fall is his interest in enticing others to rebel against heaven as he had
done. Such an understanding is evident in the version of the
myth of the fallen angels found in the book of Jubilees. The
leader of these angels, Mastema, and the angels under his authority are allowed "to execute the power of my [Mastema's]
will on the sons of men; for these are for corruption and leading astray before my judgment, for great is the wickedness of
the sons of men" (Jub 10:8). In the Testament of Reuben, the
myth of the Watchers is used to warn against the wiles of
women and to exhort the readers to avoid fornication (5:1-6:5).

The myth of the battle in heaven and the fall of Satan as
we have it in source II is compatible with the myth of the two
spirits in the Manual of Discipline from Qumran. Both function
as the aetiological or proto-metaphysical background for ethical teaching.

The combat myth in source II thus functions in an ethical
framework. By telling a story of origins, it explains the
present situation in which human beings must choose between
good and evil. The description of the activity of the fallen
angel, Satan, is an attempt to explain why humanity seems inclined to evil.

The Function of the Combat Myth in the Christian Redaction

The Re-use of Source I

Source I was attractive raw material for the Christian
redactor for two reasons. First of all, the oracle concerning
the birth and translation of the child could be read as a mysterious reference to the birth and ascension of Christ.

Secondly, source I addressed itself to a situation of
political-religious conflict which was analogous to the context
out of and for which the book of Revelation in its final form
was written. Since the narrative of source I was not tied to
individual, historical events, it could function equally well
for another, somewhat later group as a paradigm of their own
situation.

The redactor made a number of substantial modifications in the narrative about the woman and the dragon (source I). As noted in the section on the literary unity of ch. 12, the woman-dragon story seems to have had an earthly setting originally. Since we cannot be certain about how the story of source I was introduced, there is no way of determining whether or not it was expressed as a vision at the Jewish stage. In any case, the Christian redactor has incorporated the narrative in a vision account. Many of the visions in Revelation depict heavenly scenes. Thus the use of the vision form may have contributed to the transformation of the characters in the narrative from metaphors for earthly realities to heavenly beings. The combination of the narrative about the woman and the dragon with the battle in heaven also affected the setting of source I. If the dragon is to be cast down from heaven in act two, he must be in heaven in act one. Thus the combination of the two narratives also called for a heavenly setting for the first portion of source I.

It was argued above that the narrative about the woman and the dragon was composed as a figurative representation of political-religious conflict in which the opponent was cast in the role of the chaos beast. In the redaction, the process of mythicization is taken one step further. The new heavenly setting contributes to this intensification, in that the story of conflict is removed from the specifically political realm. This is accomplished by the identification of the dragon of chaos with Satan. This identification was facilitated by the equivalence of *drakōn* and *ophis* in source I (cf. 12:15 with 16). Leviathan was conceived of as a serpentine monster and could be called *nāḥāš* (LXX - *ophis*; see Isa 27:1). This serpentine character of Leviathan (*drakōn*) facilitated his identification with Satan, since Satan was associated with the *ophis* of Genesis 3 (LXX).[97]

The reinterpretation of the dragon spiritualizes and universalizes his conflict with the woman. The issue is no longer simply a nationalistic one with cosmic overtones, but one which has to do with the fundamentally dualistic nature of reality.

Another notable modification of source I is the shift in the significance of the woman effected by the addition of vs.

17. As was argued above the woman had clear and direct paradigmatic significance for the readers of the original, Jewish version of source I. In the source, the woman represented the community in a paradigmatic allegory. Vs. 17 indicates that the redactor did not understand the woman-dragon story in the same way. His readers were not intended to identify directly with the woman, but were to understand themselves as "her seed."

This contrast between the direct and indirect identification called forth by each of the versions of the story highlights the different ways in which their authors used language. In source I, the woman and the dragon are metaphors, like the beasts and the little horn in Daniel 7 and 8. They are complex metaphors, it is true, with mythic associations. But their primary function is to say something about an earthly reality by pointing out its cosmic or ultimate significance.

Already in source II and consistently in the victory song and the redactional additions, the focus is on heavenly realities. The shift is most obvious in the reinterpretation of the dragon, but is present in the treatment of the woman as well.

The depiction of the woman as Queen of Heaven in 12:1 suggests that in the Christian redaction the woman is not simply a metaphor for an earthly entity but that she is some sort of heavenly being. Exegetes who have accepted the latter interpretation have proposed various theories as to the nature of the heavenly reality. Some have suggested that the woman is the heavenly Jerusalem. There are several problems with this theory. The redactor at no point gives any hint that she is to be associated with a city: no mural crown, no mention of a mountain or any other appropriate attribute. Secondly, the motif of the nourishment of the woman in the desert does not fit the holy city interpretation. Thirdly, there is no indication that the description of the heavenly Jerusalem in ch. 21 is a continuation of ch. 12. The new Jerusalem is not, for example, associated with the desert in any way. Finally, the heavenly Jerusalem is said in 21:9-10 to be the bride of Christ. It is not impossible that the redactor would depict the holy city as both mother and bride of the messiah, but it is unlikely.

Ernst Lohmeyer proposed that the woman of ch. 12 is per-
sonfied wisdom.[98] This theory is attractive for several reasons. The well-developed tradition of ḥokmāh/sophia as a
heavenly woman provides an excellent analogy to the sort of
heavenly reality ascribed to the woman by the Christian redactor. This hypothesis makes sense of the designation of the
followers of Jesus as the offspring of the woman: they are the
children of wisdom.[99] Finally there is a tradition that the
end-time will be characterized by the withdrawal of wisdom from
human society,[100] which corresponds to the motif of the woman's
flight.

But there are decisive arguments against this interpretation. Lohmeyer posits an eschatological myth according to
which wisdom would descend from heaven at the end time, seek a
dwelling place among men, but be repelled by the unrighteous-
ness she meets everywhere. So she withdraws either to some
specially prepared or unknown place, presumably until the end
of the period of tribulation.[101] But this myth is a scholarly
construct based on the conflation of two quite different myths.
One is the eschatological motif of the disappearance of wisdom
as one of the signs of the end, found in 4 Ezra and 2 Apoc
Baruch. The other is the quite uneschatological myth about
wisdom coming down from heaven seeking a place to dwell on
earth. In one version (1 Enoch 42), she does not find one and
returns to her place in heaven. In other versions she descends
to dwell in Israel (Sir 24) or in wise individuals (by implication, Wisdom 1:4-5; cf. 7:7). Thus, the wisdom tradition does
not provide nearly as good a parallel to Revelation 12 as Lohmeyer claimed. Furthermore, this hypothesis does not explain
the motif of nourishing, nor does it adequately account for the
desert motif.

A further suggestion for the significance of the woman in
the present form of ch. 12 is that she is a symbol for the eschatological community of salvation, which has already appeared
on earth as the Church. The import of the symbol is that the
Church is by nature a supra-earthly, heavenly entity.[102] This
interpretation has the same weakness as older attempts to understand the woman as the Church, i.e., the inability to give

a satisfactory explanation for the birth of the child (vs. 5).
It is the old problem of explaining how the Church can be the
mother of the messiah. A. Vögtle attempted to overcome this
problem by affirming that vs. 5 refers to the birth of the messiah but suggesting that the redactor was not interested in
making his vision account correspond to the sequence of historical events.[103] This explanation is not satisfactory. If the
redactor intended the characters in the story to correspond to
historical entities, we would expect the narrative to have a
minimal correspondence to the historical relationships of the
entities represented. Gollinger's solution to the problem is
to suggest that the redactor understood 12:5, not as the birth
of Jesus, nor as the eschatological appearance of the messiah,
but as an expression of the belief in the fundamental defeat of
Satan in heaven and in the continuing protection of the Church
by God against the attacks of Satan. At the same time however,
she understands 12:17 to refer to individual, historical
Christians.[104] It is unlikely, however, that the redactor
would understand one relationship involving mother and child
(the birth of the child) metaphorically and the other (the rest
of her seed) historically. Thus, an interpretation which
could elucidate both images on the same level would be preferable.

The theory which best explains the redacted ch. 12 is
that the woman is the heavenly Israel. The background of this
understanding of the woman is in the poetry of the OT. In the
book of Hosea, the relationship between the prophet and his
harlot-wife is a symbol of the relationship between Yahweh and
personified Israel.[105] The children born to Hosea and Gomer
represent the individual Israelites, the people of Israel, as
their names show: And the Lord said, "Call his name Not my
people, for you are not my people and I am not your God" (1:9).
This motif is continued in the poem of ch. 2: "Upon her children also I will have no pity, because they are children of
harlotry" (2:6; RSV 2:4). The reconciliation between Yahweh
and his spouse is to take place in the desert in a re-enactment
of the Exodus (2:16-17; RSV 2:14-15). The same image occurs in
deutero-Isaiah, where the people are addressed as sons of the

personified Israel (Isa 50:1). In the poem of Isaiah 54 (a
passage which is probably alluded to in Rev 21:9-21) personified Israel or possibly Jerusalem is addressed as the spouse of
the Lord (vss. 5-8). The many children promised to her undoubtedly represent the restored community of the early post-
exilic period.

The redactor of Revelation 12 has intensified this metaphor so that the personified Israel is a heavenly entity who
can be depicted as the Queen of Heaven (vs. 1). This intensification of the image is probably related to the ancient idea
that all earthly entities have heavenly prototypes.[106] This
conception is reflected in the priestly tradition according to
which the earthly tabernacle, and thus the temple also, was a
copy of a heavenly original. This idea seems to be reflected
in Revelation by references to the heavenly temple with its
altar and ark of the covenant.[107] In Jewish apocalyptic literature, a number of entities, most of which had earthly counterparts at least at one time, were thought to be in heaven wait-
ing to be revealed in the end-time. The heavenly Jerusalem depicted in Revelation 21 belongs to this category.

As in source I, the birth pangs of the woman represent the
eschatological woes which precede the appearance of the messiah. The woman is depicted as the heavenly Israel in the redacted ch. 12, and thus the birth of the child in vs. 5 as a
heavenly event. This heavenly event is thus the prototype of
the earthly event of the birth of Jesus. The reference to
"the rest of her seed" in vs. 17 implies another heavenly birth
which corresponds to the establishment of the Christian community. The use of the image of birth shows that the redactor
understood the establishment of the Christian community as an
eschatological event parallel to the coming of the messiah.

The Re-use of Source II

The redactional process has resulted in a fundamental
transformation of the function of source II. The description
of a primordial event has been transformed into an eschatological event. The fall of Satan, once linked to a primordial rebellion, is now linked with the exaltation of the savior of the

end-time. This transformation is effected partly by juxtaposition and partly by the hymnic commentary of vss. 10-11, where
the victory of Michael over Satan is ascribed to Christ.

The redacted source II is thus related to the widespread
apocalyptic expectation of the definitive defeat and punishment
of Satan and the reversal of the effects of his fall. In the
Testament of Levi 18 the defeat of Beliar by the "new priest"
results in a return of the pre-fall condition of creation (vss.
10-12). In the Assumption of Moses, the appearance of the
kingdom of God is linked with the annihilation of Satan (As Mos
10:1).[108] The eschatological defeat of Belial is the central
motif of the Qumran War Scroll. The main difference between
these texts and the redacted battle in heaven of Revelation 12
is that the defeat of Satan in ch. 12 is not complete. The redacted battle in heaven (12:7-9) is nearer to these eschatological texts in meaning than to the original sense of source II.
The casting of Satan out of heaven is associated in 12:10 with
the arrival of the kingdom of God. However that kingdom is not
yet manifest on earth as vs. 12 shows; the short-term effect of
the heavenly defeat of Satan is only to strengthen his power on
earth. The remark that Satan has only a "little time" (vs.
12), however, implies that the heavenly defeat is a guarantee
of the earthly, i.e., the total defeat of the adversary.

It was argued in the last section that, for the Christian
redactor, the heavenly event of the woman's giving birth is a
prototype of an earthly event. Likewise, in the redacted battle in heaven, the defeat of Satan is the heavenly reality to
which the annihilation of earthly forces of evil corresponds.
In each of these cases, the revelation of the heavenly event
clarifies the outcome of the earthly events which are still in
process. Jesus is exalted in heaven and will return to rule
the nations. The community will ultimately be rescued as the
woman has been. The earthly adversaries will eventually share
Satan's defeat.

The Hymnic Composition

The hymnic composition (vss. 10b-12) is carefully constructed, and is partially based on a parallelism of clauses.

It is composed of three strophes of four, three and four lines
each, respectively.[109]

1. *arti egeneto hē sōtēria kai hē dynamis kai hē*
   basileia tou theou hēmōn
   kai hē exousia tou christou autou
   hoti eblēthē ho katēgōr tōn adelphōn hēmōn
   ho katēgorōn autous enōpion tou theou hēmōn
   hēmeras kai nyktos.
2. *kai autoi enikēsan auton dia to haima tou arniou*
   kai dia ton logon tēs martyrias autōn
   kai ouk ēgapēsan tēn psychēn autōn achri thanatou.
3. *dia touto euphrainesthe, ouranoi kai hoi en autois*
   skēnountes.
   ouai tēn gēn kai tēn thalassan
   hoti katebē ho diabolos pros hymas echōn
   thymon megan
   eidōs hoti oligon kairon echei.

There is some rhyming within each strophe: (1) the repetition
of *hēmōn* at or near the end of lines; (2) *arniou* and *thanatou*
at the end of lines one and three; (3) *thalassan* and *megan* at
the end of lines two and three. There is also parallelism
within each strophe of cognate words or of similar constructions: (1) the correspondence of *ho katēgorōn* and *ho katēgōr* in
lines three and four; (2) the parallelism of *dia to haima* and
dia ton logon in the first and second lines and of *enikēsan* and
ēgapēsan in the first and third lines; (3) the correspondence
of *echōn* and *echei* in lines three and four and the antithetic
parallelism of *euphrainesthe* and *ouai* and of *ouranoi* and *gēn* in
the first and second lines.

The first and third strophes are constructed in parallel
fashion. The first two lines of each describe the results of
the victory, while the last two describe the immediate cause.[110]
Grammatically speaking, the third lines of the two strophes
(which give the cause) both begin with *hoti*, while the fourth
lines begin with nominative participles, each having the same
subject, the *katēgōr*.

If we compare 12:10-12 with the OT psalms in an attempt to
determine its genre, we find that it is not a hymn in the

strict sense, i.e., a song of praise.[111] Its closest parallel
is the type Gunkel called *Siegeslieder* ("victory songs").[112]

The pattern of Rev 12:10-12 is:

1. Proclamation of salvation (vs. 10)
2. Proclamation of kingship (vs. 10)
3. Description of victory (vss. 10-11)
4. Call for rejoicing (vs. 12)

The call for rejoicing is a typical element of a victory
song.[113] The other three elements constitute a pattern which
is also present in several of the victory songs discussed by
Gunkel, e.g., Ps 46:1-8. Vss. 1-3 describe the deity as a
mah^{a}sęh, a shelter or refuge, for his people, as a helper and
rescuer. Vss. 4-5 describe the peaceful state resulting from
his aid (equivalent to *sōtēria* in Rev 12:10).[114] Vss. 9-10 describe the victory, and vss. 11-12 the exaltation (equivalent
to *basileia* in Rev 12:10). This pattern of kingship based on
victory in battle is also found in Pss 48:1-9, 76:1-10, 97:1-5,
98:1-6. The pattern also occurs in Exod 15:16-18, the "Song
of the Sea," with the addition of the motif of the building of
a sanctuary on a sacred mountain (a motif also found in Pss 48
and 76). This pattern of combat, victory and establishment of
kingship derives from the Canaanite version of the combat
myth.[115] The significance of the appearance of this pattern
in the hymn will be discussed below.

It was argued above that Rev 12:10-12 was composed by the
Christian redactor. The next task is to attempt to discover
what his intent was in adding this hymn.

The redactional addition to source II (*ho ophis ho
archaios, ho kaloumenos diabolos kai ho satanas, ho planōn tēn
oikoumenēn holēn*) and the victory song (vss. 10-12) interpret
and comment upon the battle in heaven depicted in source II.
In the process they introduce a new mythical conception: the
heavenly court presided over by the deity as king-judge and
involving the testimony of accusing and defending angels.[116]
This complex of motifs is introduced by the use of the epithets
diabolos, satanas and *katēgōr; śṭn* and *mśṭmh* are both titles
which were later used as names of the principal adversary and
leader of the fallen angels.[117] In Rev 12:9 the accumulation

of titles and epithets indicates that the author has an individual in mind to whom various traditions and epithets are being consciously attached. This process presupposes a stage in
the development of the myth of the divine court in which the
functions of accuser and defender were conceived of as resting
primarily on two individuals. In the book of Jubilees these
are primarily the Angel of the Presence and the Prince of Mastema;[118] they are Satan and the patron angel of Israel, probably Michael, in the Testaments of the Twelve Patriarchs.[119]

The texts from Qumran published so far do not refer explicitly to a judicial conflict between Michael as patron of Israel and Beliar as their accuser. In the Damascus Document,
however, the struggle of Moses and Aaron with Jannes and Jam-
bres reflects a struggle between the Prince of Lights and Belial (CD 5:18-19). This interpretation is similar to the book
of Jubilees' understanding that Moses' struggle with Pharaoh
and the Egyptian sorcerers reflects a conflict between the
Angel of the Presence and Mastema.[120] The latter story clearly
presupposes a heavenly court in which Mastema is accuser and
the Angel of the Presence is defender.[121] We can infer that
the story in the Damascus Document is based on a similar conception, and further, that the dualism of the Spirit of Truth
versus the Spirit of Deceit found elsewhere in the scrolls is
also associated with a conception of the heavenly court. It
does seem that this mythic pattern has faded into the background at Qumran somewhat, but the occurrence of the term *śṭn*
in several fragmentary contexts may be an indication that it
was still alive.[122]

The identification of the dragon in vs. 9 with *ho kaloumenos diabolos kai ho satanas* (the former being the LXX translation of *haśśāṭan* and the latter its transliteration) is
picked up again in vs. 10, the first verse of the victory song.
The repetition of the *eblēthē* in vs. 10b has the effect of
giving one more epithet to the dragon, *ho katēgōr*, which, in a
legal context, is closely related to the function of *ho satanas*.[123]

This coincidence of military and judicial conflict between
Michael and Satan which results from the redactional use of

source II is not unique. Jubilees 48 presupposes both a judicial struggle between Mastema and the Angel of the Presence
(vss. 15 and 18 contain references to Mastema's accusation of
Israel which would presumably have been countered by a defense
offered by the Angel of the Presence) as well as a military
struggle (vs. 13).[124] In the Animal Apocalypse, the judgment
of condemnation passed on the fallen angels is followed by
their being cast into the abyss by one of the archangels.[125]
This action is of course, in the context, the execution of the
sentence and thus judicial punishment. But the form the judgment takes is reminiscent of the typical issue of the combat
myth, where the victor confines the vanquished god to the underworld. The Melchizedek fragment from Qumran refers to the
eschatological judgment which Melchizedek will pronounce
against Belial and the spirits of his lot. This conviction was
then to be followed by a battle in which Melchizedek will be
aided by the heavenly ones on high.[126] Upon this battle the
kingship of Melchizedek was expected to follow,[127] just as the
dominion of Michael over the '*ēlîm* and that of Israel over all
flesh would follow the great battle described in the War
Scroll.[128] A similar motif is represented in the redaction
of Revelation 12 by the *basileia tou theou* and the *exousia tou
christou autou* (vs. 10) which follow the battle of vss. 7-9.

In Daniel 7 we find the sequence of judgment (vss. 10,
26a), destruction (vss. 11-12, 26b) and kingship (vss. 13-14,
27). As in the Animal Apocalypse, the destruction here is judicial punishment. But the mythic context of the vision is the
assembly of the gods where El passes judgment on the dispute
over kingship between Yamm and Baal. The implied antagonism in
Daniel 7 between the beasts on the one hand and the Ancient of
Days and one like a son of man on the other recalls the battles
between Yamm and Baal and between Yahweh and Leviathan. Daniel
7, as well as the texts mentioned above, thus shares the combination of combat and judicial motifs with Revelation 12.

Vs. 10 functions as a sort of climax to the story of ch.
12 thus far told. It is a heavenly proclamation whose function
is to clarify for the readers the significance of the events
narrated. The point of the proclamation of vs. 10 is that the

expulsion of the accuser (of the faithful) has made possible the initiation (*arti*) of the kingdom of God and the authority of his Christ. There is clearly some tension in that proclamation. The *śāṭan* or *katēgōr* in his judicial function is usually portrayed as subordinate to and under the control of the deity. His activity in the divine court is a threat to the faithful but not to the deity or the exercise of his power. It is the more general activity of the Evil Angel as deceiver, tempter, and destroyer, which must be put to an end to allow the new era to take effect.[129] Why then has the redactor chosen to emphasize the more narrow function of the *katēgōr*?

Source II originally described an abortive primordial rebellion which was one of the stories told to explain the origin of evil. After his defeat, Satan devoted his energies to spreading rebellion.[130] The addition to vs. 9 and vs. 10 have transformed that primordial event to the eschatological defeat of the accusing angel by the defending angel. And yet, as vs. 12 makes clear, this defeat does not lead to the complete annihilation of the power of the adversary which has permeated the order of earthly reality. It is a more limited victory, which entails Satan's loss of access to the heavenly court and thereby his office of accuser. What significance had this event for Christian readers?

Vs. 10b ("who accuses them day and night before our God") and vs. 11 indicate what the significance of the victory of Michael is for the Christians. Satan's loss of access to the heavenly court means that no further accusations can be brought against the faithful. They are safe from the threat of further indictments in the heavenly court. Their accuser is not just warded off from the divine presence temporarily, but is definitively silenced.[131]

Vs. 10b as noted above refers to the heavenly court. Vs. 11, by mentioning the testimony of the brethren and their death, indirectly brings earthly courts to mind. Here again is the motif of the heavenly prototype of an earthly entity or process. The Christians have been on trial for their faith here below, presumably before Roman magistrates. Vs. 11 indicates that their conduct in such trials and their resulting deaths,

combined with their participation in the expiation of Christ's
death, have won them acquittal in the heavenly court. Their
eternal destiny is thus assured.

The heavenly acquittal is ascribed however only to those
who "loved not their lives even unto death." It is only those
who have actually died for the faith whose eternal destiny is
assured. Vs. 12 indicates that the power of the adversary over
those still living has not yet been broken. This is the sense
of the woe spoken on the earth and sea. The woe of course includes those who dwell on earth, as the call to rejoicing of
vs. 12a was addressed to "you that dwell therein" as well as to
heaven itself. The statement that the devil knows that his
time is short indicates that his power over the faithful still
living can only be exercised for a limited time. This element
of vs. 12 most likely alludes to the three and a half times
mentioned in source I.

The hymnic passage, then, with the support of the redactional addition to vs. 9, is a rather artfully integrated commentary on the myth of the battle in heaven. The commentary
introduces a second mythic pattern, the heavenly court, which
lends itself more easily to the partially realized eschatology
of the redactor expressed in vs. 11.

The New Unity

The way in which the redactor has combined the two sources
is remarkable first of all in that he is sensitive to the ancient mythic pattern and uses it as his organizing principle.
It was noted in Chapter II that the narrative of Revelation 12
in its present form reflects the basic pattern of the combat
myth:

    A. The Dragon (vs. 3)
    B. Chaos and Disorder (vs. 4a)
    C. The Attack (vs. 4b)
    D. The Champion (vs. 5a)
    E. The Champion's "Death" (vs. 5b)
    G. Recovery of the Champion (vs. 7a)
    H. Battle Renewed and Victory (vss. 7b-9)
    I. Restoration and Confirmation of Order (vss. 10-12a)
    F. The Dragon's Reign (vss. 12b-17) [132]

The victory song, as was indicated above, reflects the pattern
of the Canaanite combat myth. Source I reflects the pattern of

the Leto-Python-Apollo myth, which is a Greek version of the
combat myth. Source II derives ultimately from the Canaanite
myth of Athtar, and is closely related to the form that myth
takes in the story of the rebellion of Satan. These two narratives and the hymn are combined in such a way that the new unity also reflects the pattern of the combat, as shown above.
The motif of vengeance on the dragon, which the reader expects
in the woman-dragon narrative, is expressed by the placement of
source II after the depiction of the rescue of the child and
the woman (vss. 5-6). In place of the child's vengeance on the
attacker, which would be usual, we find Michael the archangel
fighting on his behalf. The first part of the hymn makes explicit that the point of contention is universal kingship: *hē
basileia tou theou kai hē exousia tou christou autou* (vs. 10).

The skill of the redactor of Revelation 12 is shown in the
masterful way in which he has used the story of the fall of
Satan. On the one hand, as we have noted above, it functions
as the climax and fitting conclusion to the story of confrontation and threatened birth of source I. Secondly it initiates,
as the first scene, the eschatological drama which culminates
in 19:11-22:5.

Although a climax of sorts was reached with 12:10, the redactor is able to maintain the momentum of the story with two
devices. One is the spatial distinction of heaven and earth:
Satan has been defeated in heaven, but he is yet to be defeated
on earth (vs. 12). The other is the arrangement of source I.
He has created a proleptic ending for the story (vs. 6), and
has placed the most detailed description of the actual conflict
after source II. This placement of the rest of source I at the
end of the chapter prevents any levelling off of the dramatic
tension. Finally, the redactional addition of vs. 17 is a dis-
tinctly open-ended conclusion to the passage which points ahead
to further conflict.

The repetition of the attack on the woman by the dragon in
vss. 13-16 does not seem to have any further or distinctive
significance in comparison with the attack in vss. 1-6. The
basic similarity of the two passages is already implied by the
fact that vss. 13-16 add nothing new to what has already been

said in vs. 6. Thus the renewed attack on the woman should not
be interpreted as an earthly conflict which reflects the heavenly one described in vss. 1-6. The conflict of vss. 13-16 is
still a prototypical conflict. Its placement after the fall of
the dragon has a purely literary interest: to renew the situation of conflict as an introduction to ch. 13. The transition
to the human realm occurs only in vs. 17 with the mention of
the dragon's attack on the "rest of her seed."

The pattern of the combat myth as it appears in Revelation
12 is dominated by the figure of the dragon and his disruptive
and rebellious acts. Thus the controlling myth of the chapter
is that of the resurgence and conquering of chaos. The hymn
interprets the two narratives, which have been fused into a
single story, in judicial language. But the story itself, with
its language of conflict and battle, is a meaningful way of
expressing the experience and hope of the redactor's community.
This is clear from the fact that he returns to conflict language in vss. 13-17.

It was noted above that the reinterpretation of the woman
and the dragon as heavenly beings has the effect of shifting
the emphasis from a nationalistic conflict between the Jewish
people and Rome to a universal, cosmic conflict. Thus the expectation evoked by the redacted narrative is less closely related to the expectation of the traditional, national eschatological events of New Exodus and New Conquest. The fate of the
woman has become a more general symbol of rescue. The redactor
has also introduced references to individual Christians and
alluded to their historical situation which involves being on
trial and put to death by the Romans (vss. 10-11, 17). The
hymn makes clear that the motifs of rescue and victory are associated by the redactor with the fate of the martyrs. There
are still implications for politics in the redacted ch. 12.
The "little time" left to the dragon refers not only to the
ultimate defeat of the dragon, but in the overall context of
the book to the end of Roman power as well (cf. 12:18 and ch.
13). But the redactor has shifted the emphasis of the narrative from the nation to the individual martyr.

It is the mythic pattern of source I which dominates ch.
12 in its redacted form. This is true first of all from a

purely quantitative point of view. Thirty-four and one-half
lines of the Nestle text are devoted to the woman versus the
dragon story, while twenty-two and one-half are devoted to the
battle in heaven and the hymnic commentary combined.

Furthermore, the redactor could easily have placed all of
source I before source II and ended the passage with the victory song. Vs. 12 would have made an appropriate transition
to vs. 18 which sets the stage for ch. 13. The fact that he
instead placed source II and the song within source I emphasizes the story of source I and is an indication that its pattern has paradigmatic importance for the Christian readers.

The open-enededness of vs. 17 was pointed out above. In
fact the overall effect of ch. 12 is open-ended. The child and
the woman are rescued *temporarily*. The child is taken to the
throne of God, whence he is expected to return. The woman is
to be nourished in the desert for a predetermined length of
time (vss. 6, 14). The sojourn in the desert, even in its most
idealized form, is always a prelude to something else.

The dragon is only *partially* defeated. He is expelled
from heaven, never to return (*oude topos heurēthē autōn eti en
tō ouranō*), but woe to the earth and sea because of the wrath
of the fallen one. This partial defeat also points clearly
ahead to further events: *eidōs hoti oligon kairon echei*.

The significance of this open-ended quality of Revelation
12 will be discussed in Chapter IV.

CHAPTER III

[1]See James M. Robinson, "The Johannine Trajectory," in *Trajectories through Early Christianity* (by J. M. Robinson and Helmut Koester; Philadelphia: Fortress, 1971) 242-44.

[2]The theory that vs. 13 is redactional is supported by the fact that it refers to the child as *ton arsena* rather than maintaining the source's (*to*) *arsen*.

[3]R. H. Charles, *A Critical and Exegetical Commentary on the Revelation of St. John* (ICC; New York: Scribner's, 1920) 1. clviii, note 1.

[4]Alexandrinus reads *epi tēn kephalēn*; Sinaiticus and Ephraemi read *epi tēs kephalēs*; see Charles, *Revelation of St. John*, 2. 327; Henry Barclay Swete, *The Apocalypse of St. John*, 2nd ed. (London: Macmillan, 1907) 188.

[5]Charles, *Revelation of St. John*, 1. clviii note 1. The passages in which *hopou* occurs without *ekei* are: 2:13 (twice), 11:8, 14:4, 17:9, 20:10.

[6]Ibid., 1. clvii-viii.

[7]Ibid., clviii. See also Blass-Debrunner, 400.8.

[8]This question was first raised by Eberhard Vischer, *Die Offenbarung Johannis: Eine jüdische Apokalypse in christlicher Bearbeitung* (TU 2, 3; Leipzig: Hinrichs, 1886) 19-27. He was followed by numerous exegetes; see the discussion by Wilhelm Bousset, *Die Offenbarung Johannis* (Meyer 16; Göttingen: Vandenhoeck und Ruprecht, 1896) 132-33. Weyland independently proposed that the core of the work, including ch. 12, was originally Jewish in the *Theologisch Tijdschrift* (1886) 454-70 and *Omwerkings en Compilatie-Hypothesen toegepast op de Apocalypse van Johannes* (Groningen: Wolters, 1888). The theory was further developed by Friedrich Spitta, *Die Offenbarung des Johannes* (Halle, 1889) 125-27. Bousset himself rejected the theory (*Offenbarung Johannis*, 412-13). But Johannes Weiss and Julius Wellhausen revived the hypothesis (Weiss in his *Offenbarung des Johannes* in *Die Schriften des Neuen Testaments* [ed. Johannes Weiss; Göttingen: Vandenhoeck und Ruprecht, 1908] 2. 648; Wellhausen in his *Analyse der Offenbarung Johannis* [Abhandlungen der königlichen Gesellschaft der Wissenschaften zu Göttingen, phil.-hist. Kl., N.F. 9, 4; Berlin: Weidmann, 1907] 18-21). R. H. Charles accepted the hypothesis that the original core of ch. 12 was mythic material redacted by a Jew (*Revelation of St. John*, 1. 305-7). Ernst Lohmeyer did not believe it possible to determine specific Jewish sources used in the work (*Die Offenbarung des Johannes* [HNT 16; Tübingen: Mohr, 1926] 192). G. B. Caird seems to presuppose that the author

148

of the book of Revelation, as we now have it, adapted the mythic material directly (*A Commentary on the Revelation of St.
John the Divine* [New York: Harper and Row, 1966] 147-52); but
he gives no arguments against the Jewish hypothesis.

[9]Note the application of the text to the Davidic messiah
in Pss Sol 17:23-27 (21-25).

[10]Pierre Prigent, *Apocalypse 12: Histoire de l'exégèse*
(Beiträge zur Geschichte der biblischen Exegese 2; Tübingen:
Mohr, 1959) 8, 136.

[11]See the summary of the arguments given by Charles, *Revelation of St. John*, 1. 299-300, 308-9.

[12]See Prigent, *Apocalypse 12*, 23-27; Hildegard Gollinger,
Das "Grosse Zeichen" von Apokalypse 12 (Stuttgarter Biblische
Monographien 11; Würzburg: Echter Verlag, 1971) 27-29.

[13]Prigent, *Apocalypse 12*, 8; Gollinger, *Grosse Zeichen*,
56-63.

[14]T Asher 7:3 (the Most High will come and break the head
of the dragon in the water); T Dan 5:10; T Levi 3:3; 1QM 1:1.

[15]2 Enoch 29:4-5; Life of Adam and Eve 12-17.

[16]1 Enoch 10, 54:6, 69:27-28, 90:20-27; cf. also Jub
10:4-11.

[17]Charles, *Revelation of St. John*, 1. 323-24.

[18]Ibid., 1. lxiii, 303-5; cf. also idem, *Studies in the
Apocalypse* (Edinburgh: Clark, 1913) 79-102.

[19]Cf. also Matt 1:18, 23 (the LXX of Isa 7:14 may have
influenced this occurrence; cf. Krister Stendahl, *The School of
St. Matthew* [Philadelphia: Fortress, 1968] 97-99); 24:19; Mark
13:17; Luke 21:23.

[20]Contra Charles, *Revelation of St. John*, 1. 305.

[21]Cf. Blass-Debrunner, 136.3.

[22]Ibid., 297.

[23]It has been demonstrated that this was the technique of
the author of Acts; see Ernst Haenchen, *The Acts of the Apos-
tles: A Commentary* (Philadelphia: Westminster, 1971) 74-75.
This flaw also lessens the utility of a recent study by Raymond
A. Martin (*Syntactical Evidence of Semitic Sources in Greek
Documents* [Septuagint and Cognate Studies 3; Missoula, Mont.:
SBL, 1974]).

[24]In rabbinic literature, the serpent of Genesis 3 is
called *haqqadmônî*, which corresponds to *ho archaios*; cf. Sotah
9b; Sanhedrin 29a; Sifre D. 323; see also Louis Ginzberg, *The

Legends of the Jews, 5. 94 note 60. In the above passages the serpent is not explicitly linked with Satan. But the serpent was only the tool of Satan according to the Apocalypse of Moses 15, the Pirke de Rabbi Eliezer 13 and the Aboth de Rabbi Nathan 2. According to 1 Enoch 69:6, Eve was tempted by Gadreel, a fallen angel. On "the ancient serpent," see also Charles, *The Revelation of St. John*, 1. 325-26.

[25]*Diabolos* and *satanas* refer to the functionary of the heavenly court whose office it is to accuse and convict human beings in heavenly trials; see Charles, *Revelation of St. John*, 1. 325-27; Strack-Billerbeck, 1. 141-44. The reference to *ho planōn tēn oikoumenēn holēn* is probably an allusion to Genesis 3; cf. the LXX of Gen 3:13--*kai eipen hē gynē ho ophis ēpatēsen me*. Satan's epithet *ho planōn*, however, may have derived from the legend of the Watchers; according to 1 Enoch, they led mankind astray; cf. 1 Enoch 7-8, 10:1-8, 54:6, 69:4-14. According to Jub 10:1-14, the demons, the sons of the Watchers, lead men astray. The two motifs (Satan's leading Eve and the Watchers leading humanity astray) are combined in 1 Enoch 69:4-14.

[26]See note 1 above.

[27]See Bruce M. Metzger, *A Textual Commentary on the Greek New Testament* (London: United Bible Societies, 1971) 748.

[28]See the discussion by Charles, *Revelation of St. John*, 1. 331.

[29]The phrase is typical of the author of Revelation; see ibid., 1. 369.

[30]Wellhausen (*Analyse*, 20-21) took vs. 17 to be part of the Jewish source and argued that the woman symbolized a Pharisaic group who fled from Jerusalem between 66 and 70 C.E. and believed that the messiah would come forth from their circle. The *loipoi*, on the other hand, referred to a group against whom the source was written, those of a Zealot persuasion who remained in the temple during the Roman siege. The most serious problem with Wellhausen's interpretation of vs. 17 is that he does not explain how the *loipoi* can be called "of her seed."

[31]See the discussion above of the motif of translation to heaven in the treatment of the Apocalypse of Adam: Chapter II, *Other Recently Proposed Parallels*.

[32]See Charles, *Revelation of St. John*, 1. 319.

[33]Ibid., 327; Strack-Billerbeck, 1. 141-42; Charles and Bousset (*Offenbarung Johannis*, 400) assume that *katēgōr* is a Hebraised form of *katēgoros*, but studies of the papyri have shown that *katēgōr* was a common colloquial formulation; cf. Arndt-Gingrich, 424.

[34]Cf. Charles (*Revelation of St. John*, 1. 329) on vs. 13.

150

[35] G. Delling, "Zum gottesdienstlichen Stil der Johannes-Apokalypse," *NovT* 3 (1959) 134-37; more recently, Klaus-Peter Jörns, *Das hymnische Evangelium* (Studien zum Neuen Testament 5; Gütersloh: Mohn, 1971) 178-79.

[36] Charles, *Revelation of St. John*, 1. 326; Jörns, *Evangelium*, 110-12; see also the bibliographical references given by Jorns (178-79 notes 49-51).

[37] Cf. 2:7, 11, 17, 26 etc.; 1:5, 5:9, 7:14; 1:2, 9, 6:9, etc.; 2:10-11.

[38] Cf. 14:8, 10, 19; 15:1, 7, etc.

[39] Charles, *Revelation of St. John*, 1. 325.

[40] Ibid., 327-28; see also 1. lxiii and clviii note 1.

[41] Ibid., 309, 328-29.

[42] Ibid., 304.

[43] Ibid., 328 and the references given there.

[44] Cf. Frank Moore Cross, *Canaanite Myth and Hebrew Epic: Essays in the History of the Religion of Israel* (Cambridge: Harvard University Press, 1973) 120.

[45] See also Job 3:8, 7:12, 9:13, 40-41; Cross, *Canaanite Myth and Hebrew Epic*, 135.

[46] Pss 74:12-17, 89:9-12, 104:26; cf. Sigmund Mowinckel, *The Psalms in Israel's Worship* (New York: Abingdon, 1967) 1. 108-9, 143-46; Cross, *Canaanite Myth and Hebrew Epic*, 135.

[47] Cross, *Canaanite Myth and Hebrew Epic*, 135-37.

[48] Patrick D. Miller, *The Divine Warrior in Early Israel* (Harvard Semitic Monographs 5; Cambridge: Harvard University Press, 1973) 74-141.

[49] Ibid., 118-21; see also W. F. Albright, "The Psalm of Habakkuk" in *Studies in Old Testament Prophecy* (ed. H. H. Rowley; Edinburgh: Clark, 1950) 8-9.

[50] Isa 30:6-7 (LXX - *mataia*). The MT is corrupt in vs. 7; the link of Egypt and Rahab is clear, although the specific nature of the comparison is obscure. Cf. Ps 87:4 (LXX - *Raab*).

[51] Jer 51:34 (Nebuchadnezzar has swallowed me *ktnyn*); Ezek 29:3-5 (Pharoah, king of Egypt, *htnyn hgdwl*; LXX - *ton drakonta ton megan*); Ezek 32:2-8 (Pharoah, king of Egypt, you are *ktnyn bymym*; LXX - *hōs drakōn ho en tē thalassē*).

[52] Ezek 29:3; cf. also 28:2, 31:10-11, 32:2, 32:12; Isa 14:4-20.

[53]Dan 7:8, 11, 20, 25; 8:9-11.

[54]Pss Sol 2:29 (25).

[55]Pss Sol 2:1-2, 26-31; cf. also 17:13.

[56]See also Pss Sol 17:11-22, which makes a similar point.

[57]John J. Collins, *The Sibylline Oracles of Egyptian Judaism* (SBL Dissertation Series 13; Missoula, Mont.: Scholars Press, 1974) 74-80.

[58]Ibid., 75.

[59]Ibid., 74-80.

[60]Sib Or 5:28-34; cf. Collins, *Sibylline Oracles*, 81-88.

[61]See especially Sib Or 5:33-34: *isazon theō auton*; see also 5:139-40: *tēs megalēs Romēs basileus megas isotheos phōs, hon, phas', autos ho Zeus eteken kai potnia Hērē*.

[62]Sib Or 5:29; cf. Wilhelm Bousset, *The Antichrist Legend* (London: Hutchinson, 1896) 152.

[63]Exod 16:4-17:7; cf. also 1 Cor 10.

[64]See also Deut 32:11-12, As Mos 10:8; the eagle metaphor is used in a more general sense in Isa 40:31, but the eschatological use of the desert motif occurs in the same chapter.

[65]Martin Hengel, *Die Zeloten* (Arbeiten zur Geschichte des Spätjudentums und Urchristentums 1; Leiden: Brill, 1961) 255-61.

[66]1 Mac 2:28-29, 2 Mac 5:27, Pss Sol 17:16-17.

[67]1QS 8:14; cf. Frank Moore Cross, *The Ancient Library of Qumran and Modern Biblical Studies* (Garden City, N.Y.: Doubleday, 1961) 78 note 36a.

[68]1QM 1:1-3; cf. Peter von der Osten-Sacken, *Gott und Belial* (Studien zur Umwelt des Neuen Testaments 6; Göttingen: Vandenhoeck und Ruprecht, 1969) 30-41.

[69]Josephus *Ant.* 22.97-99; cf. Hengel, *Zeloten*, 235-36; Emil Schürer, *The History of the Jewish People in the Age of Jesus Christ* (rev. and ed. Geza Vermes and Fergus Millar; Edinburgh: Clark, 1973) 1. 456.

[70]A very similar movement, whose expectations were probably the same as those of Theudas, arose about a decade later. Cf. Josephus *JW* 2.259; Hengel, *Zeloten*, 236.

[71]Josephus *Ant.* 20.169; *JW* 2.261; Hengel, *Zeloten*, 236-37; Schürer, *History*, 1. 464.

[72]Sir 48:9-10; cf. Ulrich B. Müller, *Messias und Menschensohn in jüdischen Apokalypsen und in der Offenbarung des Johannes* (Gütersloh: Mohn, 1972) 184-87. See also 1 Enoch 46:2-3, 62:7; 4 Ezra 13:26, 52; cf. Müller, *Messias und Menschensohn*, 47-51, 147-54.

[73]The phrase in Daniel 7:25 means three and a half years; see H. Louis Ginsberg, *Studies in Daniel* (New York: Jewish Theological Seminary of America, 1948) 1.

[74]Dan 12:6-7, 7:25-27, 8:14, 9:27.

[75]The citation is the writer's translation of Strack-Billerbeck, 2. 284-85; the text is P^{e}siq 49b.

[76]Swete, *Apocalypse of St. John*, 148-49.

[77]Ibid., 151.

[78]Ibid., 155.

[79]Ibid., 157.

[80]Ibid., 159.

[81]Wellhausen, *Analyse*, 20-21.

[82]Stanislas Giet, *L'Apocalypse et l'histoire* (Paris: Presses Universitaires de France, 1957) 110-11.

[83]Lohmeyer, *Offenbarung des Johannes*, 103.

[84]Ibid., 103-4, 105.

[85]Ibid., 106.

[86]Edwin Honig, *Dark Conceit: The Making of Allegory* (Evanston: Northwestern University Press, 1959) 12.

[87]Translation is from C. K. Barrett, *The New Testament Background: Selected Documents* (New York: Harper and Row, 1961) 8.

[88]On the date of Revelation, see the discussion in Feine-Behm-Kümmel, 327-29. There is no unambiguous internal evidence as to date. What evidence there is is useless as long as the history of the redaction of the work has not been thoroughly studied. Most scholars accept the traditional dating frist attested by Irenaeus, which assigns the work to the latter part of Domitian's reign (90-95); see the discussion by Elisabeth Schüssler Fiorenza, "Apocalyptic and Gnosis in the Book of Revelation," *JBL* 92 (1973) 565.

[89]Rev 1:4, 9, 11; 2:1, 8, 12, 18, 24; 3:1, 7, 14.

[90]Hans Conzelmann, "Die Mutter der Weisheit," in *Zeit und Geschichte* (ed. E. Dinkler; Tübingen: Mohr, 1964) 225.

[91]Collins, *Sibylline Oracles*, 40-41.

[92]Ibid., 61-63.

[93]Ben Zion Wacholder, *Eupolemus: A Study of Judaeo-Greek Literature* (Cincinnati: Hebrew Union College, 1974) 104-5, 287-88.

[94]Life of Adam and Eve 12-17.

[95]2 Enoch 29:1-5; this tradition is reflected in Jude 6.

[96]On the Watchers, see 1 Enoch 10:6-16; 12-16; 69:4; Jub 4:15, 22; T Reuben 5:1-6:5; T Naph 3:5; 2 Enoch 7, 18.

[97]See above, note 24.

[98]Lohmeyer, *Offenbarung des Johannes*, 102-3.

[99]Cf. Luke 7:35.

[100]Cf. 4 Ezra 5:9-10, 2 Apoc Bar 48:36.

[101]Lohmeyer, *Offenbarung des Johannes*, 102.

[102]Gollinger, *Grosse Zeichen*, 69-70, 180-81.

[103]Vögtle's theory is summarized by Gollinger, ibid., 70.

[104]Ibid., 179.

[105]Hos 1:2, 2:4-5 (RSV 2:2-3).

[106]Müller, *Messias und Menschensohn*, 47-48; Robert G. Hamerton-Kelly, *Pre-existence, Wisdom, and the Son of Man* (Cambridge: Cambridge University Press, 1973) 15-21.

[107]Rev 6:9, 7:15, 8:3, 9:13, 11:19, 15:5-8, 16:1.

[108]Cf. 1 Enoch 90:20-27.

[109]Lohmeyer (*Offenbarung des Johannes*, 102) divides the passage into 3 strophes of 6, 4 and 6 lines respectively. His division seems to be quite arbitrary, especially for the first strophe. One could begin a new line with *kai hē basileia* giving 5 lines, but the separation of a sixth line would result in a torso of a line: either *ho katēgorōn autous* or *hēmeras kai nyktos*. The method followed here is to begin a new line with the beginning of each new clause.

[110]Ibid.

[111]Sigmund Mowinckel, *The Psalms in Israel's Worship* (New York: Abingdon, 1967) 1. 81; Hermann Gunkel and Joachim Begrich, *Einleitung in die Psalmen: Die Gattungen der religiösen Lyrik Israels*, 2nd ed. (HKAT supplementary vol.; Göttingen: Vandenhoeck und Ruprecht, 1966) 32-94.

[112] Gunkel and Begrich, *Einleitung*, 311-14.

[113] Cf. Pss 97:12, 98:1; Exod 15:2.

[114] Even if *sōtēria* means victory here (so Charles, *Revelation of St. John*, 1. 326), it would still have the connotations of the usual benefits which follow victory.

[115] Cross, *Canaanite Myth and Hebrew Epic*, 142-43.

[116] This conception has its roots in ancient Semitic myth which involved a council of the gods. See Cross, *Ancient Library*, 213-15, especially 214 note 32; Miller, *Divine Warrior*, 8-74; Marvin Pope, *Job* (AB; Garden City, N.Y.: Doubleday, 1965) 9-11.

[117] Pope, *Job*, 9; cf. Zech 3:1-5.

[118] Jub 17:15-16; 18:9-12; 48:2-4, 9-13, 15-19; cf. George Nickelsburg, *Resurrection, Immortality and Eternal Life in Intertestamental Judaism* (Harvard Theological Studies 26; Cambridge: Harvard University Press, 1972) 12-13; Otto Betz, *Der Paraklet* (Arbeiten zur Geschichte des Spätjudentums und Urchristentums 2; Leiden: Brill, 1963) 54, 59-63.

[119] T Levi 5:6; cf. Nickelsburg, *Resurrection*, 13-14; Betz, *Paraklet*, 63-64.

[120] Jub 48:9-13.

[121] Jub 48:15, 18; cf. 17:15-18:12.

[122] 1QH f4, 6; f45, 3; 1QSb 1:8. Cf. E. L. Sukenik, *The Dead Sea Scrolls of the Hebrew University* (Jerusalem: Hebrew University and Magnes Press, 1955) 35-58 and plates 35-58.

[123] See above, note 33.

[124] See Nickelsburg's discussion of Daniel 12 (*Resurrection*, 11-12).

[125] 1 Enoch 90:20-27.

[126] 11QMelchizedek 9-15; cf. A. S. van der Woude, "Melchizedek als himmlische Erlösergestalt in den neugefundenen eschatologischen Midraschen aus Qumran Höhle 11," *OTS* 14 (1965) 354-73; M. de Jonge and A. S. van der Woude, "11QMelchizedek and the New Testament," *NTS* 12 (1966) 301-26, especially 302-5; see also von der Osten-Sacken, *Gott und Belial*, 206-10; Joseph A. Fitzmyer, "Further Light on Melchizedek from Qumran Cave 11," *Essays on the Semitic Background of the New Testament* (Sources for Biblical Study 5; Missoula, Mont.: Scholars Press, 1974) 245-67.

[127] 11QMelchizedek 15, 24-26; cf. de Jonge and van der Woude, "11QMelchizedek," 305.

[128] 1QM 17:7-8.

[129] 1QS, *passim*; As Mos 10:1, Rev 21:4.

[130] Life of Adam and Eve 12-17; 1 Enoch 9:6-11, 54:6, 69:1-15, especially 4-5; 2 Enoch 18:35, 31:3-8.

[131] Cf. 1 Enoch 40:7, Jub 48.

[132] See Chapter II, *The Pattern of the Combat Myth and Revelation 12.*

CHAPTER IV

THE ESCHATOLOGICAL ADVERSARY

The purpose of Chapters IV and V is to show that Revelation 12 introduces the second half of the body of the book (12-22:5) and that, in doing so, provides a mythic framework most clearly for the second half of the body of the work, but for the entire book as well. Chapter IV will show that this is the case with regard to the theme of the eschatological adversary. Chapter V will show that the pattern of the combat myth, which is the controlling structure of Revelation 12, also provides the structure of the book as a whole. This organizing pattern is most clear at the end of the book, but its influence is visible elsewhere as well.

That Revelation 12 introduces the second great cycle of vision accounts (12-22:5) is clear from a number of points of view. From the point of view of literary structure, ch. 12 begins a new sequence since it follows the audition and vision associated with the seventh trumpet (11:15-19). 11:19 thus marks an ending and 12:1 a beginning. It was argued in Chapter I that this new beginning is not just one of the five cycles of visions,[1] but rather marks the opening of the second great half of the body of the work.[2] There are two main literary signals that this is the case. First, 11:19 is the first natural break in the action since 4:1. In chs. 4-5 the scroll with seven seals is introduced. The unsealing of the scroll is described from 6:1-8:1. But there is no break at 8:1, since the effect of the unsealing of the seventh seal is the appearance of the angels with the trumpets. Thus 4:1-11:19 is tightly integrated by its focus on the scroll with seven seals.[3] The second signal is the new commission vision of ch. 10, which points ahead, not to ch. 11, but to ch. 12 and what follows.[4]

The introductory character of ch. 12 is also clear from the open-endedness of the narrative.[5] The messianic office of the child is announced in 12:5, but fulfilled only in 19:15. The dragon is defeated in heaven in 12:8-9, but his definitive defeat and punishment are described only in 20:10. The

157

statement that the dragon went away to make war on the rest of
the seed of the woman reintroduces the persecution theme, which
plays an important role in the second great cycle of visions,
and culminates in the vision of the martyrs in the thousand
year reign (20:4).[6]

Cosmic Dualism

The narrative of ch. 12 provides the mythic framework for
the unfolding of the second great cycle of vision accounts.
That mythic framework is characterized first of all by a cosmic
dualism.[7] The situation of conflict in which the apocalyptist's community found itself is described in ch. 12 as a cosmic conflict. The confrontation is portrayed upon the universal canvas of the heavens and the antagonist is Satan himself.

Now this cosmic dualism is characteristic of the entire
book and is especially emphasized in the second great cycle of
visions (12-22:5). All who are not followers of the Lamb are
in the camp of Satan and the beast. This is said most clearly
of the Roman empire which is characterized in 13:2 and 4 as the
instrument of Satan.[8]

A similar attitude toward at least some Jews is reflected
in the seven messages. Those Jews with whom some of the apocalyptist's addressees are in conflict, the synagogues of Smyrna
and Philadelphia are each called *synagōgē tou satana* (2:9,
3:9). The use of this phrase reflects a dualistic sectarian
mentality similar to that of the Qumran sect. In the Qumran
scrolls the inclusive term *'ēdāh* (congregation) is used for the
totality of the members of the sect.[9] The same term in a construct relation with "Belial" refers at least to the adversaries of the sect and possibly to all non-members.[10] The phrase
synagōgē tou satana in Rev 2:9 and 3:9 is equivalent to the
former expression, *'dt bly'l*; except perhaps for the specificity of *synagōgē*, which seems to be closer to the term *yḥd*.
The latter was used for the particular community or settlement
at Qumran.[11] But the form of expression used in Rev 3:9 indicates that the underlying conception is a general, dualistic
one of contrast between the *synagōgē tou satana* and, presumably, the *synagōgē tou kyriou*. The Jews in Philadelphia are

said to be *ek tēs synagōgēs tou satana*. The underlying conception then is not that of a number of synagogue communities who have opted for Satan and thus become *synagōgai tou satana*; but rather the more clearly dualistic notion expressed by the implicit opposition between the *synagōgē tou satana* and the *synagōgē tou kyriou* and parallel to the contrast at Qumran between the congregation of God[12] (of Israel[13] or of the Poor[14]) and the congregation of Belial.[15]

This hint that all human beings are divided into two groups is made explicit already in the first great cycle of vision accounts (4-11). On the one hand there are the servants of God who are sealed on the forehead (7:3).[16] On the other hand, there are all the rest of humanity--those who do not have the seal of God upon their foreheads (9:4). The former are to be preserved from the "angelic" (9:11, 14-15) plagues inflicted upon human beings and the earth, while these plagues are specifically directed against the latter (9:4-6; cf. 3:10). This dualistic division of humanity is clear but quite general. The radicalness of the dichotomy is maintained in the second great cycle of visions (12-22:5) but the two groups are characterized more specifically.

In chs. 12-22:5 it becomes clear that all humanity is divided into worshippers of the Lamb and worshippers of the beast. In 13:8 it is said that all those on earth whose names are not written in the book of life of the Lamb will worship the beast. These worshippers are marked with the *charagma* of the beast (13:16), which is set over against the *sphragis* of the living God (7:2).[17] The ultimate fate of this portion of humanity is announced almost immediately (14:9-11)--eternal torment in fire and sulphur. But before that definitive punishment, they will have to bear the plagues of the wrath of God. It was noted above that the plagues in the first great vision cycle (particularly the plague of locusts associated with the fifth trumpet--9:4) were directed against those who did not have the seal of God. This theme is picked up and made more specific in ch. 16 which describes the plagues of the seven bowls. The first is directed against those "who have the mark of the beast and who worship his image" (16:2). The fifth plague is directed against the kingdom of the beast (16:10).

The theme enunciated in 13:8 (that the dwellers on earth whose names are not in the book of life will worship the beast) is taken up again in 17:8. Here it is said that they will marvel (*thaumasthēsontai*) at the beast. The fate of the followers of the beast is described in ch. 19: defeat in battle with the Lamb, being slain with the sword (19:21). Their ultimate fate, as predicted in 14:9-11, is described in 20:15. At the final judgment, any one whose name was not found in the book of life was thrown into the lake of fire (cf. 13:8, 17:8).

Contrasted with the followers of the beast are the followers of the Lamb. They are to be preserved from the plagues of the wrath of God (3:10, 7:3, 9:4). Those who do *not* worship the beast will share in the first resurrection and the messianic reign (20:4). Rather than the mark of the beast, they will bear the name of the Lamb on their foreheads (22:4; cf. 3:12, 7:3). Finally, the fate of those who *are* in the book of life of the Lamb is a blessed existence in the holy city Jerusalem come down from heaven (21:27).

This dichotomy of all humanity based on loyalty to the Lamb versus loyalty to the beast is most characteristic of the second great vision cycle (12-22:5). After the description of the last judgment in 20:11-15, we find, alongside the continuation of that particular brand of dualism, a more ethical type of dualism as well. In 21:7-8, *ho nikōn* is contrasted with those guilty of a list of vices.[18] In 21:27 those who are written in the Lamb's book of life are contrasted with any one who practices abomination or falsehood. This ethicizing of the dualism expressed in the visions continues in the epistolary epilogue (22:6-21). In 22:11 the unjust and the defiled are contrasted with the just and the holy. Finally, in 22:14-15, those who wash their robes (cf. 7:14) are contrasted with those guilty of a list of vices (in part similar to that of 21:7).[19]

The sectarian dualism expressed in the book is primarily shaped by the combat myth. It must be seen in the context of the idea that the present time is characterized by a universal struggle between the allies of God and the forces of Satan. The most characteristic shape of this conflict is competition between the rule of Christ and the rule of the beast, i.e., the

Roman empire.[20] The two are incompatible; thus one must choose
a side and suffer the consequences. This dualism is somewhat
ethicized since each "side" is implicitly associated with good
or evil. But there is no reflection upon this association; it
is simply assumed.

The Role of Satan

It was argued in Chapter II that the two sources used by
the redactor of Revelation 12 (the narrative about the woman
and the dragon, and the story of the battle in heaven) each
have their roots in the ancient Near Eastern combat myth.[21]
The new composition, the redacted ch. 12, is also dominated by
the pattern of the combat myth and the latter is the context in
which Revelation 12 should be read.[22] The combat myth is also
the mythic context for the entire second great cycle of vision
accounts; it provides the mythic framework not only for ch. 12,
but for the rest of the book as well.

This point may be briefly illustrated by pointing out how
the role of Satan in the book is determined by the combat myth.
In ch. 12, Satan's role as *katēgōr* in the heavenly court is
subordinated to his role as warrior.[23] His activity on earth
after having been cast down is characterized as waging war on
those who observe the commands of God and hold the witness of
Jesus (12:17). The subsequent activities of Satan are all dominated by battle language. In ch. 13 he bestows power and authority on the beast who wages war on the saints (13:7) and
eventually on Christ (19:19). In 16:13 Satan, aided by the two
beasts, assembles the kings of the whole world for battle (16:
13-14). His final exploit is to gather Gog and Magog for battle against those enjoying the messianic kingdom (20:7-10).
Especially noteworthy for the point under discussion is the
fact that the traditional motif of Satan as the deceiver is interpreted in military terms. Deceiving the nations is equated
with gathering them for battle (20:8).

The Beast from the Sea

Besides the characterization of Satan as an agent of battle in this section (12-22:5), there are a number of motifs

characteristic of the ancient Near Eastern combat myth. The
first of these is the description of the beast from the sea in
ch. 13:1-10. The first thing the interpreter must reckon with
is that the author of this passage is making use of the book of
Daniel. In Daniel 7 four beasts rise out of the sea, each different from the other (7:3). In Revelation 13 a single beast
rises out of the sea which combines salient characteristics of
each of the four beasts of Daniel 7.[24] The beast of Rev 13:1
has ten horns. The only beast said to have horns in Daniel 7
is the fourth, which has ten (vs. 7). The beast of Rev 13:1
has seven heads. The total number of heads of the beasts in
Daniel 7 is also seven. Now the vision of the four beasts in
Dan 7:2-7 is not simply an historical allegory using arbitrar-
ily chosen images. Rather, the motif of beasts rising out of
the sea reflects the ancient Near Eastern combat myth.[25] The
effect of depicting the four kingdoms as beasts of watery chaos
in Daniel 7 is to characterize them as rebellious and as mani-
festations of chaos rather than order.

The motif of rebellion is a very frequent feature of the
combat myth. The reason for combat is most often the attempt
of one god or group of gods to usurp the kingship or power of
another god or group of gods.[26] The rebellion is often accom-
panied by or expressed in inordinately prideful statements.[27]
This is the sense of the "great things" spoken by the little
horn in Dan 7:8, 11 and 20. The point is more clearly expressed in the interpretation of the vision: He shall speak words
against the Most High... (7:25). This element is picked up in
Rev 13:5 in an apparent allusion to Dan 7:8 and/or 20: (kai
edothē autō) stoma laloun megala ....[28] The subsequent statements (Rev 13:5b-6), however, do not seem to allude to anything
in Daniel 7, but can be explained as a paraphrasing summary of
Dan 8:10-14; cf. 8:25.[29] These passages vividly reflect a myth
about a battle in heaven involving stars.[30] There explicit
language of rebellion (vss. 11, 25) and attack (vs. 10) is
used. The rebellion is against the śar haṣṣābā'/śar śārîm, who
in the present context is God himself.[31] The attack is made on
heavenly beings, angels or stars.[32]

If we compare Dan 8:10-14 with Rev 13:5b-6 we find a number of common elements. The Daniel passage includes an attack on heavenly beings (vs. 10), a rebellion against God (vs. 11), interference with the temple cult (vs. 11)[33] and an indication of how long this situation will continue (vs. 14). The Revelation passage refers to blasphemy against those who dwell in heaven (vs. 6), blasphemies against God (vs. 6), blasphemy against the dwelling of God (*tēn skēnēn autou*, vs. 6), and an indication of how long the beast will exercise authority (vs. 5b).[34]

It seems then that in Rev 13:5b-6 the highly mythical statements of Daniel 8 are alluded to and softened. Instead of a direct rebellion against God himself, blasphemies against him and his name are mentioned. The rest of vs. 6 is difficult because of textual and interpretive problems. The better attested and more difficult reading is: ...*blasphēmēsai...kai tēn skēnēn autou, tous en tō ouranō skēnountas*.[35] In Dan 8:11 reference is made to the earthly temple. In the present form of Rev 13:6, however, the earthly temple is not referred to. The phrase *tous en tō ouranō skēnountas*, if we accept the reading given above, seems to be in apposition to *tēn skēnēn autou*. However the author's intent here should be explicated in detail,[36] it is at least clear that the *skēnē* of God is a heavenly entity. This lack of interest in the earthly temple is surprising given the inclusion of 11:1-2 and the rich possibilities of historical allusion in the first century C.E. It is probably to be explained as a result of alienation from the historical Jerusalem (cf. 11:8) and the possibly related lack of interest in the continuation or re-establishment of the temple cult (cf. 21:22).

The fact that the author of 13:1-10 is dependent on Daniel is no reason to deny the importance of the combat myth as the context in which the passage must be understood.[37] Two important elements of that myth are determinative of the nature and function of the beast in this passage: its origin in watery chaos and the acts of rebellion.

That the beast in Rev 13:1-10 should be interpreted in the context of the combat myth is supported by the contrast

between the beast from the sea (vs. 1) and the beast from the
land (*ek tēs gēs*; vs. 11). However much one might wish to dispute Gunkel's exegesis at particular points, his suggestion
that the two beasts in Revelation 13 reflect the mythic tradition concerning Leviathan and Behemoth is illuminating and has
rightly won widespread support.[38] One of his basic insights
was that Leviathan and Behemoth in Job 40-41 are mythological
creatures who were defeated in battle by God in primordial
time, are constantly held in check by him, and may still make
attacks on God's creation from time to time.[39] The ongoing
battle between God and these beasts is thus a mythological expression of the constant tension between creation and chaos.
This line of interpretation of Job 40-41 has been widely accepted, refined and updated.[40]

Gunkel's argument with regard to Revelation 13 was that
here, as in many other cases, the ancient combat myth has been
transformed from a primordial myth into an eschatological
myth.[41] With regard to the particular point under discussion,
the Leviathan and Behemoth motif, the transformation involves
the shift of the battle with the two beasts from the time of
creation to the end-time. Such a shift is already present in
Isa 27:1: "In that day the Lord with his hard and great and
strong sword will punish Leviathan the fleeing serpent, Leviathan the twisting serpent, and he will slay the dragon that is
in the sea." The shift also seems to be reflected in the book
of Daniel, especially ch. 7. This end-time slaying of Leviathan is well attested in rabbinic literature. According to one
text, the righteous will enjoy the spectacle of a contest between the two beasts in the time to come.[42] According to
another, Gabriel will arrange a hunt for Leviathan. Gabriel,
however, will not prevail over the beast, for only his maker
can do so.[43]

A third passage says that God will command Leviathan to
battle with the "bull of the wilderness," and both will per-
ish.[44] In the first of these three passages it is also said
that the two beasts will furnish not only sport but also food
for the righteous in the messianic age. The idea that the
faithful would have these beasts for an eschatological banquet

is attested in apocalyptic writings.[45] The presence of this
motif may be an indication that the idea of an eschatological
battle with Leviathan and Behemoth was current at that time,
i.e., the end of the first century C.E.[46] Given that the originally primordial battle in heaven between Michael and Satan is
adapted to an eschatological context in Revelation 12, it
should not be surprising to find eschatological adversaries in
ch. 13 depicted as the primordial beasts of chaos, Leviathan
and Behemoth.

Support for the hypothesis that Rev 13:1 and 11 are alluding to Leviathan and Behemoth comes from the fact that the association of the two beasts with the sea and the land, respectively, was fairly widespread in apocalyptic literature. In
1 Enoch 60:9 it is said that Leviathan dwells in the abysses of
the sea, while Behemoth dwells in the dry land of the wilderness.[47] According to 4 Ezra 6:49-52 the sea could not hold
both monsters, so Leviathan was assigned to the sea, the
seventh part of the earth, and Behemoth was given one of the
six parts of the dry land.[48] Finally, 2 Apoc Bar 29:4 says
that when the messiah is revealed, Behemoth will be revealed
from his place (on earth?) and Leviathan shall ascend from the
sea. This association of the beasts with the land and sea is
also attested in rabbinic literature.[49] Given that this is a
fairly standard motif, it is more likely that it is the background for the sea/land contrast in Revelation 13, than some
geographical allegorical intent.[50]

The Beast from the Abyss

That the *thērion to anabainon ek tēs abyssou* in Rev 11:7
is a form of the chaos beast of the combat myth needs little
argument since the work of Gunkel.[51] That he is called *thērion*
may be the influence of Dan 7:3, but the term is used for the
chaos monster elsewhere as well.[52] The motif of the beast *ascending* from the sea/abyss is the particular formulation given
to the mythic tradition by the author of Daniel 7, which then
seems to have exercised an influence on subsequent texts.[53]
The original context of the motif becomes clear again in the
formulation of 2 Apoc Bar 29:4, "And Behemoth shall be revealed

from his place and Leviathan shall ascend from the sea...."[54]
The name Leviathan used here makes clear that the beast derives
from the ancient combat myth.[55] The term *abyssos* reflects the
ancient myth as much as the term *thalassa*. *Abyssos* is the term
regularly used in the LXX to translate $t^e h\hat{o}m$. $T^e h\hat{o}m$ is related
to the Accadian *Ti'āmat* and thus to the ancient Mesopotamian
combat/creation myth.[56] $T^e hom$ is often used in parallelism
with $y\bar{a}m$.[57] Both are associated with the marine monsters mentioned in the OT who function as the adversaries of Yahweh in
contexts where the experience of Israel is expressed in mythic
terms. At times $t^e h\hat{o}m$ and $y\bar{a}m$ seem to be identified with the
various beasts; at times they are their habitat.[58]

One must then ask what function this chaos beast has in
Rev 11:1-13. The interpretation of this passage is notoriously
difficult.[59] There are a number of indications that the apocalyptist made use of a written source or sources in the composition of 11:1-13.[60] If sources were used, they were most
likely redacted to some extent by the author of the book in its
present form.[61]

Bousset argued that 11:3-13 is a partially redacted fragment from the tradition concerning the Antichrist.[62] He further attempted to demonstrate that this Antichrist tradition is
of Jewish origin and that it was already well developed by the
time the book of Revelation was written.[63] If such was the
case, according to Bousset, then much of the material dealing
with the Antichrist in later Christian writings need not be
assumed to be dependent on the book of Revelation, but probably
attests independently to older, Jewish Antichrist tradition.[64]
R. H. Charles is the only scholar since Bousset who has significantly furthered the discussion of the Antichrist tradition.[65]

The two studies share a terminological difficulty. First,
the term "Antichrist" is used even in non-messianic contexts.
Such usage is often confusing and sometimes misleading. Second, Charles distinguishes between the Antichrist, Beliar and
Nero myths. Such distinctions are important for tracing the
history of traditions and their relationships. But if they are
held absolutely, the similarities between the various myths are
obscured. In an attempt to overcome these problems, the term

"eschatological adversary" will be used here as the general
term which best describes the phenomenon.[66]

A further problem characteristic of Bousset's work is his
operating assumption that motifs in later Christian writings
which are similar to elements of the book of Revelation are independent witnesses to the Antichrist tradition. It is not
methodologically sound to adopt what should be an hypothesis
in each individual case as a general axiom. Related to this
assumption is the tendency to deemphasize the extent and significance of the creative contribution of the author of the
book of Revelation.

The latter tendency weakened Bousset's interpretation of
Rev 11:7. He admits the possibility that the phrase *to thērion
to anabainon ek tēs abyssou* is a redactional element, but goes
on to say that the verse must have spoken originally of a
"dämonischen Macht" which killed the two witnesses.[67] Charles
is much more cautious on this point and in effect says that it
is not possible to reconstruct what sort of adversary may have
been described in the source.[68]

Bousset is certainly right that 11:3-13 must be understood
in the context of the contemporary expectation of the appearance of an eschatological adversary in Jerusalem.[69] But his
statements that the beast in 11:7 cannot be interpreted as a
proleptic reference to the beasts of chs. 13 and 17, and that
the former appears independently in a distinct context, need to
be qualified.[70] The overall context and events of 11:3-13 are
distinctive when compared to the rest of the book, but the origin and function of the beast in 11:7 have close parallels in
chs. 13 and 17. The phrase *to thērion to anabainon ek tēs
abyssou* is paralleled by *to thērion...mellei anabainein ek tēs
abyssou* in 17:8; the *poiēsei met' autōn polemon kai nikēsei
autous* is paralleled by *kai edothē autō poiēsai polemon meta
tōn hagiōn kai nikēsai autous* in 13:7.[71] Now it is of course
conceivable that 11:7 was part of the source and that the author of the book in its present form alluded to that verse in
the other two passages. There are several arguments which can
be made against that hypothesis. First, the ascent of the
beast from the abyss does not have a particularly coherent

168

connection with its context in ch. 11. Second, the contemporary passages (cited in note 69) which speak of an eschatological adversary appearing in Jerusalem do not depict that adversary in bestial form nor as ascending from the abyss. Third, the parallel passages which Bousset cites, which do have an adversary ascending from the abyss, are late. The possibility that the presence of this motif is due to the influence of the book of Revelation cannot simply be disregarded.

The only text contemporary with or earlier than Revelation which could be said to refer to an adversary ascending from the abyss is 2 Thes 2:3. Such an interpretation of the passage would be based on a particular translation of *huios tēs apōleias*, one of the epithets applied to the eschatological adversary in 2 Thes 2:3-10; namely "one from the abyss" or "one from Hades," or some such. Bousset implies such an interpretation by citing 2 Thes 2:3 along with the later passages referred to above which clearly associate the adversary with the abyss.[72] But this interpretation of 2 Thes 2:3 must be rejected because the phrase elsewhere regularly means "one destined for destruction."[73] The latter translation makes good sense for the statement that the beast *eis apōleian hypagei* in 17:8, 11. The statement does not mean that the beast comes from and will return to the abyss, but rather that he comes from the abyss and is destined for eternal destruction in the lake of fire (19:20, 20:10). Further, the fact that the angel of the abyss is given the epithet *apollyōn* (9:11) does not imply an identity of *abyssos* and *apōleia*.

The only texts other than Revelation which do say that the adversary will ascend from the abyss are late. The texts cited by Bousset in this connection are:

1. A Syriac sermon attributed to Ephraem, entitled *De fine extremo* (*De Agog et Magog et de fine consummatione*).[74] Bousset refers to this text with the abbreviation Ephraem Syrus.[75] He refers to Ephraem Syrus 7 (actually it is ch. 8) which says that the Antichrist will come from the underworld (Abaddon).[76] The text reads: *wnpq n't' 'l 'r'' mn 'bdn' 'wl'.*[77]

2. The earliest extant complete commentary in Greek on
the book of Revelation is that by Andreas, bishop of
Caesarea, in the second half of the fifth century.
Andreas comments on Rev 11:7--*ho antichristos ho ek
tōn skoteinōn kai bythiou tēs gēs chōriōn exiōn*, in
hois ho diabolos katadedikastai.[78]

3. The Greek apocalypse of Esdras.[79] Bousset cites
Apoc Esdras 27: *autos anabēsetai gar ho antikeimenos
tois anthrōpois apo tōn tartarōn kai endeixetai polla
tois anthrōpois.*[80]

It is doubtful that Ephraem's sermon reflects tradition
independent of the book of Revelation. If this work is in fact
by Ephraem, it is likely that this motif derives from the book
of Revelation, since there is evidence that he knew and used
the latter.[81]

Andreas' comment does go beyond the book of Revelation to
the extent that it identifies the beast in Rev 11:7 as the
Antichrist. But the statement that he comes from the lower regions of the earth seems to be a simple paraphrase of the Revelation text.

The situation is most complex with the Apocalypse of Esdras, since some commentators have argued that the present
apocalypse is a Christian redaction of an earlier Jewish work.[82]
In discussing the date of the work, Denis adopts this hypothesis, in that he mentions a ninth century date as a possibility
for the Christian redaction, but allows that the Jewish parts
may go back to the early second century.[83] But the passage
which Bousset cites (Apoc Esdras 27 = 3:15 in Riessler) belongs
to a section which Riessler assigns to the Christian redaction.[84] Since the passage is suspected of being late and
Christian, it is dubious evidence for the association of the
eschatological adversary with the abyss independently of the
book of Revelation.

The intent of this examination of the evidence for Bousset's interpretation is not to assert that these passages are
literary borrowings from Revelation. The point at issue is to
what extent the Antichrist tradition studied by Bousset was an
oral tradition *independent of* Revelation. The variety of

expression in the passages cited above is an indication that
the tradition was not a literary one in a rigid or mechanical
sense.[85] The evidence in this case seems to be best explained
as resulting from a process in part literary, in part oral.
The author of Revelation had at his disposal the book of Daniel
and probably a written source reflected in Rev 11:3-13. His
contribution was to combine the contemporary tradition about an
eschatological adversary expected to appear in Jerusalem with
the myth about the chaos beast from the abyss, possibly inspired by the form that myth took in Daniel 7. The result of
this process (Revelation 11) then became part of oral tradition
and reappears in various forms in later literary works. The
hypothesis that Daniel 7 influenced the process described above
is supported by the fact that the phrase *poiēsei met' autōn
polemon kai nikēsei autous* in the same verse is an allusion to
Dan 7:21.[86]

Thus Rev 11:7 does not seem to have been part of a source
used by the author of the book as we now have it. Its particular depiction of the eschatological adversary owes something to
Daniel 7, but does not simply reflect a contemporary and widespread idea of how the Antichrist will come. Rather it seems
to be the composition of the author of Revelation.

The Signification of the Beasts

If Rev 11:7 is most likely the composition of the author
of Revelation in its present form, the question then arises how
the beast of 11:7 relates to those mentioned in chs. 13 and 17.
First of all, it is clear that the beast of 11:7 and that of
ch. 17 are identical. The equivalence of *to thērion to anabainon ek tēs abyssou* (11:7) and *to thērion...mellei anabainein ek
tēs abyssou* (17:8) is sufficient indication of this identity.

We must then ask how the beast of ch. 17 relates to that
of ch. 13. According to 13:1, that beast arises out of the
sea, while 17:8 and 11:7 describe a beast from the abyss. It
was noted above that *tᵉhôm* and *yām*, and thus *abyssos* and *thalassa* in the LXX, are very closely related in the OT texts which
reflect the chaos/combat myth. In other words, *to thērion to
anabainon ek tēs abyssou* (11:7) and *ek tēs thalassēs thērion*

anabainon (13:1) are equivalent for all intents and purposes in a mythic context. Furthermore a comparison of what is said concerning the beast of 13:1-10 with the description of the beast of ch. 17 shows that the two are identical. There are differences in the two descriptions, but they are not such as to make a distinction between the two beasts necessary. The similarities and differences can be best illustrated by a synoptic list of characteristics.

chapter 13	chapter 17
a *beast* (*thērion*) arising from the sea (1)	a scarlet *beast* (*thērion*) (3)
ten horns (1)	*ten horns* (3, 7)
seven heads (1)	*seven heads* (3, 7)
ten diadems on horns (1)	
(a) *blasphemous name(s)* on his heads (1)	full of *names of blasphemy* (3)
[combination of traits from Dan 7:4-6] (2)	a woman sitting on the beast (3, 7)
one of heads wounded and healed (3)	the beast was and is not and will ascend from the abyss (8)
	the beast goes to destruction (8, 11)
the whole earth will be amazed after the beast	*the dwellers on the earth will be amazed when they see the beast* (8)...
they will worship the beast (4)	
all *the dwellers on the earth who are not in the book* will worship the beast (8)	*who are not in the book* (8)

A further point of similarity between the two passages is not easily shown on such a chart. In both chapters there is an equivalence expressed between the beast and one of its heads. In 13:3 it is said that *one of the heads* of the beast (was) as if slaughtered unto death, and its fatal wound was healed. Then in the description of the activity of the second beast it is said of the *first beast* that its fatal wound was healed (13: 12). Again in 13:14 it is the *first beast* (not one of his heads) who has a wound of the sword and lived (or returned to life). In ch. 17 a similar equivalence is apparent. In vs. 10 the beast's seven heads are identified as seven kings, five of whom have fallen, one is, and one has not yet come. Then in vs. 11 it is said that the beast itself is an eighth. In the context, this must mean that the beast is identified with whoever will reign as the eighth in the series of kings. In the same verse it is said that the eighth is also *ek tōn hepta*. In other words, the eighth king will be in some sense identical with one of the seven kings who preceded him. Thus we have the beast (the eighth) identified with one of its heads (the seven).

The significance of this similarity can only be assessed in the context of a discussion of the signification of the beast(s) in chs. 13 and 17. Whether or not and to what extent the beasts in these two chapters can be interpreted as historical allegory has long been a point of contention among exegetes.[87]

The Beast as Rome

E. Lohmeyer provides a modern example of an interpretation which denies historical allegory entirely. But this line of interpretation has been widely criticized.[88] The author of Revelation 13 is making use of Daniel 7, as was noted above and as Lohmeyer admits.[89] Since the model of Revelation 13 is a passage which uses mythic language to interpret a religio-political conflict, a reader familiar with that prototype is inclined to read Revelation 13 in the same light. Lohmeyer's arguments against this approach to the text are not compelling. He asserts, for example, that because the beast described in Rev 13:1-2 combines features distributed among four different beasts in Daniel 7, the former can have no relation to the historical situation.[90] The conflation of the beasts in Revelation 13 certainly shows that the author had less interest in the schematization of history than the author of Daniel 7 had, but it by no means follows that his work has no historical-allegorical interest.

Lohmeyer's treatment of the statement ascribed to the worshippers of the beast is no more persuasive. They say "Who is like the beast, and who is able to war with it?" The first clause seems to reflect a common OT expression, usually applied to God himself.[91] Lohmeyer asserts that this expression is applied only to "göttlichen und widergöttlichen Wesen" in late

Judaism (no references given). He submits, on this basis, that
the expression could not be applied to an earthly power.[92]
This argument overlooks the fact that the passage in question
is a parody.[93] Even if elsewhere the expression were used only
of God, it would not follow that it could not apply here to a
human being or institution. Rather, it would make the irony of
its use here even more intense.[94]

Lohmeyer compares Rev 13:5 with Dan 7:8 and 20 and notes
that in the latter it is the "eleventh horn" which "blasphemes,"
while in the former it is the beast itself which does so. He
concludes that the Daniel passages make sense only as historical allegory, while the Revelation passage cannot at all be
taken as such.[95] This is certainly faulty logic. The Daniel
passages do clearly call for an historical-allegorical interpretation. An interest is shown not only in referring to a
particular historical person, but also in placing that person
in an historical sequence. The Revelation passage is not interested in such an historical sequence. But that lack of interest does not exclude the possibility that the beast of Rev
13:1-2 also has an historical referent.

Finally, one last argument which Lohmeyer gives to show
that the first beast of Revelation 13 cannot be interpreted as
Rome is that the identification of the fourth beast of Daniel 7
with Rome is first attested explicitly in rabbinic literature.[96]
This statement is quite misleading. Josephus, though somewhat
circumspectly for obvious reasons, provides ample evidence that
the fourth kingdom of Daniel 7 was regularly interpreted as
Rome in his day.[97] In 4 Ezra 12:10-12 the fourth beast of
Daniel 7 is reinterpreted as Rome, indirectly but quite clearly.[98] 2 Apoc Bar 39:3-7 is not directly alluding to Daniel 7,
but there the four kingdom sequence is adopted and the fourth
is clearly Rome.[99]

Given that its prototype (Daniel 7) and its near-contem-
poraries (4 Ezra 11-12 and 2 Apoc Bar 36-40), all belonging to
the same genre,[100] have a historical-political interest, it is
reasonable to expect that Rev 13:1-10 does as well. The arguments against such an interpretation presented by Lohmeyer are
not compelling. The question then presents itself whether an
approach which takes such an historical-political interest

seriously can provide a coherent interpretation of the beast in
13:1-10 and its relationship to the beast of ch. 17 (which is
identical with that of 11:7 as noted above).

The Beast as Nero

In ch. 17 the heads of the beast are explicitly identified
as kings.[101] One would expect then, that in ch. 13, where one
of the heads is singled out for discussion, the heads should be
similarly understood. Then the head which is *hōs esphagmenēn
eis thanaton* (13:3) is most naturally to be taken as one of the
Roman emperors. Whether this element refers to the actual death
of an emperor or to a serious illness from which an emperor later recovered has been disputed.[102] The vivid use of the word
"sword" in vs. 14 would seem to exclude the latter possibility.
The parallel between the head of the beast which was *hōs esphagmenēn* and the *arnion...hōs esphagmenon* (5:6) would seem to imply that by the head of the beast an individual who had actually died is meant. Since the wound and healing of the head
seems to be a parody of the death and resurrection of Jesus, it
is unlikely that the former refers to a crisis and resolution
in the empire itself, e.g., those which followed the deaths of
Julius Caesar and Nero.[103] The force of the parody requires an
individual who not only died but also rose from the dead. The
only emperor who could conceivably be cast in this role is Nero.
He died a violent death, from a self-inflicted dagger wound.
The ground was prepared for the second part of the parody by
the legend of Nero's return.[104]

The hypothesis that the wounded head refers to Nero is
supported by the fact that the number of the beast in 13:18
can be very plausibly explained as a reference to Nero. First
of all, the use of the word *psēphizein* is an indication that
the number involves the process of gematria, i.e., adding the
numerical values of the letters of a word.[105] Secondly, the
most natural way to understand *arithmos gar anthrōpou estin*
(13:18) is that the number relates to the name of some human
individual.[106] The only other occasion where an interpretation
is said to require *sophia* and *nous* is 17:9. There the interpretation involves an historical-geographical referent--the
seven hills of Rome. Finally, the solution *nrwn qsr* (= 666)

also explains the variant reading 616 by positing *nrw qsr* which
would reflect the Latin form of the name Nero. Most manuscripts which read 616 are Latin witnesses.[107] The spelling
nrwn qsr has been confirmed by an Aramaic document from
Murabba'at.[108]

The importance of Nero for the interpretation of ch. 13 is
reinforced by the fact that an otherwise puzzling element in
ch. 17 can be explained as an allusion to the Nero legend.
That is the prophecy in 17:16-17 that the beast and the ten
horns will destroy the harlot. The harlot is clearly identified as the city of Rome by the reference to the seven hills in
vs. 9 and by the statement that she is the great city which has
dominion over the kings of the earth (vs. 18). The identification is also supported by the fact that Babylon was a cryptic
name for Rome in the Jewish Sibylline tradition, as well as
among Christians.[109] In vs. 16 it is said that the beast and
the ten horns (= kings) will hate the harlot, make her desolate
and naked, devour her flesh, and burn her with fire. This
prophecy is closely related to a Jewish Sibylline oracle describing what Nero would do on his return: He will immediately
seize her because of whom he himself perished. And he shall
destroy many men and great tyrants and shall burn all men as
none other ever did (5:367-69).[110] This passage also reflects
the contemporary expectation that Nero would return to regain
power in Rome and destroy his enemies.[111]

Thus, the beast in Rev 13:1-10 is best understood as the
fourth kingdom of Daniel, reinterpreted to refer to Rome, and
the wounded head as Nero. There is, as was noted above, a certain fluidity in the imagery, whereby the beast and the wounded
head are conflated. The Roman empire is suggested to the reader at the outset, then attention is called to the wounded head,
which brings Nero to mind. Finally, references to the beast
which was wounded and yet lived lead the reader to take the
beast as the returned Nero. Since the Nero legend is also reflected in ch. 17, the eighth king is best understood as the
returned Nero. Now it becomes clear that a parallel is intended between the image of the wound which is healed in ch. 13 and
the "is not and is about to ascend from the abyss" in ch. 17.

Both refer to the fact that Nero has died, but that he will return to life; i.e., return from Sheol.[112] There is an antithesis established here between Jesus who has died, is now exalted
in heaven as the Christ, whence he will descend to earth on the
clouds or on a white horse (1:7, 19:11); and Nero who has died,
is now in the abyss = Sheol, whence he will ascend to earth to
slay the two witnesses, make war on the saints, destroy Rome
and finally do battle with Christ.

This antithesis clarifies the variation in vocabulary regarding the origin of the beast. In 13:1, where dependence on
Daniel is greatest, *thalassa* is the particular form of chaos
chosen. In 11:7 and 17:8 the term *abyssos* is used because of
its equivalence with Sheol which better expresses the antithesis to the Christ of heaven.

Thus, the particular way in which the author of the book
of Revelation has adopted the Nero legend involves the conception of a dying and rising Nero of sorts. Now many exegetes
have assumed that this was one widespread stage in the development of the Nero legend.[113] Under this assumption those exegetes refer to a legend of Nero redivivus which was current
toward the end of the first century, and which the author of
Revelation supposedly adopted.[114] But it seems rather that
this particular form of the Nero legend is peculiar to the book
of Revelation.

The Nero Legend

To demonstrate this, the development of the Nero legend
must be briefly reviewed.[115] When it became clear to Nero that
he could no longer remain in power, he vacillated between suicide, flight, and throwing himself upon the mercy of Galba or
of the Roman people. He considered fleeing to Parthia as well
as beseeching the people of Rome for the prefecture of Egypt
(Suetonius *Nero* 47). When he finally committed suicide, it was
outside the city of Rome and the circumstances of his death
were not widely known at the time (Suetonius 48-49). The vague
circumstances of his death, as well as his popularity in some
quarters, gave rise to the legend that he had in fact escaped
death.[116] The fact that Nero had considered fleeing to the

Parthians soon evoked the legend that he had done so. Linked
to that belief was the expectation that he would return with
Parthian armies to regain his power as emperor of Rome and to
destroy his enemies.[117] The intensity and longlivedness of
this expectation is shown by the series of pretenders who appeared from 69 to 88.[118] The legend of Nero's return seems to
have arisen among and awakened greatest responses from those
who had been sympathetic to Nero. Such sympathizers were to be
found mostly in the East, particularly in Greece and Parthia.[119]
The legend of Nero's return in those quarters seems to have
arisen as a form of anti-Roman propaganda, in the framework of
the age-old conflict of East and West. In such a context, for
the peoples of the East, the expectation of Nero's return functioned as a sort of savior myth.[120]

It is important to note that in the references to the Nero
legend in the Greek and Latin authors there is no indication
that the legend involved the return of Nero from the dead. The
presupposition of this form of the legend was that Nero had not
in fact died, but was living somewhere in secrecy, preparing to
regain power. Even in the time of Trajan the belief that Nero
was still alive persisted; this fact is attested by Dio Chrysostom.[121] The persistence of the belief is not surprising
since Nero was only 31 or 32 when he died in 68.[122]

The legend was then adopted in certain Jewish circles
which produced Sibylline oracles. The earliest datable references to the Nero legend in the Sibylline collection are those
of book 4.[123] In a context of oracles foretelling the ruin of
various cities, consisting mainly of prophecies of their subjugation to Rome, the destruction of Jerusalem is "foretold."
The text continues, "And then from Italy a great king, like a
fugitive slave, shall flee unseen, unheard of, over the passage
of the Euphrates...." (4:119-20).[124] This king is then identified by a reference to matricide, and the text goes on to describe the struggle for the throne of Rome, "...when he has run
away beyond the Parthian land" (124). The destruction of the
temple by Titus is then alluded to and various other events,
concluding with the eruption of Vesuvius, which is characterized as punishment of Italy for the destruction of the temple.

The text goes on, "And to the west shall come the strife of
gathering war, and the exile from Rome, brandishing a mighty
sword, crossing the Euphrates with many myriads" (137-39).
There follow oracles against three localities, and then the
following statement: "There shall come to Asia great wealth
which Rome once stole for herself and stored in her rich
treasure-house. And twofold and more shall she restore to
Asia, and then there shall be a surfeit of war" (145-48). This
statement expresses the expected result of the return of Nero.
It shows that in the fourth Sibylline book, composed a dozen
years or so after the death of Nero and not much more than a
decade after the destruction of the temple, the Nero legend has
simply been taken over in its original form as anti-Roman propaganda. Nero is assumed to be alive. Although his matricide
and general wickedness are noted, he is not cast in the role of
any sort of demonic being nor eschatological adversary.[125]

There are a number of oracles in the fifth book which refer to the return of Nero.[126] The final redaction of this book
was made during the reign of Hadrian.[127] In this book the Nero
legend is taken over as well, but is modified in such a way as
to reverse its original intent. Instead of a savior, Nero is
cast as the eschatological adversary.[128] This is most clear in
5:93-110 and 361-84. In the former oracle, Nero, as "the Persian," will lay Alexandria waste and then approach Jerusalem
to sack it. But God will intervene by sending a king to defeat
him. In the second oracle, Nero's return coincides with "the
last time," and the battle he initiates is the final battle.

Besides the ascription of these eschatological deeds to
Nero, his person is mythicized in the fifth book in other ways.
The motif of the rebellion against God, characteristic of the
combat myth and of OT passages which reflect it,[129] is associated with Nero in 5:28-34: "Then he shall return, making himself equal to God: but *God* shall convince him that he is not"
(33-34). The description of Nero as "a godlike man, to whom,
they say, Zeus himself gave birth and our lady Hera" (139-40)
is certainly ironic, as the context shows. The statement is
followed by a sarcastic reference to his penchant for public
performance, a jibe at his artistic ability, and a remark about

his many murders. The cutting of the isthmus at Corinth was also seen as *hybris*.[130]

Finally, the actual deeds of Nero's career as well as the havoc he was expected to cause upon his return are described with a kind of poetic hyperbole which has the effect of making him a superhuman being. Certain elements in this category are derived from the language of the chaos/combat myth.[131] The most obvious of these is the statement applied to Nero that *toutou gar phanentos <ho>lē ktisis exetinachthē....* (5:152).[132] The manuscripts read *phanentos* here. Alexandre and Volkmann[133] emend to *prophanentos*; Lanchester emends to *thaneontos*.[134] No emendation seems necessary. The sense seems to be that Nero's rule was a time of chaos rather than order. This interpretation is supported by the statement that Nero "shall throw all into confusion" (5:30).

Now of the five passages in Sib Or 5 which refer to Nero, three of them clearly reflect the belief that Nero is alive somewhere in the East. In the first passage (5:28-34) a brief description of Nero's career is followed by the comment: *all' estai kai aistos oloiios*[135] *eit' anakampsei isazōn theō auton* (5:33-34). The sense seems to be that even when Nero has fallen from power, he will still be destructive, in that he will be seeking allies and readying for battle. Neither the being "unseen" nor the "returning" here imply that Nero is thought to have died.[136]

A second passage shows even more clearly that Nero is thought of as still living. This is 5:137-54. The passage opens with a short summary of Nero's deeds as emperor. Then follows the statement: "A terrible and shameless king will flee from Babylon, whom all mortals and excellent men despise....He will come to the Medes and to the kings of the Persians, the ones whom he first desired and to whom he gave glory, making his den with these wicked men against a true people" (5:143-49).[137] Babylon here is most likely a reference to Rome. In the immediate context (150-51) a reference is made to the destruction of the temple. By analogy with the first destruction, the power responsible for the deed is called Babylon. Also, a few lines later (158-61), it is said that a star will fall from heaven and burn the deep sea, Babylon itself and the land of Italy. The association of Babylon and Italy makes clear that Babylon stands for Rome. Thus the passage under discussion refers to Nero's flight from Rome to the East, which is presumed to have happened rather than his suicide.

A third passage (5:214-27) makes use of mythological language but does not at all imply that Nero is thought to have died. The passage opens with an exhortation to Corinth to mourn her fate (214): "For when...the three sister Fates lead him who now flees by guile beyond the bank of the isthmus on high so that all may see him who once cut the rock...he will destroy and smite your land, as is predetermined" (215-19).[138] The point here seems to be the contrast between the present hiddenness and future manifestation of Nero, as well as between the deed which was welcomed by Corinth (the attempt to cut a canal through the isthmus) and the fated destruction which Nero would wreak on the city on his return. The way in which Nero's present hiddenness is described--fleeing guilefully beyond the isthmus--is better understood as a reference to Nero's sojourn among the Parthians rather than among the dead.

The fourth passage in question (5:93-110) speaks about "the Persian" who will come and destroy Alexandria and then turn to attack Jerusalem. The most probable interpretation of the passage is that it refers to Nero's return in alliance with the Parthians who were also referred to as Persians.[139] Nero's role here is certainly eschatological in that he is cast in opposition to the king sent from God (108). But there is no indication that Nero is thought to have died nor that his return is from the dead.

The fifth passage (5:361-84) is the one usually referred to as an example of the Nero redivivus myth. The text reads: "There shall be at the last time, about the waning of the moon, a world-convulsing war deceitful in guilefulness. And there shall come from the ends of the earth (*hēxei d' ek peratōn gaiēs*) a matricide fleeing and devising sharp-edged plans in his mind. He shall ruin all the earth....That for which he perished he shall seize at once (*hēs charin ōleto t'autos, helei tautēn parachrēma*). And he shall destroy many men and great tyrants, and shall burn all men as none other ever did..." (361-69). Now the *ōleto* here might be understood as a reference to the death of Nero. The basic meaning of *ollymai* of living beings is to die, especially a violent death. But it can also mean to be undone, to be ruined.[140] For several reasons, it seems best to understand *ōleto* here not as a reference to the death of Nero, but rather to his fall from power. First of all, the description of the return *ek peratōn gaiēs* reflects the idea that Nero is in the far East somewhere rather than in Sheol. Secondly, 5:143 and 216 refer explicitly to the flight of Nero, which presupposes the legend that he fled Rome to the Parthians rather than committing suicide. If *ōleto* were taken here as referring to the death of Nero, it would be the only such reference in the entire fifth book, which refers to Nero five times. It seems then that the passage refers to Nero's fall from power, to his loss of the throne and of the city of Rome, which he is expected to recover upon his return (*hēs charin ōletō...helei tautēn parachrēma*).

In the passages in the Sibylline corpus noted so far, there have been two basic ways in which the Nero legend was adapted. In the fourth book, the legend is simply incorporated in its non-Jewish, eastern form as anti-Roman propaganda. The Jewish adapter does not utilize the possibilities of the legend for depicting Nero as a savior-king, but neither does he reverse this role to portray him as an eschatological adversary. The latter adaptation is characteristic of the fifth book. Nero is mythicized and given the role of eschatological adversary. In both forms of the myth, Nero is presumed to be still alive; thus neither can appropriately be called a "Nero redivivus" myth.

There is possibly a third way in which the Nero legend was adapted by the Jewish Sibylline tradition. The statement in book 3:63 that Beliar will come afterwards *ek de Sebastēnōn* may be translated either "from the inhabitants of Sebaste (Samaria)" or "from the line of Augustus."[141] The latter is more likely since Nero appears numerous times in the Sibylline collection, whereas Samaria appears nowhere else.[142] If the second is the better translation, then this text is evidence for the identification of Nero with Beliar in the Sibylline tradition. This would be the highest degree of mythicization of Nero in the Jewish portions of the Sibylline bookš. The text goes on to describe the activities of the returned Nero (assuming the second of the two possible translations). This second Neronic career is characterized by cosmic signs, raising the dead, and deceiving mortals so that they put their trust in him. To this particular mythic formulation it makes no difference whether Nero committed suicide or fled to the Parthians. The point is that the returned Nero (regardless of the place from which he returns) will in some sense be Beliar.[143]

The identification of Nero and Beliar is also found in the Ascension of Isaiah (Mart Isa) 4:2-4. A number of commentators have concluded that 3:13-5:1 is a Christian interpolation into a Jewish work, the narrative of the martyrdom of Isaiah.[144] This narrative is of uncertain date, but the tradition regarding the manner of execution of the prophet described in it seems to be reflected in Heb 11:37. Thus a first century date is possible, but not certain. This martyrdom of Isaiah was allegedly combined with a Christian work which describes a revelatory vision of Isaiah. The theoretical martyrdom consists of chs. 1-5 (excluding interpolations); the vision comprises 6-10 (ch. 11 was subsequently joined to the work). The vision or ascension portion(6-10) has been tentatively assigned to the second century.[145]

The text of interest here reads as follows:

> "And now Hezekiah and Jasub, my son, these are the days of the completion (?) of the world. And after it has come to its consummation, Beliar, the great prince, the king of this world who has ruled it since it came into being, shall descend; he will come down from his firmament in the form of a man, a lawless king, a slayer of his mother, who himself (even) this king will persecute the plant which the Twelve Apostles of the Beloved have planted; and one of the twelve will be delivered into his hand.--This ruler will thus come in the likeness of that king and there will come with him all the powers of this world...."[146]

There follows a description of the activity of the returned Nero = Beliar which is similar to that in Sib Or 3:64-70. It

consists in working cosmic signs, acting and speaking in the
name of the "Beloved" (= Christ), claiming to be God, setting
up his image in every city, and receiving the worship of all
the people in the world.

In his discussion of this passage (4:2-4) Charles has certainly shown that a date toward the end of the first century is
not impossible.[147] One of the arguments which Charles uses to
specify the date is that, since the passage looks upon Nero's
history (i.e., his career as emperor) as past, it is thus evidence for the abandonment of the belief that Nero was still
alive.[148] Surely such argumentation is not cogent.

The identification of Nero with Beliar in this passage includes the actual historical career of Nero as emperor. Neither this passage nor Sib Or 3:63 show any interest in the
event of Nero's death nor in his sojourn in the underworld.
There is thus no interest in either work in a Nero redivivus,
i.e., in a Nero returning from the dead.

The legend of Nero's return was adopted by Jewish and
Christian writers in various ways. The interest in the death
of Nero and thus in his return as a return from the dead seems
to be peculiar to the book of Revelation. This distinctive expression of the Nero legend was evidently formulated by the
author of the book in its present form in order to characterize
Nero, the agent of Satan, as the mirror image in an antithetical sense of Christ, the agent of God.

The Significance of the Nero Legend

In Chapter III the use of the combat myth in Revelation 12
was elucidated. The attack of the dragon on the woman reflects
the phase of the combat myth called the dragon's reign, in
which the chaos beast threatens the hero's mother.[149] That
element of the combat myth is used in Revelation 12 to characterize the religious-political conflict in which the author
and his first readers were engaged.[150] That conflict is given
universal and cosmic significance by the identification of the
dragon with Satan.[151] The use of the combat myth interprets
the conflict experienced by the community as a resurgence of
chaos, and gives the expected rescue a cosmogonic character.

The rescue will involve the re-establishment of order, a new
creation.

Function

The combat myth functions in a similar way in chs. 13 and
17. The association of the chaos beast with the Roman empire
characterizes the power of Rome and the society it has established as a threat to order, peace and prosperity rather than
their foundation. The combat myth regularly involves a struggle for kingship. In the archaic myths, this kingship was understood as a kingship over the assembly of the gods. At all
stages ultimate power and the commensurate recognition are at
stake. Thus when faced with such a struggle the people, as the
gods of old, must take sides. The persecution which the first
readers were experiencing is characterized in chs. 13 and 17 as
part of this cosmic struggle for kingship; the war on the saints
is part of the threat, the act of rebellion of the chaos beast
as it attempts to usurp power.

The fluidity of reference or signification of the beast
was noted above.[152] The beast signifies both the Roman empire
in general and Nero in particular. Although the use of figurative language is different in each case, the effect here is
similar to that of Daniel 7-12. The saints are confronted with
an institution, a collective power, whose threat manifests itself most clearly and acutely in an individual ruler.

A further difference between Revelation and Daniel 7-12 is
that Antiochus Epiphanes was the actual, living antagonist of
his community at the time the author of the visions of Daniel
was writing. He apparently expected the eschatological turning
point to involve the death of Antiochus.[153] The author of Revelation, on the other hand, was evidently aware of the fact
that Nero had died some twenty years prior to the time he was
writing.[154] Both Daniel and Revelation might be said to involve political eschatology, since the great battle(s) of the
end involve the defeat of religious-political adversaries in
both cases. The concreteness and historical rootedness of this
eschatology is evident in Daniel which was written in the midst
of such a conflict. The book of Revelation achieves a similar
concreteness by the incorporation of the Nero legend.

The aim of the author of Revelation seems to have been to characterize the contemporary situation as a dualistic struggle in which his readers must take sides and firmly resist the powers of chaos expressed in the form of persecution.[155] The adoption of the Nero legend lent a great deal to this characterization in terms of concrete appeal to the imagination, urgency deriving from a direct link to current expectation of Nero's return, and symbolic power in the antithetical structure of the dualistic imagery. First of all, Nero was a well-known, flamboyant figure, who for Christians already had the character of an adversary because of his famous persecution of the Christians of Rome subsequent to the great fire.[156] That fact along with his well-known claims to divinity and intensive cultivation of the ruler cult made his assimilation to Antiochus Epiphanes in the form of the rebellious chaos beast very plausible.

Secondly, the expectation of Nero's return was probably a well known phenomenon in Asia Minor at the time Revelation was written, if not still widely held. The first pretender, who appeared in 69,[157] was based for a time on an island in the Aegean, Cynthos. He was disposed of by the Roman governor of Galatia and Pamphylia, and his remains were carried first to Asia (presumably the Roman province on the west coast of Asia Minor), and from there to Rome. According to Tacitus, the appearance of this pretender aroused terror in Achaia and Asia; thus knowledge of the incident must have been widespread.[158] Other pretender(s) allied themselves with the Parthians and at least one of these was active in Asia Minor as well.[159]

Thirdly, the radical dualistic nature of the conflict was expressed by the author of Revelation by characterizing Nero, and thus Rome indirectly, as the antitype both to God and to Christ. The statement in Rev 17:8 that *to thērion...ēn kai ouk estin kai parestai* is a double parody. It parodies God himself first of all who is *ho ōn kai ho ēn kai ho erchomenos* (1:4, 8; 4:8). It is also a parody of Jesus who lived on earth, is now exalted in heaven and will come soon with the clouds (1:7; 3:11; 16:15; 22:7, 12; 22:20).[160] There is a second coming of Nero as well as of Christ. By means of that motif and others

the beast, Nero, is characterized as an Antichrist figure,
though the term *antichristos* is not used. The beast of 13:1
has ten diadems; Christ, returning as Divine Warrior wears many
diadems (19:12). Written on the beast are blasphemous names
(13:1, 17:3); Christ is inscribed with a secret name (19:12)
and with royal titles (19:16). This motif is certainly meant
to contrast Rome's illegitimate claims to royal power and divine honors with the legitimate claim of Christ. Finally, and
most strikingly, the death and resurrection of Jesus is paro-
died by the wound of the beast which was healed (13:3), by its
ascent from the abyss (11:7, 17:8); i.e., by Nero redivivus.
The Nero legend thus functions to clarify who the adversary is
and what the issues are in the struggle.

It was noted above (note 155) that in ch. 13 the depiction
of Nero and Rome as the chaos beast is combined with an exhortation to the readers to endure persecution (13:9-10). It
would seem then that the combat myth in chs. 13 and 17 (cf.
17:6) functions to identify the ruling power with the forces of
chaos and thus to awaken and reinforce resistance to that power
in the readers. This resistance is of a passive nature as the
high value placed on martyrdom shows.[161] But it is nonetheless
a powerfully expressed ideology of intellectual and spiritual
resistance. The cosmic dualism discussed above, which divides
all humanity into worshippers of the Lamb and worshippers of
the beast is similar to the Zealot theological-political principle that the Kingdom of God and the Kingdom of Caesar are incompatible.[162] The expectation of the destruction of the earth
is related to the situation of religious-political conflict.
The destruction will be, at least in part, vengeance for the
blood of the martyrs.[163] The present order, natural and
social, has been corrupted by the influence of Rome.[164] The
earth must thus be purged in preparation for the creation of a
new heaven and a new earth.

The depiction of Nero as the chaos beast is thus part of
a cosmic ideology which interprets a situation of conflict and
urges a policy of passive resistance and martyrdom.

The Fusion of Diverse Traditions

In Chapter II it was argued that the mythic motifs and
patterns used in Revelation 12 could not have been derived from

any single religious tradition. Most significantly, it did
not seem possible to interpret the passage strictly within an
ancient Near Eastern-Israelite-Jewish continuum. It seemed
rather that the author was deliberately choosing to be international by composing his narrative with elements taken from a
variety of cultural contexts. The adoption of the Nero legend
in Revelation 13 and 17[165] is a further example of the way the
apocalyptist drew upon the non-Jewish culture of his environment. He not only alluded to a current political legend, but
placed it at the center of the book's eschatological schema.
This was accomplished by casting Nero in the role of Antichrist.

It might be objected that the author of Revelation did not
borrow a non-Jewish, anti-Roman legend directly, but rather
that he was simply dependent on the Jewish Sibylline tradition.
In response to this objection it can be said first of all, that
only the two references to Nero in the fourth sibyl are clearly
older than the book of Revelation.[166] As was pointed out
above, these passages are only eschatological to the extent
that the non-Jewish legend was. Nero will avenge the East on
Rome. He is not yet an eschatological adversary.[167] The *ter-*
minus ante quem for the oracles regarding Nero in the fifth
sibyl is 132 C.E.[168] It can be reasonably supposed that the
Nero oracles are at least somewhat earlier, that they were
written at a time when the expectation of Nero's return was
still lively. It is not unlikely that these oracles are contemporary with Revelation. In any case, even if the relevant
oracles of the fifth sibyl were earlier than Revelation, there
is no indication of literary dependence. The similarities are
general and details differ. In each case Nero is an eschatological adversary, but with different characteristics. No mention is made in Revelation of certain traits of Nero which are
emphasized in the sibyls; for example, Nero's matricide (Sib
Or 4:121; 5:30, 142) and his association with the destruction
of the Jerusalem temple (indirectly in 4:115-27; directly in
5:150). The emphasis on Nero's return from the dead in Revelation does not derive from the Jewish Sibylline tradition as was
pointed out above. Thus it would seem best to regard the

adoption of the Nero legend by the fifth sibyl and by Revelation as analogous phenomena, rather than to posit dependence.
The fact that the respective authors proceeded in a similar
manner to transform the hero or savior Nero into an eschatological adversary shows that the author of Revelation was not
unique in his tendency to fuse diverse traditions. The writers
of Jewish Sibylline oracles were also willing and able to in-
corporate elements of the legends and myths of their non-Jewish
contemporaries.[169]

The clear and intense interest in the figure of Nero expressed in Revelation 13 and 17 may shed some light on one aspect of the fusion of diverse traditions noted in Revelation
12. It was argued in Chapter II that the narrative about the
dragon's attack on the woman in Revelation 12 is an adaptation
of the myth about Python's attack on Leto at the time of the
birth of her son Apollo. The question naturally arises why
this particular mythic pattern was adopted.

Caird suggested that the myth reflected in Revelation 12
was deliberately adopted and rewritten to contradict its current political application.[170] It is not the emperor who is
the dragon-slayer, the victor who embodies the triumph of order
over chaos, of light over darkness, but it is the messiah who
has the legitimate claim to this role. Caird is essentially
correct on this point, which can be further specified and elucidated. It was argued in Chapter II that the Leto-Python myth
was adopted first of all in a Jewish context. No clear evidence was discovered for the date or provenance of this adaptation. Since the source was available to the author of Revelation, a first century date in Asia Minor was tentatively proposed.[171] It was argued that the function of this adaptation
in its original Jewish context was primarily political. It was
the mythicized expression of the religious-political conflict
of the Jews with Rome.[172] Caird's suggestion would fit very
well with this interpretation. The rule of Augustus was celebrated as a golden age and as the rule of Apollo.[173] The
Apollo myths and cult were made to function as political propaganda for the empire.[174] Augustus himself was thought of as
the son of Apollo, as a popular legend regarding his birth

shows.[175] Since Augustus was the model for later emperors, a
dissident Jew might express opposition to Rome at any time in
the first century by co-opting Apollonian motifs.

The author of the book of Revelation as we now have it
found this mythic adaptation very useful for his own purposes.
The power of Rome was for him the rebellion of the chaos beast,
the power of the eschatological adversary which would reach its
zenith with the return of Nero. The polemical use of the myth
of Apollo's birth would be of particular interest because of
Nero's well known self-identification with Apollo.[176] Tacitus
says that there was a popular legend about snakes (*dracones*)
guarding Nero in his infancy. He comments that Nero assimilated this tale to foreign miracles in that he claimed there was
only one snake. The comment is obscure; Nero may have compared
the incident to the myth about the attack of Python.[177] As in
the time of Augustus, the myths and cult of Apollo were used
during Nero's reign as imperial propaganda.[178] Nero associated
his own person with Apollo much more blatantly than Augustus
had done. He established a special corps of youths (over 5,000
according to Suetonius *Nero* 20) called Augustiani, who were to
lead the applause at Nero's public appearances. Dio Cassius
quotes their acclamations twice; in 62.20.5 they cry out, "*Ho
kalos Kaisar, ho Apollōn, ho Augoustos, heis hōs Pythios. ma
se, Kaisar, oudeis se nika.*" At Nero's triumphal entry into
Rome after participating in the Greek games, he is hailed among
other things as Pythian victor and Apollo (Dio Cassius 63.20.5).
The procession ended at Apollo's temple on the Palatine where
Nero dedicated his wreaths to the god.[179]

Nero justified his singing career by saying that singing
is sacred to Apollo.[180] He set up several statues of himself
playing the lyre (Suetonius *Nero* 25) and issued a number of
coins depicting Apollo playing his lyre. The coin type had
been used by Augustus and was thus traditional and respectable.
But given Nero's propensity for lyre-playing and the acclamations of the Augustiani, the self-flattery and claims to divinity were unmistakable.[181]

The identification of Nero with Apollo was known in the
East as well as Rome. After Nero liberated Greece, a number of

Greek cities issued decrees thanking the emperor. The decree
passed by Acraephiae in Boeotia has been found. It praises
Nero as the New Sun (*neos Hēlios epilampsas tois Hellēsin*), as
Apollo and as Zeus the Liberator.[182] The governor of Egypt
issued coins depicting the Pythian Apollo to celebrate Nero's
victories in the Greek games.[183]

By incorporating and reinterpreting the Jewish source
which used the Apollo myth to depict the birth of the messiah,
the author of Revelation formulated a further element in the
antithesis of Christ and Nero. The claims of the Apollonian
Nero are rejected by the depiction of Christ as the true
bringer of order and light.

NOTES

CHAPTER IV

[1]See Chapter I, *The Overall Plan of the Book.*

[2]Chapter I, *The Two Scrolls as an Organizing Principle.*

[3]Chapter I, d. *Relation of Content of Scroll to Visions.*

[4]Chapter I, a. *The Content of the Little Scroll.*

[5]See Chapter I, c. *The Unity of Chs. 12-22,* and Chapter III, *The New Unity.*

[6]See 13:7, 10, 15; 17:6; 18:20, 24; 19:2; 20:4.

[7]See Chapter III, *The Re-use of Source I.*

[8]The appropriateness of interpreting the beast of 13:1-10 as the Roman empire will be argued below; see *The Beast as Rome.*

[9]Frank M. Cross, *The Ancient Library of Qumran and Modern Biblical Studies,* rev. ed. (Garden City, N.Y.: Doubleday, 1961) 79-80.

[10]1QH 2:22: *'dt bly'l;* compare the similar and probably equivalent expressions in 1QS 5:1; 1QM 15:9, 13; 1QH 2:32, 6:5, 7:34; CD 1:12. On the use of "Belial" in the Qumran documents, see Hans Walter Huppenbauer, "Belial in den Qumrantexten," *TZ* 15 (1959) 81-89.

[11]On *yhd* see Cross, *Ancient Library,* 79. T. H. Gaster ("Satan," *IDB* 4. 227) thinks that *synagōgē* in Rev 3:9 is equivalent to *'ēdāh,* since *synagōgē* is used to translate *'ēdāh* by the LXX.

[12]1QM 4:9.

[13]1QSa 1:1, 20; 2:12.

[14]4 QpPs37 2:10; cf. 1QpHab 12:3. See Cross, *Ancient Library,* 84-85.

[15]Compare the contrast between the "men of the community (*yahad*)" and the "congregation (*'ēdāh*) of the men of perversion" in 1QS 5:1-2.

[16]The sealing of the servants of God on the forehead (*sphragisōmen...epi tōn metōpōn autōn*--7:3) before the onset of the plagues recalls Ezekiel 9, where those who mourned the defilement of the temple are marked on the forehead to preserve them from the angels about to destroy Jerusalem (*dos to sēmeion epi ta metōpa tōn andrōn....--9:4* LXX).

[17]See Charles, *Revelation of St. John*, 1. 363; E. -B.
Allo, *Saint Jean: L'Apocalypse*, 4th ed. (Paris: Gabalda, 1933)
211; Heinrich Kraft, *Die Offenbarung des Johannes*, (HNT 16a;
Tübingen: Mohr, 1974) 181. The image of two eschatological
marks, one for salvation, one for destruction is also used in
Pss Sol 15:8-10 (6-9). The terms are *to sēmeion tou theou* and
to sēmeion tēs apōleias. The term *charagma* may have been
chosen by the author of Revelation or the tradition he uses
here because it was the technical term for the imperial stamp;
cf. Adolf Deissmann, *Light From the Ancient East* (New York:
Harper and Row, [1927]) 341 and Fig. 62. The term *sphragis* may
have been chosen because of its use in association with circum-
cision and baptism. For references see Gottfried Fitzer,
"*Sphragis ktl.*," *TDNT* 7 (1971) 947, 949, 952.

[18]*Ho nikōn*: cf. 2:7, 17, 26; 3:5, 12, 21. On 21:7-8, see
Anton Vögtle, *Die Tugend- und Lasterkataloge im Neuen Testament*
(NTAbh 16; Münster: Aschendorff, 1936) 12, 37-38, 202; Ehrhard
Kamlah, *Die Form der katalogischen Paränese im Neuen Testament*
(Wissenschaftliche Untersuchungen zum Neuen Testament 7; Tüb-
ingen: Mohr, 1964) 21-23, 160; P. Prigent, "Une trace de litur-
gie judéo-chrétienne dans le chapitre XII de l'Apocalypse de
Jean," *RSR* 60 (1972) 165-72.

[19]See Vögtle, *Die Tugend- und Lasterkataloge*, 12, 37-38,
202; Kamlah, *Die Form der katalogischen Paränese*, 21-23, 160.

[20]See note 8 above.

[21]See Chapter II, *The Dragon's Attack on the Woman* and *The
Battle in Heaven*.

[22]See Chapter III, *The New Unity*.

[23]Ibid.

[24]On the similarities of wording and content, see Charles,
Revelation of St. John, 1. 345.

[25]Aage Bentzen, *Daniel*, 2nd ed. (HAT 19; Tübingen: Mohr,
1952) 59; see also J. A. Emerton, "The Origin of the Son of Man
Imagery," *JTS* 9 (1958) 228, 230, 232. The seven heads of the
beast of 13:1 may also reflect an ancient mythic tradition; see
Chapter II, *Mythological Parallels to the Dragon as Chaos Monster*.

[26]See the introductory portion of Chapter II, *Mythological Parallels to the Dragon...* and *The Battle in Heaven*.

[27]Cf. Ezek 28:2, 29:3 and Isa 14:4-20. For further OT
passages which reflect this motif, see Hermann Gunkel, *Schöpfung und Chaos in Urzeit und Endzeit* (Göttingen: Vandenhoeck
und Ruprecht, 1895) 84.

[28]The LXX and the version of Theodotion both read...*stoma
laloun megala*...in Dan 7:8 and 20.

[29]So Bousset, *Offenbarung Johannis*, 421.

[30]See Chapter II, *Mythological Parallels to the Dragon*....

[31]This is clear because of the indication that the continual burnt offering is made to him (Dan 8:11); Bentzen, *Daniel*, 70; M. Delcor, *Le Livre de Daniel* (SB; Paris: Gabalda, 1971) 173.

[32]Bentzen, *Daniel*, 70; John J. Collins, "The Son of Man and the Saints of the Most High in the Book of Daniel," *JBL* 93 (1971) 56-63.

[33]Bentzen, *Daniel*, 70; Delcor, *Daniel*, 174-75.

[34]The two indications of time are not exactly equivalent. The 2300 evenings and mornings of Dan 8:14 are 1150 days. If one counts 30 days to a month, this would be a little more than 38 months compared to the 42 months of Rev 13:5. The latter would seem to correspond more accurately to the 3-1/2 times (= years) of Dan 7:25 (cf. Rev 12:14). But the 2300 evenings and mornings of Dan 8:14 were probably intended to be equivalent to the 3-1/2 times of 7:25 and 12:7. Cf. Bentzen, *Daniel*, 52 (note to 7:25), 67, 71. According to Delcor, the time of desecration of the temple given in Dan 8:14 is not intended to be the same length of time as the persecution (7:25) (*Daniel*, 177). See the recent discussion on the time designations in Daniel by Hans Burgmann, "Die vier Endzeittermine im Danielbuch," *ZAW* 86 (1974) 543-50.

[35]See the discussion in Metzger, *A Textual Commentary*, 748-49.

[36]See the discussion in Charles, *Revelation of St. John*, 1. 352-53; Allo opts for a spiritual interpretation—the dwelling of God in the hearts of the saints (*L'Apocalypse*, 208).

[37]Allo made too sharp a distinction between historical allegory and mythic motifs. His interpretation of Daniel 7 and Rev 13:1-10 is thus one-sided; cf. *L'Apocalypse*, 222. See Chapter III on the use of the marine monsters and the combat myth to interpret historical events (*The Traditional Function of the Dragon* and *Revelation 12 as Allegorical Narrative*).

[38]Gunkel's thesis has been adopted, with varying opinions on its centrality, by Charles, *Revelation of St. John*, 1. 358; Lohmeyer, *Offenbarung des Johannes*, 111; G. B. Caird, *A Commentary on the Revelation of St. John the Divine* (New York: Harper and Row, 1966) 161; Kraft, *Offenbarung des Johannes*, 179. Gunkel's interpretation is rejected by Allo, *L'Apocalypse*, 223; and by Bousset, *Offenbarung Johannis*, 435-36.

[39]Gunkel, *Schöpfung und Chaos*, 51-61, especially 56, 58, 60-61.

[40]See Marvin H. Pope, *Job* (AB; Garden City, N.Y.: Doubleday, 1973); on possible prototypes of Behemoth in Ugaritic myth, see pages 321-22. See also Mary K. Wakeman, *God's Battle with the Monster* (Leiden: Brill, 1973), especially chapters IV (The Sea-Monster), V, VI (The Earth-Monster) and VII.

[41]Gunkel, *Schöpfung und Chaos*, 360, 362, 367.

[42]*Midrash Rabba Leviticus* 13:3. This text and the following two are cited by Pope, *Job*, 324-25.

[43]*bBaba Bathra* 75a.

[44]*Pesiqta de Rab Kahana* 188b.

[45]4 Ezra 6:52; 2 Apoc Bar 29:4. This tradition is reflected in the MT of Ps 74:14--"Thou didst crush the heads of Leviathan, thou didst give him as food for the people" (translation from RSV note).

[46]On the dating of 4 Ezra and the Syriac Apocalypse of Baruch, see D. S. Russell, *The Method and Message of Jewish Apocalyptic* (Philadelphia: Westminster, 1964) 62-65.

[47]The translation here paraphrased is that of Charles in *APOT*, 2. 224.

[48]*Et dedisti Beemoth unam partem quae siccata est tertio die, ut inhabitet in ea, ubi sunt montes mille; Leviatae autem dedisti septimam partem humidam....* Text cited from Bruno Violet, *Die Esra-Apokalypse (IV Esra)* (GCS 18; Leipzig: Hinrichs, 1910) 120.

[49]References are given by Lohmeyer, *Offenbarung des Johannes*, 111.

[50]Several commentators combine the mythical and geographical-allegorical interpretations, e.g., Caird, *A Commentary on Revelation*, 161-62. He cites 4 Ezra 11 as an example of a vision in which the motif of a beast coming from the sea has a clearly geographical reference. His argument for this interpretation rests on the fact that the eagle has none of the mythical associations with the cosmic deep which Leviathan has. But it is not at all obvious in the vision account nor in the interpretation (4 Ezra 12:10-39) that the image of the eagle coming up from the sea is meant to be understood geographically. In fact, that interpretation is made rather unlikely by the interpretation given for the coming up out of the sea of the "man" in the following vision account: "Just as no one can explore or know what is in the depths of the sea, so no one on earth can see my Son...except in the time of his day" (13:52, RSV).

[51]Gunkel, *Schöpfung und Chaos*, 360-61. This interpretation is allowed by Bousset for the beast in 17:8 (*Offenbarung Johannis*, 480, note 2).

[52]Dan 7:5 (LXX): *kai idou...allo thērion*; see also Ps 68: 31 (68:30 RSV) and the numerous other texts cited by Gunkel, *Schöpfung und Chaos*, 329.

[53]Namely Rev 13:1; 4 Ezra 11:1, 13:3; 2 Apoc Bar 29:4.

[54]The translation is that of R. H. Charles, *APOT*, 2. 497.

[55]See Chapter II, *Mythological Parallels to the Dragon*....

[56]Gunkel, *Schöpfung und Chaos*, 360-61; cf. also 21-29. That there are vestiges of the Mesopotamian myth in Genesis 1 is accepted by W. F. Albright (*Yahweh and the Gods of Canaan* [Garden City, N.Y.: Doubleday, 1969] 184-85). See also Wakeman, *God's Battle with the Monster*, 86-87.

[57]See for example Isa 51:10, Job 28:14, Ps 33:7 (LXX Ps 32:7 - *abyssos/thalassa*).

[58]See Gunkel, *Schöpfung und Chaos*, 69, 370. In Ps 74:13 (LXX 73:13) *yām* and *tannīnîm* seem to be equivalent (LXX *thalassa* and *drakōn*). In Isa 51:9-10, slaying *Rahab/tannīn* is parallel to drying up *yām/tᵉhôm*. On Isa 51:9-10 and the combat myth, see Cross, *Canaanite Myth and Hebrew Epic*, 108.

[59]See the summary discussion of the problematic of the chapter and the brief history of its exegesis in Josef Ernst, *Die eschatologischen Gegenspieler in den Schriften des Neuen Testaments* (Biblische Untersuchungen 3; Regensburg: Verlag Friedrich Pustet, 1967) 124-26.

[60]First, the only very external connection between verses 1-2 and 3-13 which consists in the fact that both passages refer to the historical Jerusalem; see Bultmann's comments in his review of Lohmeyer's commentary in *TLZ* 52 (1927) 507. The repetition of the two differently formulated but equivalent time periods is an indication of a literary seam; the repetition serves to link the two passages. Second, the passage 11: 3-13 is linguistically distinctive in comparison to the rest of the book. Charles adduces a great number of arguments on this score, also for verses 1-2 (*Revelation of St. John*, 1. 271-73), many of which are not compelling. A few, however, are noteworthy. *Ptōma* is used for "corpse" in vss. 8 and 9, whereas *nekros* is used in this sense in 16:3. *Theōrein* is used in vss. 11 and 12 which occurs no where else in the book; *blepein* or *horan* are the terms used elsewhere. In vs. 6 *hosakis ean* is used to denote indefinite frequency, whereas *hotan* is used in the same sense in 4:9; the former appears nowhere else in the book. Finally, *hē polis hē megalē* is used in vs. 8 of Jerusalem, whereas elsewhere in the book, it is used only of Rome. Third, the facts that the content of the passage (1-13) is distinctive with regard to the rest of the book and that it gives the impression of fragmentariness support the hypothesis that a source or sources are being used here.

[61]The use of the image of lampstands in vs. 4 is reminiscent of the extensive use of the image in the opening vision
and the seven messages; cf. 1:12-13, 20; 2:1, 5. The *hopou kai
ho kyrios autōn estaurōthē* in vs. 8 looks like a redactional
aside, and is compatible with the style of the book elsewhere
(with the exception of 12:6, 14 which come from a source; see
Chapter III); Charles, *Revelation of St. John*, 1. 287. Finally, vs. 7 reflects ideas and diction found elsewhere in the
book and was probably composed, as a whole or in part, by the
author of the book in its present form. See the discussion in
the text below. Note also that *telein*, used in this verse in
connection with the completion of the testimony of the two witnesses, is used several times elsewhere in the book for the
completion of a period of time or phase of the eschatological
drama; see 15:1, 8; 20:3, 5, 7; possibly also 10:7. On 11:7 as
the work of the apocalyptist-redactor, see Charles, *Revelation
of St. John*, 1. 285.

[62]Bousset, *Offenbarung Johannis*, 383; see also idem, *Der
Antichrist* (Göttingen: Vandenhoeck und Ruprecht, 1895) 11-13.

[63]Bousset, *Offenbarung Johannis*, 384-85.

[64]Bousset, *Der Antichrist*, 18-19. See for example, his
treatment of Rev 13:16-17 in *Offenbarung Johannis*, 427-28 and
Der Antichrist, 132-33.

[65]R. H. Charles, *The Ascension of Isaiah* (London: Black,
1900) li-lxxiii; and *Revelation of St. John*, 2. 76-87. See the
summaries and critiques of Bousset's and Charles' studies on
the Antichrist myth(s) in Ernst, *Die eschatologischen Gegenspieler*, 283-92. For Bousset's later comments on the subject,
see *Die Religion des Judentums im späthellenistischen Zeitalter*
(ed. Hugo Gressmann; HNT 21; Tübingen: Mohr, 1926) 254-56; and
"Antichrist," *Encyclopedia of Religion and Ethics* (ed. James
Hastings; New York: Scribner's, 1908) 1. 578-81. Notable later
studies include Béda Rigaux, *L'Antéchrist et l'opposition au
royaume messianique dans l'Ancien et le Nouveau Testament*
(Gembloux: Duculot, 1932). Studies important for background
are K. L. Schmidt, "Lucifer als gefallene Engelmacht," *TZ* 7
(1951) 161-79; Victor Maag, "B^eli̇ja'al im Alten Testament," *TZ*
21 (1965) 287-99. The Qumran texts have provided new data on
the subject. Relevant studies include H. W. Huppenbauer,
"Belial in den Qumrantexten"; Peter von der Osten-Sacken, *Gott
und Belial* (Studien zur Umwelt des Neuen Testaments 6; Götting-
en: Vandenhoeck und Ruprecht, 1969); J. T. Milik, "Milkisedek
et Milkiresa' dans les anciens écrits juifs et chrétiens," *JJS*
23 (1972) 95-144; J. T. Milik, "4QVisions de 'Amram et une
citation d'Origène (Planches I-II)," *RB* 79 (1972) 77-97. See
also Michael Stone, "Antichrist," *Jewish Encyclopedia* 3 (1971)
59-62.

[66]Josef Ernst's term *eschatologische Gegenspieler* is used
with a similar intent; see *Die eschatologischen Gegenspieler*,
X-XI.

[67]Bousset, *Der Antichrist*, 11.

[68]Charles, *Revelation of St. John*, 1. 285-86.

[69]Bousset, *Offenbarung Johannis*, 384-85; the supporting texts are Mark 13:14 and parallels, 2 Thes 2:3-12, As Mos 10.

[70]Ibid., 378.

[71]A number of usually reliable manuscripts omit this clause from 13:7. But this omission is probably due to haplography. See the discussion in Metzger, *A Textual Commentary*, 749.

[72]Bousset, *Der Antichrist*, 99.

[73]See Walter Bauer, *A Greek-English Lexicon of the New Testament*, 4th ed. rev. (trans. and adapted by W. F. Arndt and F. W. Gingrich; Chicago: University of Chicago Press, 1957) 103. See also B. Rigaux, *Saint Paul: Les Epitres aux Thessaloniciens* (Paris: Gabalda, 1956) 657-58; Ernst, *Die eschatologischen Gegenspieler*, 35.

[74]Thomas Joseph Lamy, *Sancti Ephraem Syri Hymni et Sermones* (Mechlinia: Dessain, 1889) 3. 187-212; see the discussion of this text by Bousset, *Der Antichrist*, 35-38; he considers this sermon to be authentic except for a few interpolations and dates it to about 373.

[75]Bousset, *Der Antichrist*, 75.

[76]Ibid., 99.

[77]Lamy, *Sancti Ephraem Syri*, 203.

[78]Bousset, *Der Antichrist*, 99; on the commentary of Andreas, see *Offenbarung Johannis*, 68.

[79]For editions, translations and studies, see Albert-Marie Denis, *Introduction aux pseudepigraphs grecs d'Ancien Testament* (Studia in Veteris Testamenti Pseudepigrapha 1; Leiden: Brill, 1970) 91-93.

[80]Bousset, *Der Antichrist*, 99 note 2.

[81]See the discussion by Bousset, *Offenbarung Johannis*, 21.

[82]Paul Volz, *Die Eschatologie der jüdischen Gemeinde* (Tübingen: Mohr, 1934) 50; Paul Riessler, *Altjüdisches Schrifttum ausserhalb der Bibel* (Augsburg: Filser, 1928) 1243.

[83]Denis, *Introduction*, 93.

[84]3:11-15; cf. Riessler, *Altjüdisches Schrifttum*, 1273.

[85]The variety consists, for example, in expressions equivalent to *abyssos*; in Ephraem Syrus *abaddon* is used. Andreas speaks of the dark and deep regions of the earth, while the Apocalypse of Esdras refers to Tartarus.

[86]See Charles, *Revelation of St. John*, 1. 286; Allo, *L'Apocalypse*, 152; Kraft, *Offenbarung des Johannes*, 157.

[87]See the discussion in Gunkel, *Schöpfung und Chaos*, 230-33; he agrees with earlier exegetes who interpreted the beast of ch. 13 as the Roman empire and the woman of ch. 17 as the city of Rome. But he cautions that the fact that the author intended those two images as historical allegory does not mean that the exegete is allowed to allegorize every detail in the two vision accounts. Gunkel does allow the allegorical interpretation both of the ten horns and the seven heads in 13:1; i.e., he admits that both images refer to a series of kings, and furthermore, that the wounded head refers to the fate of an individual king (342). But he objected strenuously to the interpretation of 666 (13:18) as a reference to a particular emperor (374-78). Bousset follows Gunkel in taking the ten horns and seven heads allegorically (though he interprets their significance for the chapter differently) (416, 418). He disagrees with Gunkel in that he takes the rising out of the sea (13:1) and the rising out of the earth (13:11) allegorically, as well as the number 666 (416, 424, 428-30). Charles follows Gunkel and Bousset on the allegorical interpretation of the beast (13:1) and of the woman of ch. 17 (*Revelation of St. John*, 1. 333; 2. 54). He interprets the seven heads allegorically as referring to Roman emperors, but, contra Bousset, takes the ten horns as an archaic survival, meaningless in the present context (1. 346-47). Charles also agrees with Gunkel and Bousset in taking the wounded head allegorically, and with Bousset on the 666 (1. 348-50; 364-68). Charles does not take the rising out of the sea allegorically (1. 345), but he does so interpret the rising out of the land (1. 357). Most subsequent commentators take this line of interpretation at least for some of the images; cf. Allo, *L'Apocalypse*, 204, 206, 235, 288-89; Bonsirven allows the allegorical interpretation of the beast of 13:1 as the Roman empire and the woman of ch. 17 as Rome, but only as symbols of the power of the Antichrist; in this interpretation he follows Allo, *L'Apocalypse*, 289 (Joseph Bonsirven, *L'Apocalypse* [Verbum Salutis 16; Paris: Beauchesne, 1951] 230, 270-71); Johannes Behm, *Die Offenbarung des Johannes* (NTD 11; Göttingen: Vandenhoeck und Ruprecht, 1953) 73-74, 91-93; Lucien Cerfaux and Jules Cambier, *L'Apocalypse* (Lectio Divina 17; Paris: Les Editions du Cerf, 1955) 121-22, 152-53; G. B. Caird, *A Commentary on Revelation*, 161-65, 213, 216-17, 219; Charles Brütsch, *Die Offenbarung Jesu Christi* (3 vols.; Zürcher Bibel Kommentare; Zürich: Zwingli, 1970) 108, 116, 118, 140, 223, 251; Kraft, *Offenbarung*, 175-76 (the wounded head is Domitian), 185, 217-18, 221-22. Notable exceptions to this approach are Lohmeyer, *Offenbarung des Johannes*, 107-12, 135-44; Mathias Rissi, *Zeit und Geschichte in der Offenbarung des Johannes* (Zürich: Zwingli, 1952) 79; *Was ist und was geschehen soll danach* (ATANT 46; Zürich: Zwingli, 1965)

69-70; J. Sickenberger, "Die Johannesapokalypse und Rom," *BZ* 17 (1926) 270-82, and *Erklärung der Johannesapokalypse* (Bonn: Hanstein, 1942); J. Freundorfer, *Die Apokalypse des Apostels Johannes und die hellenistische Kosmologie und Astrologie* (Biblische Studien 33, 1; Freiburg: Herder, 1929).

[88]See in particular, R. Bultmann's review of Lohmeyer's commentary in *TLZ* 52 (1927) 505-12, especially 510-11.

[89]Lohmeyer, *Offenbarung des Johannes*, 111.

[90]Ibid., 107-8.

[91]The references are given by Charles, *Revelation of St. John*, 1. 351.

[92]Lohmeyer, *Offenbarung des Johannes*, 109. Of course such language is applied to the political adversaries of Yahweh and Israel in the OT; cf. Isa 47:8, 10; Ezek 27:3, 28:2; Isa 14:12-14.

[93]Kraft elucidates this aspect well (*Offenbarung des Johannes*, 176).

[94]Lohmeyer's argument would seem to be refuted by the fact that in the Mart Isa 4:6-8 comparable OT language, usually addressed to God, is applied to the returning Nero. Nero here is identified with Beliar and thus highly mythicized, but the link to the historical person is not broken. This passage will be discussed in more detail below.

[95]Lohmeyer, *Offenbarung des Johannes*, 109.

[96]Ibid., 112.

[97]See the discussion by David Flusser, "The four empires in the Fourth Sibyl and in the Book of Daniel," *Israel Oriental Studies* 2 (1972) 158-59; see also Ernst, *Die eschatologischen Gegenspieler*, 132; Bentzen, *Daniel*, 33.

[98]Bentzen, *Daniel*, 65; see also 33; Flusser, "The four empires," 158; G. H. Box in Charles, *APOT*, 2. 609, 613; Ernst, *Die eschatologischen Gegenspieler*, 132.

[99]Charles, *APOT*, 2. 501; Flusser, "The four empires," 158.

[100]They are all vision accounts.

[101]In vs. 9 or 10, depending how the verses are divided. On the question of the identification of the kings mentioned here, see Lyder Brun, "Die römischen Kaiser in der Apokalypse," *ZNW* 26 (1927) 128-51; A. Strobel, "Abfassung und Geschichtstheologie der Apokalypse nach Kap 17, 9-12," *NTS* 10 (1964) 433-45; and B. Reicke, "Die jüdische Apokalyptik und die johanneische Tiervision," *RSR* 60 (1972) 175-81.

[102]See the discussion by Bousset, *Offenbarung Johannis*, 434 and that by Charles, *Revelation of St. John*, 1. 349-50.

[103]So Gunkel, opting for Caesar; *Schöpfung und Chaos*, 355; see the discussion in Charles (*Revelation of St. John*, 1. 349) for other older commentators who took this view. Caird combines this interpretation with that based on the legend of Nero's return (*A Commentary on Revelation*, 164-65). Kraft adopts this interpretation but applies it to the crisis following Domitian's death (*Offenbarung des Johannes*, 176).

[104]A recent discussion of the Nero legend may be found in John J. Collins, *The Sibylline Oracles of Egyptian Judaism* (SBL Dissertation Series 13; Missoula, Mont.: Scholars Press, 1974) 80-87; for bibliography, see 188, note 47. See also Michael Grant, *Nero* (New York: American Heritage Press, 1970) 250-51.

[105]See Iamblichus *Theol. Ar.* 64; Ernst, *Die eschatologischen Gegenspieler*, 141; Kraft, *Offenbarung des Johannes*, 183.

[106]The argument that the phrase *arithmos anthrōpou* should be translated "a human number," or "an ordinary number" is not compelling. This interpretation is based on a comparison of this verse with 21:17. There an angel measures the wall of the new Jerusalem which is said to be 144 cubits *metron anthrōpou, ho estin aggelou*. It is argued by those who take this position that here an angelic method of reckoning is contrasted with a human method. This contrast is not explicit in the text. In fact the point may be that the same *method* of reckoning is used, i.e., a cubit = the length of the forearm. But when an angel is measuring, the cubit is larger, since an angel's forearm (in the form in which they appear to human beings) is longer than a man's! See the discussion by Caird (*A Commentary on Revelation*, 273). In any case some modification of the usual measurement is implied. But in 13:18 there is no hint that any sort of contrast with another type of number is intended. Gunkel adopted this position (*Schöpfung und Chaos*, 376); he was followed by Lohmeyer (*Offenbarung des Johannes*, 115). See the discussion in Charles for older commentators who supported this view and for a critique of it (*Revelation of St. John*, 1. 364-65); Ernst also rejects this interpretation (*Die eschatologischen Gegenspieler*, 142).

[107]See the discussions in Bousset, *Offenbarung Johannis*, 428-30; Charles, *Revelation of St. John*, 1. 364-68.

[108]D. R. Hillers, "Rev 13:18 and a Scroll from Murabba'at," *BASOR* 170 (1963) 65.

[109]See the discussion of Sib Or 5:137-54 below. See also 1 Pet 5:13 and the discussion and list of passages in Charles, *Revelation of St. John*, 2. 14.

[110]For the motif of devouring flesh associated with Nero's return, see Sib Or 5:222-24.

[111]See Bousset, *Offenbarung Johannis*, 474-80; Charles, *Revelation of St. John*, 2. 71-72.

[112]For *abyssos* as equivalent to Sheol, see Jonah 2:6 and Ps 70 (71):20 (LXX).

[113]Bousset, *Offenbarung Johannis*, 419; Ernst, *Die eschatologischen Gegenspieler*, 147; Charles, *Revelation of St. John*, 2. 83-85; so also lately Reicke, "Die johanneische Tiervision," 182-83; and Dominique Cuss, *Imperial Cult and Honorary Terms in the New Testament* (Paradosis 23; Fribourg: The University Press, 1974) 92.

[114]Bousset, *Offenbarung Johannis*, 419, 467, 477-78; R. H. Charles, *Ascension of Isaiah*, lxxii; Ernst (*Die eschatologischen Gegenspieler*, 147) does not use the term "Nero redivivus," but he adopts the idea behind the term and assumes that it is present in Sib Or 5:28-34, 214-27. His position is very similar to Charles'. The term "redivivus" should of course be reserved for someone thought to be returning from the dead.

[115]The relevant ancient texts are Suetonius *The Lives of the Caesars* 6 (*Nero*) 47-57, especially 57; Tacitus *The Histories* 1.2, 2.8-9; Dio Cassius 63.9, 66.19.3; Dio Chrysostom *Orations* 21.10.

[116]See also Tacitus *The Histories* 2.8; A. Momigliano, "Nero," *CAH* 10 (Cambridge: Cambridge University Press, 1934) 741.

[117]See the discussion in Charles, *Revelation of St. John*, 2. 80-81. Note that at least one of those who pretended to be Nero sought refuge and military aid from the Parthians; see Tacitus *The Histories* 1.2; Dio Cassius 66.19.3; Joann. Antioch. (fr. 104 Muell.--text and translation printed with the Dio Cassius passage in the LCL edition); Suetonius *Nero* 57.

[118]The date of the appearance of the last attested pretender is uncertain. Dio reports that a false Nero by the name of Terentius Maximus appeared during the reign of Titus and sought and received support from the Parthians. Suetonius mentions a pretender who appeared when he himself was a young man. He dates this appearance to twenty years after Nero's death (i.e., in 88). This man, according to Suetonius, was vigorously supported by the Parthians (*Nero* 57). The critical questions are whether these two writers refer to the same pretender; and if so, whose date is to be preferred. It would seem that Suetonius is reliable for events in his own lifetime.

[119]See Momigliano, "Nero," 741-42. On the positive attitude to Nero among Greeks, see Grant, *Nero*, 251.

[120]See the discussion in Collins, *Sibylline Oracles*, 81-82. The oracle of Hystaspes also seems to reflect this East-West antagonism; see John R. Hinnells, "The Zoroastrian Doctrine of Salvation in the Roman World," in *Man and His Salvation: Studies in Memory of S. G. F. Brandon* (ed. E. J. Sharpe and J. R. Hinnells; Manchester: The University Press, 1973) 125-48. Bousset overlooked this central function of the original Nero legend. He comments that the legend was originally "römisch-national"

(*Offenbarung Johannis*, 475). It is true that Nero was regretted in some quarters of the West as the last of the Julio-Claudian line, but this phenomenon seems to have had limited importance (cf. Momigliano, "Nero," 741).

[121]Cf. Suetonius *Nero* 57; Tacitus *The Histories* 2.8; see also Joann. Antioch. fr. 104 (see note 117); Dio Chrysostom *Orations* 21.10.

[122]According to Dio Chrysostom, in his time everyone wished Nero were alive and most believed it. Charles is certainly right that this is an exaggeration, but it is evidence that at least some people in the time of Trajan believed that Nero was still alive. See Charles, *Ascension of Isaiah*, lix and the criticism of his remark and its implications by Collins, *Sibylline Oracles*, 189 note 58. Momigliano takes the statement of Chrysostom seriously ("Nero," 742).

[123]The fourth Sibylline book was composed about 80 C.E.; it is dated by the last datable event mentioned, the eruption of Vesuvius in 79. See Flusser, "The four empires," 148; and John J. Collins, "The Place of the Fourth Sibyl in the Development of the Jewish Sibyllina," *JJS* 25 (1974) 365-80.

[124]The translation of the Sibylline books cited is that of H. C. O. Lanchester, "The Sibylline Oracles," in Charles, *APOT*, 2. 368-406, unless otherwise indicated.

[125]Flusser, "The four empires," 148 note 2; 151-52. This form of the legend, which does not go beyond the form apparently reflected by the Greek and Latin writers, is also the form the Nero legend takes in the eighth Sibylline book; cf. 8:65-72 and 139-59. A translation is given in Edgar Hennecke and Wilhelm Schneemelcher, *New Testament Apocrypha* (Philadelphia: Westminster, 1965) 2. 727, 729-30.

[126]5:28-34, 93-110, 137-54, 214-27, 361-84.

[127]Collins, *Sibylline Oracles*, 75.

[128]Ibid., 82.

[129]See Chapter III, *The Battle in Heaven*, and above, *The Beast from the Sea*.

[130]Collins, *Sibylline Oracles*, 192 note 76.

[131]The shaking of all creation belongs to the motif of the theophany of the Divine Warrior; cf. Cross, *Canaanite Myth and Hebrew Epic*, 155-57.

[132]The Greek text is cited according to the edition of Johannes Geffcken, *Die Oracula Sibyllina* (GCS 8; Leipzig: Hinrichs, 1902) 111. The manuscripts read *hē ktisis*, but *holē* is necessary for the meter; so emended by Charles Alexandre. For bibliographical details on his edition, see Geffcken, *Oracula Sibyllina*, XIII-XIV.

[133]On the edition by Volkmann, see Geffcken, *Oracula Sibyllina*, XVI.

[134]See Lanchester's remarks in Charles, *APOT*, 2. 400.

[135]Some manuscripts read *oloigios*; others *ho logios*; Geffcken adopts Friedlieb's emendation (*oloiios*). For bibliographical details on Friedlieb's edition, see Geffcken, *Oracula Sibyllina*, XIV-XV.

[136]Charles argues that this passage describes Nero redivivus because the author is writing two generations after Nero's death (*Ascension of Isaiah*, lxxii). First of all it should be noted that this passage was redacted in the time of Hadrian, but very likely contains material written at an earlier time (cf. Collins, *Sibylline Oracles*, 75, 94-95). The redactor may well have received this review of history in written form, coming to an end with the reign of an emperor before his own time. He would naturally then have updated the review. In any case the passage regarding Nero (5:28-34) shows no interest in nor awareness of Nero's death nor conception of Nero's return from the underworld.

[137]Translation by the writer.

[138]Translation by the writer.

[139]Collins, *Sibylline Oracles*, 84.

[140]See H. G. Liddell and R. Scott, *A Greek-English Lexicon* (Oxford: Clarendon, 1966) 1217; for example, Aeschylus *Persae* 1016.

[141]Translations by the writer.

[142]Collins, *Sibylline Oracles*, 86.

[143]According to Charles, the text presumes that Nero is still alive (*Ascension of Isaiah*, lxviii).

[144]The exceptions are F. C. Burkitt and Vacher Burch; see the introductory notes by J. Flemming and H. Duensing in Hennecke-Schneemelcher, 2. 642-43. See also the discussion in Charles, *Ascension of Isaiah*, xxxvi-xxxviii; Charles himself argues that 3:13b-4:18 is an independent work which he labels the Testament of Hezekiah (*Ascension of Isaiah*, xlii-xliii).

[145]Hennecke-Schneemelcher, 2. 642-43.

[146]Translation from Hennecke-Schneemelcher, 2. 648-49.

[147]Charles, *Ascension of Isaiah*, lxx-lxxii.

[148]Ibid., lxx; he goes on to conclude that the passage must be dated after 88, when the last pretender appeared. Given the weakness of the premise, this conclusion is not justified.

[149]See Chapter II, *The Dragon's Attack on the Woman*.

[150]Chapter III, *The New Unity*.

[151]Chapter III, *The Re-use of Source I*.

[152]See above, *The Signification of the Beasts*.

[153]Cf. Dan 11:40-45 which predicts the death of Antiochus, and opens "At the time of the end...."

[154]Nero died in 68; a date of about 90-96 for the composition of Revelation is presupposed here. The images applied to Nero by our author (the wound, the ascent from the abyss) are more easily understood on the author's assumption of Nero's death than of his flight.

[155]This is evident from the placement of the exhortation of 13:9-10 in the context of the depiction of the Roman empire as the chaos beast raised up by Satan.

[156]See the discussions by Momigliano, "Nero," 722-26; and Grant, *Nero*, 151-61.

[157]See Momigliano, "Nero," 741.

[158]Cf. Tacitus *Histories* 2.8-9.

[159]According to Dio Cassius (66.19.3), Terentius Maximus, who claimed to be Nero during the reign of Titus, was an Asiatic and gained a number of followers in Asia; cf. Grant, *Nero*, 250. See also notes 117 and 118 above.

[160]See the discussion above, *The Beast as Nero*.

[161]Cf. 6:9-11, where the association of the souls with the heavenly altar seems to imply that their deaths are sacrifices offered to God (Charles, *Revelation of St. John*, 1. 172-74); 20:4-6. The term "martyr" is used here of one who has died rather than act contrary to his or her religious convictions; this use does not imply that the term is already a technical one in Revelation (see the discussion of this issue above in Chapter I, d. *The Seven Bowls*).

[162]Josephus *JW* 2.118, 433; 7.323, 410.

[163]Rev 16:5-7; 19:2; cf. 18:20, 24.

[164]Rev 19:2--"He (God) judged the great harlot who corrupted the earth with her fornication...." The solidarity of the natural and social realms is implied here; the earth is corrupt because of the perverse character of the social order as determined by Rome. On the idea that unrighteous behavior of humanity can corrupt the elements, see H. D. Betz, "On the Problem of the Religio-Historical Understanding of Apocalypticism," *Journal for Theology and the Church* 6 (New York: Herder, 1969) 143-53.

[165]The Nero legend is also reflected in Rev 9:13-19, 16: 12-16 and 19:11-21, as will be shown in Chapter V.

[166]On the date of the fourth sibyl, see above, note 123.

[167]See above, note 125.

[168]Collins, *Sibylline Oracles*, 94.

[169]See the chapter on "The Syncretism of the Sibyllina," in ibid., 97-115.

[170]Caird, *A Commentary on Revelation*, 148.

[171]Chapter III, *Date and Provenance of Source I.*

[172]Chapter III, *The Function of the Combat Myth in Source I.*

[173]Virgil *Ecologue* 4.10-14.

[174]Jean Gagé, *Apollon romain* (Bibliothèque des écoles françaises d'Athènes et de Rome 182; Paris: Boccard, 1955) 583-637.

[175]Suetonius *Lives* 2 (*Augustus*) 94.

[176]This point was emphasized by William K. Hedrick in commenting on Caird's remark in the former's dissertation ("The Sources and Use of the Imagery in Apocalypse 12" [Diss., Graduate Theological Union, 1970] 148-49).

[177]Tacitus *Annals* 11.11. The legend is also mentioned by Suetonius (*Nero* 6) and by Dio Cassius (61.2). The passages are quoted synoptically by Kurt Heinz, *Das Bild Kaiser Neros bei Seneca, Tacitus, Sueton und Cassius Dio* (Biel: Graphische Anstalt Schüler AG, 1948) 14. See also Hildebrandt, "Das römische Antichristentum zur Zeit der Offenbarung Johannis und des 5 sibyllinischen Buches," *Zeitschrift für wissenschaftliche Theologie* 17 (1874) 67. Grant infers that the reference was to a myth about Hercules, who strangled a serpent sent to kill him (*Nero*, 186).

[178]Gagé, *Apollon romain*, 650-82.

[179]See the discussions by Henry Bardon, *Les Empereurs et les lettres latines d'Auguste à Hadrien* (Paris: Société d'Edition 'Les Belles Lettres', 1940) 198; Dominique Cuss, *Imperial Cult and Honorary Terms*, 77-80; Gagé, *Apollon romain*, 660-61; Grant, *Nero*, 101, 233.

[180]Tacitus *Annals* 14.14; cf. Grant, *Nero*, 101.

[181]See the discussions by Grant, *Nero*, 207; Gagé, *Apollon romain*, 650. On the coins which depict Nero as Apollo, see Edward A. Sydenham, *The Coinage of Nero* (London: Spink,

1920) 14-15, 35-38, 72-76; a number of these coins are repro-
duced by Grant, *Nero*, 207, 209, 218 (only the obverse of the
latter two coins is pictured, whereas the Apollo motif is on
the reverse).

[182]See Gagé, *Apollon romain*, 654 and note 2; Grant, *Nero*,
232.

[183]Grant, *Nero*, 231.

CHAPTER V

THE PATTERN OF THE COMBAT MYTH IN THE BOOK OF REVELATION

The search for a common pattern in religious phenomena as
an aid in understanding individual texts and their relationships to other texts is one of the fundamental options of interpretation: the search for similarities. The weaknesses of
this approach are tendencies to over-simplification, over-
emphasis on similarities so that significant differences are
overlooked, and the fallacy that similarity always implies dependence or influence. These weaknesses characterized an early
attempt to explain the similarities between Babylonian texts
and the Old Testament. This attempt was the suggestion made by
the so-called "pan-Babylonian school" that all religious and
cultic symbolism derives from the Babylonian world view. This
movement was severely criticized but had an extensive influence
on subsequent scholarship.[1] Another, more successful attempt
to explain the similarities among religious texts of various
cultures of the ancient Near East was that of what came to be
called the "myth and ritual school," led by S. H. Hooke in Eng-
land and Sigmund Mowinckel in Scandanavia.[2] The basic thesis
of this group was that there was a common "ritual pattern" in
the ancient East associated in each culture with a major annual
festival. This pattern, as formulated by Hooke, has the following elements:

    a. The dramatic representation of the death and resur-
       rection of the god
    b. The recitation or symbolic representation of the
       myth of creation
    c. The ritual combat, in which the triumph of the
       god over his enemies was depicted
    d. The sacred marriage
    e. The triumphal procession, in which the king played
       the part of the god followed by a train of lesser
       gods or visiting deities[3]

The primary focus of the research of this school has been
on the psalms and the royal cult. According to Mowinckel,
there was an annual festival during the monarchy in which the
enthronement of Yahweh was celebrated. This festival was
heavily influenced by the Canaanite New Year festival which had

essentially the same ritual pattern as the festival at Babylon.[4] The basic insight of the myth and ritual school, that
the royal cult of Israel must be understood in the framework of
the royal and agricultural festivals of her neighbors, has won
widespread acceptance, although many significant details are
disputed. The major unresolved problem was how the royal cult
related to traditions about the Exodus and Conquest and the
cult of the league. It is this issue which Frank M. Cross has
addressed in his studies of Canaanite and early Hebrew poetry.[5]
He has isolated an archaic mythic pattern which is particularly
characteristic of Canaanite (Ugaritic) poetry, but is still
discernible in the victory hymns of the league. The elements
of this pattern are:

    a. The Divine Warrior goes forth to battle against chaos.
    b. Nature convulses at the manifestation of the Warrior's
       wrath.
    c. The warrior-god returns to take up kingship among the
       gods and is enthroned on his mountain.
    d. The Divine Warrior utters his voice from his temple;
       fertility results.[6]

Cross has also traced motifs and themes related to this pattern, particularly the motif of the storm theophany, from the
time of the league down to proto-apocalyptic texts of the sixth
century.[7] The imagery of the theophany of the divine warrior
in the old hymns and the royal psalms reappears in proto-
apocalyptic texts to describe the coming of the divine warrior
in eschatological warfare.[8]

    Paul D. Hanson has shown that what he calls the mythic or
ritual pattern of the conflict myth of the ancient Near East is
reflected not only in the hymns of the league and the royal
psalms but also in a number of proto-apocalyptic texts, e.g.,
Zechariah 9.[9] The structure of Zechariah 9 as interpreted by
Hanson is as follows:

    a. Conflict-Victory (1-7)
    b. Temple Secured (8)
    c. Victory Shout and Procession (9)
    d. Manifestation of Yahweh's Universal Reign (10)
    e. Salvation: Captives Released (11-13)
    f. Theophany of Divine Warrior (14)
    g. Sacrifice and Banquet (15)
    h. Fertility of Restored Order (16-17)[10]

This structure is then compared with the mythic pattern reflected in the *Enuma elish*, the Baal-Yamm conflict, Exodus 15 and Judges 5.[11] Not every text has all the elements found in the other texts, and the order varies, but the elements listed are typical. Hanson's formulation of the pattern of the *Enuma elish* is quoted here as representative:

a. Threat (I:109 - II:91)
b. Combat-Victory (IV:33-122)
c. Theophany of the Divine Warrior (IV:39-60)
d. Salvation of the Gods (IV:123-46; VI:1-44; cf. VI:126-57, 149-51)
e. Fertility of the Restored Order (V:1-66; cf. VII:1-2, 59-83)
f. Procession and Victory Shout (V:67-89)
g. Temple Built for Marduk (V:117-56; VI:45-68)
h. Banquet (VI:69-94)
i. Manifestation of Marduk's Universal Reign (anticipated: IV:3-18; manifested: VI:95 - VII:144)[12]

This basic mythic pattern as isolated by Cross and Hanson from Ugaritic and OT texts is not unique to those traditions. The pattern was also present in Mesopotamian mythic texts as Hanson notes.[13] But the essential elements of the pattern were even more widespread. Joseph Fontenrose has shown that the same basic structure of the combat myth is discernible in Sumerian-Babylonian, Hittite, Canaanite-Ugaritic, Greek and Egyptian myths.[14] Many of the texts which reflect the pattern were current in the Hellenistic and Roman periods.[15] Thus one can speak of a mythic pattern of combat which was widespread in the early Imperial period. The pattern was reflected in a variety of forms, but the fundamental similarities were clear enough. Even if one is not prepared to accept Fontenrose's theory that all the variants derive ultimately from a single source,[16] he has at least shown convincingly that the various combat myths are structurally or phenomenologically similar. Thus any one form of the combat myth would have been cross-culturally intelligible.

The fundamental elements of the pattern as isolated by Fontenrose are:

a. The Dragon Pair - the opponent is often a pair of dragons or beasts
b. Chaos and Disorder - forces which the opponent represents

c. The Attack
d. The Champion
e. The Champion's Death
f. The Dragon's Reign
g. Recovery of the Champion
h. Battle Renewed and Victory
i. Restoration and Confirmation of Order[17]

The Dragon Pair, Chaos and Disorder, and The Attack (Fontenrose) correspond to the threat of chaos in the first element of Cross' and Hanson's patterns. The Champion, Recovery, and Victory (Fontenrose) correspond to Theophany of the Divine Warrior (Cross and Hanson) and Combat-Victory (Hanson). Restoration and Confirmation of Order (Fontenrose) correspond to kingship and Fertility of the Restored Order (Cross and Hanson) and Salvation and Manifestation of Universal Reign (Hanson).

The book of Revelation has often been mentioned as a work in which many archaic mythic motifs reappear. The best known and only systematic attempt to demonstrate this is Hermann Gunkel's *Schöpfung und Chaos*.[18] S. H. Hooke went a step further and suggested "...that the general plan to which the apocalyptic visions conform is based on the early myth and ritual pattern referred to [of the ancient East], and is evidence for its persistence long after the social structure and outlook of the early civilizations which had given birth to it had decayed and passed away."[19] Unfortunately, Hooke's attempt to demonstrate this remains on the most general level and is very brief--less than two pages are devoted to the book of Revelation![20]

But Hooke's intuition was in fact correct with regard to the book of Revelation. The ancient mythic pattern discussed above, which was still current in the early Imperial period, is clearly discernible in Revelation.

In the discussion of the structure of Revelation in Chapter I, it was argued that the five series of visions in the body of the book (4-22:5) recapitulate the same eschatological pattern involving persecution of the faithful, punishment of the nations, i.e., the adversaries of God and his people, followed by salvation of the elect.[21] There are a number of proleptic, elliptic and veiled events in the earlier series which are only comprehensible as allusions to events described in greater detail in the later series.[22] This state of affairs is

paralleled by the fact that the pattern of the combat myth is
reflected in each series; in a fragmentary way in the earlier
series, but in a quite detailed and striking manner in the last
two series.

The Pattern in the First Series of Visions
The Heavenly Scene and the Scroll

H. P. Müller's study of the mythological and OT background
of Revelation 5:1-5 concentrates primarily on discerning a
tradition-critical pattern characteristic of the motif of the
"himmlische Ratsversammlung."[23] Müller finds this pattern in
Rev 5:1-5, Isaiah 6, 1 Kings 22, the legend of Keret from
Ugarit, and a number of Mesopotamian texts. The pattern consists of three elements:

1. A question addressed by the divine king to the
   assembled gods, seeking a volunteer for a specific
   task
2. Bewilderment of the assembled gods
3. Commission of the volunteer

The question of the angel in Rev 5:2--"Who is worthy to
open the scroll and to break its seals?"--reflects the first
element (cf. Isa 6:8). The second element is expressed in the
statement that no one was able to open the scroll and in the
seer's reaction (5:3-4). The third element appears in the
elder's designation of the one "worthy" of the task (5:5).

Müller's study is helpful in its demonstration that Revelation 4-5 can be interpreted in an illuminating way in the context of the ancient motif of the assembly of the gods. His
emphasis on the traditio-critical pattern, however, prevented
him from realizing the full potential of his approach. In his
discussion of the Myth of Zu, Müller notes the parallel with
Rev 5:1-5 with regard to the three point pattern mentioned
above, but does not note other important points of contact.[24]
He returns to this myth in a footnote near the end of his article and briefly indicates what light it might cast on Revelation 5.[25]

The first way in which Müller's work should be supplement-
ed is to note that in at least two of the texts which reflect

the pattern he has isolated, the task involved is doing battle
with the rebellious chaos beast. In the Myth of Zu, Anu asks
the gods of the land, "Which of the gods shall slay Zu?"[26] The
question form does not appear in the *Enuma elish*, but the pattern is reflected in Anshar's request to several gods in turn
to do battle with Tiamat.[27]

The second point to be noted is that in both of these
texts, the rebellion of the chaos beast involves the Tablets of
Fate or Tablets of Destinies. Kingship over the gods, and thus
universal power, seem to be linked to the possession of these
tablets.[28] Tiamat set up Kingu as king of the gods to replace
her slain consort Apsu. She elevated him in rank in various
ways and then said:

> "I have cast for thee the spell, exalting thee in
>   the Assembly of the gods.
> To counsel all the gods I have given thee full power.
> Verily, thou art supreme, my only consort art thou!
> Thy utterance shall prevail over all the Anunnaki!"

The text continues:

> She gave him the Tablets of Fate, fastened on his breast:
> "As for thee thy command shall be unchangeable, [Thy
>   word] shall endure!"
> As soon as Kingu was elevated, possessed of [the rank
>   of Anu],
> For the gods, his (variant: her) sons, [they decreed]
>   the fate:
> "Your word shall make the fire subside,
> Shall humble the 'Power-Weapon,' so potent in (its)
>   sweep!"[29]

When Marduk agreed to do battle with Tiamat, his condition
was that he be given the power over the fates, i.e., the kingship over the gods which Kingu had usurped. He addressed
Anshar:

> "Creator of the gods, destiny of the great gods,
> If I indeed as your avenger,
> Am to vanquish Tiamat and save your lives,
> Set up the Assembly, proclaim supreme my destiny!
> When jointly in Ubshukinna (the Assembly Hall) you have
>   sat down rejoicing,
> Let my word, instead of you, determine the fates.
> Unalterable shall be what I may bring into being;
> Neither recalled nor changed shall be the command
>   of my lips."[30]

When Marduk had defeated Tiamat and Kingu, he "took from him the Tablets of Fate, not rightfully his, sealed them with a seal and fastened (them) on his breast."[31] After creating the cosmos from the carcass of Tiamat, Marduk gave the Tablet of Destinies, which he had taken from Kingu, to Anu. But it is Marduk who is subsequently king of the gods in Anu's stead.[32]

In the Myth of Zu, the link between possession of the Tablets of Destinies and Enlilship, or kingship over the gods, is equally clear. The bird-god Zu, apparently associated with the underworld,[33] expresses his plan of rebellion as follows:

> "I will take the divine tablets of destinies, I,
> And the decrees of all the gods I will rule!
> I will make firm my throne and be the master of the norms,
> I will direct the totality of all the Igigi."[34]

The ending of this myth is still unknown, but by analogy with the *Enuma elish*, one can surmise that the god who ultimately defeated Zu took possession of the tablets and became king of the gods.

This association of dominion with a written document does not appear in the OT passages cited by Müller which reflect the motif of the divine council (Isaiah 6, 1 Kings 22). Daniel 7 also reflects the divine council motif and involves written documents as well: "...the court sat in judgment and the books were opened" (Dan 7:10).[35] This combination of motifs is also present in Revelation 4-5, where the Lamb is allowed to open the scroll with the seven seals.

The ancient mythic idea of heavenly books or tablets is present in the Biblical and apocryphal literature in a variety of forms. There is some overlap, but it seems that these forms can be categorized into three basic types:

1. A list of names in heaven which contains the names of the righteous or the elect destined for salvation
2. Books or heavenly tablets where all the deeds of human beings are recorded; these books will be the basis of the eschatological judgment
3. Books or heavenly tablets which decree, predict and/or control future events[36]

The books of Dan 7:10 are not explicitly identified. Since, however, the scene is described as a court sitting in judgment, it is likely that they are books of judgment in which deeds are recorded (type 2). The Animal Apocalypse (1 Enoch 85-90), roughly contemporary with Daniel 7, also contains a judgment scene where books are opened (90:20). One aspect of this judgment is the condemnation of the seventy "shepherds" into whose care Israel had been entrusted (90:22-23, 25). These "shepherds" are most likely heavenly beings, since human beings are regularly depicted as animals in this work. These heavenly beings are associated with various political powers, since it is said that they delivered the sheep to wild beasts (89:65-68, 90:2-18). These wild beasts are clearly the nations to which Israel had been subjected from the Babylonians to the Seleucids. One of the books opened at the judgment is the record kept, presumably by another heavenly being, of the deeds of the seventy shepherds (89:61-64, 70-71). This record is to be a testimony against the shepherds (89:63). Completed portions are sealed (89:71), presumably to preserve them intact until the judgment.

The similarity of the four beasts in Daniel 7, representing four kingdoms ranging from Babylon to the Seleucids, to the seventy shepherds in the Animal Apocalypse is evident. In both cases the Babylonians are represented by one or more lions (cf. Dan 7:4 with 1 Enoch 89:65-67). This analogy makes it quite likely that the books in Dan 7:10 are books of judgment (type 2).

The other two types of heavenly books are mentioned in Daniel as well. The first type, the list of the names of the righteous elect, occurs in 12:1. Those whose names are in "the book" will be delivered from the time of trouble at the end. The third type, books which contain the events of the future, occurs in 10:21. An angel, probably Gabriel (cf. 9:21), tells Daniel that he will reveal to him what is inscribed in the book of truth. This remark characterizes the narrative of eschatological events which follows (11:2-12:4) as the content of this book of truth (cf. 11:2).

Revelation 4-5 differs from Daniel 7 in that the former is not described as a judgment scene. The scroll with the seven seals is not explicitly identified. Daniel 7 may be the model for Revelation 4-5, since they share the setting in the divine council and the juxtaposition of an enthroned high god with a second heavenly figure who is being inaugurated into some sort of office.[37] In Daniel 7 the office is clearly kingship. In Revelation 5 the nature of the office is not so clear. A number of exegetes have argued that Revelation 5 is an enthronement scene.[38] The implication of this line of interpretation is that the office is kingship. But W. C. van Unnik has shown that this interpretation is not very well supported by the text. A number of details one would expect to find if it were an enthronement scene are lacking, e.g., royal symbols such as a sceptre or crown, mention of the Lamb's elevation or enthronement, or even some indication of a change in the Lamb's status.[39] The acclamation of 5:9-10 describes the work already accomplished by the Lamb. The only change or new element introduced in Revelation 5 is the acclamation of the Lamb's worthiness for the act of opening the scroll. The other acclamations (5:12, 13) are quite general and certainly do not ascribe kingship to the Lamb explicitly.

But there is a good analogue to Revelation 4-5 in the *Enuma elish*. Marduk appears before the assembly of the gods after he has agreed to battle Tiamat, but before the combat has taken place.[40] He is proclaimed king, enthroned and vested. Even though he does not yet possess the Tablets of Fate, the gods say, "...Thy decree is unrivaled, thy command is Anu" (IV:4).

The restraint with regard to kingship language in Revelation 5 is puzzling in view of the chapter's similarity on other points to the pattern of the combat myth, and especially in light of the explicit references to the enthronement and kingdom of Christ elsewhere in the book (3:21, 11:15, 12:5). The explanation seems to lie in the particular structuring principle used by the author. Revelation does not simply reflect the pattern of the combat myth as found in any particular mythic text. Rather, the pattern is used in a cyclical, recapitulatory way, as will be shown below. Revelation 4-5 introduces the first series of visions (4:1-8:5) as well as the entire first great cycle of visions (4:1-11:19). The combat-victory is described for the first time in this first great cycle in

11:18. In connection with that victory the kingship of Christ
is proclaimed (11:15). Thus, the lack of explicit kingship
language in ch. 5 is due to the fact that the Lamb's appropria-
tion of the scroll is only a proleptic establishment of his
kingship over the world, though the praise accorded him by
"every Creature" (5:13) shows that the full establishment of
that kingship is not in doubt. The enthronement of Christ in
3:21 is best explained as a reference to the kingship of Christ
in heaven, similar to the sense of 12:5 and 10.

Thus, even though the kingship of the Lamb in Revelation 5
is a qualified one, the scroll with the seven seals does reflect the ancient motif of the Tablets of Fate which symbolize
power to rule.

The scroll with the seven seals has other associations as
well. The Tablets of Fate in Mesopotamia represented the order
in the cosmos expressed both in nature and in legitimate rule.
When Zu stole the tablets, "The norms were suspended."[41] The
victory of Marduk is followed by creation.[42] The motif of the
fertility of the restored order is not absent in Revelation as
we shall see below. But the scroll of ch. 5 is more directly
related to the later apocalyptic development of the myth of
heavenly tablets, i.e., the book which decrees future events
(type 3). This is evident from the effects of the opening of
the book: the revelation of the events of the end-time.

A further distinctive element in Revelation 5 has been
elucidated by van Unnik.[43] This is the use of the term *axios*
in connection with the opening of the scroll (5:2, 9). Van
Unnik has shown that the term was widely used in the Graeco-
Roman world in the context of regulating the approach to the
sacred. One had to be tested or initiated before approaching
holy or esoteric books and other objects, or before being ad-
mitted to sacred ceremonies or a holy community. As a close
parallel to Revelation 5, he cites Wis 3:1-8 where worthiness
results from passing the test of suffering and death.[44] The
hymnic passage of Rev 5:9-10 defines the Lamb's worthiness as
the result of his atoning death. Thus the motif in Revelation
5 is well grounded in the Christian kerygma and its interpretation of worthiness has Jewish precedent. But like the pattern

of the combat myth, the prerequisite of "worthiness" for approaching a sacred book is language which would have been meaningful to any reader in the Graeco-Roman world.

The Seven Seals

The pattern of the combat myth is present in fragmentary
form in the first series of visions (4-8:5). The opening
scene, chs. 4-5, reflects various elements of the combat myth,
as was shown above. In the visions associated with the opening
of the seven seals, four elements of the mythic pattern are
present.

The first occurs in the vision following the fifth seal,
which describes the souls of those who have been slain for the
word of God and for the witness they had held (6:9-11). This
indirect reference to persecution expresses the element of
Threat, element (a) in Hanson's schema. The persecution theme
is directly linked to the chaos beast in 13:7, "Also it was
allowed to make war on the saints and to conquer them."

The second element is related to the opening of the sixth
seal, which is followed by cosmic disturbances (6:12-14).
These cosmic disturbances reflect the Theophany of the Divine
Warrior, Hanson's element (c), Cross's (b). The quaking of the
earth and the flattening of mountains are typical motifs in
such theophanies.[45] Darkening of the sun, moon and stars is
associated with Yahweh's battle with the dragon (identified
with Pharoah) in Ezek 32:1-8. Rev 6:13-14 is an allusion to
Isa 34:3-4 which is a war song reflecting the ancient combat
myth.[46] These cosmic disturbances are a proleptic revelation
of "the great day of their [enthroned one and the Lamb, cf.
chs. 4-5] wrath" (6:17). The actual Combat-Victory is not described in this series.

The third element appears immediately following the theophany of 6:12-17, i.e., the Salvation [of the faithful], element (d) in Hanson's schema. The 144,000 of 7:1-8 are saved by
the protection of a divine seal from the plagues against earth
and sea (7:2-3). The multitude of 7:9-17 is described in a
heavenly scene of victory and bliss subsequent to the "great
tribulation" (7:14). The fourth element, the Fertility of the

Restored Order--Hanson's element (e), Cross's (d)--is reflected
in vss. 16-17. Hunger, thirst and the scorching heat of the
sun will not disturb them; the Lamb will guide them to springs
of living water.

The pattern as reflected in the first series of visions in
Revelation thus has the following elements (using the elements
of Hanson's schema):

a. Threat (6:9-11)
c. Theophany of the Divine Warrior (6:12-17)
d. Salvation (7:1-15)
e. Fertility of the Restored Order (7:16-17)

The Pattern in the Second Series of Visions

The pattern of the combat myth is also reflected in the
series of visions associated with the seven trumpets. The
first element--the Threat--is present in a veiled manner. Os-
tensibly, the events following the fifth and sixth trumpets are
plagues like those following the first four trumpets. It is
evident, however, that the first four trumpets involve plagues
against the natural world, while the fifth and sixth are directed against humanity. It was pointed out in Chapter I that the
sixth seal (9:13-19) is a veiled allusion to the battle described more fully in the sixth bowl (16:12-16) and in the last
series of visions (19:19-21).[47] For those readers familiar
with the Nero legend, the reference to the river Euphrates as
the place of origin of the cavalry (9:14-16) would call to mind
the expectation that Nero would return from Parthia with an
army.[48] The sixth trumpet thus reveals proleptically the appearance of Nero as Antichrist, and so functions as Threat (for
the elect) in a veiled manner.

Four further elements of the combat pattern are present in
summary form in the heavenly acclamations of 11:15, 17-18.
First, in 11:15 loud voices proclaim, "The kingdom of the world
has become the kingdom of our Lord and of his Christ, and he
shall reign for ever and ever." This proclamation corresponds
to the mythic element of the Victory Shout, Hanson's element
(f). The scene in the *Enuma elish* in the divine assembly following Marduk's victory over Tiamat is similar:

Being [assem]bled, all the Igigi bowed down,
While everyone of the Anunnaki kissed his feet,
[...] their assembly to do obeisance,
They stood [before h]im, bowed (and said:) "He is the
    king!"[49]

This proclamation of kingship (Rev 11:15) is repeated by the
twenty-four elders in vs. 17, "We give thanks...that thou hast
taken thy great power and begun to reign."

Second, the Combat-Victory is briefly related in vs. 18,
"The nations raged, but thy wrath came, and the time...for destroying the destroyers of the earth." Third, the Salvation of
the faithful is described in the same verse, "...[and the time
came] for rewarding thy servants, the prophets and saints, and
those who fear thy name, both small and great...."

Fourth, the Theophany of the Divine Warrior is transformed
in 11:19 into a theophanic revelation of the ark of the covenant in the heavenly temple. Besides the earthquake, the theophanic elements particularly characteristic of the storm god
are present here: lightning, thunder and hail.[50]

The pattern of the combat myth is thus reflected in the
series of visions associated with the seven trumpets by the
following elements:

a. Threat (9:13-19)
f. Victory Shout (11:15, 17)
b. Combat-Victory (11:18a,d)
d. Salvation (11:18c)
c. Theophany (11:19)

The Pattern in the Third Series of Visions

The third series of vision accounts consists of 12:1-15:4.
In the discussion of ch. 12, it was pointed out that the entire
pattern of the combat myth is present in that chapter.[51] The
significance of that fact will be discussed below.

The rest of the series of visions also reflects the pattern in capsule form. Ch. 13 clearly expresses the Threat element. The chaos beast from the sea, identified with Nero redivivus, threatens the faithful with persecution. This is explicit in vss. 7 and 9-10. The chaos beast from the land also
threatens the elect in that it has the power to cause those who

refuse to worship the beast to be slain (vs. 15). Again the
persecution is interpreted as the threat of chaos.

It was pointed out earlier that 14:14-20 is a proleptic
and veiled description of the battle of 19:11-21. Thus 14:14-
20 expresses the element of Combat-Victory in an allusive way.
Finally, 15:2-4 reflects the element of Salvation in that it
describes those who have conquered in heaven before the throne
of God.[52] It is a more concise version of the scene depicted
in 7:9-17.

Thus the mythic pattern as reflected in 13:1-15:4 is as
follows:

    a. Threat (13:1-18 especially vss. 7, 9-10, 15)
    b. Combat-Victory (14:14-20)
    d. Salvation (15:2-4)

The Pattern in the Fourth Series of Visions

The fourth series of visions consists of the seven bowls
and associated visions plus the Babylon appendix. The pattern
of the combat myth is present in a very fragmentary form in the
seven bowls, but the entire pattern is clearly present in the
Babylon appendix (17:1-19:10).

The Seven Bowls

The vision following the sixth bowl (16:12-16) describes
preparations for a great battle. The description of the beast
(Nero) assembling kings from the East for battle, as well as
mention of the Euphrates, would call the legend of Nero's return to mind for the first readers.[53] Thus this passage alludes proximately to the prediction of Nero's destruction of
Rome in 17:16-17, and ultimately to the battle between Christ
and Nero redivivus in 19:11-21. Since only the preparations
for battle are described here, this passage reflects the Threat
element.

The cosmic disturbances which follow the pouring out of
the seventh bowl reflect the Theophany of the Divine Warrior.
Here the elements of the storm god's theophany present in 11:19
are combined with the more general cosmic disturbances mentioned in 6:12-14. The statement *gegonen* in 16:17 reflects

very tersely the Victory Shout, while vs. 19 is a capsule description of Combat-Victory.

Thus the pattern as reflected in the seven bowls consists of the following elements:

a. Threat (16:12-16)
f. Victory Shout (16:17)
c. Theophany (16:18, 20-21)
b. Combat-Victory (16:19)

The Babylon Appendix

a. *Threat.* In the Babylon appendix, it should be noted first of all that much of ch. 17 is devoted to depicting the threat posed by the beast and the harlot. Vs. 3 describes the beast as full of blasphemous names. This motif recalls the description of the activity of the beast from the sea in 13: 5-7. There blasphemy is one element in the rebellion of the chaos beast against heaven, described in terms reminiscent of Daniel 7-8 and whose roots are ultimately in the ancient combat myth.[54] Thus the beast of 17:3 manifests a threat against God himself. In view of the discussion of the signification of the beast above, it is clear that this rebellion, this resurgence of chaos, is ascribed to the Roman empire. In 17:6 it is said that the woman was drunk with the blood of the saints and of the martyrs of Jesus. Here a threat is also expressed; this time in an explicit reference to persecution. As the rebellion of the beast from the sea involved making war on the saints (13:7), so also here; chaos is manifested in persecution. Finally, the threat is expressed in the *parousia* of the beast (predicted in 17:8) and his assembling the ten kings as allies in preparation for making war on the Lamb (vss. 12-13).

b. *Combat-Victory.* The Combat-Victory is described in 17:14--"They will make war on the Lamb, and the Lamb will conquer them...." It is evident that in ch. 17 two battles and thus two victories are described. The first is the one just mentioned, the battle between the Lamb on the one hand, and the beast and his allies on the other. Vs. 14 seems to be a proleptic reference to the great battle described in 19:19-20. The various formulations of the threat (17:3, 6, 8, 12-13) are followed by an assurance of ultimate victory (17:14). The second battle mentioned is the attack of the beast and his allies on the harlot, which, as was indicated above, reflects the expectation of Nero's return with Parthian allies to regain possession of Rome.[55] If the beast is to be defeated by the Lamb and cast into the lake of fire (17:14, 19:20), then this battle against Rome must take place before the beast's battle with the Lamb. This observation led Charles to suggest "that the text is deranged and composite--being based on two Sources." He suggested that the proper order of the last part of the chapter is vss. 11-13, 17, 16, 14.[56] Whatever the materials may have been with which the apocalyptist was working, the reason for the arrangement of these verses is clear from the context. Ch. 18 is a collection of rather disparate material which both mourns and celebrates the fall of Babylon. Immediately preceding the introduction to this collection (18:1) is the prediction in veiled terms of the destruction of Rome by Nero and the Parthian kings (17:16-17). 17:18 clarifies just who this harlot is. The destruction of Rome is thus to precede the second coming of Christ as divine warrior. For this reason, the reference to the battle with the Lamb is placed first in proleptic fashion, so that vss. 16-18 could serve as the chronological introduction to ch. 18.

c. *Victory Shout*. Even though the fall of Babylon does not result from the battle of the Lamb, it is brought about by God as part of his purpose (17:17). Thus it is celebrated with a Victory Shout in 18:1-3: "Fallen, fallen is Babylon the great!" The Victory Shout is picked up again in 19:1-5. The victory is celebrated as an expression of the glory and power of God (vs. 1) and of his just judgment (vs. 2). It is seen as vengeance for the blood of those fallen in persecution (vs. 2). The character of this section as victory shout is perhaps most vividly expressed in 19:3--"Hallelujah! The smoke from her goes up for ever and ever."

In 19:6 we find an acclamation of kingship: "Alleluia, for the Lord [our] God, the Pantocrator, reigns (*ebasileusen*)." This element is a typical form taken by the victory shout.[57]

In part of the passage of the *Enuma elish* listed by Hanson as
the manifestation of Marduk's reign, it is said that Anu placed
the royal throne before the assembly of the gods. They pronounce among themselves a curse. Then it is said, "When they
had granted him [Marduk] the exercise of kingship of the gods,
they confirmed him in dominion over the gods of heaven and
earth."[58] Both Rev 19:6 and the *Enuma elish* passage come under
the category of enthronement.[59] The enthronement motif in acclamation form appears in the Baal cycle: "Thou'lt take thine
eternal kingdom, Thine everlasting dominion."[60] Compare Exod
15:18, "Yahweh will reign forever and ever."[61] The acclamation
of kingship is part of element (c) of Cross's formulation of
the pattern: The warrior-god returns to take up kingship and is
enthroned on his mountain (cf. Exod 15:17).

d. *Sacred Marriage.* The next element in the pattern
reflected in Rev 17:1-19:10 is the *hieros gamos.* It appears in
19:7 with the announcement that the marriage of the Lamb has
come.[62] This element is not specifically mentioned in the
studies of Cross and Hanson. The reason it is not mentioned
seems to be twofold. First, the sacred marriage does not occur
in the available forms of the *Enuma elish.* Second, this particular motif does not appear in the OT passages which reflect
the pattern of the combat myth. But the motif does seem to
have exercised some influence on Israelite-Jewish religion.[63]
Although the sacred marriage is not mentioned in the *Enuma
elish*, there is evidence that it formed part of the celebration
of the New Year festival, at least at certain periods.[64] A
number of Sumerian texts have been preserved which seem to be
related to the cultic practice of sacred marriage.[65] A ritual
of sacred marriage was associated with victory in combat at the
Edfu festival of ancient Egypt.[66]

Actually, the sacred marriage is one specific aspect of
one of the typical elements of the ancient mythic pattern,
namely, the fertility which follows the Combat-Victory and/or
the establishment of the kingship of the god. The sacred marriage as a form or symbol of fertility is attested in the Ugaritic texts. A number of commentators agree that such an interpretation should be given to a passage which describes the

lovemaking of Baal and Anat. A second passage probably belongs
with that one, which describes the birth of offspring to the
divine couple.[67] There is less agreement on a second text. It
describes Baal's mating with a cow or heifer who bears him offspring. Given the similarity of this text to the one just discussed, it should very likely be taken as a reference to Baal's
powers of fertility which have a cosmic significance.[68] A
third mythic passage, "The Birth of the Gods Dawn and Dusk,"
involves El's seduction of two goddesses. Kapelrud believes
that the text was used cultically in connection with the *hieros
gamos*, probably during the New Year festival.[69] There has been
speculation that two legendary texts might have been associated
with the cultic practice of sacred marriage. In any case, they
illustrate the importance of the marriage theme and its association with fertility at Ugarit.[70]

e. *Banquet*. Finally, the marriage supper of the Lamb
(19:9) corresponds to the Banquet, element (h) in the pattern
isolated by Hanson. The Banquet motif is also part of the
ritual pattern of the Baal cycle, where it follows temple
building as in the *Enuma elish*.[71]

The mythic pattern then as manifested in Rev 17:1-19:10 is
as follows:

a. Threat (17:3, 6, 8, 12-13)
b. Combat-Victory (17:14)
f. Victory Shout (18:1-3, 19:1-5, 19:6)
e. Fertility/Sacred Marriage (19:7)
h. Banquet (19:9)

The Pattern in the Fifth and Last Series of Visions
Theophany of the Divine Warrior

The last series of visions in the book of Revelation (19:
11-22:5) opens with the Theophany of the Divine Warrior and his
heavenly armies (19:11-16). The allusion to Isa 63:1-6 in 19:
13 and 15 is evidence of the link between this passage and older divine warrior hymns. Isa 63:1-6 itself is already an eschatological transformation of the archaic hymns.[72] It still
manifests the archaic motif of the "March in the South."[73] *Ta
strateumata [ta] en tō ouranō* (19:14) reflects the epithet

yahwęh 'ᵉlōhê ṣᵉbā'ôt, which belongs to the archaic holy war tradition.[74] This motif seems to have a background in the hosts of El and Baal.[75]

Banquet

In Rev 19:17-18, 21b we find a quite different formulation of the banquet motif from that of 19:9. Here *to deipnon to mega tou theou* (19:17) consists of a feast for birds on the flesh of kings, captains, etc., of all the enemies about to be slain by the divine warrior. The passage has a clear relation to Ezek 39:17-20 where the eschatological battle is to be followed by a feast for the birds of every sort and the beasts of the field on the flesh of the mighty, the blood of the princes of the earth. In the Ezekiel passage the banquet is explicitly referred to as a sacrificial feast; the bodies of the mighty and the princes are equated with rams, lambs, goats etc. (vs. 18). The same equivalence is made in Isa 34:1-7 of the nations to be slain by the divine warrior, of their corpses and blood with the fat and blood of sacrificial animals. Isa 34:7 makes clear that this sacrificial banquet has roots in the conception of fertility following victory in combat: "...Their land shall be soaked with blood, and their soil made rich with fat."[76] The Ugaritic text which describes Anat's slaughter of "picked fighters," her wading in their blood, and then bathing in dew, rain and fatness of the earth is relevant here.[77] Her attack on Mot is also of interest:

> She seizes the Godly Mot--
>   With sword she doth cleave him
> With fan she doth winnow him--
>   With fire she doth burn him.
> With hand-mill she grinds him--
>   In the field she doth sow him.
> Birds eat his remnants,
>   Consuming his portions,
>   Flitting from remnant to remnant.[78]

The fertility aspect is clear here. Mot, who represents or personifies death and sterility, is slain and sown as grain.[79]

Threat and Combat-Victory

In this last vision series there are three instances of Combat-Victory: 19:19-21a, 20:1-3 and 20:7-10. The first and

third, 19:19 and 20:8-9a, depict the Threat, while 19:20-21a
and 20:9b-10 describe the Combat-Victory. The second passage
is the most archaic. In the ancient combat myth the victorious
god often confined his defeated foe to the earth as opposed
to heaven, in the underworld, at the foot of or under a mountain or volcano.[80] Note, for example, how Anat treats the
dragon, presumably after defeating him:

> In the land of Mḫnm he (the dragon) swirled the sea
> His double tongue licked the heavens;
> His double tail swirled the sea.
> She fixed the unmuzzled dragon;
> She bound him to the heights of Leba[non].[81]

Manifestation of Kingship

The element of the Manifestation of Kingship or Universal
Reign takes the form of the messianic reign (20:4-6) in this
series of visions. Here the ancient concept of the life-giving
power of the king is expressed in resurrection language rather
than fertility language.

Fertility of the Restored Order and Sacred Marriage

The motif of the Fertility of the Restored Order is present in the last series of visions in a variety of ways. In
21:2, 9 the fertility motif takes the form of the Sacred Marriage. The function of this motif in the context of this last
series of visions will be further discussed below.

The fertility motif is also present in the form of creation (21:1). The victory of Marduk over Tiamat is followed in
the *Enuma elish* by his creation of heaven and earth.[82] The
combats of Baal and Anat are cosmogonic.[83]

The river of the water of life and the tree of life in
22:1-2 also express the fertility theme.[84]

The statement in 21:1 *kai hē thalassa ouk estin eti* is a
particularly archaic motif. This remark in the context of a
new creation evidences the consciousness that Sea (= Yamm) is
somehow the adversary of order. It goes beyond the ancient
mythic texts in its presupposition that the adversary will be
completely annihilated. In the *Enuma elish*, Tiamat is not

annihilated; rather her body is the stuff from which the cosmos
is created.[85] When Baal overcomes Yamm with the clubs Kothar
wa-Khasis fashioned for him, he is inclined to annihilate his
foe. But Ashtoreth rebukes him:

> "'For shame, O Puissant [Baal];
>   For shame, O Rider of the Clouds!
> For our captive is Prin[ce Yamm],
>   Our captive is Judge Nahar.'
> As [the word] left [her mouth],
>   Puissant Baal was ashamed..."[86]

The text is too fragmentary to be read from this point on, but
apparently Yamm was not annihilated. Elsewhere, when victory
over Yamm is described, terms like "muzzling" and "binding" imply that he was limited in his power, but not utterly destroyed.[87]

In the OT both motifs of binding and slaying are present.
In Job 40:25-32 (41:1-8 RSV) Leviathan is described as God's
captive, as bound. In Isa 51:9 and Ps 74:13 the marine monster
is split or cut in pieces as was Tiamat. In the eschatological
passage T Levi 18, the binding motif reappears. The "new
priest" will bind Beliar (18:12). In 1 Enoch the wicked angels' fate is similar in part to that of Satan in Revelation.
In both cases the punishment is in two stages: first binding
and then eternal punishment in fire.[88] In 1 Enoch the binding
is primordial, whereas in Revelation, both the binding and
eternal punishment are eschatological.

The stark annihilation of the adversary implied by Rev
21:1 has a parallel in As Mos 10:1--"And then his kingdom shall
appear throughout all His creation, And then Satan shall be no
more, And sorrow shall depart with him."[89] The motif of the
destruction of Sea in Rev 21:1 then reflects the idea found in
at least one other apocalyptic text that the adversary (usually
Satan or evil) will be totally and utterly defeated. But the
fact that the adversary is designated as Sea shows that the
author of Revelation was in touch with some contemporary form
of the Semitic mythic pattern. It is unlikely that a statement
like Rev 21:1 could have been simply derived from the OT.

Temple-Building and Salvation

In the Mesopotamian and Ugaritic myths, the Combat-Victory is followed by the building of a temple for the victorious god, which is his possession and dwelling place and from which he will rule; Hanson's element (g), implied by Cross's (c). In the *Enuma elish* (V:121-30, VI:51-58, 70-73) there is an equivalence between the shrine of Marduk, Esagila or Esangil, and the city Babylon. The shrine of Marduk is not associated with a mountain, but it is called high, lofty and elevated because of its stagetower or ziggurat construction.[90] Its top reaches nearly to heaven.[91] This temple in Babylon has a cosmic significance in that it is the stopping place of the gods as they journey from their dwelling in the sweet waters under the earth (Apsu) to heaven for assemblies and back home again. Thus it is the point which unites the underworld, earth and heaven. So the temple of Marduk, and thus Babylon as well, is the center of the world.[92]

In the Ugaritic texts, probably after Baal has defeated Yamm and clearly only after obtaining leave from El, he commissions Kothar wa-Khasis to build him a temple-palace on Mt. Zaphon.[93] The Israelites apparently took over terms like "holy abode" and "mount of thy possession" from Canaanite oral literature to designate the various shrines of Yahweh. Finally this language was applied to Mount Zion, the temple mount, which took on cosmic characteristics.[94]

The element of Temple-Building appears in the last series of visions in Revelation in the form of the descent of the new Jerusalem (21:2, 9). There are a number of indications that the descent of the holy city fills the role of the establishment of the king-god's temple, even though it is explicitly said that it contains no temple (21:22). First of all, the association of Jerusalem with Mt. Zion and the temple, geographically, historically and traditionally means that each automatically carries connotations of the others in a symbolic context. Thus, even apart from the temple, Jerusalem is specially the abode of the Lord (cf. Ezek 48:35). Secondly, the temple derives much of its importance from the fact that the Lord dwells there, is enthroned there, and can be approached

by his devotees there.[95] The new Jerusalem functions in all
three of these ways (21:3; 22:1, 3b; 22:3c-4).

In 21:4 the new life in the presence of the Lord is described. This verse reflects a further element of the mythic
pattern, Salvation of the Gods, Hanson's element (d), which appears as the Salvation of Israel in Zech 9:11-13 and elsewhere.[96] This salvation is described in 21:4 with language
drawn from Isaiah. One of the passages alluded to is Isa 25:
6-8. There salvation is described in more directly mythical
terms. The Lord will swallow up death forever (25:8) as Mot
swallowed Baal.[97] The Lord's wiping away the tears of his
people is paralleled by his holding a great banquet on Mt.
Zion. In its present context, this banquet follows the Lord's
victory over an alien city (Isa 25:1-5).

A further indication that the new Jerusalem functions as
the temple once did is the fact that the Jerusalem appendix is
modeled in part on Ezekiel 40-48. The earlier prophet was carried by the hand of the Lord to a high mountain to view the
ideal city, which was to function as a model for the restoration (Ezek 40:1-2). So also John is carried by the Spirit to
a high mountain to observe the descent of the new Jerusalem
(Rev 21:10). "A man" appeared to Ezekiel to guide him through
the structure, carrying a measuring reed. John also has a
guide with a measuring rod.[98] The bulk of Ezekiel's vision
concerned the temple (40:5-47:12), while John's concerns only
the city. But a number of motifs from Ezekiel 40-48 are reflected in the Jerusalem appendix. That nothing unclean should
enter the city (Rev 21:27) reflects the concept of cultic pur-
ity particularly associated with the temple (cf. Ezek 43:7-9,
44:5-9). The river flowing from the throne and the leaves for
healing in Rev 22:1-2 reflect the river issuing from the temple
and the healing leaves of Ezek 47:1-12. It seems clear then
that all the salvific effects of life and fertility associated
with the sanctuaries of the gods in ancient myth and with the
temple in the OT are associated with the new Jerusalem in Revelation.

Sacred Marriage

In this last series of visions the transformed Temple-Building motif is combined in a unique way with the Sacred Marriage theme by the identification of the holy city with the bride of the Lamb (21:2, 9). There was of course already a long tradition of regarding cities as women or goddesses.[99] The particular cluster of motifs found here and their interrelationships seem best explained by supposing that one of the literary models of the Jerusalem appendix (and of 21:2 as well) was Isaiah 54. If we assume that the apocalyptist was familiar with this poem and considered it a prophetic promise addressed to Jerusalem, a number of elements in this vision are clarified. First of all, the identification of the bride of the Lamb with the new Jerusalem is analogous to the poetic image of Jerusalem as the Lord's spouse in Isa 54:5-8.[100] Secondly, the construction of the new Jerusalem out of precious materials may have been suggested by the promise of 54:11-12; "...I will set your stones in antimony, and lay your foundations with sapphires [or lapis lazuli]. I will make your pinnacles agate, your gates of carbuncles, and all your wall of precious stones."[101] That Isa 54:11-12 in particular may have had an influence on Rev 21:19-21 is supported by the fact that the text was apparently interpreted eschatologically at Qumran. In fragments of a commentary on Isaiah, it appears that the new Jerusalem was interpreted allegorically to refer to the "Congregation of His elect." The gates of carbuncles, for example, are interpreted as the leaders of the tribes of Israel.[102] The fact that the names of the twelve apostles of the Lamb are written on the twelve foundations of the city may be an indication that the new Jerusalem in Revelation is also symbolic of the (Christian) community.[103]

The mythic pattern then as manifested in Rev 19:11-22:5 is as follows:

c. Theophany of the Divine Warrior (19:11-16)
h. Banquet (19:17-18, 21b)
a. Threat (19:19, 20:8-9a)
b. Combat-Victory (19:20-21a, 20:1-3, 20:9b-10)
i. Manifestation of Kingship (20:4-6)

e. Fertility of the Restored Order (21:1, 22:1-2)
   as Sacred Marriage (21:2, 9)
g. "Temple"-Building (21:2, 21:9-27)
d. Salvation (21:4)

Revelation 12 as Paradigm of the Book of Revelation

Ch. 12 has a pivotal position in the book, first of all, because it is a midpoint structurally speaking as the introduction to the second great cycle of visions. It is pivotal also because it makes explicit for the first time that the combat myth is the conceptual framework which underlies the book as a whole. Satan is mentioned five times in the seven messages.[104] This fact is already an indication that the author is working within a dualistic framework. In the first great cycle of visions (4:1-11:19), there are indications that the pattern of the combat myth is a structuring principle. But there is no clarity about the nature of the adversary. In the first series the Threat is expressed by a reference to persecution but the agents of the persecution are not mentioned (6:9-11). The Theophany of that series (6:12-17) seems to be directed against the kings of the earth, among others (6:15), a general reference which neither clarifies the historical situation addressed, if any, nor the mythic context of the passage. The situation is much the same in the second series. The Threat (9:1-11, 13-19) is veiled and mysterious. The Combat-Victory (11:18a,d) is against the nations. The abrupt and unprepared appearance of the beast from the abyss in 11:7 is the first unmistakable indication that the mythic context in which these visions must be understood is the combat myth, involving the rebellion and defeat of the chaos beast.[105] This reference, however, is allusive rather than elucidating. It serves to increase suspense and point ahead. In chs. 13 and 17 it becomes clear that the combat myth is being used to interpret a religious-political conflict. The chaos beast/Antichrist is a mythicized Roman emperor.[106]

The mythic context of combat and chaos is first systematically introduced in ch. 12. At this crucial point the author mentions Satan for the first time in the visions and identifies

him with the chaos beast par excellence, the dragon (12:9).
This identification shows that for the author of Revelation the
threat of the Roman empire is not a random, accidental or isolated event. The disorder experienced is not due to the whim
of one or more evil human beings. Rather, the persecution
facing the author and his first readers is part of a universal
and systematic rebellion of chaos against order. The epithet
ho ophis ho archaios applied to Satan in 12:9 alludes to the
serpent of Gen 3:1, and thus indicates that the conflict began
in primordial time.

The paradigmatic character of Revelation 12 for the book
as a whole may be illustrated in terms of the pattern of the
combat myth. That pattern is repeated in each series of visions and in fullest form at the end. Such repetition is characteristic of mythic language and is an indication that the
structure of the events narrated is the "message," rather than
the particular details of any one story or image.[107] The over-
coming of the Threat, the defeat of chaos and the re-establish-
ing of order is thus the fundamental significance of each of
the cycles of visions and of Revelation as a whole. The paradigmatic nature of ch. 12 is evident in the fact that the pattern of the combat myth is reflected in quite full form within
this single chapter. The following elements of the pattern are
present in Revelation 12:

a. Threat (vss. 3-4)
d. Salvation (vss. 5-6)
b. Combat-Victory (vss. 7-9)
f. Victory Shout (vss. 10-12)

The attack of the dragon on the woman (vss. 3-4) reflects
and interprets the experience of the author (in this case redactor) and his community. It is homologous with the other
images expressive of Threat in the book: the attack of the
dragon on the seed of the woman (12:17), the war of the beast
on the saints (13:7, 9-10), the persecution of the saints by
the harlot (17:6), and the persecution alluded to in 6:9-11.
The wars waged by the beast and his allies on the Lamb and by
Satan on the saints during the messianic reign seem to be projections of the fundamental experience of persecution. These
projections draw heavily upon mythic images as does Rev 12:3-4.

It was shown (in Chapter III) that Revelation 12, in its redacted form, makes use of the combat myth to interpret a situation of persecution. The issue is no longer seen as a national struggle between the Jews and Rome, but as a more individualized conflict in which the possibility of martyrdom is emphasized. This shift in perspective is expressed by the reference to the dragon's making war on the rest of the woman's "seed" (vs. 17) and especially by the allusion to earthly trials and executions in the hymnic composition (vs. 11). The way in which the combat myth functions in ch. 12 is characteristic of Revelation as a whole.

In ch. 13, as noted earlier, the Roman empire, particularly as represented by Nero, is depicted as the chaos beast rebelling against God himself. That rebellion includes hostile actions toward the saints (vs. 7). Ch. 13:9-10 breaks out of the vision form with an allusion to Jer 15:2: "If any one is to be taken captive, to captivity he goes; if any one is to be slain with the sword, with the sword he must be slain."[108] This allusion is framed by two direct addresses to the readers: "If any one has an ear, let him hear," and "This is the endurance and the faith of the saints." The former is a formula used repeatedly in the messages to the seven churches and would thus be an especially clear signal for a direct, hortatory address to the readers.

This allusion to Jeremiah implies that the stance which the readers are encouraged to adopt is one of passive resistance. This impression is reinforced by the fact that the imagery of combat is used in such a way as to exclude the people from any active role in battle. In contrast to the Qumran War Scroll, the people are not expected to take part in the eschatological battle.

But the faithful are allowed some role in bringing about the eschatological fulfillment. The role of the people is illuminated already in the fifth seal (6:9-11). The souls under the altar ask the holy and true ruler, "How long until you will pass judgment and avenge our blood upon those who dwell upon the earth?" (vs. 10). They are told that they have only a little time to wait, until the number of their fellow servants,

who are to be killed as they have been, is complete (vs. 11).
This dialogue is important in two ways for understanding how
the combat myth functions in Revelation. First of all it indicates that the divine victory in the combat, which involves the
defeat of the adversary and his allies as well as the destruction of the earth, is interpreted as divine judgment and vengeance for the deaths of the martyrs. Secondly, if there is a
fixed number of martyrs who must meet their deaths before the
end can come, then each martyr's death brings the eschaton
closer. This idea is a non-violent kind of synergism which
contrasts with the Zealot policy of fighting to bring in the
kingdom.[109] It is similar to the theology of the Assumption of
Moses, where the voluntary deaths of Taxo and his sons in effect bring about the manifestation of the Kingdom of God.[110]

The combat myth in Revelation thus functions to reinforce
resistance to Rome and to inspire willingness for martyrdom.
It does this by depicting for the readers the ultimate resolution of the conflict in which they are involved, i.e., their
own ultimate salvation and the eventual defeat and destruction
of their adversaries.

Reading or hearing the book of Revelation would provide a
proleptic experience of victory. We noted in Chapter I that
Revelation was probably read in the worship service. The locus
then for this preliminary experience of victory was probably
the cult. A further observation supports this theory. In the
discussion of recapitulation in Chapter I, it was noted that
most of the recurring visions of the salvation of the faithful
involve a liturgical setting. It is striking that every vision
of salvation which *precedes* the depiction of the final battle
(19:11-20:3) involves a liturgical element, while those which
follow do not (20:4-6, 21:1-22:5). This apparent distinction
between the present, proleptic experience of salvation and the
future, ultimate salvation, suggests that the liturgy was the
locus of the proleptic experience of salvation in the communities of the author and his first readers. It was in that context that fellowship with God and the Lamb was experienced in a
preliminary form and that the hope for a more complete eschatological salvation was articulated and nurtured.

CHAPTER V

[1]See the discussion in Sigmund Mowinckel, *The Psalms in Israel's Worship* (New York: Abingdon, 1967) 2. 240; see also Thomas Fawcett, *Hebrew Myth and Christian Gospel* (London: SCM, 1973) 18.

[2]The program of this movement was announced in a volume of essays edited by S. H. Hooke, *Myth and Ritual* (London: Oxford University Press, 1933). The discussion was continued in two further volumes of essays, also edited by Hooke, *The Labyrinth* (London: SPCK, 1935) and *Myth, Ritual, and Kingship* (Oxford: Clarendon, 1958). See also the characterizations of the movement by Mowinckel, *The Psalms*, 2. 240 and Fawcett, *Hebrew Myth and Christian Gospel*, 17-18.

[3]Hooke, *Myth and Ritual*, 8; see also the essay by C. J. Gadd in the same volume, 46-59.

[4]Mowinckel, *The Psalms*, 1. 132, 134; in his earlier work, Mowinckel argued from the Babylonian texts. On the later work of the myth and ritual school with critique, see Cross, *Canaanite Myth and Hebrew Epic*, 79-83.

[5]Cross, *Canaanite Myth and Hebrew Epic*, 79-90.

[6]Ibid., 162-63; the elements of the pattern as Cross formulates them are paraphrased here.

[7]Ibid., 169-77.

[8]Ibid., 170.

[9]Paul D. Hanson, "Zechariah 9 and the Recapitulation of an Ancient Ritual Pattern," *JBL* 92 (1973) 54-59; now see also *The Dawn of Apocalyptic* (Philadelphia: Fortress, 1975) 292-324.

[10]Hanson, "Zechariah 9," 53; numbering added. See also *Dawn of Apocalyptic*, 315-16.

[11]Hanson, "Zechariah 9," 54-56; *Dawn of Apocalyptic*, 299-303.

[12]Hanson, "Zechariah 9," 54; numbering added; *Dawn of Apocalyptic*, 302.

[13]Hanson, "Zechariah 9," 54-55; *Dawn of Apocalyptic*, 302-3.

[14]Joseph Fontenrose, *Python: A Study of Delphic Myth and Its Origins* (Berkeley: University of California Press, 1959) 1-11, 77-93, 122-24, 132-38, 151-64, 178-84, 209-16, 262-73.

[15]The currency of the Canaanite-Ugaritic pattern in the
Hellenistic and Roman periods is attested by the work of Philo
Byblius on the Phoenician religion and by his source, Sanchun-
iathon. Fragments of Philo Byblius are preserved by Eusebius
Praeparatio evangelica 1.9-10. See the studies by C. Clemen,
Die phönikische Religion nach Philo von Byblos (Mittheilungen
der vorderasiatisch-ägyptischen Gesellschaft 42.3; Leipzig:
Hinrichs, 1939); O. Eissfeldt, *Ras Schamra und Sanchunjaton*
(Halle: Niemeyer, 1939); *Sanchunjaton von Berut und Ilumilku
von Ugarit* (Halle: Niemeyer, 1952); Lynn R. Clapham, "Sanchuniathon: The First Two Cycles" (Ph.D. diss., 1969). The myths
concerning the combats of Apollo and Zeus are well attested
from the Hellenistic through the Byzantine periods. For references see Fontenrose, *Python*, 21, 70-76. The Egyptian combat
myth is attested by Plutarch *Moralia* 355D-358E; see also
Herodotus 2.144; 2.156; Diodorus Siculus 1.21.2-7, 1.88.4-6.

[16]Fontenrose, *Python*, 1-3, 145, 176, 177, 262.

[17]Ibid., 262-64. The pattern is quoted more fully above,
Chapter II, *The Pattern of the Combat Myth and Revelation 12*.

[18]Gunkel, *Schöpfung und Chaos*, 171-398; see also Hans-
Peter Müller, "Die himmlische Ratsversammlung. Motivgeschichtliches zu Apc 5:1-5," *ZNW* 54 (1963) 254-67.

[19]S. H. Hooke, "The Myth and Ritual Pattern in Jewish and
Christian Apocalyptic," in *The Labyrinth*, 213-33; the quotation
is from 213.

[20]Ibid., 232-33. Hooke's implication that the triumphal procession of the Babylonian New Year festival is reflected in the book of Revelation (233) seems to be an example of
eisegesis.

[21]See above, Chapter I, *Recapitulation in the Five Series*.

[22]Ibid.

[23]See note 18 above.

[24]Müller, "Die himmlische Ratsversammlung," 262-63.

[25]Ibid., 266 note 39; the importance of the Myth of Zu for
Revelation was apparently brought to Müller's attention by
Traugott Holtz whom he cites in this note. Holtz discussed the
point very briefly in the first edition of his book on the
Christology of Revelation, published in 1962. His comments
were republished in the second edition (*Die Christologie der
Apokalypse des Johannes* [TU 85; Berlin: Akademie, 1971] 36 and
note 2) with a brief discussion of Müller's article (248, addition to page 36, note 2).

[26]OB version 2.9; translation by E. A. Speiser, *ANET*, 111;
cf. the Assyrian version 2.27-30; *ANET*, 113.

[27] *Enuma elish* II; translation by E. A. Speiser, *ANET*, 63-64.

[28] On the Tablets of Destinies see Bruno Meissner, *Babylonien und Assyrien* (Kulturgeschichtliche Bibliothek 1.4; Heidelberg: Winter, 1925) 7, 124; Heinrich Zimmern, *Das babylonische Neujahrsfest* (Der alte Orient 25.3; Leipzig: Hinrichs, 1926); Geo Widengren, *The Ascension of the Apostle and the Heavenly Book* (*King and Saviour III*) (UUA 1950:7; Uppsala: Lundequistska, 1950) 7-21; Leo Koep, *Das himmlische Buch in Antike und Christentum* (Theophaneia 8; Bonn: Hanstein, 1952) 4, note 3; S. M. Paul, "Heavenly Tablets and the Book of Life," *Journal of the Ancient Near Eastern Society of Columbia University* 5 (1973) 345-53.

[29] *Enuma elish* I:152-61; *ANET*, 62-63.

[30] *Enuma elish* II:122-29; *ANET*, 64.

[31] *Enuma elish* IV:121-22; *ANET*, 67.

[32] *Enuma elish* V:69-70, 85-89; VI:91-104; *ANESTP*, 502-3.

[33] See Speiser's introduction and note 1, *ANET*, 111.

[34] The Myth of Zu, Assyrian version, 2.12-15; *ANET*, 112-13.

[35] That Daniel 7 reflects the ancient mythic motif of the divine council is held by Cross (*Canaanite Myth and Hebrew Epic*, 17, 165-66, note 86) and Bentzen (*Daniel*, 61).

[36] (1) This form is the most common in the OT and NT: Exod 32:32; Isa 4:3; Ezek 13:9; Mal 3:16; Ps 69:29 (MT; 69:28 RSV); Phil 4:3; Rev 3:5, 13:8, 17:8, 20:12b (*allo biblion...ho estin tēs zōēs*), 20:15, 21:27; 1 Enoch 108:3; on the concept of the "book of Life" at Qumran, see Friedrich Nötscher, "Himmlische Bücher und Schicksalsglaube in Qumran," *RQ* 1 (1959) 405-11; reprinted in *Vom Alten zum Neuen Testament* (Bonner Biblische Beiträge 17; Bonn: Hanstein, 1962) 72-79. (2) Jubilees 5:13-18, 28:6 (...and the man who does so, they set down guilt against him in heaven...); 1 Enoch 81:4, 90:20; Rev 20:12 (...*kai biblia enoichthēsan...kai ekrithēsan hoi nekroi ek tōn gegrammenōn en tois bibliois kata ta erga autōn*). T Levi 5:4 probably belongs here, but may be an example of the third type. (3) Jubilees 16:9, 23:32; 1 Enoch 81:1, 93:1-2 (Apocalypse of Weeks), 103:2, 106:19, 108:7. Related to this type is the idea that eternally valid commandments of God are engraved on heavenly tablets; cf. Jubilees 6:31, 28:6 (that no one should give his younger daughter before the elder).

[37] On the mythic prototypes of the two figures, see J. A. Emerton, "The Origin of the Son of Man Imagery," *JTS* 9 (1958) 225-42. On the interpretation of the one like a son of man and his role in Daniel, see John J. Collins, "The Son of Man and the Saints of the Most High in the Book of Daniel," *JBL* 93 (1974) 50-66.

[38]For example, Lohmeyer, *Offenbarung des Johannes*, 48-49; Holtz, *Die Christologie der Apokalypse*, 27-29; Kraft, *Offenbarung des Johannes*, 103, 111-12; Elisabeth Schüssler Fiorenza, *Priester für Gott* (NTAbh 7; Münster: Aschendorff, 1972) 274-75.

[39]W. C. van Unnik, "Worthy is the Lamb. The Background of Apoc 5," *Mélanges bibliques en hommage au R. P. Béda Rigaux* (eds. A. Descamps and A. de Halleux; Gembloux: Duculot, 1970) 446-48.

[40]*Enuma elish* III:131-IV:34; *ANET*, 66.

[41]OB version 2.1; *ANET*, 111.

[42]*Enuma elish* IV:135-V:66; *ANET*, 67-68 and *ANESTP*, 501-2.

[43]Van Unnik, "Worthy is the Lamb," 448-61.

[44]Ibid., 458.

[45]Cf. Judg 5:4-5; Pss 18:8, 68:8-9; Hab 3:6. See the discussion in Cross, *Canaanite Myth and Hebrew Epic*, 100-1, 155-59. Baal's voice makes the mountains quake (*CTA*, 4.7.31; *ANET*, 135).

[46]See Cross, *Canaanite Myth and Hebrew Epic*, 175.

[47]See Chapter I, *Recapitulation in the Five Series*, b. *The Seven Trumpets*.

[48]See Chapter IV, *The Nero Legend*.

[49]*Enuma elish* V:85-88; *ANESTP*, 502. See also *CTA*, 4.4-5. 40-46; *ANET*, 133: "Thy [El] decree is: our king's Puissant Baal, Our sovereign second to none..."

[50]The three elements are present in the theophany of Yahweh as storm god in Ps 18:13-15; cf. Cross, *Canaanite Myth and Hebrew Epic*, 159; the Ugaritic parallels are cited on 147-49.

[51]See Chapter II, *The Pattern of the Combat Myth and Revelation 12*.

[52]Compare 15:2 (standing beside the sea of glass) with 4:6.

[53]See Chapter IV, *The Nero Legend*.

[54]See Chapter IV, *The Beast from the Sea*.

[55]See Chapter IV, *The Nero Legend*.

[56]Charles, *Revelation of St. John*, 2. 58, 61.

[57]See above, *The Pattern in the Second Series of Visions*.

[58]*ANET*, 514; see also V:88; *ANESTP*, 502.

[59]See Mowinckel on the relation of what he terms the "enthronement psalms" (e.g., Psalms 47, 93, 96) and the ancient Near Eastern myths (*The Psalms*, 1. 106-16); see also Hanson on Psalms 29, 47 and 48 ("Zechariah 9," 57-58; *Dawn of Apocalyptic*, 307-8).

[60]*CTA*, 2.4.9-10; *ANET*, 131; cf. Cross, *Canaanite Myth and Hebrew Epic*, 114. This passage is included by Hanson in his reconstruction of the ritual structure of the Baal-Yamm conflict under the element "Manifestation of Baal's Universal Reign (anticipated)" ("Zechariah 9," 55). The acclamation is spoken by Kothar wa-Khasis; his prediction seems to be fulfilled by a later passage: "Baal seats him [on] his kingdom's [throne], upon his dominion's [seat]" (*CTA*, 6.6.33-35; *ANET*, 141). The text is discussed by Peter J. van Zijl, *Baal: A Study of Texts in Connexion with Baal in the Ugaritic Epics* (Alter Orient und Altes Testament 10; Neukirchen-Vluyn: Verlag Butzon und Bercker Kevelaer, 1972) 237-38.

[61]This acclamation is part of the mythic pattern reflected by Exodus 15; cf. Cross, *Canaanite Myth and Hebrew Epic*, 142.

[62]On the sacred marriage, see Lewis Farnell, *Greece and Babylon* (Edinburgh: Clark, 1911) 263-68; Albrecht Dieterich, *Eine Mithrasliturgie*, 3rd ed., (ed. Otto Weinreich; Leipzig: Teubner, 1923) 121-34; Samuel Angus, *The Mystery-Religions and Christianity* (New York: Scribner's, 1925) 112-17; Samuel Noah Kramer, *The Sacred Marriage Rite* (Bloomington, Ind.: Indiana University Press, 1969). On nuptial imagery in the OT and early Christianity, see Claude Chavasse, *The Bride of Christ* (London: Faber, 1940); I. A. Muirhead, "The Bride of Christ," *SJT* 5 (1952) 175-87; R. A. Batey, *New Testament Nuptial Imagery* (Leiden: Brill, 1971).

[63]The sacred marriage is possibly the background for the prophetic image of the marriage of Yahweh with Israel: cf. Hos 2:19; Isa 54:5-6; Ezek 16:8. See Robert B. Coote, "The Serpent and Sacred Marriage in Northwest Semitic Tradition" (Ph.D. diss., Harvard University, 1972). The Song of Songs may reflect the practice and poetry of the sacred marriage rite; see Theodore H. Robinson, "Hebrew Myths," in S. H. Hooke, *Myth and Ritual*, 185, where older literature is cited; and S. N. Kramer, "The Sacred Marriage and Solomon's Song of Songs," in *The Sacred Marriage Rite*, 85-106. In a recent study, J. Cheryl Exum concludes that if the Song of Songs is based on previously extant songs, they have been thoroughly reworked into the author's intentional literary design ("A Literary and Structural Analysis of the Song of Songs," *ZAW* 85 [1973] 78).

[64]See C. J. Gadd, "Babylonian Myth and Ritual," in S. H. Hooke, *Myth and Ritual*, 56-57.

[65]See "Love-Song to a King," *ANET*, 496; "Sumerian Sacred Marriage Texts," *ANESTP*, 637-45. See also the cylinder inscription B of Gudea, which describes the sacred marriage of

Ningirsu and Bau which brings prosperity to Lagash; discussed by Hooke, *Myth and Ritual*, 10.

[66]See A. M. Blackman, "Myth and Ritual in Ancient Egypt," in Hooke, *Myth and Ritual*, 34.

[67]*CTA*, 10; *ANET*, 142; see the discussions by Arvid S. Kapelrud, *Baal in the Ras Shamra Texts* (Copenhagen: Gad, 1952) 67-68; John Gray, *The Legacy of Canaan* (Supplements to Vetus Testamentum 5; Leiden: Brill, 1957) 68-70; van Zijl, *Baal*, 243-54, especially 253; Richard J. Clifford, *The Cosmic Mountain in Canaan and the Old Testament* (Harvard Semitic Monographs 4; Cambridge: Harvard University Press, 1972) 76. See also Clifford's discussion of *Ugaritica*, V; RS 24.245, 11.5-10 as a reference to a *hieros gamos* following the enthronement of Baal (*Cosmic Mountain*, 77-78).

[68]*CTA*, 5.5.17-21; *ANET*, 139; see Kapelrud, *Baal*, 68-69, 121; Gray, *Legacy*, 50; van Zijl, *Baal*, 172-75. The fact that animal names were used in Ugaritic to designate heroes makes it likely that the cow or heifer here refers to Baal's consort, probably Anat; on this use of animal names, see P. D. Miller, "Animal Names as Designations in Ugaritic and Hebrew," *Ugarit-Forschungen* 2 (1971) 177-86.

[69]Kapelrud, *Baal* 70-71; Gray connects the text with "seasonal rites observed by the primitive community"; *Legacy*, 12.

[70]On the Keret legend, see Gray, *Legacy*, 15; on the tale of Aqhat, see van Zijl, *Baal*, 265-80.

[71]*CTA*, 4.6.39-59; *ANET*, 134.

[72]Cross, *Canaanite Myth and Hebrew Epic*, 144, 229 note 42.

[73]Clifford, *Cosmic Mountain*, 119 note 23.

[74]Cross, *Canaanite Myth and Hebrew Epic*, 70.

[75]Patrick D. Miller, *The Divine Warrior in Early Israel* (Harvard Semitic Monographs 5; Cambridge: Harvard University Press, 1973) 18-20, 155.

[76]On the relationship of bloody sacrifice, banquet and fertility, see Hanson, "Zechariah 9," 46-47 note 25; *Dawn of Apocalyptic*, 322.

[77]*CTA*, 3.2; *ANET*, 136; see the study by John Gray, "The Wrath of God in Canaanite and Hebrew Literature," *Bulletin of the Manchester University Egyptian and Oriental Society* 25 (1947-53) 9-19, referred to by Hanson ("Zechariah 9," 46-47 note 25).

[78]*CTA*, 6.2.31-38; *ANET*, 140.

[79]See the discussion by Kapelrud, *Baal*, 125-26; Cross, *Canaanite Myth and Hebrew Epic*, 118; for other commentators who interpret the passage from the point of view of agricultural fertility as well as for discussion of other points of view, cf. van Zijl, *Baal*, 225-26. A banquet for the creatures of the wilderness is closely linked to God's defeat of Leviathan in Ps 74:14. The MT reads "for the people"; cf. the tradition about the eschatological banquet in which Leviathan and Behemoth would be food for the just; see Chapter IV, *The Beast from the Sea*.

[80]See Chapter II, *The Battle in Heaven*.

[81]*PRU*, II.3.3-11; translation cited is by Cross, *Canaanite Myth and Hebrew Epic*, 119; the "f" which transforms "licks" into "flicks" on page 119 of Professor Cross's book is a typographical error (personal communication).

[82]*Enuma elish* IV:130-V:66; *ANET*, 67-68; *ANESTP*, 501-2.

[83]See the discussion by Cross, *Canaanite Myth and Hebrew Epic*, 120.

[84]The water of life reflects the mythic emphasis on the fertile waters of rain, dew and rivers. Cf. *Enuma elish* V:49, 54-55, 58; on Baal, see Kapelrud, *Baal*, 93-98.

[85]*Enuma elish* V; *ANET*, 67-68; *ANESTP*, 501-2. In Sib Or 5:155-61 the burning up of the sea is part of the divine punishment for the destruction of Jerusalem; in Sib Or 5:447-56 the drying up of the sea is one of the disasters of "the last time"; its counterpart is that great Asia will become water. The former text is analogous to Revelation in its apparent association of the sea with Babylon, adversary of God's people.

[86]*CTA*, 2.28-30; *ANET*, 131. Cross' quite different translation (*Canaanite Myth and Hebrew Epic*, 115-16) emphasizes the defeat of Yamm, but does not imply his total annihilation as subsequent statements on 116 show.

[87]See the text quoted above, in which Anat's binding the dragon to the heights of Lebanon is mentioned. See also *CTA*, 3.4.30-50; *ANET*, 137.

[88]Cf. 1 Enoch 10:4-16, 90:20-27.

[89]Translation cited is by Charles, *APOT*, 2. 421. In As Mos 10:6, the sea's retiring into the abyss is one of the cosmic disturbances resulting from the theophany of the Divine Warrior; for the suggestion that As Mos 10:3-10 is a divine warrior hymn, see Adela Yarbro Collins, "Composition and Redaction of the Testament of Moses 10," *HTR*, forthcoming.

[90]This is most clear in Alexander Heidel's translation, *The Babylonian Genesis* (Chicago: University of Chicago Press, 1951) 48-49.

[91]If Esharra in VI:66 refers to heaven; contra Heidel, *Babylonian Genesis*, 49.

[92]See the discussion in Clifford, *Cosmic Mountain*, 17-21.

[93]*CTA*, 4.5.116-19; *ANET*, 134; see the discussion in Clifford, *Cosmic Mountain*, 60-61.

[94]Cf. Cross, *Canaanite Myth and Hebrew Epic*, 125, 142; Clifford, *Cosmic Mountain*, 131, 141-60.

[95]Cf., for example, Ezek 43:7.

[96]See Hanson, "Zechariah 9," 53, 56; *Dawn of Apocalyptic*, 301, 303, 305-8, 311-13, 315, 321.

[97]Cf. *CTA*, 5.2.1-5; *ANET*, 138.

[98]Ezek 40:3-4; Rev 21:15-17; *ho estin aggelou* of Rev 22:17 may very well be an exegetical comment, making explicit that "the man" of Ezek 40:3 is to be understood as an angel. See the discussion in Chapter IV, note 106.

[99]The most obvious contemporary example was the cult of Roma; OT examples of cities as women include Ezek 16:3-45 (Jerusalem), vs. 46 (Sodom and Samaria); Isaiah 47, Jer 50:42, Zech 2:7 (Babylon); Isa 62, 66:7-11, Micah 4:9-13 (Jerusalem/Zion). See Aloysius Fitzgerald, "The Mythological Background for the Presentation of Jerusalem as a Queen and False Worship as Adultery in the OT," *CBQ* 34 (1972) 403-16.

[100]The image also appears, in a less explicit way, in Isa 62:4-5.

[101]Other texts and traditions have certainly had an influence on the list of twelve precious stones with which the twelve foundations of the wall of the city were adorned (21: 19-20). The breastplate of the high priest was to be set with twelve precious stones which correspond more or less to the list here (cf. Exod 28:17-21, 39:10-13). Josephus and Philo interpreted the stones on the high priest's breastplate as representing the signs of the zodiac. See the discussion in Charles, *Revelation of St. John*, 2. 159, 165-69.

[102]See J. M. Allegro, "More Isaiah Commentaries from Qumran's Fourth Cave," *JBL* 77 (1958) 220-21. 4QpIsa[d] fgt. 1 is especially interesting for Rev 21:9-21 because it combines references to the stones of the high priest's breastplate with its interpretation of Isa 54:11-12 (lines 3-5). On the New Jerusalem as the Qumran community, see also 1QS 8:5-10 (alluding to Isa 28:16).

[103]Compare the statement in Rev 3:12 that the one who conquers will become a pillar in the temple of God. Cf. also 1 Cor 3:10-17, Eph 2:19-22.

[104] 2:9, 2:10, 2:13, 2:24, 3:9.

[105] See Chapter IV, *The Beast from the Abyss.*

[106] See Chapter IV, *The Beast as Nero.*

[107] See Chapter I, *Why Recapitulation?*

[108] On the textual problem in 13:10, see Charles, *Revelation of St. John*, 1. 355-57; see also the discussion above, Chapter I, c. *The Unity of Chs. 12-22.*

[109] Josephus *Ant.* 18.5; Martin Hengel, *Die Zeloten* (Leiden: Brill, 1961) 129-31.

[110] As Mos 9-10; J. Licht, "Taxo, or the Apocalyptic Doctrine of Vengeance," *JJS* 12 (1961) 95-103.

APPENDIX

It was argued in Chapter II that the mythic pattern of
source I derives from the myth about Leto's giving birth to
Apollo while pursued by Python. It was shown in Chapter III
that this mythic pattern was first adapted for a Jewish context
before being incorporated into this Christian apocalypse.
Since the final redaction of the book of Revelation took place
somewhere in western Asia Minor, it was hypothesized that the
Jewish adaptation of the myth also took place in that region.
This hypothesis cannot, of course, be proven; but it is the
purpose of this appendix to give external support to that theory by showing that the particular mythic pattern we are concerned with was well enough known and widespread enough in
western Asia Minor in the first centuries B.C.E. and C.E. for a
Jew living in that area to have been familiar with it.

There is a wealth of material, literary and monumental,
which attests the various mythological traditions about Leto.[1]
What is of interest here is the particular motif of Python's
attack on Leto and the attestation of that motif in western
Asia Minor.

The earliest literary evidence of this motif is Lucan's
mention of it in his work on the civil war, which he published
in 62 or 63 C.E.:

> There [Parnassus] Apollo, with yet unpracticed
> shafts, laid low the Python and so avenged his
> mother who had been driven forth when great with
> child.[2]

This reference shows that Leto was commonly associated with the
dragon Python in the early Imperial period. Lucan links this
mythic pattern with Apollo's takeover of the oracle at Delphi.[3]
But the birthplace of Apollo was often placed elsewhere, most
often on Delos.[4]

Tacitus and Strabo provide evidence for the fact that,
alongside Delos, Ephesus was a strong contender for the honor
of the title of Apollo's birthplace. Tacitus, writing about
100 C.E., reports that when Tiberius made a general inquiry (22
C.E.) about rights of asylum in connection with temples in Asia

Minor, ambassadors from Ephesus made known that their most ancient religious traditions were associated with Ortygia (a
sacred grove just outside Ephesus, as Strabo tells us) where
Leto had given birth to Apollo and Artemis, leaning on an olive
tree.[5]

Strabo (writing at some time between 44 B.C.E. and 21
C.E.)[6] says that near Ephesus, by the Panormus harbor where the
temple of the Ephesian Artemis is, lies Ortygia, a magnificent
grove crossed by the Cenchrius River, where Leto is said to
have bathed herself after her travail.[7] He says that this
grove was the scene of the birth of the twin gods and that
Curetes assisted Leto in concealing the birth from Hera's
jealous notice by making a great din.[8] He notes that (in his
own time) there were several temples in the grove, some ancient
and some "of latter times."[9] In one of the later temples is a
work of Scopas depicting Leto holding a sceptre and Ortygia
(the nymph who assisted with the birth) standing next to her
holding the two children. Finally, he says that a general festival was held there annually, involving feasts, drinking par-
ties and certain mystic rites.[10] It is clear that we have here
the fusion of certain Greek traditions and rites with indigen-
ous rituals of Asia Minor.[11]

These quotations are important for our discussion as evidence of the first century C.E. that the mythic pattern described by Lucan was known in Asia Minor. While neither of
them explicitly mentions Python, we can assume that his conflict with Leto was part of the mythic tradition known at Ortygia. This assumption is supported by Strabo's reference to
Hera's jealousy which is associated with Python's attack in our
literary sources.[12]

Further literary evidence for the mythic pattern we are
concerned with comes from the second century C.E. The most
detailed account we have is that preserved in Latin in the so-
called *Fabulae* of Hyginus. Hyginus himself probably wrote at
some time between 138 and 192, i.e., under the Antonines.[13]
But he based his work on Greek sources which probably go back
at least to the first century C.E.

Lucian of Samosata refers to the mythic conflict of Leto
with Python twice. In the *Dialogues of the Sea-gods* he has
Iris commission Poseidon by order of Zeus to make the wandering
island Delos firm as a place for Leto to give birth. Poseidon
orders the Tritons to give Leto passage to the island, and predicts that the infants will take vengeance, as soon as they are
born, on the dragon (*drakōn*) that is now terrifying their
mother.[14] This version has much in common with that of Hyginus: the envy of Hera, the aid of Poseidon, the wandering island. *The Dialogues of the Sea-gods* is to be dated somewhere
between 140 and 180 C.E.[15]

The other occasion on which Lucian refers to the mythic
pattern in question is in his treatise *On the Dance* (37-38):

> Let this be the range we prescribe for the dancer's
> learning, and let him know thoroughly all that lies
> within it: the castration of Uranus...and after
> that, the errancy of Delos, the travail of Leto,
> the killing of Pytho....[16]

Lucian's work itself is to be dated to 162-165 C.E.[17]
However, the practice of pantomimic dancing is considerably
older. According to Lucian, the art began to reach its perfec-
tion in the time of Augustus.[18] Thus both the mythic pattern
(as we know from other evidence) as well as the practice of
enacting it in dance are probably a good deal earlier than
Lucian.

These then are the major early literary sources for our
mythic pattern and its association with Ephesus. Since the
primary cult at Ephesus was that of Artemis, and since Leto is
the mother of Artemis, it is not surprising to find a Leto cult
in Ephesus as well. But Leto traditions and cult were by no
means confined to Ephesus in the Asia Minor area. Artemis and
Apollo were worshipped throughout the region, and Leto was often honored along with them. Major sites for the honor of
Apollo were Pergamum where he was honored as the father of
Asclepius, and Didyma and Claros, where he was consulted as
giver of oracles.

We have clear monumental evidence from a number of cities
of western Asia Minor that the myth of Python's attack on Leto
was known.

LYDIA

Ephesus

We have already discussed the references of Strabo (*Geogr.* 14.639-40 = 14.1.20) and Tacitus (*Ann.* 3.61) to mythic traditions and cult involving Leto at Ephesus. See Wehrli's article for a discussion of the ancient evidence and for references to Ephesian coins depicting Leto.[19]

There is evidence for a temple of the Pythian Apollo at Ephesus.[20]

In the sixth and fifth centuries B.C.E. there developed in Greek vase-painting the representation of Leto fleeing from Python, carrying her two children who shoot their arrows at the dragon from their mother's arms.[21] This representational type was probably used later as the basis for a bronze statue at Delphi, which was copied in two marble works.[22] The type then became popular in the Roman Imperial period in various cities of Asia Minor, and was frequently imprinted on their coins. One such coin was minted at Ephesus under Hadrian.[23]

Another coin depicting Leto holding her two children was minted at Ephesus under Antoninus Pius, but it may have been based on a different representational type, i.e., Leto as nursing mother.[24]

CARIA

Magnesia on the Maeander

A coin minted at Magnesia under Hadrian bears the representation of Leto fleeing carrying her two children, who shoot their arrows, presumably at Python.[25] This is the same representation which appeared on coins of Ephesus of the same date (see above).

Miletus

A coin of Miletus bears on the reverse the same representation of Leto as the coin from Magnesia discussed above. On the obverse are two busts who have been tentatively identified as Marcus Aurelius and Commodus; the coin would thus seem to date from c. 161-180 C.E.[26]

Another coin, though even later than the one just discussed, is mentioned here because it shows so clearly the motif
of the attack of the divine children against the pursuer. This
coin bears the bust of Balbinus (emperor for a brief time in
238 C.E.) on the obverse, and the fleeing Leto with children on
the reverse. Each divine child is depicted as holding a bow
and drawing an arrow from a quiver.[27]

Didyma by Miletus

Zeus and Leto were important deities in Didyma already in
the third century B.C.E. This is shown by an inscription from
Cos which says that the *hieros gamos* of Zeus and Leto took
place at Didyma.[28] Their position of honor seems to have en-
dured, since they were especially honored during the joint
reign of Diocletian and Maximian, as will be noted below.

In an inscription of the early second century C.E., Apollo
is addressed as *Lētoidēs*.[29]

Between 286 and 293 C.E., i.e., under the joint emperors
Diocletian and Maximian, two statues were erected in Didyma,
each with its own base with identical dedicatory inscriptions
on each base. The images are said to be of Zeus and of Leto
together with the twin gods. The text begins to be fragmentary
at the mention of the twin gods, so we can only conjecture how
they were described. The editor suggests, on the basis of the
coin types, that the statue of Leto probably depicted her as
fleeing and the children possibly as shooting arrows.[30]

In addition to this unequivocal evidence for the myth of
Python's attack on Leto, there is general attestation for the
cults of "Apollo Pythios," Apollo as son of Leto, and of Leto
herself. The existence of these cults may imply the currency
of the Leto-Python-Apollo myth, but this is not certain. The
relevant data follows in summary form:

MYSIA

Pergamum

Apollo Pythios was worshipped at Pergamum from about the
second century B.C.E. until at least the time of Hadrian.[31]

Pausanias mentions a sanctuary dedicated to the god which he calls a *Pythion*.[32] This sanctuary is attested by an inscription which dates to about 133 B.C.E. A structure at Pergamum has been identified as this *Pythion* and seems to have been built between 197 and 160 B.C.E.[33]

Near the *Asclepieion* at Pergamum an altar stone was found with an inscription dedicating an *oiōnoskopion* (a place where auguries are taken) to *Pythios Phoibos*. The script dates from the time of Trajan or Hadrian.[34]

Now apparently Leto, along with Apollo and Artemis, was honored at the *Asclepieion* at Pergamum. An altar was found there with a dedication to Leto offered by an *archiereus* (presumably a high priest of the official city cults, not of Leto). Unfortunately, this dedication does not seem to be datable by the script, but the office of the donor is attested from the time of Caesar to the time of Trajan.[35]

SPORADES

Rhodes

In volume 65 of the Annual of the British School at Athens, P. M. Fraser published one new inscription and re-edited two previously published ones. The third inscription discussed is said to have been founded by M. Segre near the sanctuary of Apollo Pythios.[36]

Sikinos

Sikinos is an island in the Sporades, as is Patmos, where the author of the book of Revelation was exiled, according to tradition.

A proxeny decree was found on Sikinos (*IG* XII, 5, 24) by Ludwig Ross in the early part of this century. The decree honored Aischylos of Paros and was to be set up in the sanctuary of the Pythian Apollo. Ross dated the inscription to the end of the third, beginning of the second century B.C.E.[37]

CARIA

Apollonia by Salbacus

A coin minted here depicts Apollo and Artemis with a goddess; Louis Robert suggests that the goddess is Leto.[38] The coin was minted between 161 and 169 C.E.[39]

Physcus

According to Strabo (*Geogr.* 14.652 = 14.2.4) there was a sacred grove or precinct (*alsos*) of Leto in Physcus.

Wehrli refers to a dedicatory inscription to Leto from this locality, but does not give the date.[40]

Caunus

An inscription found at Caunus, on the mainland opposite Rhodes, contains an oracle of Apollo Gryneios. In the oracle Apollo is referred to as *Lētous Phoibon*; i.e., as son of Leto, as in the inscription from Didyma.[41] G. E. Bean gives as a *terminus ante quem* the Rhodian domination of Caunus in the first century B.C.E.[42]

Calynda

Strabo (*Geogr.* 14.651 = 14.2.2) says that there was a sacred grove or precinct (*alsos*) of Leto near the city of Calynda. The grove was near a temple (*hieron*) of Artemis.

PHRYGIA

Laodicea ad Lycum

Laodicea was one of the seven cities addressed in the opening chapters of the book of Revelation.

A number of inscriptions discovered at Claros mention the "prophet of Pythian Apollo" from Laodicea who regularly led a delegation from his town to consult the oracle at Claros.[43]

LYCIA

Xanthus

Strabo mentions a *Lētōon* on the Xanthus River near the city of Xanthus, which he says is the largest city of Lycia.[44]

The worship of Leto was particularly strong and widespread in Lycia.[45]

This completes our brief survey of evidence for the Leto-Python-Apollo myth in western Asia Minor from the late Hellenistic and early Roman periods. It should now be clear that mythic traditions and cultic activities which reflect the myth related by Hyginus (*Fab*. 140) were widespread in the region and at the time that the Jewish adaptation of that myth was probably made.

As is argued in Chapter III, source I (the Jewish adaptation of the Leto myth) did not contain the heavenly symbolism which now appears in Rev 12:1. The heavenly attributes were given to the woman by the Christian redactor. He understood the woman as the heavenly Israel and it was thus natural for him to describe her with language inspired by Isis as *regina caeli*.

It is not surprising that a mythic pattern concerning Leto was enriched with the iconography of Isis. The Oxyrhynchus Litany, dated to the first or second century C.E., testifies for Lycia at least that Isis and Leto were identified.[46]

In the Isis aretalogies, which were current in the late Hellenistic and early Imperial periods, Isis is associated with the sun. In the aretalogy found at Cyme (a city once controlled by the Attalids of Pergamum, then a free city under Roman domination belonging to the conventus of Smyrna[47]), Isis says that she accompanies the sun in its course.[48] In the period of the late kingdom in Egypt Isis is called the "female sun," the "second sun," and "companion of the sun."[49]

In *CIG* 5115, Isis is called "rosy-breasted" (*rhodosternos*). At Tenedos (an island off the coast of Troas) she was called the "name of the sun," according to the Oxyrhynchus Litany.[50] The association of Isis with the moon is reflected in the iconography of coins from Asia Minor, where she sometimes appears with a half moon on her shoulders. Such coins were minted at Aphrodisias and Heraclea by Salbacus in Caria; at Bageis in Lydia; at Hyrgaleia, Themisonium and Tripolis in Phrygia.[51]

If the Christian apocalyptist who gave the book of Revelation its present form did in fact draw upon language used to
depict Isis in his description of his own *regina caeli*, Isis
traditions must have been part of his environment. It is the
purpose of the following pages to assemble epigraphical and
numismatic evidence to show that the Isis cult was very firmly
rooted and widespread in western Asia Minor during the first
and early second centuries C.E.

The pioneer in an examination of this sort is Georges
Lafaye whose study of 1884 examined the origins of the Sarapis
cult in Alexandria and the spread of the worship of Sarapis,
Isis, Harpocrates and Anubis to Greece and Italy.[52] Further
work was done by Wilhelm Drexler (1889), Adolf Rusch (1906),
T. A. Brady (1935), M. P. Nilsson (1950).[53] Since the publication of Nilsson's *Geschichte der griechischen Religion*, two
very useful works have appeared. The first is an article by
David Magie in which he has collected both numismatic and in-
scriptional evidence for cults of the Egyptian deities in Asia
Minor, an undertaking which had not been attempted since Drexler. The second is Ladilaus Vidman's collection of inscriptions relating to the worship of the Egyptian deities outside
Egypt.[54] The Brill series, Etudes préliminaires aux religions
orientales dans l'empire romain, edited by M. J. Vermaseren,
has also produced some useful tools and studies in the last
several years.[55]

The following discussion contains evidence from these
earlier studies which is relevant for the time period and geographical area with which we are concerned. An attempt will be
made to update Magie and Vidman in light of subsequent discov-
eries.

MYSIA

Cyzicus

At Cyzicus, an important port of northern Mysia, the worship of Isis and Sarapis was well established in the first century B.C.E. Two inscriptions, tentatively assigned to the
first century B.C.E., make dedications to Sarapis and Isis in

the names of their worshippers (each inscription contains a
list of names; one, fourteen).[56]

A third inscription, dated to the first century B.C.E., is
a dedication to Sarapis and Isis of a statue.[57]

A fourth inscription of uncertain date is on a small altar
and dedicates it to Isis.[58]

Hamamlu

An inscription found in this town to the south of Cyzicus
on a small base is a dedication to *Isis karpophoros*. It has
been dated generally to the Roman period.[59]

Pergamum

The earliest evidence of an Isis cult in Pergamum is an
inscription dated to the first century C.E. which says that two
hieraphoroi (their names are given; one is a man, one a woman)
have dedicated statues of Sarapis, Isis and a number of other
deities and performed a number of other actions relating to the
cult.[60]

The Oxyrhynchus Litany referred to above, which dates to
the late first or early second century C.E., refers to Isis as
en Pergamō despotis.[61] This epithet is an indication that the
Isis cult had a substantial following in Pergamum toward the
end of the first century C.E.

Pitane

A coin was minted in Pitane sometime in the first or second century C.E. which depicts, on the obverse, the goddess
Roma wearing the headdress of Isis.[62]

LYDIA

Aegae

Hadrian's wife Sabina was honored by her husband with a
special coinage in 128 C.E. with the title 'Augusta' and again
after her death in 136 or 137 C.E.[63] Aegae (German, Aigai), an
Aeolian city, minted a coin depicting Sabina on the obverse and
the standing Isis on the reverse, probably between 128 and 137
C.E.[64]

Cyme

Cyme also minted coins in honor of Sabina. Two of these depict Isis, clothed, wearing the Egyptian headdress, with the infant Horus on one arm and grasping a scepter with the other.[65]

Clazomenae

A coin of Clazomenae minted under Trajan depicts the wreathed head of the emperor on the obverse and the city goddess on the reverse. In the right hand of the goddess is a tiny figure of Isis.[66]

Sardis

Drexler reports references to a coin minted at Sardis in honor of Agrippina (about 55 C.E.) which depicted the standing figure of Isis on the reverse. He also notes two coins, also from Sardis, honoring Octavia, the wife of Nero (before 62 C.E.). Both depict Isis on the reverse, walking and holding a spear.[67]

Magnesia ad Sipylum

In this city, which lies across some low mountains to the northeast of Smyrna, an inscription was found in 1935 which is a dedication to Sarapis and Isis, followed by the name of the priest and a list of *therapeutai*. The dedication dates from the second century B.C.E.; the names were added in the first or second century C.E.[68]

Ephesus

The Sarapis-Isis cult was flourishing in Ephesus in the the second century C.E. as the large basilica-style temple near the harbor dedicated to the Egyptian deities shows.[69] But there is clear, though not abundant evidence that their cult existed there in the first half of the third century B.C.E. and was well established in the first century B.C.E.

A dedication was found in the Ephesus area (exact location unknown) which is generally dated to the early third century B.C.E. This dedication is to Sarapis, Isis, Anubis and the deities who share their temple. This is possibly an indication

that a sanctuary of the Egyptian deities existed in Ephesus
already in the third century B.C.E.[70]

A white marble pillar, published after Magie's article,
was found in a pavement in front of the library at Ephesus.[71]
The pillar is inscribed with ...*Sarapidi anethēken*. The script
has been dated to the first century B.C.E. The inscription is
evidence for the continuation of the worship of Sarapis into
the first century B.C.E. The worship of Isis most likely also
continued into the first century B.C.E., since coins of Ephesus
of that period contain Isis motifs. Four *cistophoroi* from
Ephesus, dating between 91 and 82 B.C.E., bear the headdress of
Isis on the reverse.[72] Another Ephesian coin was minted under
the praetor C. Fannius in 48 B.C.E., also with the *cista mysti-
ca* on the obverse. On the reverse are two snakes around a
small temple. There is a statue above the temple; on the right
a torch, on the left the headdress of Isis.[73]

A priest of Isis (*[Is]ios Zōsim[os]*) is mentioned in a
list of priests in an inscription from Ephesus dated to the
time of Hadrian.[74]

Tralles

A votive tablet of white marble was found in Tralles which
mentions a priest of Isis and Sarapis.[75] It has been dated to
the Roman period.

A coin of Sabina (128-137 C.E.; see above on Aegae) from
Tralles depicts Isis standing and holding Harpocrates on her
left arm.[76]

Magnesia on the Maeander

A number of coins dating from the Roman Imperial period
have been found which depict the bust of Sarapis on the obverse
and the standing figure of Isis on the reverse.[77]

Priene

An altar was discovered at Priene in what appears to be a
chapel dedicated to Isis. On the altar is a dedicatory inscription which reads: *Isidos*, *Sarapidos*, *Anoubidos*. The chapel, altar and inscription have been dated to the third century
B.C.E.[78]

A temenos, dating from the same period, has also been found at Priene.[79]

An inscription, dated to about 200 B.C.E., discusses the cult of Sarapis, Isis, and the gods with them and what items their priest should receive as his due.[80]

Finally, a round altar was found in the chapel mentioned above, dedicated to Sarapis, Isis, Anubis, Harpocrates and the unconquered Heracles. The *terminus post quem* for the dating of this altar is 100 B.C.E.[81]

Heraclea Latmus

A dedicatory inscription to Sarapis, Isis, and Anubis from Nestor and the *thiasitai* was discovered at Heraclea. Unfortunately this inscription has not been dated.[82]

Didyma

An inscription was found in the ruins of the Apollo temple at Didyma which has been dated to c. 288-87 B.C.E.[83] It seems to be some sort of an inventory and mentions a *phialē* of Osiris.

A further inscription, which is a dedication of *Theodōro[s] Nikiou* to Sarapis, Isis and Anubis, has been found at Didyma and dated to the period from 150-100 B.C.E.[84]

Olymus

In an inscription from Olymus, which dates from about 84 B.C.E., a priest of Isis is mentioned.[85]

Mylasa

In an inscription from Mylasa dating to the first century B.C.E., a priest of Isis is mentioned.[86] Another inscription, of the Imperial period, mentions a *neōkoros* of Isis.[87]

Iasus

An inscription found at Iasus and dated to the Roman period is a dedication of an altar to Anubis, Isis Pelagia and Isis Bubastis.[88]

A further inscription dating from the Imperial period has been identified as a *lex sacra* issued by the *neōkoros Menecratēs* at the command of Sarapis, Isis and Anubis.[89]

Myndus

Myndus minted coins in the second or first century B.C.E. which bear on the obverse the head of Sarapis and on the reverse, with the names of the magistrates, the headdress of Isis.[90]

A number of coins minted by this city in the second or first century B.C.E. depict the head of Zeus in a laurel wreath on the obverse and the headdress of Isis on the reverse.[91]

Halicarnassus

An inscription which dates from the first century B.C.E. or C.E. was discovered at Halicarnassus which is evidence for a cult of Isis and Sarapis there during that period.[92]

Coins, like those of Myndus mentioned above, were minted in Halicarnassus in the second or first century B.C.E., which depict the head of Sarapis on the obverse and the headdress of Isis on the reverse.[93]

PHRYGIA

Synnada

A coin from Synnada, unfortunately undated, has been published by the British Academy in London, which depicts a bearded Heracles on the obverse and Isis on the reverse. In her right hand is a *sistrum*; in her left, a *situla*.[94]

Laodicea

Three coins minted at Laodicea under Augustus (28 B.C.E.-14 C.E.) are especially interesting for our purposes since they combine the attributes of Isis with those of Apollo. They depict the head of Apollo with a laurel wreath and/or lyre on the obverse and the headdress of Isis on the reverse.[95]

A coin minted here under Domitian depicts the bearded *Dēmos* on the obverse and the headdress of Isis over an altar on the reverse.[96]

Themisonium

A coin from Themisonium, unfortunately undated, depicts Sarapis on the obverse and Isis on the reverse with a half moon on her shoulders. In her uplifted right hand is the *sistrum*; in her left, the *situla*.[97]

LYCIA

Myra

Two coins minted at Myra (undated) are similar to the Augustan coins from Laodicea in that they combine attributes of Isis and Apollo. They depict the laureate head of Apollo with bow and quiver on the obverse and the headdress of Isis in the left field of the reverse.[98]

The cult of Isis at Myra in the first or second century C.E. is attested by the Oxyrhynchus Litany, which indicates that the goddess was revered there as *kednē* and *eleutheria*.[99]

Maskytes

Two coins minted in Maskytes in the second or first century B.C.E. depict Artemis (one, the bust; the other, the head) with a bow (and, in one case, a quiver) on the obverse and on the reverse, in association with a deer, the headdress of Isis.[100]

Phaselis

In Phaselis we find again coins which link Apollo and Isis. In the second or first century B.C.E. coins were minted here which depict the head of Apollo on the obverse and the headdress of Isis along with a lyre and torch on the reverse.[101]

SPORADES

Lesbos: Mytilenae

A dedicatory inscription to Isis Pelagia was found in Mytilenae which dates to the first century B.C.E. or C.E.[102]

A fragmentary inscription probably mentions a priestess of Isis; this inscription has been dated to the first century C.E.[103]

Finally, a dedication was made here to Sarapis as Zeus Helios and to Isis (*tē kyra Isidi*) by a citizen of Alexandria during the Imperial period, possibly in the second century C.E.[104]

Chios

An inscription dating from the Roman period was discovered here. It is a dedication to Sarapis, Isis, Anubis, Harpocrates and the *theoi synnaoi*.[105]

Cos

An inscription of the first century C.E. mentions a priest of Isis and Sarapis.[106]

Chalce

An inscription of Chalce, dating to the second or first century B.C.E., refers to an offering made to Sarapis and Isis by command.[107]

Rhodes

Rhodes city. In 88 B.C.E., when Rhodes was attacked by Mithradates VI of Pontus, there was a *hieron* of Isis in the capital city.[108]

An inscription, dated tentatively to the second century B.C.E., refers to a priest of Isis and Bubastis.[109] A group of *Isiastai* at Rhodes city is attested by an inscription of the first century B.C.E.[110] A *charisterion* was erected to *Isis Soteira* in Rhodes city probably in the first century B.C.E.[111]

Coins of the later second or early first century B.C.E. minted in Rhodes city depict the radiate Sarapis or Helios on the obverse and the headdress of Isis on the reverse.[112]

Camirus. An altar was found here which was apparently dedicated originally to Vesta (Hestia) in the second century B.C.E. and later rededicated to Sarapis and Isis (probably in the first century C.E.).[113]

Lindus. In 10 C.E. a priest was honored with a gold crown in Lindus by devotees of Isis and Sarapis (*hypo Eisiast[an Sera]p[ia]st[a]n*).[114] In the same year his wife (a priestess) and their son were honored by the same group(s).[115]

This collection and survey of epigraphical and numismatic evidence for the Isis cult has shown that Isis was known and worshipped in the last century B.C.E. and the first century C.E. along the western coast of Asia Minor from Cyzicus (Mysia)

in the north to Rhodes and its dependencies in the south, and
in many inland cities such as Laodicea, Themisonium and Synnada
(Phrygia).

It is probable then that any Jew or Christian living in
western Asia Minor in the first century C.E. was familiar not
merely with the existence of an Isis cult, but also with her
iconography and mythic traditions.

It is also interesting to note that Isis was very well
known in the Hellenistic and Roman periods as the mother of
Horus-Harpocrates, and was often depicted holding or nursing
the divine infant, madonna-style.[116] Monuments of this sort
have been discovered in Cyme, Tralles, Iasus, Perge and
Delos,[117] so we may infer that this iconographical type was
well-known in western Asia Minor in the Graeco-Roman period.

NOTES

APPENDIX

[1]For the various forms, history, and occurrences of the
Leto myth, see the following studies: Theodor Schreiber,
*Apollon Pythoktonos. Ein Beitrag zur griechischen Religions-
und Kunstgeschichte* (Leipzig: Engelmann, 1879); Otto Gruppe,
*Die griechischen Culte und Mythen in ihren Beziehungen zu den
orientalischen Religionen*, vol. 1: *Einleitung* (Leipzig: Teub-
ner, 1887) 553, 535-36, 539; Albrecht Dieterich, *Abraxas:
Studien zur Religionsgeschichte des spätern Altertums* (Leipzig:
Teubner, 1891) 116-22; Enmann, "Leto," in Roscher, 2.2. 1959-71;
B. Sauer, "Leto in der Kunst," in Roscher, 2.2. 1971-80; Ludwig
Preller and Carl Robert, *Griechische Mythologie*, 4th ed. (Ber-
lin: Weidmann, 1894-1926) 1. 233-38; Charles Picard, *Ephèse et
Claros: Recherches sur les sanctuaires et les cultes de l'Ionie
du Nord* (Paris: Boccard, 1922); Wehrli, "Leto," PW Supple-
mentband 5. 555-76; H. J. Rose, *A Handbook of Greek Mythology*,
5th rev. ed. (London: Methuen, 1953) 103, 114, 134-37; Joseph
Fontenrose, *Python: A Study of Delphic Myth and Its Origins*
(Berkeley and Los Angeles: University of California Press,
1959) 18, 21, 56-57, 189-90, 550; Walter F. Otto, "Mythos von
Leto, dem Drachen und der Geburt," *Das Wort der Antike* (ed.
Kurt von Fritz; Stuttgart: Klett, 1962) 90-128.

[2]Cf. William B. Anderson, "Lucan," *OCD*, 514. Translation
cited is from LCL of Lucan 5.79-81:

> *Ultor ibi expulsae, premeret cum viscera partus, matris,
> adhuc rudibus Paean Pythona sagittis explicuit, cum
> regna Themis tripodasque teneret.*

[3]Cf. Fontenrose, *Python*, 13-22.

[4]See Otto, "Mythos von Leto," *passim*.

[5]*Ann*. 3.61; cf. Martin P. Nilsson, *Geschichte der
griechischen Religion*, vol. 2: *Die hellenistische und römische
Zeit* (München: Beck, 1950) 325, 350-51.

[6]Eric H. Warmington, "Strabo (2)," *OCD*, 863.

[7]*Geogr*. 14.639-40 (14.1.20).

[8]On the Curetes, cf. Nilsson, *Geschichte*, 2. 351 and
literature cited there.

[9]14.640 (14.1.20): *tōn d'hysteron genomenōn*.

[10]*Ibid*.: *panēgyris d' entautha synteleitai kat' etos,
ethei de tini hoi neoi philokalousi, malista peri tas entautha
euōchias lamprynomenoi· tote de kai tōn kourētōn archeion syna-
gei symposia, kai tinas mystikas thysias epitelei.*

264

[11]Cf. Nilsson, *Geschichte*, 2. 351.

[12]Cf. Hyginus *Fab.* 140; Lucian *Dial. mar.* 9(10) = 314-16.

[13]Cf. H. J. Rose, "Mythographers," *OCD*, 594.

[14]Lucian *Dial. mar.* 9(10) = 314-16.

[15]Walter M. Edwards, "Lucian," *OCD*, 515.

[16]The translation cited is from the LCL; *toutō gar tō diastēmati periōristhō hēmin hē tou orchēstou polymathia kai ta dio mesou malista istō, Ouranou tomēn...kai meta tauta Dēlou planēn kai Lētous ōdinas kai Pythōnos anairesin....*

[17]See the introduction to *The Dance* by A. M. Harmon in LCL, *Lucian*, vol. 5. 209.

[18]Ibid. See also the article "Pantomimus," by William Beare, *OCD*, 643-44.

[19]Wehrli, "Leto," 557-58.

[20]Schreiber, *Apollon*, 68.

[21]Sauer, "Leto in der Kunst," 1972-74.

[22]Ibid., 1974.

[23]Ibid.

[24]Cf. A. Löbbecke, "Griechische Münzen aus meiner Sammlung IV," *Zeitschrift für Numismatik* 17 (1890) 1-26.

[25]Barclay V. Head, *A Catalogue of the Greek Coins in the British Museum: Catalogue of the Greek Coins of Ionia* (ed. R. S. Poole; Bologna: A. Forni-Editore, 1964) 165, no. 55.

[26]Ibid., 200, no. 158.

[27]Ibid., no. 164.

[28]Albert Rehm, *Didyma*, part 2: *Die Inschriften* (general ed. Theodor Wiegand, Deutsches Archäologisches Institut; ed. of this vol., Richard Harder; Berlin: Mann, 1958) 116. Cf. also Wehrli, "Leto," 557.

[29]Rehm, *Didyma* 2. 168, no. 223A.

[30]Ibid., 115-17, nos. 89-90.

[31]Cf. Erwin Ohlemutz, *Die Kulte und Heiligtümer der Götter in Pergamon* (Darmstadt: Wissenschaftliche Buchgesellschaft, 1968) 7-8; cf. also L. Robert, *Etudes anatoliennes* (Paris: Boccard, 1937) 72-73.

[32] Pausanias 9.35.7.

[33] Ohlemutz, *Die Kulte*, 9-12.

[34] Christian Habicht, *Altertümer von Pergamon*, vol. 8, 3: *Die Inschriften des Asklepieions* (Berlin: de Gruyter, 1969) 129-30, no. 115; cf. Ohlemutz, *Die Kulte*, 13.

[35] Habicht, *Die Inschriften*, 132-33, no. 120; cf. Ohlemutz, *Die Kulte*, 12.

[36] *Annual of the British School at Athens* 65 (1970) 31-36.

[37] When Ross discovered the inscription it was built into a Doric temple which he identified as the temple of the Pythian Apollo (Ludwig Ross, *Inselreisen*, vol. 1 [ed. F. Hiller von Gaertringen et al.; Halle: Niemeyer, 1912] 129-32; cf. A. Frantz, H. A. Thomson, and J. Travlos, "The 'Temple of Apollon Pythios' on Sikinos," *AJA* 73 [1969] 397-422, pls. 97-114).

[38] Louis Robert, *Monnaies grecques* (Centre de recherches d'histoire et de philologie 1, Hautes études numismatiques 2; Geneva: Librairie Droz, 1967) 89 and note 6.

[39] *Sylloge Nummorum Graecorum Deutschland, Sammlung von Aulock*, vol. 7: *Karien* (ed. K. Kraft and D. Kienast; Berlin: Mann, 1962) no. 2491 (Lucius Verus).

[40] Wehrli, "Leto," 555.

[41] See above, note 29.

[42] G. E. Bean, "Notes and Inscriptions from Caunus [Part 2]," *JHS* 74 (1954), inscription no. 21, 85-87; cf. also R. Merkelbach, "Ein Orakel des gryneischen Apollon," *Zeitschrift für Papyrologie und Epigraphik* 5 (1970) 48.

[43] J. Des Gagniers et al., *Laodicée du Lycos, le Nymphée, campagnes 1961-63* (Université Laval, Recherches archéologiques, Série 1: Fouilles; Quebec: Presses de l'Université Laval, 1969) 298-303.

[44] *Geogr.* 14.665-66 (14.3.6).

[45] Wehrli, "Leto," 555-56 and 573.

[46] Published as No. 1380 in *The Oxyrhynchus Papyri*, Part XI, 190-220. Isis is called *en Lykia Lētō* in lines 78-79 (197).

[47] A. H. M. Jones, *The Cities of the Eastern Roman Provinces*, 2nd ed. (Oxford: Clarendon Press, 1971) 28, 33, 47, 53, 79.

[48]*Egō paredreuō tē(i) tou hēliou poreia(i)*. Text republished by Jan Bergman, *Ich bin Isis: Studien zum memphitischen Hintergrund der griechischen Isisaretalogien* (Acta Universitatis Upsaliensis, Historia Religionum 3; Uppsala: Universitetet, 1968) 301-3.

[49]Bergman, *Ich bin Isis*, 162.

[50]*Pap. Oxy.* 1380, 112-13 (198).

[51]Drexler, "Isis," 437.

[52]Georges Lafaye, *Histoire du culte des divinités d'Alexandrie* (Paris: Thorin, 1884).

[53]Wilhelm Drexler, "Der Isis- und Sarapis-Cultus in Kleinasien," *Numismatische Zeitschrift* 21 (1889) 1-234 and 385-92 and "Isis: ausserägyptische Kulte," in Roscher, 2. 373-548; Adolf Rusch, *De Serapide et Iside in Graecia Cultis* (Berlin: H. S. Hermann, 1906); see the review of Rusch by A. J. Reinach in *RHR* 60 (1909) 94-95; Thomas A. Brady, *The Reception of the Egyptian Cults by the Greeks (330-30 B.C.)* (*The University of Missouri Studies* 10, No. 1; 1935); Martin P. Nilsson, *Geschichte*, 2. 118-19, 597-613 and *passim*.

[54]David Magie, "Egyptian Deities in Asia Minor in Inscriptions and on Coins," *AJA* Series 2, 57 (1953) 163-87; Ladilaus Vidman, *Sylloge inscriptionum religionis Isiacae et Sarapiacae* (Religionsgeschichtliche Versuche und Vorarbeiten 28; Berlin: de Gruyter, 1969); P. M. Fraser discusses the Hellenistic evidence for the spread of the cult of Sarapis (and related deities) in the islands of the Aegean and in Asia Minor in his "Two Studies on the Cult of Sarapis in the Hellenistic World," *Opuscula Atheniensia* 3 (Skrifter utgivna av Svenska Institutet i Athen 4°, 7; Lund: Gleerup, 1960) 24-37.

[55]Volume 15 in the series is Regina Salditt-Trappmann, *Tempel der ägyptischen Götter in Griechenland und an der Westküste Kleinasiens* (Leiden: Brill, 1970); vol. 18 is J. Leclant, *Inventaire bibliographique des Isiaca: A-D* (Leiden: Brill, 1972); vol. 26 is F. Dunand, *Le Culte d'Isis dans le basin oriental de la Méditerranée*, vol. 3: *Le Culte d'Isis en Asie mineure* (Leiden: Brill, 1973); and vol. 46 is G. J. F. Kater-Sibbes, *A Preliminary Catalogue of Sarapis Monuments* (Leiden: Brill, 1973).

[56]Vidman, *Sylloge*, 163, No. 318, 319; cf. Magie, "Egyptian Deities," 176 and note 128; and Dunand, *Le Culte d'Isis*, 101 and note 1.

[57]Vidman, *Sylloge*, 163-64, No. 320; Dunand, *Le Culte d'Isis*, 101 and note 3.

[58]Vidman, *Sylloge*, 164, No. 321; cf. Magie, "Egyptian Deities," 176 and note 128; and Dunand, *Le Culte d'Isis*, 101 and note 4.

[59]Vidman, *Sylloge*, 162-63, No. 317; cf. Dunand, *Le Culte d'Isis*, 104 and note 1.

[60]Vidman, *Sylloge*, 161, No. 313; cf. Magie, "Egyptian Deities," 175 and note 124; cf. also Ohlemutz, *Die Kulte*, 273; and Dunand, *Le Culte d'Isis*, 93-94.

[61]*Pap. Oxy.* 1380, 108 (198).

[62]*SNGD*, vol. 4: *Mysien* (ed. K. Kraft; Berlin: Mann, 1960) table 44, no. 1431.

[63]C. H. V. Sutherland, "Sabina," *OCD*, 785.

[64]*SNGD*, vol. 16: *Nachtrag II: Mysien, Troas, Aeolis, Lesbos* (Berlin: Mann, 1966) table 265, no. 7674.

[65]Drexler, "Der Isis- und Sarapis-Cultus," 65-66.

[66]Ibid., 76-77.

[67]Ibid., 150.

[68]Vidman, *Sylloge*, 158, No. 307; Magie, "Egyptian Deities," 174 note 110. Note the error or misprint in Magie's text concerning the attestation (in the second century *after* Christ) of the Sarapis-Isis cult in Magnesia; the cult is already attested in the second century *before* Christ by the dedication itself; cf. Dunand, *Le Culte d'Isis*, 80-81.

[69]See Magie, "Egyptian Deities," 173 and the literature he cites in note 98; see also Wilhelm Alzinger, "Ephesos. B. Archaeologischer Teil," PW Supplementband 12. 1652-54; Joseph Keil, "Denkmäler des Sarapiskultes in Ephesus," *Anzeiger der Akademie der Wissenschaften, Wien* 17 (1954) 217-28; Salditt-Trappmann, *Tempel der ägyptischen Götter*, 26-32.

[70]Vidman, *Sylloge*, 153, No. 296; cf. Magie, "Egyptian Deities," 173 and note 97; cf. also Dunand, *Le Culte d'Isis*, 67-69.

[71]Vidman, *Sylloge*, 154, No. 298 and literature there cited.

[72]Cf. Magie, "Egyptian Deities," 173 and his reference to the work of Pinder (1855) in note 97. See also the *Sylloge Nummorum Graecorum: The Burton Y. Berry Collection*, vol. 1, part 2: *Megaris to Egypt* (New York: The American Numismatic Society, 1962) plate 40, no. 1059.

[73]*SNGD*, vol. 6: *Ionien* (Berlin: Mann, 1960) table 57, no. 1868; cf. Dunand, *Le Culte d'Isis*, 68 and note 2.

[74]Vidman, *Sylloge*, 154-55, No. 300; cf. Dunand, *Le Culte d'Isis*, 69-70 and note 1.

[75]...*hierea Eisidos kai Sarapidos*...; Vidman, *Sylloge*, 152-53, No. 295; cf. Dunand, *Le Culte d'Isis*, 79 and note 3.

[76]Drexler, "Der Isis- und Sarapis-Cultus," 156.

[77]Magie, "Egyptian Deities," 173; coins dated generally to the Imperial period, note 93; coins dated from the rule of Severus to that of Gordian, note 94; cf. Dunand, *Le Culte d'Isis*, 66 and note 2 (and the references cited there).

[78]Vidman, *Sylloge*, 149, No. 290 and literature there cited; cf. also Magie, "Egyptian Deities," 173 and note 91; and Dunand, *Le Culte d'Isis*, 54.

[79]Cf. Salditt-Trappmann, *Tempel*, 45-46 and plan 5 at the end of the book.

[80]Vidman, *Sylloge*, 149-50, No. 291; cf. Magie, "Egyptian Deities," 172-73 and note 90; and Dunand, *Le Culte d'Isis*, 56.

[81]Vidman, *Sylloge*, 151, No. 292; cf. Magie, "Egyptian Deities," 173 and note 91.

[82]Vidman, *Sylloge*, 147, No. 285 and the literature there cited; cf. also Dunand, *Le Culte d'Isis*, 53 and note 4.

[83]Vidman, *Sylloge*, 148-49, No. 289; cf. Magie, "Egyptian Deities," 173-74 and note 100; cf. Dunand, *Le Culte d'Isis*, 49-50.

[84]Vidman, *Sylloge*, 149, No. 289a; cf. Dunand, *Le Culte d'Isis*, 50.

[85]Vidman, *Sylloge*, 143-44, No. 278 (*hiereōs Eisios*); cf. Magie, "Egyptian Deities," 171, note 81; see also Dunand, *Le Culte d'Isis*, 39.

[86]Vidman, *Sylloge*, 142-43, No. 276 (*hierea Isidos*); cf. Magie, "Egyptian Deities," 171, note 81; see also Dunand, *Le Culte d'Isis*, 37.

[87]Vidman, *Sylloge*, 143, No. 277; cf. Magie, "Egyptian Deities," 171, note 81; see also Dunand, *Le Culte d'Isis*, 38.

[88]Vidman, *Sylloge*, 141, No. 274; cf. Dunand, *Le Culte d'Isis*, 40-42.

[89]Vidman, *Sylloge*, 141, No. 274a; cf. Dunand, *Le Culte d'Isis*, 39-40, who dates the inscription to the Hellenistic period.

[90]Cf. Magie, "Egyptian Deities," 171 and note 78.

[91]*Sylloge Nummorum Graecorum*, vol. 4: *Fitzwilliam Museum, Leake and General Collections*, part 6: *Asia Minor-Phrygia* (British Academy; London: Oxford University Press, 1965) plate

92, no. 4729; cf. also Drexler, "Der Isis- und Sarapis-Cultus," 136; *SNGD*, vol. 7, table 83, nos. 2635, 2636; see also Dunand, *Le Culte d'Isis*, 35 and note 6 (and the references given there).

[92]Vidman, *Sylloge*, 140, No. 272; cf. P. M. Fraser, "Two Studies," 34, note 5; cf. also Dunand, *Le Culte d'Isis*, 35 and note 1.

[93]Cf. Magie, "Egyptian Deities," 171 and note 77; see also Dunand, *Le Culte d'Isis*, 34 and note 4 (where further literature is cited).

[94]*SNGB*, vol. 4, part 6, plate 100, no. 5010. Drexler lists two coins of this type from Synnada. He identifies the male head on one as Akamas, the mythical founder of the city, and the other as Thynnaros. He does not suggest dates for either coin ("Der Isis- und Sarapis-Cultus," 177-78).

[95]*SNGD*, vol. 9: *Phrygien* (ed. H.-W. Ritter; Berlin: Mann, 1964) table 124, nos. 3806, 3807, 3808; cf. Dunand, *Le Culte d'Isis*, 46 and note 10 (and the references cited there).

[96]*SNGD*, vol. 9, table 125, no. 3814; cf. Dunand, *Le Culte d'Isis*, 46-47 and note 1 (and the references cited there).

[97]*SNGB*, vol. 4, part 6, plate 100, no. 5012; cf. Drexler, "Der Isis- und Sarapis-Cultus," 180-81.

[98]*SNGA*, vol. 1, part 2, plate 45, nos. 1196, 1197; cf. Dunand, *Le Culte d'Isis*, 5.

[99]*Pap. Oxy.* 1380, 79-80 (197).

[100]*SNGD*, vol. 10: *Lykien* (Berlin: Mann, 1964) table 142, nos. 4342, 4362.

[101]*SNGD*, vol. 10, table 144, nos. 4437, 4438; cf. Dunand, *Le Culte d'Isis*, 5 (and literature cited there).

[102]Vidman, *Sylloge*, 134, No. 259; cf. Dunand, *Le Culte d'Isis*, 98 and note 5.

[103]Vidman, *Sylloge*, 134, No. 260; cf. Dunand, *Le Culte d'Isis*, 98 and note 2.

[104]Vidman, *Sylloge*, 135, No. 261; on inscriptions No. 259-61, cf. Magie, "Egyptian Deities," 175 and note 114; see also Dunand, *Le Culte d'Isis*, 99 and note 1.

[105]Vidman, *Sylloge*, 134, No. 257; cf. Magie, "Egyptian Deities," 174 and note 113; Fraser, "Two Studies," 25, note 4; and Dunand, *Le Culte d'Isis*, 77.

[106]Vidman, *Sylloge*, 131, No. 249; cf. Magie, "Egyptian Deities," 171 and note 73; see also Dunand, *Le Culte d'Isis*, 31.

[107]Vidman, *Sylloge*, 128, No. 241; cf. Magie, "Egyptian Deities," 170 and note 67.

[108]For a chronological survey of the evidence for the Isis cult in Rhodes city, cf. Dunand, *Le Culte d'Isis*, 18-24. Cf. Magie, "Egyptian Deities," 170 and note 60; see also Dunand, *Le Culte d'Isis*, 21 and notes 5 and 6.

[109]Vidman, *Sylloge*, 101-2, No. 173; cf. Magie, "Egyptian Deities," 170 and note 61.

[110]Vidman, *Sylloge*, 103-5, No. 177; cf. Magie, "Egyptian Deities," 170 and note 63; and Dunand, *Le Culte d'Isis*, 23 and notes 1 and 2.

[111]Vidman, *Sylloge*, 104, No. 179; cf. Magie, "Egyptian Deities," 170 and note 61.

[112]Cf. Magie, "Egyptian Deities," 170 and note 65. A coin of this type from Rhodes, though undated, was published in *SNGA*, vol. 1, part 2, plate 42, no. 1131. See also *SNGB*, vol. 4, part 6, plate 94, nos. 4813, 4814, 4817; cf. Dunand, *Le Culte d'Isis*, 21 and note 3 (where further references are given).

[113]Vidman, *Sylloge*, 113, No. 199; cf. Dunand, *Le Culte d'Isis*, 27 and note 5.

[114]Vidman, *Sylloge*, 127, No. 238.

[115]Vidman, *Sylloge*, 128-29; No. 239; cf. Dunand, *Le Culte d'Isis*, 26 and note 5.

[116]Cf. Hans W. Müller, "Isis mit dem Horuskinde," *Münchner Jahrbuch der bildenden Kunst*, Series 3, 14 (Munich: Prestel, 1963) 7-38.

[117]V. Tran Tam Tinh and Yvette Labrecque, *Isis lactans* (Etudes préliminaires aux religions orientales dans l'empire romain 37; Leiden: Brill, 1973); see the map at the end of the book.

BIBLIOGRAPHY

Albright, W. F. "Anath and the Dragon." *BASOR* 84 (1941) 14-17.

_____. "Are the Ephod and the Teraphim Mentioned in Ugaritic Literature?" *BASOR* 83 (1941) 39-42.

_____. "Baal-Zephon." In *Festschrift Alfred Bertholet*, edited by Walter Baumgartner et al. Tübingen: Mohr, 1950.

_____. "The Psalm of Habakkuk." In *Studies in Old Testament Prophecy*, edited by H. H. Rowley. Edinburgh: Clark, 1950.

_____. *Yahweh and the Gods of Canaan*. Garden City, N.Y.: Doubleday, 1969.

Allegro, J. M. "More Isaiah Commentaries from Qumran's Fourth Cave." *JBL* 77 (1958) 215-21.

Allo, E.-B. *Saint Jean: L'Apocalypse*. 4th ed., rev. EBib. Paris: Gabalda, 1933.

Angus, Samuel. *The Mystery-Religions and Christianity*. New York: Scribner's, 1925.

Anthes, Rudolf. "Mythology in Ancient Egypt." In *Mythologies of the Ancient World*, edited by Samuel N. Kramer. Garden City, N.Y.: Doubleday, 1961.

Attridge, Harold W., and Oden, Robert A., eds. *De Dea Syria*. SBL Texts and Translations. Missoula, Mont.: Scholars Press, 1976.

Bardon, Henry. *Les Empereurs et les lettres latines d'Auguste à Hadrien*. Paris: Société d'Edition 'Les Belles Lettres,' 1940.

Barrett, C. K. *The New Testament Background: Selected Documents*. New York: Harper and Row, 1961.

Batey, R. A. *New Testament Nuptial Imagery*. Leiden: Brill, 1971.

Baumgarten, J., and Mansoor, M. "Studies in the New *Hodayot* (Thanksgiving Hymns) - II." *JBL* 74 (1955) 188-95.

Bean, G. E. "Notes and Inscriptions from Caunus [Part 2]." *JHS* 74 (1954) 85-110.

Behm, Johannes. *Die Offenbarung des Johannes*. NTD 11. Göttingen: Vandenhoeck und Ruprecht, 1953.

Bentzen, Aage. *Daniel*. 2nd ed. HAT 19. Tübingen: Mohr, 1952.

Bergman, Jan. *Ich bin Isis: Studien zum memphitischen Hintergrund der griechischen Isisaretalogien*. Acta Universitatis Upsaliensis, Historia Religionum 3. Uppsala: Universitetet, 1968.

Betz, Otto. "Das Volk seiner Kraft: Zur Auslegung der Qumrânhodajah III, 1-18." *NTS* 5 (1958) 67-75.

_____. *Der Paraklet*. Arbeiten zur Geschichte des Spätjudentums und Urchristentums 2. Leiden: Brill, 1963.

_____. "Die Geburt der Gemeinde durch den Lehrer." *NTS* 3 (1956/57) 314-26.

Blackman, A. M. "Myth and Ritual in Ancient Egypt." In *Myth and Ritual*, edited by S. H. Hooke. London: Oxford University Press, 1933.

Böhlig, Alexander, and Labib, Pahor. *Koptischgnostische Apokalypsen aus Codex V von Nag Hammadi....Wissenschaftliche Zeitschrift der Martin-Luther-Universität Halle-Wittenberg*, Sonderband. Halle: Martin-Luther-Universität Halle-Wittenberg, 1963.

Boismard, M. E. "'L'Apocalypse,' ou 'les apocalypses' de S. Jean." *RB* 56 (1949) 507-27.

Boll, Franz. *Aus der Offenbarung Johannis: Hellenistische Studien zum Weltbild der Apokalypse*. Stoicheia 1. Leipzig: Teubner, 1914.

Bonnet, Hans. *Reallexikon der ägyptischen Religionsgeschichte*. Berlin: de Gruyter, 1952.

Bonsirven, Joseph. *L'Apocalypse*. Verbum Salutis 16. Paris: Beauchesne, 1951.

Bornkamm, Günther. "Die Komposition der apokalyptischen Visionen in der Offenbarung Johannis." *ZNW* 36 (1937) 132-49. Reprint in *Studien zu Antike und Urchristentum: Gesammelte Aufsätze Band II*. BEvT 28. Munich: Kaiser, 1959.

_____. "*Mystērion, myeō*." *TDNT* 4 (1967) 802-28.

_____. "On the Understanding of Worship." *Early Christian Experience*. New York: Harper and Row, 1969.

Bousset, Wilhelm. "Antichrist." In *Encyclopaedia of Religion and Ethics*, edited by James Hastings. Vol. 1. New York: Scribner's, 1908.

_____. *Die Offenbarung Johannis*. Meyer 16, 5th ed. Göttingen: Vandenhoeck und Ruprecht, 1896.

_____. *Die Religion des Judentums im späthellenistischen Zeitalter*. Edited by Hugo Gressmann. HNT 21. Tübingen: Mohr, 1926.

Bousset, Wilhelm. *The Antichrist Legend*. London: Hutchinson, 1896. Translation of *Der Antichrist*. Göttingen: Vandenhoeck und Ruprecht, 1895.

Bowman, John W. "The Revelation to John: Its Dramatic Structure and Message." *Int* 9 (1955) 436-53.

Brady, Thomas. *The Reception of the Egyptian Cults by the Greeks (330-30 B.C.)*. *The University of Missouri Studies* 10, 1, 1935.

Braun, F. M. "La Femme vêtue de soleil (Apoc. XII): Etat du problème." *Revue Thomiste* 55 (1955) 639-69.

Braun, Herbert. *Qumran und das Neue Testament*. Vol. 1. Tübingen: Mohr, 1966.

Breech, Earl. "These Fragments I Have Shored against My Ruins: The Form and Function of 4 Ezra." *JBL* 92 (1973) 267-74.

Brown, Raymond E. *The Semitic Background of the Term "Mystery" in the New Testament*. Facet Books, Biblical Series 21. Philadelphia: Fortress, 1968.

Brownlee, W. H. "Messianic Motifs of Qumran and the NT." *NTS* 3 (1956/57) 12-30, 195-210.

Brox, N. *Zeuge und Märtyrer*. Munich: Kösel Verlag, 1961.

Brütsch, Charles. *Die Offenbarung Jesu Christi*. 3 vols. Zürcher Bibelkommentare. Zürich: Zwingli, 1970.

Brun, Lyder. "Die römischen Kaiser in der Apokalypse." *ZNW* 26 (1927) 128-51.

Buck, Adriaan de. *The Egyptian Coffin Texts*. Vol. 2. The University of Chicago Oriental Institute Publications 49. Chicago: University of Chicago Press, 1938.

Budge, E. A. Wallis. *Egyptian Literature*. Vol. 1, *Legends of the Gods: The Egyptian Texts*. London: K. Paul, Trench, Trübner, 1912.

_____. *From Fetish to God in Ancient Egypt*. Oxford: Oxford University Press, H. Milford, 1934.

_____. *The Gods of the Egyptians; or, Studies in Egyptian Mythology*. Vol. 2. Chicago: Open Court, 1904. Reprint, New York: Dover Publications, 1969.

Bultmann, Rudolf. Review of Lohmeyer. *TLZ* 52 (1927) 505-12.

Burgmann, Hans. "Die vier Endzeittermine im Danielbuch." *ZAW* 86 (1974) 543-50.

Caird, G. B. *A Commentary on the Revelation of St. John the Divine*. New York: Harper and Row, 1966.

274

Cerfaux, Lucien, and Cambier, Jules. *L'Apocalypse*. Lectio
Divina 17. Paris: Les Editions du Cerf, 1955.

Chamberlain, J. V. "Another Qumran Thanksgiving Psalm" and
"Further Elucidation of a Messianic Thanksgiving Psalm
from Qumran." *JNES* 14 (1955) 32-41, 181-82.

Charles, R. H. *A Critical and Exegetical Commentary on the Revelation of St. John*. 2 vols. ICC. New York: Scribner's,
1920.

_____. *Studies in the Apocalypse*. Edinburgh: Clark, 1913.

_____. *The Ascension of Isaiah*. London: Black, 1900.

Chavasse, Claude. *The Bride of Christ*. London: Faber, 1940.

Clapham, Lynn R. "Sanchuniathon: The First Two Cycles." Ph.D.
dissertation, Harvard University, 1969.

Clemen, C. *Die phönikische Religion nach Philo von Byblos*.
Mittheilungen der vorderasiatisch-ägyptischen Gesellschaft
42.3. Leipzig: Hinrichs, 1939.

Clifford, Richard J. *The Cosmic Mountain in Canaan and the Old
Testament*. Harvard Semitic Monographs 4. Cambridge:
Harvard University Press, 1972.

Cole, Percival R. *Later Roman Education in Ausonius, Capella
and the Theodosian Code*. New York: Teachers College,
Columbia University, 1909. Reprint, New York: AMS, 1972.

Collart, Paul. *Nonnos de Panopolis: Etudes sur la composition
et le texte des Dionysiaques*. Le Caire: Impr. de l'Institut français d'archéologie orientale, 1930.

Collins, Adela Yarbro. "Composition and Redaction of the Testament of Moses 10." *HTR*, forthcoming.

Collins, John J. "The Place of the Fourth Sibyl in the Development of the Jewish Sibyllina." *JJS* 25 (1974) 365-80.

_____. *The Sibylline Oracles of Egyptian Judaism*. SBL
Dissertation Series 13. Missoula, Mont.: Scholars Press,
1974.

_____. "The Son of Man and the Saints of the Most High in
the Book of Daniel." *JBL* 93 (1974) 50-66.

Conzelmann, Hans. "Die Mutter der Weisheit." In *Zeit und Geschichte*, edited by E. Dinkler. Tübingen: Mohr, 1964.

Coote, Robert B. "The Serpent and Sacred Marriage in Northwest
Semitic Tradition." Ph.D. dissertation, Harvard University, 1972.

Cross, Frank Moore, Jr. *Canaanite Myth and Hebrew Epic: Essays in the History of the Religion of Israel.* Cambridge: Harvard University Press, 1973.

_____. *The Ancient Library of Qumran and Modern Biblical Studies.* Rev. ed. Garden City, N.Y.: Doubleday, 1961.

Cumont, Franz. "Dea Syria." In PW 4. 2236-43.

Cuss, Dominique. *Imperial Cult and Honorary Terms in the New Testament.* Paradosis 23. Fribourg: The University Press, 1974.

Danielou, Jean. Review of Böhlig-Labib. *RSR* 54 (1966) 291-93.

Deichgräber, Reinhard. *Gotteshymnus und Christushymnus in der frühen Christenheit: Untersuchungen zur Form, Sprache und Stil der frühchristlichen Hymnen.* Studien zur Umwelt des Neuen Testaments 5. Göttingen: Vandenhoeck und Ruprecht, 1967.

Deissmann, Adolf. *Light from the Ancient East.* Translated by L. R. M. Strachan from the 4th German ed. New York: Harper and Row, [1927].

Delcor, Matthias. *Le Livre de Daniel.* SB. Paris: Gabalda, 1971.

_____. "Un Psaume messianique de Qumran." In *Mélanges bibliques rédigés en l'honneur de André Robert.* Travaux de l'Institut Catholique de Paris 4. Paris: Bloud et Gay, 1957.

Delling, Gerhard. "Zum gottesdienstlichen Stil der Johannes-Apokalypse." *NovT* 3 (1959) 107-37.

Denis, Albert-Marie. *Introduction aux pseudepigraphs grecs d'Ancien Testament.* Studia in Veteris Testamenti Pseudepigrapha 1. Leiden: Brill, 1970.

Des Gagniers, J., et al. *Laodicée du Lycos, le Nymphée, campagnes, 1961-63.* Université Laval, Recherches archéologiques, Série 1: Fouilles. Quebec: Presses de l'Université Laval, 1969.

Dieterich, Albrecht. *Abraxas: Studien zur Religionsgeschichte des spätern Altertums.* Leipzig: Teubner, 1891.

_____. *Eine Mithrasliturgie.* 3rd ed. Edited by Otto Weinreich. Leipzig: Teubner, 1923.

Doty, William G. *Letters in Primitive Christianity.* Guides to Biblical Scholarship, New Testament Series. Philadelphia: Fortress, 1973.

Drexler, Wilhelm. "Der Isis- und Sarapis-Cultus in Kleinasien." *Numismatische Zeitschrift* 21 (1889) 1-234 and 385-92.

Drexler, Wilhelm. "Isis: ausserägyptische Kulte." In Roscher, 2. 373-548.

Driver, G. R. *Canaanite Myths and Legends*. Old Testament Studies 3. Edinburgh: Clark, 1956.

Drummond, James. *The Jewish Messiah*.... London: Longmans, Green and Co., 1877.

Dunand, F. *Le Culte d'Isis dans le basin oriental de la Méditerranée*. Vol. 3, *Le Culte d'Isis en Asie mineure*. Etudes préliminaires aux religions orientales dans l'empire romain 26. Leiden: Brill, 1973.

Dupont-Sommer, A. "La Mère du Messie et la mère de l'aspic dans un hymne de Qoumrân." *RHR* 147 (1955) 174-88.

Dupuis, E. *L'Origine de tous les cultes*. Paris, 1794.

Eissfeldt, Otto. *Ras Schamra und Sanchunjaton*. Halle: Niemeyer, 1939.

_____. *Sanchunjaton von Berut und Ilumilku von Ugarit*. Halle: Niemeyer, 1952.

Emerton, J. A. "The Origin of the Son of Man Imagery." *JTS* 9 (1958) 225-42.

Enmann. "Leto." In Roscher, 2. 1959-71.

Ernst, Josef. *Die eschatologischen Gegenspieler in den Schriften des Neuen Testaments*. Biblische Untersuchungen 3. Regensburg: Verlag Friedrich Pustet, 1967.

Exum, J. Cheryl. "A Literary and Structural Analysis of the Song of Songs." *ZAW* 85 (1973) 45-79.

Farnell, Lewis. *Greece and Babylon*. Edinburgh: Clark, 1911.

Farrer, Austin. *A Rebirth of Images: The Making of St. John's Apocalypse*. Westminster: Dacre, 1949.

_____. *The Revelation of St. John the Divine*. Oxford: Clarendon, 1964.

Fawcett, Thomas. *Hebrew Myth and Christian Gospel*. London: SCM, 1973.

Festugière, A.-J. "A propos des arétalogies d'Isis." *HTR* 42 (1949) 209-34.

Feuillet, André. *L'Apocalypse: Etat de la question*. Studia Neotestamentica Subsidia 3. Paris: Desclée, 1963.

_____. "Le Messie et sa mère d'après le chapitre XII de l'Apocalypse." *RB* 66 (1959) 55-86.

Feuillet, Andre. "La Moisson et la vendange de l'Apocalypse
(14, 14-20). La Signification chrétienne de la révélation
johannique." *NRT* 94 (1972) 225-50.

Fiorenza, Elisabeth Schüssler. "Apocalyptic and Gnosis in the
Book of Revelation." *JBL* 92 (1973) 565-81.

_____. "The Eschatology and Composition of the Apocalypse."
CBQ 30 (1968) 537-69.

_____. *Priester für Gott: Studien zum Herrschafts- und
Priestermotiv in der Apokalypse.* NTAbh N. F., 7.
Münster: Aschendorff, 1972.

Fitzer, Gottfried. *"Sphragis."* *TDNT* 7 (1971) 939-53.

Fitzgerald, Aloysius. "The Mythological Background for the
Presentation of Jerusalem as a Queen and False Worship as
Adultery in the OT." *CBQ* 34 (1972) 403-16.

Fitzmyer, Joseph A. "Further Light on Melchizedek from Qumran
Cave 11." In *Essays on the Semitic Background of the New
Testament.* Sources for Biblical Study 5. Missoula, Mont.:
Scholars Press, 1974.

Fleischer, Robert. *Artemis von Ephesos und verwandte Kultstatuen aus Anatolien und Syrien.* Etudes préliminaires
aux religions orientales dans l'empire romain 35. Leiden:
Brill, 1973.

Flemming, J., and Duensing, H. "The Ascension of Isaiah." In
Hennecke-Schneemelcher 2. 642-43.

Flusser, David. "The four empires in the Fourth Sibyl and in
the Book of Daniel." *Israel Oriental Studies* 2 (1972)
148-75.

Fontenrose, Joseph. *Python: A Study of Delphic Myth and Its
Origins.* Berkeley: University of California Press, 1959.

Ford, J. Massingberd. "The Divorce Bill of the Lamb and the
Scroll of the Suspected Adultress. A Note on Apoc. 5, 1
and 10, 8-11." *JSJ* 2 (1971) 136-39.

Frantz, A., Thomson, H. A., and Travlos, J. "The 'Temple of
Apollon Pythios' on Sikinos." *AJA* 73 (1969) 397-422.

Fraser, P. M. "Greek-Phoenician Bi-lingual Inscriptions from
Rhodes." *Annual of the British School at Athens* 65 (1970)
31-36.

_____. "Two Studies on the Cult of Sarapis in the Hellenis-
tic World." *Opuscula Atheniensia* 3. Skrifter utgivna
av Svenska Institutet i Athen 4°, 7. Lund: Gleerup, 1960.

Freundorfer, J. *Die Apokalypse des Apostels Johannes und die hellenistische Kosmologie und Astrologie.* Biblische Studien 33, 1. Freiburg: Herder, 1929.

Funk, Robert W. *Language, Hermeneutic, and Word of God: The Problem of Language in the New Testament and Contemporary Theology.* New York: Harper and Row, 1966.

Gadd, C. J. "Babylonian Myth and Ritual." In *Myth and Ritual,* edited by S. H. Hooke. London: Oxford University Press, 1933.

Gagé, Jean. *Apollon romain.* Bibliothèque des écoles françaises d'Athènes et de Rome 182. Paris: Boccard, 1955.

Geffcken, Johannes. *Die Oracula Sibyllina.* GCS 8. Leipzig: Hinrichs, 1902.

Giblin, Charles. "Structural and Thematic Correlations in the Theology of Revelation 16-22." *Bib* 55 (1974) 487-504.

Giet, Stanislas. *L'Apocalypse et l'histoire: Etude historique sur l'Apocalypse johannique.* Paris: Presses Universitaires de France, 1957.

Ginsberg, H. Louis. *Studies in Daniel.* Texts and Studies of the Jewish Theological Seminary of America 14. New York: Jewish Theological Seminary of America, 1948.

Ginzberg, Louis. *The Legends of the Jews.* 7 vols. Philadelphia: Jewish Publication Society, 1909-55.

Glueck, Nelson. *Deities and Dolphins.* New York: Farrar, Strauss and Giroux, 1965.

Goetze, A. "The City Khalbi and the Khapiru People." *BASOR* 79 (1940) 32-33.

Golenishchev, Vladimir S. *Die Metternichstele in der Originalgrösse.* Leipzig: Engelmann, 1877.

Gollinger, Hildegard. *Das "Grosse Zeichen" von Apokalypse 12.* Stuttgarter Biblische Monographien 11. Würzburg: Echter Verlag, 1971.

Gordon, Cyrus H. "Canaanite Mythology." In *Mythologies of the Ancient World,* edited by Samuel N. Kramer. Garden City, N.Y.: Doubleday, 1961.

_____. *Ugaritic Literature.* Rome: Pontificium Institutum Biblicum, 1949.

Grant, Michael. *Nero.* New York: American Heritage Press, 1970.

Gray, John. *The Legacy of Canaan: The Ras Shamra Texts and Their Relevance to the Old Testament.* VTSup 5. Leiden: Brill, 1957.

Gray, John. "The Wrath of God in Canaanite and Hebrew Literature." *Bulletin of the Manchester University Egyptian and Oriental Society* 25 (1947-53) 9-19.

Greenfield, J. Review of Kaiser. *JBL* 80 (1961) 91-92.

Griffiths, J. Gwyn. *The Conflict of Horus and Seth, from Egyptian and Classical Sources*. Liverpool: Liverpool University Press, 1960.

_____. *Apuleius of Madauros: The Isis Book (Metamorphoses, Book XI)*. Etudes préliminaires aux Religions orientales dans l'empire romain 39; Leiden: Brill, 1976.

_____. *Plutarch's "De Iside et Osiride"*. N.p.: University of Wales Press, 1970.

Grueber, Herbert A., ed. *Coins of the Roman Republic in the British Museum*. London: Printed by order of the Trustees, 1910.

Gruppe, Otto. *Die griechischen Culte und Mythen in ihren Beziehungen zu den orientalischen Religionen*. Vol. 1, *Einleitung*. Leipzig: Teubner, 1887.

Güterbock, Hans. "Hittite Mythology." In *Mythologies of the Ancient World*, edited by Samuel N. Kramer. Garden City, N.Y.: Doubleday, 1961.

_____. "The Hittite Version of the Hurrian Kumarbi Myths: Oriental Forerunners of Hesiod." *AJA* 52 (1948) 123-34.

_____. *Kumarbi*. Istanbuler Schriften 16. Zürich: Europa Verlag, 1946.

Gundel, Hans. "Zodiakos: Der Tierkreis in der Antike." *PW* 10A. 462-709.

Gunkel, Hermann. *Schöpfung und Chaos in Urzeit und Endzeit: Eine religionsgeschichtliche Untersuchung über Gen 1 und Ap Joh 12*. Göttingen: Vandenhoeck und Ruprecht, 1895.

_____. *Zum religionsgeschichtlichen Verständnis des Neuen Testaments*. FRLANT 1, 1. Göttingen: Vandenhoeck und Ruprecht, 1903.

_____, and Begrich, Joachim. *Einleitung in die Psalmen: Die Gattungen der religiösen Lyrik Israels*. 2nd ed. HKAT supplementary vol. Göttingen: Vandenhoeck und Ruprecht, 1966.

Habicht, Christian. *Altertümer von Pergamon*. Vol. 8, 3, *Die Inschriften des Asklepieions*. Berlin: de Gruyter, 1969.

Haenchen, Ernst. *The Acts of the Apostles: A Commentary*. Philadelphia: Westminster, 1971.

Hamerton-Kelly, Robert G. *Pre-existence, Wisdom, and the Son of Man*. Cambridge: Cambridge University Press, 1973.

Hanson, Paul D. *The Dawn of Apocalyptic*. Philadelphia: Fortress, 1975.

_____. "Zechariah 9 and the Recapitulation of an Ancient Ritual Pattern." *JBL* 92 (1973) 37-59.

Harder, R. *Karpokrates von Chalkis und die memphitische Isis-propaganda*. Abhandlungen der preussischen Akademie der Wissenschaften zu Berlin, phil-hist Kl. 14. Berlin: de Gruyter, 1943.

Harris, J. Rendel. *The Apology of Aristides on behalf of the Christians*. Texts and Studies 1, 1. Cambridge: Cambridge University Press, 1891.

Haussig, Hans Wilhelm, ed. *Wörterbuch der Mythologie*. Vol. 1, 1, *Götter und Mythen im Vorderen Orient*. Stuttgart: Klett, 1965.

Head, Barclay V. *A Catalogue of the Greek Coins in the British Museum: Catalogue of the Greek Coins of Ionia*, edited by R. S. Poole. Bologna: A. Forni-Editore, 1964.

Hedrick, William K. "The Sources and Use of the Imagery in Apocalypse 12." Dissertation, Graduate Theological Union, 1970.

Heidel, Alexander. *The Babylonian Genesis: The Story of Creation*. 2nd ed. Chicago: University of Chicago Press, 1951.

Heinz, Kurt. *Das Bild Kaiser Neros bei Seneca, Tacitus, Sueton und Cassius Dio*. Biel: Graphische Anstalt Schüler AG, 1948.

Hengel, Martin. *Die Zeloten*. Arbeiten zur Geschichte des Spätjudentums und Urchristentums 1. Leiden: Brill, 1961.

Hennecke, Edgar, and Schneemelcher, Wilhelm. *New Testament Apocrypha*. Vol. 2. Philadelphia: Westminster, 1965.

Hildebrandt. "Das römische Antichristentum zur Zeit der Offenbarung Johannis und des 5 sibyllinischen Buches." *Zeitschrift für Wissenschaftliche Theologie* 17 (1874) 57-95.

Hillers, D. R. "Rev 13:18 and a Scroll from Murabba'at." *BASOR* 170 (1963) 65.

Hinnells, John R. "The Zoroastrian Doctrine of Salvation in the Roman World." In *Man and His Salvation: Studies in Memory of S. G. F. Brandon*, edited by E. J. Sharpe and J. R. Hinnells. Manchester: The University Press, 1973.

Höfner, Maria. "Allat (Lāt, 'Ilat)." In *Wörterbuch der Mythologie*, edited by H. W. Haussig (see Haussig).

Hofmann, Karl-Martin. *Philema Hagion*. Gütersloh: Der Rufer Evangelischer Verlag, 1938.

Holtz, Traugott. *Die Christologie der Apokalypse des Johannes*. 2nd ed. TU 85. Berlin: Akademie, 1971.

Honig, Edwin. *Dark Conceit: The Making of Allegory*. Evanston: Northwestern University Press, 1959.

Hooke, S. H., ed. *Myth and Ritual*. London: Oxford University Press, 1933.

_____. *Myth, Ritual, and Kingship*. Oxford: Clarendon, 1958.

_____. *The Labyrinth*. London: SPCK, 1935.

Huppenbauer, Hans Walter. "Belial in den Qumrantexten." *Theologische Zeitschrift* 15 (1959) 81-89.

Huschke, E. *Das Buch mit sieben Siegeln in der Offenbarung St. Johannis 5, 1 u. folg.* Leipzig: Naumann, 1860.

Jacobsen, Thorkild. "Mesopotamia." In *The Intellectual Adventure of Ancient Man*. By H[enri] Frankfort et al. Chicago: University of Chicago Press, 1946.

_____. "The Battle between Marduk and Tiamat." *JAOS* 88 (1968) 104-8.

Jörns, Klaus-Peter. *Das hymnische Evangelium: Untersuchungen zu Aufbau, Funktion, und Herkunft der hymnische Stücke in der Johannesoffenbarung*. Studien zum Neuen Testament 5. Gütersloh: Mohn, 1971.

Jones, A. H. M. *The Cities of the Eastern Roman Provinces*. 2nd ed. Oxford: Clarendon Press, 1971.

Jones, Bruce W. "More about the Apocalypse as Apocalyptic." *JBL* 87 (1968) 325-27.

Jonge, M. de, and Woude, A. S. van der. "11Q Melchizedek and the New Testament." *NTS* 12 (1966) 301-26.

Kaiser, Otto. *Die mythische Bedeutung des Meeres in Ägypten, Ugarit und Israel*. BZAW 78. Töpelmann, 1959. 2nd ed., 1962.

Kallas, James. "The Apocalypse--An Apocalyptic Book?" *JBL* 86 (1967) 69-80.

Kamlah, Ehrhard. *Die Form der katalogischen Paränese im Neuen Testament*. Wissenschaftliche Untersuchungen zum Neuen Testament 7. Tübingen: Mohr, 1964.

282

Kapelrud, Arvid S. *Baal in the Ras Shamra Texts.* Copenhagen: Gad, 1952.

Kassing, Altfrid Th. *Die Kirche und Maria: Ihr Verhältnis im 12. Kapitel der Apokalypse.* Düsseldorf: Patmos Verlag, 1958.

Kater-Sibbes, G. J. F. *A Preliminary Catalogue of Sarapis Monuments.* Etudes préliminaires aux religions orientales dans l'empire romain 46. Leiden: Brill, 1973.

Kees, H. "Seth." In PW 2, 4. 1896-1922.

Keil, Joseph. "Denkmäler des Sarapiskultes in Ephesus." *Anzeiger der Akademie der Wissenschaften, Wien* 17 (1954) 217-28.

Keydell, Rudolf. "Eine Nonnos-Analyse." *L'Antiquité classique* 1 (1932) 173-202.

_____. "Nonnos (15)." In PW 17. 904-20.

_____. "Peisandros (12)." In PW 37. 145-46.

_____. "Zur Komposition der Bücher 13-40 der Dionysiaca des Nonnos." *Hermes* 62 (1927) 343-434.

Koch, Klaus. *The Rediscovery of Apocalyptic: A Polemical Work on a Neglected Area of Biblical Studies and Its Damaging Effects on Theology and Philosophy.* SBT, 2nd Series 2. Naperville, Ill.: Allenson, 1972.

Koehler, Reinhold. *Über die Dionysiaka des Nonnos von Panopolis.* Halle: Pfeffer, 1853.

Koep, Leo. *Das himmlische Buch in Antike und Christentum.* Theophaneia 8. Bonn: Hanstein, 1952.

Koster, Willem J. W., ed. *Scholia in Aristophanem.* Groningen: Wolters, 1960-62.

Kraft, Heinrich. *Die Offenbarung des Johannes.* HNT 16a. Tübingen: Mohr, 1974.

_____. "Zur Offenbarung des Johannes." *ThRu* N.F. 38 (1973) 81-98.

Kramer, Samuel N. "Mythology of Sumer and Akkad." In *Mythologies of the Ancient World,* edited by Samuel N. Kramer. Garden City, N.Y.: Doubleday, 1961.

_____. *The Sacred Marriage Rite.* Bloomington, Ind.: Indiana University Press, 1969.

Lafaye, Georges. *Histoire du culte des divinités d'Alexandrie.* Paris: Thorin, 1884.

Lamy, Thomas Joseph. *Sancti Ephraem Syri Hymni et Sermones.*
Vol. 3. Mechlinia: Dessain, 1889.

Lanchester, H. C. O. "The Sibylline Oracles." In Charles,
APOT, 2. 368-406.

Leclant, J. *Inventaire bibliographique des Isiaca: A-D.*
Etudes préliminaires aux religions orientales dans l'empire romain 18. Leiden: Brill, 1972.

Lesky, Albin. *Hethitische Texte und griechischer Mythos.*
Anzeiger der österreichischen Akademie der Wissenschaften
9 (1950) 137-59.

Lévi-Strauss, Claude. "The Structural Study of Myth." *Structural Anthropology.* New York: Basic Books, 1963.

Licht, J. "Taxo, or the Apocalyptic Doctrine of Vengeance."
JJS 12 (1961) 95-103.

Lietzmann, Hans. *Mass and Lord's Supper: A Study in the History of the Liturgy.* Leiden: Brill, 1955.

Lind, L. R. "Un-Hellenic Elements in the Dionysiaca." *L'Antiquité classique* 7 (1938) 57-65.

_____. "Un-Hellenic Elements in the Subject Matter of the
Dionysiaca of Nonnos." *Classical Weekly* 29 (1935) 17-20.

Lindblom, Johannes. "Die Gesichte der Johannesapokalypse."
In *Gesichte und Offenbarungen: Vorstellungen von göttlichen Weisungen und übernatürlichen Erscheinungen im
ältesten Christentum.* Skrifter utgivna av Kungl. Humanistiska Vetenskapssamfundet i Lund 65. Lund: Gleerup,
1968.

Löbbecke, A. "Griechische Münzen aus meiner Sammlung IV."
Zeitschrift für Numismatik 17 (1890) 1-26.

Lohfink, Gerhard. *Die Himmelfahrt Jesu: Untersuchungen zu den
Himmelfahrts- und Erhöhungstexten bei Lukas.* Munich:
Kösel Verlag, 1971.

Lohmeyer, Ernst. *Die Offenbarung des Johannes.* HNT 16.
Tübingen: Mohr, 1926.

Lohse, Eduard. *Die Offenbarung des Johannes.* NTD 11, 10th ed.
Göttingen: Vandenhoeck und Ruprecht, 1971.

Maag, Victor. "B^{e}lĭja'al im Alten Testament." *Theologische
Zeitschrift* 21 (1965) 287-99.

MacRae, George W. "The Apocalypse of Adam Reconsidered." In
*The Society of Biblical Literature...Book of Seminar
Papers...,* edited by Lane C. McGaughy. Vol. 2. Missoula,
Mont.: SBL, 1972.

MacRae, George W. "The Coptic Gnostic Apocalypse of Adam." *HeyJ* 6 (1965) 27-35.

Magie, David. "Egyptian Deities in Asia Minor in Inscriptions and on Coins." *AJA* Series 2, 57 (1953) 163-87.

Marquardt, Joachim. *Das Privatleben der Römer.* Handbuch der römischen Alterthümer 7, 2nd ed. Leipzig: Hirzel, 1886.

Martin, Raymond A. *Syntactical Evidence of Semitic Sources in Greek Documents.* Septuagint and Cognate Studies 3. Missoula, Mont.: SBL, 1974.

Meeks, Wayne. "The Man from Heaven in Johannine Sectarianism." *JBL* 91 (1972) 44-72.

Meissner, Bruno. *Babylonien und Assyrien.* Kulturgeschichtliche Bibliothek 1.4. Heidelberg: Winter, 1925.

Merkelbach, R. "Ein Orakel des gryneischen Apollon." *Zeitschrift für Papyrologie und Epigraphik* 5 (1970) 48.

Metzger, Bruce M. *A Textual Commentary on the Greek New Testament.* London: United Bible Societies, 1971.

Meyer, Ed. "Astarte (*Astartē*)." In Roscher, 1. 645-55.

Milik, J. T. "4QVisions de 'Amram et une citation d'Origène (Planches I-II)." *RB* 79 (1972) 77-97.

_____. "Milkisedek et Milkiresa' dans les anciens écrits juifs et chrétiens." *JJS* 23 (1972) 95-144.

Miller, Patrick D. *The Divine Warrior in Early Israel.* Harvard Semitic Monographs 5. Cambridge: Harvard University Press, 1973.

_____. "Animal Names as Designations in Ugaritic and Hebrew." *Ugarit-Forschungen* 2 (1971) 177-86.

Miltner, Franz. *Ephesos: Stadt der Artemis und des Johannes.* Vienna: F. Deuticke, 1958.

Mionnet, Théodore Edme. *Description de médailles antiques, grecques et romaines.* Vol. 3. Paris: Impr. de Testu, 1806-13.

Momigliano, A. "Nero." *CAH* 10. 702-42. Cambridge: Cambridge University Press, 1934.

Mowinckel, Sigmund. "Some Remarks on Hodayot 39:5-20." *JBL* 75 (1956) 265-76.

_____. *The Psalms in Israel's Worship.* 2 vols. New York: Abingdon, 1967.

Mras, Karl, ed. *Die Praeparatio evangelica*. *Eusebius Werke*, vol. 8. GCS 43, 1-2. Berlin: Akademie, 1954-56.

Müller, Dieter. *Ägypten und die griechischen Isis-Aretalogien*. Abhandlungen der sächsischen Akademie der Wissenschaften zu Leipzig, phil-hist Kl. 53, 1. Berlin: Akademie, 1961.

Müller, Hans-Peter. "Die himmlische Ratsversammlung. Motivgeschichtliches zu Apc 5:1-5." *ZNW* 54 (1963) 254-67.

Müller, Hans W. "Isis mit dem Horuskinde." *Münchner Jahrbuch der bildenden Kunst* Series 3, 14. Munich: Prestel, 1963.

Müller, Ulrich B. *Messias und Menschensohn in jüdischen Apokalypsen und in der Offenbarung Johannes*. Studien zum Neuen Testament 6. Gütersloh: Mohn, 1972.

Münster, Maria. *Untersuchungen zur Göttin Isis: Vom Alten Reich bis zum Ende des Neuen Reiches*. Münchner Ägyptologische Studien 11. Berlin: B. Hessling, 1968.

Muirhead, I. A. "The Bride of Christ." *SJT* 5 (1952) 175-87.

Nickelsburg, George. *Resurrection, Immortality and Eternal Life in Intertestamental Judaism*. Harvard Theological Studies 26. Cambridge: Harvard University Press, 1972.

Nilsson, Martin P. *Geschichte der griechischen Religion*. Vol. 2, *Die hellenistische und römische Zeit*. Munich: Beck, 1950.

Nötscher, Friedrich. "Himmlische Bücher und Schicksalsglaube in Qumran." *RQ* 1 (1959) 405-11. Reprint, in *Vom Alten zum Neuen Testament*. Bonner Biblische Beiträge 17. Bonn: Hanstein, 1962.

Nonnus Panopolitanus. *Dionysiaca*. Edited by Rudolfus Keydell. Berlin: Weidmann, 1959.

Oberhummer, E. "Urania." PW 9A^1. 935-41.

Oden, Robert A. "Studies in Lucian's *De Syria Dea*." Ph.D. dissertation, Harvard University, 1975. Forthcoming in the Harvard Semitic Monograph series.

Ohlemutz, Erwin. *Die Kulte und Heiligtümer der Götter in Pergamon*. Darmstadt: Wissenschaftliche Buchgesellschaft, 1968.

Orbe, Antonio. Review of Böhlig-Labib. *Greg* 46 (1965) 169-72.

O'Rourke, J. J. "The Hymns of the Apocalypse." *CBQ* 30 (1968) 399-409.

Osten-Sacken, Peter von der. *Gott und Belial*. Studien zur Umwelt des Neuen Testaments 6. Göttingen: Vandenhoeck und Ruprecht, 1969.

Otten, Heinrich. *Mythen vom Gotte Kumarbi*. Deutsche Akademie der Wissenschaften zu Berlin, Institut für Orientforschung 3. Berlin: Akademie, 1950.

Otto, Walter F. "Mythen von Leto, dem Drachen und der Geburt." In *Das Wort der Antike*, edited by Kurt von Fritz. Stuttgart: Klett, 1962.

Oxyrhynchus Papyri. Edited by B. Grenfell, A. S. Hunt et al. Vol. 17-. London: Egypt Exploration Society, 1898-.

Paul, S. M. "Heavenly Tablets and the Book of Life." *Journal of the Ancient Near Eastern Society of Columbia University* 5 (1973) 345-53.

Peek, Werner. *Der Isishymnus von Andros und verwandte Texte*. Berlin: Weidmann, 1930.

Perrin, Norman. "Mark 14:62: The End Product of a Christian Pesher Tradition?" In *A Modern Pilgrimage in New Testament Christology*. Philadelphia: Fortress, 1974.

Picard, Charles. *Ephèse et Claros: Recherches sur les sanctuaires et les cultes de l'Ionie du Nord*. Bibliothèque des écoles françaises d'Athènes et de Rome...123. Paris: Boccard, 1922.

Pope, Marvin H. "*Aṯirat*." In *Wörterbuch der Mythologie*, edited by H. W. Haussig (see Haussig).

_____. "*Aṯtar*." In *Wörterbuch der Mythologie*, edited by H. W. Haussig (see Haussig).

_____. *Job*. AB 15. Garden City, N.Y.: Doubleday, 1965.

Preller, Ludwig, and Robert, Carl. *Griechische Mythologie*, 4th ed. Vol. 1. Berlin: Weidmann, 1894.

Prigent, Pierre. *Apocalypse 12: Histoire de l'exégèse*. Beiträge zur Geschichte der biblischen Exegese 2. Tübingen: Mohr, 1959.

_____. "Une Trace de liturgie judéo-chrétienne dans le chapitre XII de l'Apocalypse de Jean." *RSR* 60 (1972) 165-72.

Pritchard, James B., ed. *The Ancient Near East: Supplementary Texts and Pictures Relating to the Old Testament*. Princeton, N.J.: Princeton University Press, 1969.

_____. *Ancient Near Eastern Texts Relating to the Old Testament*. 2nd rev. ed. Princeton, N.J.: Princeton University Press, 1955.

Procksch, Otto. *Jesaia 1*. KAT 9. Leipzig: Deichert, 1930.

Rehm, Albert. *Didyma*. Part 2, *Die Inschriften*. Edited by Theodor Wiegand and Richard Harder. Deutsches Archäologisches Institut. Berlin: Mann, 1958.

Reicke, B. "Die jüdische Apokalyptik und die johanneische Tiervision." *RSR* 60 (1972) 175-81.

Reinach, A. J. Review of Rusch. *RHR* 60 (1909) 94-95.

Ricoeur, Paul. *The Symbolism of Evil*. Boston: Beacon, 1969.

Riessler, Paul. *Altjüdisches Schrifttum ausserhalb der Bibel*. Augsburg: Filser, 1928.

Rigaux, Béda. *L'Antéchrist et l'opposition au royaume messianique dans l'Ancien et le Nouveau Testament*. Gembloux: Duculot, 1932.

_____. *Saint Paul: Les Epitres aux Thessaloniciens*. EBib. Paris: Gabalda, 1956.

Rissi, Mathias. *Was ist und was geschehen soll danach: Die Zeit- und Geschichtsauffassung der Offenbarung des Johannes*. ATANT 46. Zürich: Zwingli, 1965.

_____. *Zeit und Geschichte in der Offenbarung des Johannes*. Zürich: Zwingli, 1952.

Robert, Louis. *Etudes anatoliennes*. Paris: Boccard, 1937.

_____. *Monnaies grecques*. Centre de recherches d'histoire et de philologie 1. Hautes études numismatiques 2. Geneva: Librairie Droz, 1967.

Robinson, James M. "On the *Gattung* of Mark (and John)." In *Jesus and Man's Hope*. Pittsburgh Theological Seminary Festival on the Gospels. Pittsburgh: Pittsburgh Theological Seminary, Perspective, 1970.

_____. "The Johannine Trajectory." In *Trajectories through Early Christianity*. By J. M. Robinson and Helmut Koester. Philadelphia: Fortress, 1971.

Robinson, Theodore. "Hebrew Myths." In *Myth and Ritual*, edited by S. H. Hooke. London: Oxford University Press, 1933.

Roeder, G. "Set." In Roscher, 4. 725-84.

_____. *Urkunden zur Religion des alten Ägypten*. Religiöse Stimmen der Völker. Jena: Diederichs, 1915.

Röllig, Wolfgang. "Atargatis." In *Wörterbuch der Mythologie*, edited by H. W. Haussig (see Haussig).

Rogers, Robert W. *Cuneiform Parallels to the Old Testament.*
New York: Eaton and Mains, 1912.

Roller, Otto. "Das Buch mit sieben Siegeln." *ZNW* 36 (1937)
98-113.

Rose, H. J. *A Handbook of Greek Mythology including Its Extension to Rome.* 2nd ed. London: Methuen, 1933. 5th rev.
ed., 1953.

_____. *Hygini Fabulae.* 2nd ed. Lugduni Batavorum: A. W.
Sythoff, 1963.

Ross, Ludwig. *Inselreisen.* Vol. 1, edited by F. Hiller von
Gaertringen et al. Halle: Niemeyer, 1912.

Rousseau, F. *L'Apocalypse et le milieu prophétique du Nouveau
Testament: Structure et préhistoire du texte.* Montreal:
Bellarmin, 1971.

Rudolf, Kurt. Review of Böhlig-Labib. *TLZ* 90 (1965) 359-62.

Rusch, Adolf. *De Serapide et Iside in Graecia Cultis.* Berlin:
H. S. Hermann, 1906.

Russell, D. S. *The Method and Message of Jewish Apocalyptic:
200 BC - AD 100.* Philadelphia: Westminster, 1964.

Saffrey, H. D. "Relire l'Apocalypse à Patmos." *RB* 82 (1975)
385-417.

Salditt-Trappmann, Regina. *Tempel der ägyptischen Götter in
Griechenland und an der Westküste Kleinasiens.* Etudes
préliminaires aux religions orientales dans l'empire
romain 15. Leiden: Brill, 1970.

Sander-Hansen, C. E. *Die Texte der Metternichstele.* Analecta
Ägyptiaca 7. Copenhagen: Munksgaard, 1956.

Sattler, W. "Das Buch mit sieben Siegeln. Studien zum literarischen Aufbau der Offenbarung Johannis. II. Die Bücher
der Werke und das Buch des Lebens." *ZNW* 21 (1922) 43-54.

Sauer, B. "Leto in der Kunst." In Roscher, 2. 1971-80.

Sayce, Archibald H. *Babylonian Literature.* London: S. Bagster
and Sons, [1877].

Schlier, Heinrich. "Vom Antichrist: Zum 13. Kapitel der Offenbarung Johannis." *Theologische Aufsätze: Karl Barth zum
50. Geburtstag,* edited by E. Wolf. Munich: Kaiser, 1936.
Reprint, in *Die Zeit der Kirche: Exegetische Aufsätze und
Vorträge.* 2nd ed. Freiburg in Breisgau: Herder, 1958.

Schmidt, Johann. *Die jüdische Apokalyptik: Die Geschichte
ihrer Erforschung von den Anfängen bis zu den Textfunden
von Qumran.* Neukirchen-Vluyn: Neukirchener Verlag des
Erziehungsvereins, 1969.

Schmidt, K. L. "Lucifer als gefallene Engelmacht." *Theolog-ische Zeitschrift* 7 (1951) 161-79.

Schrader, Eberhard. *Die Keilinschriften und das Alte Testament.* 3rd ed., edited by Heinrich Zimmern and H. Winckler. Berlin: Reuther und Reichard, 1903.

Schreiber, Theodor. *Apollon Pythoktonos: Ein Beitrag zur griechischen Religions- und Kunstgeschichte.* Leipzig: Engelmann, 1879.

Schrenk, Gottlob. "*Biblos, biblion.*" *TDNT* 1 (1964) 615-20.

Schürer, Emil. *The History of the Jewish People in the Age of Jesus Christ (175 B.C.-A.D. 135).* Vol. 1, edited by G. Vermes and F. Millar. Edinburgh: Clark, 1973.

Schwab, Moses, ed. *The Talmud of Jerusalem.* Vol. 1, *Berak-hoth.* London, 1886. Reprint, New York: Hermon, 1969.

Seeberg, R. "Kuss und Kanon." *Aus Religion und Geschichte. Gesammelte Aufsätze und Vorträge.* Vol. 1. Leipzig: Deichert, 1906.

Sickenberger, Joseph. "Die Johannesapokalypse und Rom." *BZ* 17 (1926), 270-82.

_____. *Erklärung der Johannesapokalypse.* Bonn: Hanstein, 1942.

Silberman, L. H. "Language and Structure in the Hodayot (1QH 3)." *JBL* 75 (1956) 96-106.

Sister, Moses. "Die Typen der prophetischen Visionen in der Bibel." *Monatsschrift für Geschichte und Wissenschaft des Judentums* 78 (1934) 399-430.

Spitta, Friedrich. *Die Offenbarung des Johannes.* Halle, 1889.

Stegemann, Viktor. *Astrologie und Universalgeschichte: Studien und Interpretationen zu den Dionysiaka des Nonnos von Panopolis.* Stoicheia 9. Leipzig: Teubner, 1950.

Stendahl, Krister. *The School of St. Matthew.* Philadelphia: Fortress, 1968.

Stone, Michael. "Antichrist." *Jewish Encyclopedia* 3 (1971) 59-72.

Strobel, A. "Abfassung und Geschichtstheologie der Apokalypse nach Kap 17, 9-12." *NTS* 10 (1964) 433-45.

Strong, Herbert, and Garstang, John. *The Syrian Goddess: A Translation of Lucian's 'De Dea Syria' with a Life of Lucian.* London: Constable, 1913.

Sukenik, E. L. *The Dead Sea Scrolls of the Hebrew University*.
Jerusalem: Hebrew University and Magnes Press, 1955.

Swete, Henry Barclay. *The Apocalypse of St. John*. 2nd ed.
London: Macmillan, 1907.

Sydenham, Edward A. *The Coinage of Nero*. London: Spink, 1920.

Sylloge Nummorum Graecorum. Vol. 4, *Fitzwilliam Museum, Leake
and General Collections*, part 6, *Asia Minor-Phrygia*.
British Academy. London: Oxford University Press, 1965.

Sylloge Nummorum Graecorum Deutschland: Sammlung von Aulock.
Vol. 4, *Mysien*, edited by K. Kraft. Berlin: Mann, 1960.

Sylloge Nummorum Graecorum Deutschland: Sammlung von Aulock.
Vol. 6, *Ionien*. Berlin: Mann, 1960.

Sylloge Nummorum Graecorum Deutschland: Sammlung von Aulock.
Vol. 7, *Karien*, edited by K. Kraft and D. Kienast. Berlin: Mann, 1962.

Sylloge Nummorum Graecorum Deutschland: Sammlung von Aulock.
Vol. 9, *Phrygien*, edited by H.-W. Ritter. Berlin: Mann,
1964.

Sylloge Nummorum Graecorum Deutschland: Sammlung von Aulock.
Vol. 10, *Lykien*. Berlin: Mann, 1964.

Sylloge Nummorum Graecorum Deutschland: Sammlung von Aulock.
Vol. 16, *Nachtrag II: Mysien, Troas, Aeolis, Lesbos*.
Berlin: Mann, 1966.

Sylloge Nummorum Graecorum: The Burton Y. Berry Collection.
Vol. 1, part 2, *Megaris to Egypt*. New York: The American
Numismatic Society, 1962.

Te Velde, H. *Seth, God of Confusion: A Study of His Role in
Egyptian Mythology and Religion*. Probleme der Ägyptologie
6. Leiden: Brill, 1967.

Thiersch, Hermann. *Artemis Ephesia: Eine archäologische Untersuchung*. Part 1, *Katalog der erhaltenen Denkmäler*. Abhandlungen der Gesellschaft der Wissenschaften zu Götting-
en, phil-hist Kl. 3, 12. Berlin: Weidmann, 1935.

Tran Tam Tinh, V., and Labrecque, Yvette. *Isis lactans*.
Etudes préliminaires aux religions orientales dans l'empire romain 37. Leiden: Brill, 1973.

Trites, A. A. "Martys and Martyrdom in the Apocalypse: A
Semantic Study." *NovT* 15 (1973) 72-80.

Unnik, W. C. van. "'Worthy is the Lamb.' The Background of
Apoc 5." *Mélanges bibliques en hommage au R. P. Béda
Rigaux*, edited by A. Descamps and A. de Halleux. Gem-
bloux: Duculot, 1970.

291

Vanni, Ugo. *La struttura letteraria dell'Apocalisse.* Alosiana scritti...8. Rome: Herder, 1971.

Victorinus. *Commentarius in apocalypsin.* Edited by Iohannes Haussleiter. *Victorini Episcopi Petavionensis Opera.* CSEL 49. Leipzig: Freytag, 1916.

Vidman, Ladilaus. *Sylloge inscriptionum religionis Isiacae et Sarapiacae.* Religionsgeschichtliche Versuche und Vorarbeiten 28. Berlin: de Gruyter, 1969.

Violet, Bruno. *Die Esra-Apokalypse (IV Esra).* GCS 18. Leipzig: Hinrichs, 1910.

Vischer, Eberhard. *Die Offenbarung Johannis: Eine jüdische Apokalypse in christlicher Bearbeitung.* TU 2, 3. Leipzig: Hinrichs, 1886.

Vögtle, Anton. *Die Tugend- und Lasterkataloge im Neuen Testament.* NTAbh 16. Münster: Aschendorff, 1936.

Volz, Paul. *Die Eschatologie der jüdischen Gemeinde.* Tübingen: Mohr, 1934.

Wacholder, Ben Zion. *Eupolemus: A Study of Judaeo-Greek Literature.* Cincinnati: Hebrew Union College, 1974.

Wakeman, Mary K. *God's Battle with the Monster: A Study in Biblical Imagery.* Leiden: Brill, 1973.

Wallace, Howard. "Leviathan and the Beast in Revelation." In *The Biblical Archaeologist Reader.* Vol. 1, edited by G. Ernest Wright and David Noel Freedman. Garden City, N.Y.: Doubleday, 1961.

Weiss, Johannes. *Die Offenbarung des Johannes: Ein Beitrag zur Literatur- und Religionsgeschichte.* FRLANT 3. Göttingen: Vandenhoeck und Ruprecht, 1904.

_____. "Die Offenbarung des Johannes." In *Die Schriften des Neuen Testaments.* Vol. 2, edited by Johannes Weiss. Göttingen: Vandenhoeck und Ruprecht, 1908.

Wehrli. "Leto." In PW Supplementband 5. 555–76.

Wellhausen, Julius. *Analyse der Offenbarung Johannis.* Abhandlungen der königlichen Gesellschaft der Wissenschaften zu Göttingen, phil-hist. Kl., N.F. 9, 4. Berlin: Weidmann, 1907.

Wernicke, K. "Artemis." In PW 2. 1336–440.

Weyland, G. J. *Omwerkings- en Compilatie-Hypothesen toegepast op de Apocalypse van Johannes.* Groningen: Wolters, 1888.

292

Widengren, Geo. *The Ascension of the Apostle and the Heavenly Book (King and Saviour III)*. UUA 1950:7. Uppsala: Lundequistska, 1950.

_____. *Muhammad, the Apostle of God, and His Ascension (King and Saviour V)*. UUA 1955:1. Uppsala: Lundequistska, 1955.

Woude, A. S. van der. *Die messianischen Vorstellungen der Gemeinde von Qumrân*. Studia Semitica Neerlandica 3. Assen: Van Gorcum, 1957.

_____. "Melchizedek als himmlische Erlösergestalt in den neugefundenen eschatologischen Midraschen aus Qumran Höhle 11." *OTS* 14 (1965) 354-73.

Zijl, Peter J. van. *Baal: A Study of Texts in Connexion with Baal in the Ugaritic Epics*. Alter Orient und Altes Testament 10. Neukirchen-Vluyn: Butzon und Bercker Kevelaer, 1972.

Zimmern, Heinrich. *Das babylonische Neujahrsfest*. Der alte Orient 25.3. Leipzig: Hinrichs, 1926,